LIVING THE TRUTH IN LOVE

Living the Truth in Love

Pastoral Approaches to Same-Sex Attraction

Edited by
Janet E. Smith
and
Father Paul Check

IGNATIUS PRESS   SAN FRANCISCO

Cover art:
Christ as Good Shepherd, early Christian mosaic
Mausoleum of Galla Placidia, Ravenna, Italy
Scala / Art Resource, NY

Cover design by John Herreid

© 2015 by Ignatius Press, San Francisco
"Finding the Water in the Desert" © 2015 by J. Budziszewski
All rights reserved
ISBN 978-1-62164-060-8
Library of Congress Control Number 2015940332
Printed in the United States of America ∞

CONTENTS

Pastoral

FOREWORD

Archbishop Allen Vigneron, Ph.D., S.T.L.

From the first hours of his taking up the office of universal pastor, Pope Francis has called for the whole Church to invest herself completely in the urgent work of the New Evangelization. To that end the Holy Father determined that the family would be the topic during two sessions of the Synod of Bishops. For the first, which met in 2014, he determined that focus was to be the "pastoral challenges to the family in the context of evangelization".[1] He has structured the second, which will meet in October 2015, to build on what was accomplished at the first by considering "the vocation and mission of the family in the Church and the contemporary world".[2]

With these decisions, Pope Francis is signaling that a first priority in the New Evangelization must be proposing anew the light that Christ's good news sheds on family life. Progress in evangelizing our society requires doing everything in our power to strengthen the unambiguous witness that families—domestic churches—can give to the good news by their living out the Lordship of Jesus to the full.

The difficulties we face in responding to the challenges Pope Francis has set before us are daunting, given the many wounds that afflict families today. Nonetheless we must face these challenges with courage and a spirit of self-sacrifice, since the evangelization of society depends upon embracing this mission. We must also embark upon this mission with serene confidence, since it is God's own work and we are merely his agents.

---

[1] This is the title of the 2013 preparatory document for the extraordinary synod of 2014: "Pastoral Challenges to the Family in the Context of Evangelization"; available at http://www.vatican.va/roman_curia/synod/documents/rc_synod_doc_20131105_iii-assemblea-sinodo-vescovi_en.html.

[2] This is the title of the 2014 *Lineamenta* for the general assembly of the Synod of Bishops on the family to be held in October 2015: "The Vocation and Mission of the Family in the Church and the Contemporary World"; available at http://www.vatican.va/roman_curia/synod/documents/rc_synod_doc_20141209_lineamenta-xiv-assembly_en.html.

Pope Francis has called upon not only the members of the synod but also on all the People of God—clergy, religious, and lay faithful—to ponder anew on what God, both in his creating and in his revealing, has told us about his plan for families. It is in loving response to this request of the Vicar of Peter that the authors in this volume offer the fruit of their attentive listening to God's word. Specifically, these essays aim to offer insights that advance the Church's response to the questions posed by the *Lineamenta* for the 2015 meeting of the synod regarding "Pastoral Attention towards Persons with Homosexual Tendencies".[3]

A common touchstone for these essays is the firm conviction that Christ reveals man to himself. As the Fathers of the Second Vatican Council testify, "Only in the mystery of the incarnate Word does the mystery of man take on light. For Adam, the first man, was a figure of Him Who was to come (cf. Rm 5: 14), namely Christ the Lord".[4] He is, as the Liturgy says, the Word through whom the Father made the universe and by whom all have been redeemed.

As the firstborn of the human race made new by grace, the Lord Jesus has renewed every dimension of our existence, not least our being "created male and female". Being sexual is part of the very fabric of being human, and the New Adam has, by his coming, uncovered for our sinful race God's plan "from the beginning" about human sexuality (see Mt 19:4). And he offers to all the strength to live out their sexuality in accordance with the Father's plan.

In looking to assist the members of the synod in their efforts to discern how in our time the disciples of Jesus can more faithfully live out this original plan, these essays seek to remind us not to lose sight of the fact that God's plan "from the beginning" for family life and human sexuality is not first of all a set of abstract socio-political norms (though our convictions can be theoretically defended). Rather, this plan is Someone, the Eternal Word himself, in whom, by whom, and for whom the Father spoke to bring the human race into being (see 1 Cor 8:6; Gen 1:26). Were any of us who respond to Pope Francis' invitation to contribute to the work of the synod to forget that at their roots all the questions

---

[3] See *Lineamenta*, questions 54–55, http://www.vatican.va/roman_curia/synod/documents/rc_synod_doc_20141209_lineamenta-xiv-assembly_en.html.

[4] Vatican II, Pastoral Constitution on the Church in the Modern World, *Gaudium et spes*, December 7, 1965, no. 22, http://www.vatican.va/archive/hist_councils/ii_vatican_council/documents/vat-ii_cons_19651207_gaudium-et-spes_en.html.

being discussed are "Christological questions"—questions about who Jesus is and how his disciples can most faithfully imitate him—then we will have failed to stand in that bright light which offers the only secure illumination for recognizing God's truth.

A second key teaching from the Second Vatican Council that has shaped the contributions made to this volume is the "Universal Call to Holiness".[5] In their comment on Jesus' admonition to his disciples, "You, therefore, must be perfect, as your heavenly Father is perfect" (Mt 5:48), the Fathers reaffirm that all Christians are called to be saints, that "the Lord Jesus, the divine Teacher and Model of all perfection, preached holiness of life to each and everyone of His disciples of every condition."[6]

This holiness of life, given by the Spirit and cultivated in response to his workings in our hearts, means, as Saint Paul says, that we must give ourselves over to "whatever is true, whatever is honorable, whatever is just, whatever is pure, whatever is lovely, [and] whatever is gracious", as well as to what is excellent, "if there is any excellence", and what is worthy of praise, "if there is anything worthy of praise" (Phil 4:8). And in the living out of our sexuality what is excellent and worthy of praise is the virtue of chastity. "Chastity" is the name for authentic excellence in human sexuality, after the pattern of Jesus Christ.[7]

Essential to every disciple's call to share in Christ's own holiness is, then, being called to share in our Lord's chastity: to live our sexuality as a participation in his experience of sexuality as self-giving lived out in the flesh. This conviction that the universal call to holiness necessarily includes a universal call to live chastely has shaped the way this volume, in response to Pope Francis' invitation, explores questions of how those who experience same-sex attraction can best advance in the virtue of chastity and the pursuit of holiness, and how most effectively to support—as Pope Francis so often puts it, "to accompany"—them on the path to purity and holiness of life. To that end, there has been a concerted effort to include in this collection personal testimony from

---

[5]See Dogmatic Constitution on the Church, *Lumen gentium*, November 21, 1964, chapter 5, "The Universal Call to Holiness in the Church", http://www.vatican.va/archive/hist_councils/ii_vatican_council/documents/vat-ii_const_19641121_lumen-gentium_en.html.

[6]Ibid., no. 40.

[7]See *Catechism of the Catholic Church*, 2nd ed. (Washington, D.C.: Libreria Editrice Vaticana—United States Catholic Conference, 2000), nos. 2337–45.

persons with same-sex attraction and from those who are committed to accompanying them. Hearing these reports of their efforts to live out their unconditional commitment to imitating the chastity of Christ, along with the accounts of other Christians who invest themselves in helping their brothers and sisters meet these challenges, is an invaluable contribution to preparing for the synod.

One way to achieve sanctity is to be a martyr. The word "martyr" means "witness". Not all martyrdom involves being burned at the stake or beheaded. Some involves being faithful at great personal sacrifice to difficult truths that are not only rejected in one's time but that are mocked and scorned. In this age, those who are faithful to the Church's teaching on sexuality are living a kind of heroic witness. Chaste Catholics who experience same-sex attraction give a particularly powerful heroic witness to their love of truth, Christ, and the Church because they are often mocked and scorned by gay activists. So, too, is the witness of those who in their professional work tend to the needs of those who experience same-sex attraction since they are often rejected and vilified by their colleagues. The pressures from the culture at large, and even from some in the Church herself, to accept same-sex attraction as positive and to justify seeking happiness in same-sex sexual relationships are great. The courage and self-giving involved in joining one's suffering to the cross of Christ along with the joy and serenity manifested that comes with faithfulness is precisely what Pope Francis is calling for as the best way to evangelize.

While this volume is published with the 2015 assembly of the Synod of Bishops in view, I am confident that it will have a usefulness beyond that event. After the synod meets, each of us must do his or her part to share the good news of Christ about the family and human sexuality. So then, these essays are offered to all believers to help them evangelize and witness to Christ's teaching about the family and sexuality with confidence. That our sexuality has been renewed by Christ is indeed a new and renewing message that takes us beyond the messages our world offers. The truth of the gospel is bracing and challenges all of us to a higher and fuller ideal. What can seem only a "narrow way" is—in the Spirit of Christ—the way made plain, the sure path to man's flourishing in this age and to the blessedness of the life to come, promised by the New Moses on the Mount of Beatitudes.

PREFACE

Moving Forward

Janet E. Smith, Ph.D.

Many of those who defend the Church's teaching on homosexuality employ natural law arguments that stress the end and purpose of the sexual act. A short version of those arguments holds that since sexual acts engaged in by those who are the same sex cannot result in new life, those acts are not in accord with God's plan for sexuality. Arguments based on the theology of the body stress the complementarity of the sexes and maintain that those who are of the same sex cannot engage in the reciprocal, complementary, asymmetrical self-giving that God planned for sexuality. Arguments of both kinds have a great deal of philosophical and theological force, but such arguments rarely have persuasive power in our day and age and are often of little use in a pastoral setting.

We live in an age where personal experience is the chief source of truth for most people. In respect to the issue at hand, many argue that since so many people with same-sex attraction (SSA) have had positive experiences when involved in same-sex relationships that involve same-sex sexual acts, those relationships and acts must be moral. That is, many think that because they have a subjectively positive response to an experience (such as feeling affirmed by another), or because they have grown in some good quality (such as thoughtfulness or generosity), then the experiences producing good feelings or personal growth must therefore be moral and good. That conclusion, though, is unwarranted even when experience itself is the sole criterion used to assess morality, for the experiences that attend any set of choices are generally complex. For instance, those who "come out" as homosexual or gay generally initially experience a consoling sense of belonging and of affirmation, experiences their lives have often been lacking. But over time, they find that many of their real-life experiences are not conducive to the happiness that human beings are meant to experience.

More and more of those who have been involved in the same-sex lifestyle are telling their stories, stories that go far beyond feeling affirmed and growing in some good human qualities to also include experiences of loneliness, alienation, confusion, various addictions, promiscuity, multiple serial relationships, physical diseases, psychological issues, and heartbreak. Fortunately, for many there is a second chapter to that story, a beautiful story of having fallen in love with Jesus and his Church, of finding an ennobling understanding of the truth of the human person. These journeys and transformations have often been facilitated by family members and friends, as well as by counselors and spiritual directors, who have been affirming and accepting of those who experience same-sex attraction without approving of all their choices. Those who courageously face the realities of their lives and resolutely make the changes necessary—a process generally involving a significant amount of suffering—eventually find peace, not misery, in accepting the Church's teaching on sexuality. In their willingness to undergo conversions of many kinds, and in their desire to seek holiness and live lives of complete self-giving, they become witnesses of the saving power of Jesus' love and the graces he bestows on those who love him, not only to others who experience same-sex attraction, but to all who want to become more radically devoted to Christ.

This book hopes to contribute to clear thinking about good pastoral approaches to those who experience same-sex attraction. We need to understand who the human person is and why living a homosexual lifestyle ultimately cannot be satisfying. We need to learn how to listen to those with SSA as well as to love and help them. Indeed, many of our authors have done just that and are great guides. Ultimately, we want to help Catholics who love those with SSA be better friends to them, to help priests and parishes be more welcoming, and to serve better those who experience SSA.

This volume grew out of the desire to provide answers to the questions posed in the *Lineamenta* for the synod on marriage to be held in Rome in the fall of 2015:

How can the Christian community give pastoral attention to families with persons with homosexual tendencies? What are the responses that, in light of cultural sensitivities, are considered to be most appropriate? While avoiding any unjust discrimination, how can such persons receive pastoral care in these situations in light of the Gospel? How can God's will be proposed to them in their situation?[1]

We decided to try to look at these questions in a comprehensive way. We discerned that it was important that both those whose wisdom comes largely from study and those whose wisdom comes largely through lived experience work together to address the pastoral issues surrounding same-sex attraction. What is learned from study and what is learned from experience should, of course, be complementary. The wisdom of the Church comes from the wisdom of Scripture and from the systematic reflection on reality by thoughtful and holy persons. The reality that thoughtful and holy people reflect upon is the lived experience of real people—their own and that of others. The lived experience of those who experience SSA and of those who counsel and minister to them is, of course, an invaluable source of knowledge and insight for developing programs of pastoral care.

We are grateful that so many busy and talented people replied positively to our urgent requests for essays. We asked those we knew to have hearts that love the Lord, his difficult truths, and those challenged by his difficult truths. This text includes essays by philosophers and psychologists, testimonies by those who have experienced or experience SSA, an analysis of the social and Church "scene", and recommended strategies by activists.

Although everyone who writes here is committed to the understanding that same-sex sexual acts are not in accord with God's plan for sexuality, there is considerable variety in the way that the authors approach and speak about SSA. Indeed, there is some disagreement on what are good and appropriate means of counseling those with SSA and on how those who experience SSA can best live out their Christian calling. We believe that some of the differences are matters of prudence, and others perhaps are more serious. We include different positions because we believe it is important that we remain in dialogue with those who share important foundational views.

[1] Synod of Bishops, XIV Ordinary General Assembly, *Lineamenta*, "The Vocation and Mission of the Family in the Church and Contemporary World", December 2014, Part 3, question 40, http://www.vatican.va/roman_curia/synod/documents/rc_synod_doc _20141209_lineamenta-xiv-assembly_en.html.

All pastoral approaches must be grounded in an authentic anthropology, an authentic understanding of the human person. The book opens with Professor Rachel Lu's lucid presentation on Christian anthropology and its implications for understanding SSA. Dr. Bob Schuchts writes beautifully about how important it is that each person understands that he or she is made in the image and likeness of God, and shows the power of prayer in healing many of the distortions of identity in the being of each and every human being. An important contribution for the discussion on renewed appreciation of friendship as part of a life of holiness is Father Dennis Billy's essay on Aelred of Rievaulx' treatise on spiritual friendship. Professor Deborah Savage's piece breaks new and very important ground by showing that the thought of Saint John Paul II drew "lived experience" more directly into a philosophical account of the person and of moral evaluation. We close this section with two essays shaped by Thomistic natural law: Professor J. Budziszewski explains how same-sex acts undermine human fulfillment because of their disharmony with natural law, and Monsignor Livio Melina provides a tight and lucid explanation of the traditional language Church documents use to speak about same-sex attractions.

A book that hopes to be helpful for those engaging in pastoral ministry to those who experience SSA must include testimonies and wise reflections of such individuals, for unless we listen we will not be able to understand and to love well. Six authors, all Catholic and all committed to living chastely, report their experience with SSA and speak of different ways of evaluating and living with their experience. We hear from Joseph Prever, who recalls the way that friendships have shaped his life; from Dan Mattson, who ponders the permissive will of God; from Robin Beck, who boldly takes Scripture at its word about homosexuality; from Eve Tushnet, a writer for the blog *Spiritual Friendship: Musings on God, Sexuality, Relationships*, who is exploring how she and others with SSA can fulfill their calling to be gifts to others; and from David Prosen, who tells about the torment of his years in the gay lifestyle, followed by the peace he now experiences. Doug Mainwaring offers the testimony of a man with SSA who is living as a devoted husband and father. We also hear from Robert and Susan Cavera, who speak of the journey traveled by those whose children experience SSA.

Two essays by those who counsel individuals with SSA include more testimonies along with expert advice on how to counsel those with SSA.

Dr. Janelle Hallman's essay on the experience of shame felt by young people with same-sex attraction should be invaluable to counselors and parents alike. Dr. Timothy Lock provides a wealth of information, including a response to some erroneous popular claims about SSA and a marvelous explanation of both healthy and unhealthy patterns of sexual maturation. Both model gentle and loving ways of accompanying those who experience SSA. Dr. Timothy Flanigan reviews the medical risks incurred by men who have sex with men and explains that the personalist approach requires that medical doctors attend to broader needs of the patient rather than the immediate medical concerns.

And finally, we close with two essays that should help us deal better with issues concerning same-sex attraction in the public sphere and the Church. Dr. Jennifer Roback Morse argues that a disregard for the well-being of children has driven and resulted from various political, legal, and cultural developments, such as no-fault divorce and widespread access to contraception. Peter Herbeck speaks of how urgent it is that the Church speak both to the public and to her members, and gives practical advice on good methods for doing so.

We are not quite at the beginning of knowing how to serve those who experience SSA, but we certainly have a great deal more to learn. As we get better in our personal lives at relating to those with SSA and as parishes get better at being welcoming to those with SSA, we will learn more that will enable us to refine and expand our approaches. We hope that we have provided sound grounding upon which to build.

INTRODUCTION

Father Paul Check, S.T.B., S.T.L.

I will not leave you orphans.

—John 14:18, NAB

Among the many promises Jesus made to his disciples was this one: that he would not leave us orphans. As Christians, we believe the Lord fulfills this promise in many ways: through his eucharistic presence in the Church, through the leadership of the successors of the apostles in communion with Peter, through Sacred Scripture. Pope Francis and Pope Benedict XVI have reminded us that we also find the presence of Christ in his Church and among Christians: in "accompaniment"[1] and in "intellectual charity."[2]

Pope Francis emphasizes that pastoral charity takes the form of walking with our brothers and sisters in Christian friendship on their journey—on our common journey—to the Lord. We help them to discover or rediscover the treasure of God's healing mercy in the "field hospital"[3] that Jesus preached and established: the Kingdom of heaven on earth, the Church. Christian friendship is "benevolence": to will the good of the other, but not from afar, and always with the healing love of Christ as the model.

---

[1] Pontificium Consilium Pro Familia, "The Art of Accompaniment", http://www.familiam .org/pls/pcpf/v3_s2ew_consultazione.mostra_pagina?id_pagina=5703, accessed April 21, 2014.

[2] "Address of His Holiness Benedict XVI: Meeting with Catholic Educators" (Catholic University of America, Washington, D.C., April 17, 2008), http://w2.vatican.va/content /benedict-xvi/en/speeches/2008/april/documents/hf_ben-xvi_spe_20080417_cath-univ -washington.html.

[3] Andrea Tornielli, "Antonio Spadaro Interviews Francis: 'The Church Is a Field Hospital Where Wounds Are Treated'", September 19, 2013, http://vaticaninsider.lastampa.it/en/the -vatican/detail/articolo/27968/.

Pope Benedict spoke of the need for "intellectual charity",[4] from which, among other things, man would learn his true identity as a child of God, who carries "the image of God at the core of his being".[5] During his tenure as Prefect for the Congregation for the Doctrine of the Faith, Pope Benedict had warned us about the dangers of "studied ambiguity"[6]—the opposite of intellectual charity—in matters related to homosexuality. Christian friendship always shares the truth in love.

This collection of essays is a response to the calls of the two popes. Authentic pastoral care of any type follows only from an authentic Christian anthropology. When Jesus recasts the second part of the great commandment—"[L]ove one another as I have loved you" (Jn 15:12; see 13:34)—he unites truth and charity for the faithful disciple by his own example. The truth frees us—from ignorance, confusion, self-preoccupation, and malice—to love with and for the heart of Christ.

In 1980, the Servant of God Terence Cardinal Cooke recognized the need for the Church to extend her maternal charity to a group of people who often feel estranged from the Church, if not rejected. He knew that the word most often associated with the Catholic Church and homosexuality is "no". In many places, including within the Christian community, this remains sadly true. To walk lovingly with those who experience same-sex attractions, Cooke established the spiritual support groups Courage and EnCourage.

From a modest beginning over thirty years ago of seven men meeting in lower Manhattan under the guidance of Father John Harvey, O.S.F.S., the humble but faithful gatherings of the men and women of the Courage and EnCourage apostolates in the United States and other countries continue to this day, following the legacy of the wisdom and charity of Cardinal Cooke. These good souls struggle with the collision of the teachings of the Church and the challenges to those teachings posed by the times. Nevertheless, they trust that Jesus fulfills his promise not to leave them orphans, and so they accompany each other in

---

[4] "Address of His Holiness Benedict XVI", April 17, 2008.

[5] "Address of His Holiness Benedict XVI on the Occasion of Christmas Greetings to the Roman Curia", December 21, 2012, http://w2.vatican.va/content/benedict-xvi/en/speeches/2012/december/documents/hf_ben-xvi_spe_20121221_auguri-curia.html.

[6] Congregation for the Doctrine of the Faith, *Letter to the Bishops of the Catholic Church on the Pastoral Care of Homosexual Persons*, October 1, 1986, no. 14, http://www.vatican.va/roman_curia/congregations/cfaith/documents/rc_con_cfaith_doc_19861001_homosexual-persons_en.html.

Christian friendship, grounded on intellectual charity. Coming to rest in the knowledge that they are beloved sons and daughters of God, they find tremendous self-acceptance and peace. In turn, they become instruments of God's love to others.

I trust that you will find this collection of essays enlightening. I hope you will find inspiring the testimonials both of those who experience same-sex attraction and those who minister directly to them, because they "put a face" on the experience, as you will see—noble, loving, and lovable faces. I hope that this volume will give you confidence that what the Church teaches about homosexuality is much more than "no", and that it is true, consistent with all of her anthropology, and—with the power of the cross shared with fellow Christians—leads to fulfillment.

Theoretical

Eros Divided: Is There Such a Thing as Healthy Homoerotic Love?

Rachel Lu, Ph.D.

For the past several decades, the secular world has been working energetically to bury a Catholic perspective on the meaning of sex. Cultural norms have shifted dramatically over that time, while the Church has steadfastly maintained the same fundamental teaching, which is rooted not just in the Judeo-Christian tradition, but also in an appreciation of human dignity, as illuminated by natural reason.

As sometimes happens, refusing to move with the herd has left Catholics in the position of cultural "radicals". To some extent, we have embraced this. Far from capitulating to the winds of culture, many contemporary—indeed, often young—Catholics have been motivated to articulate the truth with great force and clarity as they witness the cultural decay that has followed in the wake of the sexual revolution. In our time, the choice to *follow* the Church's prescriptions concerning sex and marriage has become a deeply countercultural kind of witness. Catholics are subject to intense social and political pressure to abandon their moral views, and there is every reason to expect that more and greater sacrifices will be demanded of them in the foreseeable future.

As parents today are well aware, young people are subjected to a barrage of culturally approved falsehoods concerning sex. But in an already challenging time, one group is especially at risk: Catholics who experience same-sex attraction (SSA). They find themselves at the center of an intense cultural struggle, which threatens to disrupt their lives and endanger their souls. For the secular left, their personal struggles with homoerotic desire have become a needed tool in the effort of others to undermine the norms of marriage. Thus, more than anyone else, same-sex attracted people are bombarded with lies and false promises, which are especially insidious insofar as they prey on the particular vulnerabilities of this group. Catholics have an obligation to counter these errors with a potent combination of mercy and truth. It's painfully difficult to do in the context of a raging culture war.

There is no doubt that it can be difficult, perhaps *especially* in our time, to live as a faithful Christian while struggling with same-sex attraction. Many complain that orthodox Christians respond insensitively to the questions and challenges of brothers and sisters in Christ who experience SSA. This is true, in part, for the same reasons it's always been true: as is natural, all cultures are built on a foundation of marriage, and thus SSA is a strange and sometimes troubling phenomenon. In our time, however, aggressive secular activism may make compassion especially difficult for some. Christians today feel threatened by homosexual activist groups. There is nothing paranoid about this: crusades on behalf of "sexual liberty" have already done much to undermine religious freedom and the integrity of the family. It would be surprising if that natural anxiety didn't occasionally translate into hostility toward individuals who appear in some way to be "representatives" of the homosexual community.

Yet, that hostility, although not surprising, is often quite unfair. It clearly is not the fault of particular individuals with same-sex attraction that their existence has been so exploited by the progressive left. Individual Catholics who are striving (sometimes heroically) to live faithful, virtuous lives should not feel marginalized on account of cultural movements that are quite beyond their control. But the appropriate corrective can only be a clear explanation of Catholic sexual morals and their relevance to the issue of SSA. All Catholics (whether or not they themselves experience SSA) need to feel confident that they can resist the false teachings of the secular world, while still loving and supporting individuals who experience SSA—indeed with any sexual temptation. Moral clarity is a necessary precondition to embracing *the person* without fear of fostering moral disorder or compromising the teachings of the faith.

Points of Agreement

Catholics who address this topic generally agree on three important points. First, and most critically, people with same-sex attraction are morally precious persons, made in God's image, and ordered toward union with him in the life to come. As members of society they deserve to be treated with respect and civility, and to enjoy all the ordinary rights and duties of citizenship. As Catholics they should be regarded as members of the Body of Christ, who, like all baptized Catholics, should be encouraged to pursue holiness and to participate in the full sacramental life of the Church.

Second, people experiencing same-sex attraction are often in particular need of fellowship and pastoral support. Experiences of SSA are to a great extent involuntary and, particularly in adolescence and early adulthood, can be a significant trial and a source of self-doubt. In a Catholic culture that (for good reasons) is making a significant effort to stress the good of marriage, people who are attracted mainly or exclusively to members of their own sex may find it difficult to discern their appropriate place in a family and parish community. They deserve compassion and guidance as they work through these challenges.

The third point, which is an unchangeable point of Catholic doctrine, is that homosexual acts are morally wrong and cannot be sanctioned by the Church. In a Christian context, it cannot be questioned that marriage is *by nature* built around the complementarity of man and woman and is naturally ordered toward procreation. Thus, it is metaphysically impossible to join two people of the same sex in matrimony. (But we must keep in mind that some of those who experience same-sex attraction, precisely because fundamentally they are male and female, have found it possible to contract successful marriages and families with individuals of the opposite sex.)

Questions to Be Asked

These points can reasonably be set as foundational areas of agreement among Catholics committed to being faithful to the Church. There seems, however, to be growing controversy among these Catholics concerning three related questions. In seeking moral clarity on the issue of same-sex attraction, we must work to find suitable resolutions to these three questions, and then we will turn to the central challenging question, posed below.

First, is it appropriate for Catholics to identify openly as "homosexual", "gay", or "lesbian"? More generally, how should Catholics regard the modern tendency to recognize "sexual minorities" or "sexual identity" as real phenomena that demand a philosophical and social response?

Second, might a homosexual orientation (if that concept is indeed meaningful) be regarded as a positive thing or even a blessing? Should we view gay Christians as a healthy and positive "identity group" whose alternative perspective on sexuality has real potential to enrich the life of the Church?

Third, are there unique lifestyles or sources of personal fulfillment toward which homosexuals *in particular* should be directed? Can we say meaningful things about what a *gay Catholic life* should look like, apart from the obvious point that it should not involve homosexual sex?

These questions are clearly interrelated, and it would be impossible to address them all adequately in one essay. Nonetheless, if we can establish some basics by dealing at least to some extent with these more subsidiary questions, I believe we will be ready to address one especially challenging *central* concern, which most crucially requires a response if we are to achieve moral clarity concerning same-sex attraction: Is there a particular orientation or identity that is *defined by* SSA, which is nevertheless *in itself* a good, and *naturally* ordered toward a unique sort of fulfillment? Some contemporary Catholics seem to think that there is, and this is a significant *new* idea to which the Church must give a clear response.

It seems a near certainty that most Christians historically would have answered this critical question in the negative. Homoerotic desire has traditionally been seen as a trial, and yielding to it a sin, and most Christians (historically) would no doubt have resisted strenuously the suggestion that same-sex attracted individuals should be recognized as a positive and even celebrated "sexual minority group", with its own peculiar sexual telos. Same-sex attracted persons may choose to marry opposite-sex spouses, or they may choose to remain single and celibate. But there is no particular sort of interpersonal relationship that is uniquely appropriate to them, and homoerotic desire especially should be seen as intrinsically disordered, and not something to encourage, foster, or celebrate. Or so, it has long been thought.

The Response of the Spiritual Friendship Group

Over the past few years, however, a new movement of Christians (many of them Catholic) has endeavored to find a different approach to addressing same-sex attraction. They earnestly wish to answer the above question (Is there a particular orientation or identity that is *defined by* SSA, which is nevertheless *in itself* a good, and *naturally* ordered toward a unique sort of fulfillment?) in the affirmative, in a way that they hope also harmonizes with Catholic teaching. They try to articulate ways in which being "gay and Catholic" might in fact be a distinctive good. And they hope as well to explore possibilities for directing the unique talents and dispositions of Christians with SSA toward positive ends, including fulfilling relationships that might be specially appropriate for them.

It's difficult to define this group, especially since their questions and positions are not always formulated in a philosophically precise way. I intend to refer to them loosely as the Spiritual Friendship movement, since the blog *Spiritual Friendship* has become something of a gathering point for a number of Christians (not all of them Catholic) whose aims and arguments seem broadly consonant with the goal outlined above. *Spiritual Friendship* has no single defining orthodoxy, though all contributors evidence a real desire to live as faithful Christians, who take seriously both biblical texts and their various religious authorities. The range of topics covered is broad, and it's refreshing to see young Christians making a good-faith effort to discern how they might live virtuous Christian lives without denying the reality of their experiences of same-sex attraction.

It is unlikely that all *Spiritual Friendship* writers would be in agreement on the points I make here, and of course the views in question are not limited to them. Eve Tushnet's (a blogger on the *Spiritual Friendship* site) recent book, *Gay and Catholic: Accepting My Sexuality, Finding Community, Living My Faith,*[1] represents a significant contribution to the literature on this topic. In general, the Spiritual Friendship movement has attracted a fair amount of attention and even some sympathy among faithful Catholics seeking a better pastoral approach to the issue of same-sex attraction.

A better pastoral approach to same-sex issues is certainly a worthy goal. In this chapter, however, I will argue that the intellectual project of affirming a gay or homosexual identity *as such* (even to the point of recommending a uniquely appropriate fulfillment for members of that identity group) cannot ultimately succeed. It depends primarily on an

---

[1] Eve Tushnet, *Gay and Catholic: Accepting My Sexuality, Finding Community, Living My Faith* (Notre Dame: Ave Maria Press, 2014).

effort to separate homoerotic attraction into different components or strands, rejecting the more explicitly carnal and affirming those that are less directly related to sex. The Spiritual Friendship movement thus subdivides eros in such a way that while they acknowledge that same-sex sexual behavior is wrong, they claim that same-sex attraction is not truly disordered. This is dangerous.

The Catholic tradition consistently teaches that homoerotic attraction is *intrinsically disordered*, and natural reason, aided by a complete understanding of the meaning of erotic love and sexuality, also confirms this. The dangers of eros are not theoretical: history, literature, and direct and personal experience testify strongly to the harms of eros, even to those determined to resist its power. That being the case, we cannot in good conscience advise people to build an identity or lifestyle around relationships rooted in homoerotic attraction, even if homosexual acts are rejected as such.

When persons with same-sex attraction show a willingness to give up physical intimacy for the sake of their faith, it may seem unreasonable or even cruel to ask them to do more. Nevertheless, the fact remains that it is always dangerous to pursue erotic love in a way that fits one's own emotional needs, without the order and discipline that come naturally through the organic relationship of procreation-ordered conjugal marriage. The Spiritual Friendship movement is admirable for its willingness to accept certain "hard teachings" of the faith. But in the end it represents an unusual, but still recognizably modern, attempt to separate erotic love from its true and objective telos.

Unpacking Sexual Identity

In modern society, sexual identity terms such as "gay", "lesbian", and "homosexual" have become commonplace. The use of these terms is a significant point of controversy among faithful Catholics, and it will be helpful for advancing the argument if we can understand why. This language is obviously complex in its social significance, but it also has a tendency to bury some philosophically important questions.

Faithful Catholics who do not experience same-sex attraction are often confused as to why anyone would *wish* to self-identify as gay, given the obvious connection to disordered desire. Though most people today accept that the experience of homoerotic desire can be nonvoluntary, the decision to *broadcast* that experience clearly is voluntary and may indicate something about the person's moral commitments.

Pragmatically speaking, a person might have multiple reasons for self-describing using a sexual identity term. In general, we choose vocabulary for the sake of clarity and convenience, and a phrase like "same-sex attracted" is more verbally awkward (and less familiar in society at large) than a term like "gay". There may also be times when self-identifying as "gay" can help a same-sex attracted person to reach out to others who have similar experiences. We should be careful not to read too much into a particular person's decision whether or not to use identity language.

Nevertheless, identity language raises deeper philosophical concerns. It is often meant to imply that the named characteristic is central to the very personhood of the one described. Identity language says, in effect, "This is who I am, and you must accept these characteristics in order to accept *me*." Whereas the term "same-sex attracted" takes on a passive-voice inflection in a deliberate attempt to disconnect the *experience* from the person's true character, "gay" is more direct. Thus, there *is* a difference between calling oneself "Gay and Catholic" (the title of Eve Tushnet's recent book) and calling oneself "same-sex attracted". It is the difference between saying, "I live in Minnesota", and, "I'm a Minnesotan." One more obviously ties a particular fact about me to my self-understanding and even my very personhood.

Grammar isn't everything, of course. If a nurse asks me about my blood and I say, "I'm A-positive", do I mean to suggest that blood type is a defining feature of my identity? It's unlikely. But we don't choose terms in a vacuum, and a term like "gay" inevitably draws on a broader social and linguistic context that gives it more pointed meaning. Sexual-identity terms have become familiar in modern society as a means of identifying erotic attraction as a defining and fixed aspect of personhood.

This kind of identity claim can raise some complicated issues, particularly when we start thinking about love and social acceptance. Real love must often discriminate between sinners and sins, or sometimes between persons and their defects. Although we sometimes fantasize about finding someone who will "love me as I am", a true lover wants to see his beloved's potential fulfilled, even if this involves (as it typically does) significant change. Drawing lines between the true me and my personal defects is a necessary part of this process. It's possible to love me without loving my scoliosis; indeed, if you love me, you will surely wish to see my scoliosis cured or at least marginalized such that it has little impact on my life. Real love refuses to identify me as a person with my less admirable traits or features. Moreover, why would a person want to identify with that which is a defect?

The term "defect" may itself require more elucidation. Here I will use it somewhat broadly to describe any departure from that which we take to be normative for human beings. So, there are some defects—such as scoliosis and blindness—that most obviously relate to the physical form and may seem not to have a clear moral dimension. Others, of a more psychological nature, can incline a person to sin. Same-sex attractions, various sexual fetishes, and, say, a compulsion for gambling might all be examples. These various imperfections impact life and identity in different ways. But although they clearly differ in some respects, I don't necessarily want to distinguish these kinds of "defects" from each other too sharply. As the *Catechism of the Catholic Church* states, the homosexual orientation is not chosen, and in that respect it is like scoliosis and blindness.[2] One is not responsible for having a propensity to same-sex attractions. So it may be quite reasonable to view same-sex attraction, like scoliosis and blindness, as an unchosen feature of a person "as presently constituted", which is neither deserving of moral disapprobation as such, nor deserving of being considered a part of a person's identity.

It is clear, nevertheless, that some defects are rather easily dismissed as "non-identity-forming personal features", while others are more complicated. Let's look at a few cases that may shed light on this.

Scoliosis is a particularly easy case. It's obviously a defect (with no very evident moral dimension), but it probably isn't the sort of life-changing condition that dramatically affects my character. Anyone who loves me now would surely be able to love me just as much if I were half an inch taller and had less back pain. Some personal defects are far more complex. A trait like blindness (though clearly a defect per se) may end up shaping a person's life and character in such a way that he is genuinely ambivalent about a possible cure. Sight is clearly a good per se. But coping with the challenge of blindness might further the development of especially heroic virtues or help to foster positive relationships.

---

[2] *Catechism of the Catholic Church*, 2nd ed. (Washington, D.C.: Libreria Editrice Vaticana—United States Conference of Catholic Bishops, 2000), no. 2358.

A well-adjusted blind person might reach the point where the defect actually seems like a defining and even valued part of him.

Developmental disorders can likewise occasion much debate, even among affected persons and those who most love them. Down syndrome is clearly a defect but it seems to be a "defining" defect more than, say, scoliosis or blindness. In a sense, Down syndrome seems to make those who have it "who" they are. Down syndrome seems to show more than other defects, perhaps, that it is possible for people who suffer from developmental disorders to lead joyful lives, and to be a source of grace and goodness for others around them. But are these positives intrinsic to the condition itself? Probably not, for even with Down syndrome, which seems to blunt the effects of original sin, it does not seem right to say that condition itself is a source of the goodness but that its effects are.

Same-sex attraction is clearly another very complicated sort of case. Erotic attraction has a pervasive and far-reaching impact on a person's life and character, so it makes sense that SSA, even if not good per se, will seem far more personally defining than a condition like scoliosis. And undoubtedly some goods will come to a person because of SSA while not being rooted in it. For instance, a person with same-sex attraction may be attracted to another person of the same sex who in fact becomes instrumental in his conversion to Catholicism. It would be wrong to conclude, however, that SSA by its very nature leads people to be attracted to those who will facilitate their conversion. And, of course, those with same-sex attraction, just like those who are blind, may develop virtue, even heroic virtue, in dealing with the special challenges their conditions present.

It's important to note here that the claim that same-sex attraction is a defect does not mean it is curable by natural means—nor, of course, does it mean that it is not curable. It seems clear that even extended therapeutic efforts to change or redirect SSA are often unsuccessful, and there can be no doubt that many people experience same-sex attraction when they emphatically do not wish to. But individuals suffer from all manner of defects (physical, mental, and spiritual) that science and psychology deem incurable. We don't for that reason conclude that the blind will never see, that the lame will never walk, or that mentally ill persons can never be made whole. In the end, all of us depend on God's grace to transform us into *more* than we could ever become on our own. If we conclude that same-sex attraction is (at least *as such*) nonconducive to one's thriving, we should acknowledge it as a defect that, if not curable in this lifetime, can in the end be cured by grace.

Sexual identity terms are controversial, given that they are an important component of a broader progressive agenda. Sexual identity claims can help to undermine traditional sexual morals in a number of ways. They encourage us to view sexual desire (in all its many and varied forms) as a significant manifestation of individuality. Such desires, it is suggested, must be gratified in order for people to thrive and be personally fulfilled. In that sort of context, it seems highly unreasonable to hold conjugal marriage as *the* proper earthly context for sex and erotic love more generally. What if some people are intrinsically unsuited to such a state? What if some are "built" to find love in a different way or in another sort of sexual arrangement? Would it not be cruel to deny them that chance?

Catholic sexual ethics, on this understanding, is viewed as intrinsically bigoted, since its rejection of particular sexual lifestyles is automatically interpreted as a rejection of the persons themselves. The "sexual identity" ideal has finally developed to the point where social media recognizes no less than fifty "sexual identities", and people who fit the norm (that is, people who identify with their biological sex, while romantically pursuing members of the opposite sex) are marginalized as "cisgendered", a term that serves simultaneously to represent normalcy as one of a plethora of options and to smugly imply that it is the *least interesting* available choice.

The Spiritual Friendship movement, of course, does not sanction all of these developments. But it does draw on notions of sexual identity that have emerged from these same cultural movements. Eve Tushnet, for instance, justifies her continued use of the terms "gay" and "lesbian" by explaining that her self-identification as "lesbian" was an important step in the development of her present self-understanding. In her book she explains how, like a key turning in a lock, she came to "make sense to herself" when she "realized" that she was a lesbian.[3] In short, identifying as a lesbian is part of *who* she understands herself to be.

It's a sympathetic explanation, but for modern Christians, these defining moments take place in a context of a contemporary (and in many ways deeply defective) understanding of the significance of sexual

---

[3] Tushnet, *Gay and Catholic*, p. 15.

attraction. This is manifestly true for Tushnet, who was enmeshed in gay and lesbian culture for years before her Catholic conversion. The associations she made in that culture were, she claims, morally positive in numerous ways, which she cites as further justification of her use of identity language. But however that may be, it's surely also true that such communities have, from a Catholic perspective, a radically distorted understanding of the significance of human sexuality. It is curious that Tushnet in her book does very little to repudiate her past involvement in the gay/lesbian culture; she often seems so determined to credit some of those she met there with having helped her achieve virtue, that she fails to acknowledge that the gay/lesbian culture is based largely on seeking sinful sex.

Considering the confusion about sexual identity, it's worth stepping back to ask, is there room for an authentically *Catholic or Christian* understanding of "sexual identity"? What might that mean in a Catholic context? Even more directly to our concerns, can a desire to engage in same-sex actions be considered to be good? To be in itself conducive to other good things?

If Catholics *can* view sexual identity as a real and positive phenomenon, it must involve more than just the desire for homoerotic sex. Is there a broader and less explicitly sexual way in which such an identity might be understood? The Spiritual Friendship movement supposes that there is, and this step is critical to their larger project.

Is It Good to Be Gay?

In asking the question of whether or not it is good to be gay, it should of course be understood that we are considering only *direct* goods. As noted earlier, there are any number of ways in which bad things may indirectly lead to good. Earthly trials can often facilitate the development of virtue or provide occasions for outpourings of grace. Nevertheless, we should do our best to be clear about whether or not a trait is *in itself* consistent with personal good.

Since it is agreed among all orthodox Catholics that homosexual acts are sinful, a morally positive "gay identity" must involve something broader than just sex or the desire for it. And indeed, would-be orthodox "gay Christians" do seek to articulate an understanding of what "gay" might mean. As they would have it, "gayness" really involves a rich, organic perspective on the world that goes well beyond carnal desire. When we view sexual desire as just one (possibly minor) element in a unique "orientation" or perspective, it seems more possible to diffuse the moral issues surrounding same-sex attraction. Being gay might be a gift or a blessing (albeit one requiring particular discipline and sacrifice with respect to the physical appetites). Elizabeth Scalia has explored such a possibility and suggests that "our gay brothers and sisters" are "planned, loved-into-being 'necessary others'" whose unique gifts should be valued and cherished.[4]

Julie Rodgers, a contributor to *Spiritual Friendship*, explored a similar idea in a recent essay in which she suggested that, in fact, homosexually inclined people are only slightly more burdened than others even by the call to chastity. Her desire for other women, she explains, is only occasionally carnal in nature. Most often it manifests itself as a desire for companionship, spiritual intimacy, and "an energizing love that spills over into the kind of hospitality that actually provides guests with clean sheets and something other than protein bars."[5] There is, she agrees, some temptation to lust. But this trial is in no sense unique to gays.

> Both gay people and straight people have the capacity to lust, and both gay people and straight people have the capacity for sexual sin by having sex outside of marriage. We're on level ground when it comes to having a draw toward other people with the capacity for that longing to be sexualized, and we're on level ground in that we have a draw toward other people that can be actualized in beautiful ways that promote human flourishing through community, relationship, and service.[6]

In a follow-up post on the same forum, blogger Wesley Hill suggests[7] that this thicker concept of gay identity probably is, for him and many other same-sex attracted Catholics, a major point of departure from the

---

[4] Elizabeth Scalia, "Homosexuality: A Call to Otherness?", *First Things*, June 14, 2011, http://www.firstthings.com/web-exclusives/2011/06/homosexuality-a-call-to-otherness.

[5] Julie Rodgers, "Can the Gay Be a Good?" *Spiritual Friendship* (blog), October 23, 2014, http://spiritualfriendship.org/2014/10/23/can-the-gay-be-a-good/.

[6] Ibid.

[7] Wesley Hill, "On Disagreeing About 'Homosexuality': A Thought Experiment", *Spiritual Friendship* (blog), December 17, 2014, http://spiritualfriendship.org/2014/12/17/on-disagreeing-about-homosexuality-a-thought-experiment/.

traditional Christian understanding of sexuality. To him this doesn't appear problematic; if anything, he seems to suppose that moderns understand sexual identity much better than their Christian forbears. As he tells it, a thinker like Saint Thomas Aquinas was comfortable addressing homosexuality solely through a discussion of homosexual *acts*. But modern, self-described gay Christians are instead working within "a contemporary framework of thinking about homosexuality", and within this "new social construct", sexual desire is contextualized within the broader gay identity. This is what enables us to understand "gay" as a good or at least neutral characteristic.

An obvious question now arises: What exactly does it mean to be gay? More specifically, what is the relationship (definitionally speaking) between "being gay" and experiencing homoerotic desire? It is undeniable that same-sex attracted people have a full, rich perspective on the world, along with many gifts and insights to contribute to the Church. But are any of these other features per se a component of being *gay*? Any serious moral analysis will clearly require an answer to that question.

On a level of definitions, it's difficult to identify any defining feature of a gay identity *apart from* homoerotic attraction. Certainly, it seems true that people with same-sex attraction tend to share a range of characteristics and experiences that go well beyond sexual desire. They form communities that no doubt manifest various virtues that are not directly connected sex. Nevertheless, no one self-identifies as gay merely because he is artistic, sensitive to beauty, disposed to intimate friendship, or what have you. Likewise, any person who does experience deep-seated same-sex attraction may self-identify as "gay" without causing the least confusion. He need not meet any other criteria, nor need he have any involvement in a homosexual community. In short, a gay identity or orientation (if such a concept is meaningful at all) appears to have only one definitionally necessary identifying feature: the regular and persistent experience of homoerotic desire.

Can *that* be a good, or perhaps necessarily attendant on it? The origins of same-sex attraction have been debated at great length, and I don't intend to address or settle that issue here. For my purposes it is enough to observe that, logically, there are three possibilities for how homoerotic desire might relate to potentially positive features of a broader gay "identity". First, they might be congruous in a noncausal way (as for example if SSA and musical ability were attached to the same gene sequence). Second, there might be certain talents or personality traits that leave a person especially susceptible to same-sex attraction. Though themselves good, they might open the possibility of disordered sexual desires, and in speaking of a "gay identity" we might refer more broadly to the precipitating conditions. Third, it might be that homoerotic desire *itself* opens the door to a certain goods that would not be available without it, or is even a constitutive part of some broader good that is not possible without it.

These options are not mutually exclusive. There may be truth to any or all of them. For our present purposes, however, it is enough to observe that only the third really justifies a robust affirmation of a "gay identity" as such that brings linked goods. If there are other gifts or virtues that either precede or are congruous with homoerotic desire, it would make more sense to affirm them in their own right rather than fixating on the accompanying disordered desire. Celebrating a gay or lesbian identity *as such* only makes sense if same-sex attraction is itself a causal or constitutive part of whatever good we wish to affirm.

The Spiritual Friendship movement seems to think that it can be. This is worth examining in more detail.

Eros Divided

Sexual attraction is not reducible to lust. This is a point that the writers at *Spiritual Friendship* have made again and again. And undoubtedly, they are right. Virtually every writer who treats the subject of erotic love appreciates that it involves far more than just carnal desire.

Because faithful Christians agree that it would be lustful (and therefore a sin) to indulge carnal desire for a member of one's own sex, they try to analyze erotic desire in an effort to subdivide it. The Spiritual Friendship people hold that there are explicitly carnal elements of eros that must be condemned, but there are also feelings or attractions that are not so very carnal or perhaps not even carnal that it would be moral to indulge and even encourage, as healthy components of the sort of "spiritual friendship" they wish to own.

Eve Tushnet addresses this issue in her book, *Gay and Catholic*, when she points out that homoerotic love might motivate acts of service clearly not forbidden in the *Catechism of the Catholic Church*, such as making soup for a girlfriend.[8] One cannot but wish for a bit more detail, and happily, her fellow writers at *Spiritual Friendship* provide this with more extended meditations on the noncarnal elements of eros.

Blogger Jeremy Erickson begins his reflection by noting frankly that he agrees that "if there is *no* sexual component to a person's desire for the same sex, words like 'gay' and 'bisexual' are misleading." Nevertheless, he maintains that his desire for the other sex is not reducible to carnal desire.

> Even when I am attracted to a guy in a way that includes sexual temptation, there's a lot more going on than wanting to have sex. It typically starts in a way that is physical but not genital: I notice that the guy is nice to look at. I can find myself desiring *him*. I don't actually mean that I desire to do particular sexual things with him, but simply that I desire him in a relatively vague sense. If I have a natural opportunity to befriend him, there's an energy that my feelings bring. In fact, much of this is true even in many cases that *don't* lead to lustful thoughts, and whether I experience sexual temptation has more to do with the *intensity* of the feeling than the *kind*. It's not clear to me where precisely my experience starts to differ from a straight man's. [9]

Reading Erickson's essay, I was reminded immediately of C. S. Lewis' description of the first stirrings of eros in *The Four Loves*. He notes that eros does not *immediately* beget the desire for sex. If a man is feeling the first stirrings of eros after looking at a beautiful woman, one might ask him what he wants, and receive the answer, "To go on thinking of her."[10] The desire for sex will almost certainly follow in time (and perhaps a short time) if nothing else halts the process. But it certainly is not *reducible* to that.

Nick Roen makes a similar opening in describing his attraction to a man he calls "Rick". But he goes on to note that his initial attraction ("feeling butterflies") precipitates further desires, which are themselves quite varied in nature.

> As I noticed Rick with pleasure, the attraction produced all sorts of "I want ..." desires in me. One of those desires was a sexual desire. No,

---

[8] Tushnet, *Gay and Catholic*, p.181.

[9] Jeremy Erickson, "What 'Not Reducible' Means", *Spiritual Friendship* (blog), December 18, 2014, http://spiritualfriendship.org/2014/12/18/what-not-reducible-means/.

[10] C. S. Lewis, *The Four Loves*, 2nd ed. (Boston, Mass.: Mariner Books, 1971), p. 93.

I wasn't immediately imagining what it would be like to be in bed with him, but the seed was present. However, I also experienced many heightened desires toward Rick that had nothing to do with sex. I desired to go talk to him, shake his hand, get to know him, laugh with him, and serve him by bringing him a glass of punch. In other words, not only were the seeds of sexual desire present, but the seeds of desires for friendship, hospitality, emotional intimacy, sacrificial service, and love were there as well. All different desires, all colored by the same initial attraction.[11]

There is a naïveté to these reflections that is almost touching. It is as though these bloggers are exploring only for the very first time what it feels like to fall in love. In eros, the desire for sex and for companionship, to serve unstintingly and to possess wholly, can all be rolled together into a gloriously confusing mass of emotions. It is by no means a simple experience. But that fact, though unsurprising, is in the end not especially helpful in determining whether a particular sort of sexual expression can ever be healthy.

Roen goes on to express the hope that it might be possible to "put to death" the carnal element of his homoerotic desires, while preserving the nonsexual component of his attraction. He asks,

What of the non-sexual desires for things like friendship, hospitality, relational intimacy, and sacrificial love? In my view, it is impossible to put all of these desires to death and have any semblance of consistent friendship. For example, what if I experience an attraction toward a friend to whom I have previously been unattracted, but now suddenly find attractive? (This has happened to me many times). If I were to put to death all non-sexual desires tied to this attraction, it would be practically impossible to maintain a healthy, intimate friendship with him.[12]

Some distinctions probably need to be drawn here between a love that *begins* with erotic attraction, and a nonerotic love that has the capacity to take on a more sexualized component. In the first case, as Roen himself points out, even noncarnal desires (such as the desire to serve) are tied up in a larger set of inclinations and emotions that we might characterize as *erotic attraction.* Relationships that begin on a nonerotic foundation are

---

[11] Nick Roen, "Same-Sex Attraction in Real Life", *Spiritual Friendship* (blog), February 12, 2015, http://spiritualfriendship.org/author/roenaboat/.
[12] Ibid.

a more complicated case, and we would probably need more details to determine the correct response. Of course, it would be absurd to condemn "friendship, hospitality, relational intimacy, and sacrificial love" in all contexts (or to suggest that these also need to be reserved for marriage), merely because they can sometimes precipitate erotic desire. But the important question is, can noncarnal desires that are *rooted* in a disordered erotic attraction be healthy, fruitful, or something to encourage? Is it really possible to "put to death" the carnal element while permitting the other desires (born of the same erotic attraction) to survive?

Before addressing these questions, we should note that Roen is more aggressive than some of his fellow *Spiritual Friendship* writers even in his insistence that the "passion of the flesh" needs to be "put to death". Some think it is possible to turn even that passion toward more godly ends.

In her post "Still Looking to Desire", blogger Melinda Selmys[13] explores this possibility by discussing *rightly ordered* homoerotic desire, a phenomenon she thinks can exist. Selmys observes that homoerotic attraction, like all attraction, is the recognition of genuine goodness and beauty. Thus, it shouldn't be necessary to shun the *attraction*; what is important is putting that recognition to proper use. She compares her erotic desire for other women to the attraction Eve felt in the Garden of Eden for the fruit of the Tree of Life. Eve is correct to recognize that the fruit is good. Her error lies in the decision to eat it. Likewise, lesbians are right to see women as objectively desirable. What matters is how they subjectively experience that desire and even more how they channel that desire. Selmys states,

> My desire is not disordered in and of itself: it becomes disordered when I direct it, or allow it to direct itself, towards something which is forbidden. If it leads me to fantasize about homosexual acts, or to think of the woman as a sex object, then it becomes disordered, that is ordered towards an end which is not in conformity with Truth and with the dignity of the person. But what if I make the act of will to redirect that desire, to use it as an opportunity to give glory to God for the beauty which He has made manifest in that particular woman? Or to meditate on my desire for the one-flesh union of the entire humanum in the Eucharist

[13] Melinda Selmys, "Still Looking to Desire", *Spiritual Friendship* (blog), March 17, 2015, http://spiritualfriendship.org/2014/03/17/still-looking-to-desire/.

where there is neither Gentile nor Jew, slave nor free, woman nor man? Or as an opportunity to contemplate the relationship between the doctrines of the Communion of Saints and of the resurrection of the Body? What if, by an act of will, I take that desire and order it towards its proper end: towards the Good, the Beautiful and the True?[14]

Selmys does not precisely suggest that *carnal desire* is something to encourage. To be sure, she condemns "fantasizing about homosexual acts" and "thinking of the woman as a sex object". Yet, at the same time, she does seem to think that homoerotic desire might properly provide occasion for reflecting on "desire for the one-flesh union of the entire *humanum* in the Eucharist" (emphasis added). Does that imply that the desire for bodily union might itself be taken as a positive, if infused with sufficient theological content? Even more than Erickson or Roen, Selmys seems willing to view homoerotic attraction as a positive as such, which can reasonably be encouraged and even celebrated in the proper context.

How should Catholics respond to these efforts to subdivide homoerotic attraction into ordered and disordered components? It is a question that can only be answered in the context of a broader anthropology and sexual ethics. To determine whether homoeroticism can be a healthy expression of eros, we must ask more broadly, what *is* the healthy course of healthy eros? The literature on that question is extensive, and it would be impossible to do it justice in this one essay. Nevertheless, looking at a few particularly helpful texts may be enough to illustrate the concerns Catholics should have about the attempt to subdivide eros as a justification of same-sex attraction.

Eros and Human Love

It may be worth taking a moment, at the outset of this section, to recall how our discussion of eros stands in relation to the larger project of *Spiritual Friendship* and other same-sex attracted Catholics. Same-sex attraction is clearly a real phenomenon, with real implications for the lives of those who experience it. But if it can be part of a unique and positive sexual identity, then it might also seem that gay Christians ought to

---

[14] Ibid.

be directed toward some uniquely appropriate lifestyle or relationship, which is uniquely suited to them in a way that conjugal marriage cannot be. And, of course, that is precisely what the Spiritual Friendship movement is all about: promoting friendship as a relationship for which those with SSA are particularly suited.

Clearly, this is a difficult subject. It would be cruel and silly to suggest that same-sex attracted people cannot have friends. But it's also fairly clear that, in entertaining the possibility of special, erotically tinged friendship, *Spiritual Friendship* writers are looking for a relationship that would be unique to same-sex attracted people, which has no natural counterpart among the married, or among single people who nevertheless are attracted to the opposite sex.

Virtually everyone, it is true, has the capacity for erotic attractions of an unhealthy kind, and we don't for that reason suppose that friendship should be forbidden (or allowed only among those who have *absolutely no* potential for illicit attraction). A married person, for instance, can properly form friendships with members of both sexes. But opposite-sex friends (assuming they are not eligible for romantic involvement) generally understand the importance of setting prudent boundaries on their level of intimacy. What reasonable husband would permit his wife to enter into an intimate "spiritual friendship" with another man? What wife, upon hearing that her husband was erotically attracted to another woman, would be satisfied with the assurance that their special friendship was nonphysical?

As a general rule, we advise people to *pull away* from those toward whom they feel illicit attraction. If homoerotic attraction is agreed to be disordered, it would seem appropriate to set similar boundaries on friendships that are potentially dangerous for one or both people involved. Same-sex attracted people can have same-sex friends, just as married people can have opposite-sex friends. But it would seem most prudent for them to set reasonable boundaries on their levels of intimacy, much as married people ought to do with their opposite-sex friends. That clearly is not the aim of many of the writers of *Spiritual Friendship*.

Why does this matter for single and celibate people, when they have no spouse or children to betray? It matters, first and foremost, because a disordered love will be spiritually detrimental to the lover himself, and secondarily because *all* disordered relationships have the potential to affect others in a negative way. Within a Catholic sexual ethics the primary question is not whether all affected parties consent or who else will be hurt, but rather, is this kind of love consonant with real love and respect for all involved persons, including the lover himself?

Eros, as the Church Fathers always understood, is replete with spiritual dangers. As the most intense and beguiling of human loves, it tempts us to use, possess, and idolize others. It runs roughshod over the boundaries of ordinary decorum and common sense. No other love leaves us so vulnerable to self-deception and betrayal.

Given these manifold dangers, Christians have always understood the importance of providing secure guidelines for romantic relationships. Friendship is by nature a looser and more varied arrangement. (It's no accident that *spiritual friendship* can be contemplated only under this more flexible category). But friendship is also a more disinterested, and less possessive, love than what many "gay Christians" seem to be contemplating. Tushnet and others write about the "lost art" of friendship, by which they seem to mean that our friendships are too superficial and (in some cases at least) ought to be deeper, more committed, and more spiritually and emotionally intense. But especially in the context of the reflections quoted in the last section, it begins to seem that what is wanted is not *friendship* but rather a peculiar sort of erotic love.

Erotic love is all of the things that Tushnet seems to want in a friendship: intense, consuming, and disposed to serious commitment. It is also dangerous, especially when it is untethered from its natural and approved course. And precisely because it is so bewitching, it has a strong tendency to diminish our capacity for disinterested rational thought. It's not safe to rely on people to sift through the elements of their own erotic attachments; almost certainly, a person in love doesn't fully grasp the longer-term implications or the short-term dangers of his high-flown feelings. That's why the Church takes it upon herself to educate lovers, urging them to embrace self-consciously the natural ends of erotic attachment.

Karol Wojtyla (now better known as Saint John Paul II) addressed this topic at great length in his book *Love and Responsibility*. Wojtyla understands the sexual urge to be a "natural drive" or "vector of aspiration", which pushes us to participate in the perpetuation of the species, and at the same time provides a kind of raw material for interpersonal erotic love. Wojtyla makes clear that the sexual urge is more than just an "instinct". Individuals, because they are *persons*, are attracted to particular others, not merely as sexual objects, but rather as unique and precious individuals worthy of love. Our capacity for interpersonal love enables us to "personalize" erotic attraction, and to act deliberately on the plane of love instead of being ruled by carnal desire. But because eros is by its nature infused with the sexual urge (being built on the "raw material" that the sexual urge provides), it's essential that erotic love be developed in a way that self-consciously recognizes and embraces the true purpose of the sexual urge.[15]

The sexual urge is connected in a special way with the natural order of existence, which is the divine order inasmuch as it is realized under the continuous influence of God the Creator. A man and a woman through their conjugal life and a full sexual relationship agree to take a special part in the work of creation.[16]

What that means is that couples should commit themselves voluntarily to participating in the continuance of the human race as a common good between them and as a return to God for all he has showered upon them. In marriage a man and woman give themselves wholly to one another, but as a couple they also jointly present themselves to God and society as the foundation of a new family. That role (and its attendant obligations) gives meaning and structure to their shared life and also serves as a check on the many spiritual temptations attendant on erotic love.

> The proper end of the sexual urge is the existence of the species *Homo*, its continuation, and love between persons, between man and woman, is shaped and channeled one might say, by that purpose and the material it provides. It can therefore take its correct shape only in so far as it develops in close harmony with the proper purpose of the sexual urge. An outright conflict with that purpose will also perturb and undermine love between persons. People sometimes find this purpose a nuisance and try to circumvent it by artificial means. Such means must, however, have a damaging effect on love between persons, which in this context is most intimately involved in the use of the sexual urge.[17]

Several components of this account are of relevance to our present discussion. In the first place, Wojtyla agrees that the sexual urge is itself

---

[15] Karol Wojtyla, *Love and Responsibility*, rev. ed. (San Francisco: Ignatius Press, 1993), p. 56.
[16] See ibid.
[17] Ibid., p. 53.

a natural and pervasive part of man's life, which touches many elements of man's experience. He would certainly agree that that "vector of aspiration" gives rise to more than just carnal desire. At the same time, he also suggests that actions motivated by the sexual urge need to be in keeping with its true purpose, namely, bringing forth of new persons. What that means is that a "full sexual relationship" (in a conjugal context) should not merely be seen as one available outlet for the sexual urge. It is *the* appropriate outlet, at least in the realm of merely personal relationships. Thus, it would be gravely erroneous to see sex merely as a *perk* of marriage.

In the appropriate context, sex can do much to *ward off* the more dangerous perversions to which erotic love can tend. C. S. Lewis expounds on this idea in his book *The Four Loves*. Noting how young people often regard seriousness about sex as a kind of prophylactic against immorality, he suggests that in fact it's probably much better to diffuse the mystique of sex with a healthy appreciation for its more ridiculous side. Even before it pushes us onward to the absorbing realities of pregnancy, birth, and parenthood, sex brings eros back to earth with the very literal meshing of physical bodies. The temptation to elevate one's beloved to godlike status cannot long survive such a test.[18]

Like Wojtyla, Lewis notes the natural tendency of eros to sweep lovers up in something that is intrinsically bigger than they themselves can fully recognize or comprehend. Wojtyla has argued that we must deliberately act as rational and loving beings by understanding and accepting the true purpose of the sexual urge and acting in accord with its natural ends. Lewis makes a similar suggestion by pointing out that couples in love adopt "roles": of Mother Earth and Father Sky, of Zeus and Hera, and ultimately of Christ and his Church. Where friends try to appreciate one another in their unique personhood, lovers step into preset "places" for which both their bodies and their souls have been ordered. Understanding that it is not for them to dictate the proper shape of eros, they instead embrace it for what it is and do their best to live up to the attendant commitments.

Eros, having made his gigantic promise and shown you in glimpses what its performance would be like, has "done his stuff." He, like a godparent,

---

[18] Lewis, *Four Loves*, pp. 111–13.

makes the vows; it is we who must keep them. It is we who must labor to bring our daily life into even closer accordance with what the glimpses have revealed. We must do the works of Eros when Eros is not present. This all good lovers know.[19]

Lewis also gives some warning of what can happen when eros refuses to follow the course prescribed for it.

Thus Eros, like the other loves, but more strikingly because of his strength, sweetness, terror and high port, reveals his true status. He cannot be what, nevertheless, he must be if he is to remain Eros. He needs help; therefore he needs to be ruled. The god dies or becomes a demon unless he obeys God. It would be well in such a case if he always died. But he may live on, mercilessly chaining together two mutual tormentors, each raw all over with the poison of hate-in-love, each ravenous to receive and implacably refusing to give, jealous, suspicious, resentful, struggling for the upper hand, determined to be free and to allow no freedom, living on "scenes." Read *Anna Karenina,* and do not fancy that such things happen only in Russia. The lovers' old hyperbole of "eating" each other can come horribly near to the truth.[20]

These words might serve as a helpful warning to anyone who would recommend erotically motivated "spiritual friendships" as an appropriate alternative for same-sex attracted Christians who yearn for the stability and intimacy of marriage. Erotic love, as countless individuals have discovered to their sorrow, is an unforgiving master. Unlinked from its natural path, it can do enormous damage, not only to bodies, but also to minds and souls. What is to prevent spiritual friendships from going down this same path? Do its proponents really suppose that they can tame erotic love through a formal renunciation of the carnal?

Spiritual Friendship as a Modern Phenomenon

Understanding the hazards of erotic love, the Church has for centuries prescribed marriage to lovers of every stripe as the only fitting

[19] Ibid., p.115.
[20] Ibid.

natural fulfillment of erotic love. Modern people look for every possible excuse to rebel against this natural order, complaining that it doesn't fit their particular needs and interests, and their more specifically tailored arrangements. Thus we find couples living together or continuing sexual relationships for various lengths of time, depending on their feelings and extraneous interests. Some have children without marrying or deliberately set out to raise children alone, with a same-sex partner, or in groups of three or more. Others marry but use contraceptives to delay childbearing, perhaps indefinitely.

In the eyes of the world it now seems outrageous and even cruel to suggest that people might be *morally obliged* to order their erotic proclivities according to its natural teleology. Erotic attraction, sexual expression, marriage, and domestic life can be arranged in all manner of ways, and who (they ask) is harmed by this, so long as all the relevant parties consent? In reality, the consequences of our widespread rejection of the conjugal pattern have become painfully obvious. Disordered erotic love has begotten a tidal wave of misery and social unrest, but it is difficult to find our way back when the meaning and purpose of sex have been mostly forgotten.

It might seem odd to classify "spiritual friendship" together with other disordered forms of eros that are quite obviously more appetitive and base. There is clearly a significant component of self-discipline to an erotically tinged "friendship" that assiduously avoids physical intimacy, let alone one that is directed to the mutual pursuit of transcendent goods. Nevertheless, it should be clear from the previous section that in a Catholic understanding, mere discipline is not enough. Erotic love that refuses to follow the appropriate natural order will not be salutary, and here we see that "spiritual friendship" is characteristically modern, insofar as it seeks approval for nonconjugal expressions of erotic desire. And as with all other permutations of the Church's recommended pattern for romantic or erotically tinged love, we can only suppose that this form of love will be spiritually injurious in ways that lovers themselves do not initially anticipate.

What should we recommend, then, to those who experience same-sex attraction as a seemingly settled disposition? Others are better equipped to answer this question than I, but perhaps the most fitting general comment is that there is no single recommendation that can be made to all who struggle with this one particular trial. Everyone should avoid relationships built on disordered attraction; that obligation is indeed universal. But this requirement is merely negative, and (as Tushnet rightly stresses in her book) a fulfilled life centers around service and around *positive* commitments to others and to God. Persons experiencing same-sex attraction should, of course, seek to make their lives about something other than the avoidance of homoerotic desire. But we shouldn't necessarily try to supply simple answers as to what that something should be.

For all Catholics, it is important to learn how to articulate the truths of the faith in ways that are sensitive, loving, and also clear. No one should be made to feel uniquely sinful or fallen on account of experiences that are nonvoluntary. And every baptized person should be assured that he does indeed have unique gifts to contribute to the Body of the Church. We simply need to keep working to discern what those might be, in a way that is consistent with a Catholic understanding of rightly ordered love.

Restoring Wholeness in Christ

Bob Schuchts, Ph.D.

I see clearly that the thing the Church needs most today is the ability to heal wounds.... I see the Church as a field hospital after battle.... Heal the wounds, heal the wounds.... And you have to start from the ground up.

—Pope Francis, *America Magazine*, March 2014

All of us have been wounded by the ravages of sin, either our own sins or the sin of others. Likewise, we all desperately need salvation. We need Jesus, the Physician of our souls and bodies, to heal our wounds and to restore us to wholeness.[1] This is the central message of the gospel and the essential mission of the Church.[2] Pope Francis continues to reiterate this central message of the gospel and Church teaching with simple and evocative images. If the Church is a field hospital, her clergy, religious ministers, and lay ministers are the medics, each a wounded healer,[3] called to assist those wounded in battle.

Over the past thirty-five years, I have accompanied hundreds of individuals and families on their paths toward *wholeness and holiness*. The healing journeys of individuals with same-sex attractions (SSA) are unique in some ways, but overall, their process of transformation is remarkably similar to all the other families and individuals with whom I have journeyed.

At times, those suffering with unwanted SSA or other disordered sexual desires have come to me looking to "fix" their problem, but discover that their desires and attractions cannot be simply "prayed away", as if

---

[1] See *Catechism of the Catholic Church*, 2nd ed. (Washington, D.C.: Libreria Editrice Vaticana—United States Catholic Conference, 2000), no. 1509 (hereafter, cited as *CCC*).

[2] Benedict XVI, *Jesus of Nazareth* (New York: Doubleday, 2007), p. 176.

[3] See Henri Nouwen, *The Wounded Healer* (New York: Doubleday, 1979).

by magic. This is one reason why "healing" has received such skepticism among those with SSA. People are rightly skeptical that one can pray SSA away. Many have tried and failed, believing that enough novenas or healing Masses will get rid of their unwanted desires.

Genuine healing, on the other hand, is aimed at helping the person with unwanted SSA to turn to the Lord and ask the Lord to show him what in his life has caused various kinds of brokenness in his being. For instance, has he been nursing unforgiveness or anger at someone who greatly hurt him? Has he come to believe he is unlovable or incapable of loving? Spiritual counselors have found that many of the problems that a person experiences, such as depression, are often rooted in such life experiences and attitudes. Prayer helps to discover the sources of problems, an essential step in the longer process of complete healing.

In a similar way, those with SSA and their families soon discover that these desires are really symptoms revealing a much more fundamental brokenness, one we all share in some way. Father Emiliano Tardif, a priest who ministered healing to thousands in the name of Jesus, reveals the source of this brokenness: "In the healing ministry, we are not dealing with symptoms, but with the cause of the problems.... Wounds caused by a lack of love or a distortion of love, are often at the root of our brokenness."[4]

Each of us shares an insatiable hunger for true love and meaning in life, and each of us has been wounded by the lack or distortion of love in our own lives. As Saint John Paul II was fond of saying, our lives are senseless without love, but with love our lives become meaningful and fulfilling, freeing us to become who we really are.[5] It took me many years to discover this essential truth: *only love heals at the deepest level.* Certainly different forms of counseling and psychotherapy can be enormously helpful both in helping us discover wounds and healing wounds, but, at root, everyone needs to be healed of the break from God caused by original sin and also from subsequent sins and harms. The Father's love is the key ingredient to every problem we face, because only in the light of God's love do we come to discover our wholeness in Christ, as

[4] Fr. Emiliano Tardif, *Jesus Lives Today* (South Bend, Ind.: Greenlawn Press, 1989), p. 73.

[5] See John Paul II, *Redeemer of Man*, March 4, 1979, no. 10, http://w2.vatican.va/content /john-paul-ii/en/encyclicals/documents/hf_jp-ii_enc_04031979_redemptor-hominis.html; John Paul II, *Letter to Families*, February 2, 1994, no. 11, http://w2.vatican.va/content/john -paul-ii/en/letters/1994/documents/hf_jp-ii_let_02021994_families.html.

well as our true identity as the Father's beloved sons and daughters. This discovery was strikingly emphasized by Pope Benedict XVI in *Jesus of Nazareth* as he closely examined Jesus' healing ministry in the Gospels. With conciseness and spiritual insight he observed: "Whoever wishes to heal man must see him in his wholeness and know that his ultimate healing can only be God's love."[6] This is a profound and life-changing assertion, worthy of deep pondering.

We must realize that we are *persons* first of all, created in the image and likeness of God, male and female (see Gen 1:28). Any labels that attempt to categorize us to the contrary fail to see us in the wholeness God intended. In God's eyes, there are no "queers", "fagots", "gays", or "lesbians", any more than there are "homophobes", 'bigots", "bisexuals" or "straights". These labels may describe certain elements or traits of brokenness, but they do not ultimately facilitate healing in people or relationships. Rather, they tend to inflict additional injury, deepen our sense of shame or pride, and reinforce the divisions that separate us from one another. They do not lead us to wholeness in Christ, nor do they help us see one another rightly.

A Catholic Worldview

A genuinely Catholic worldview sees all reality through the perspective of wholeness in Christ. Indeed, the word "Catholic" literally means "according to the whole". We believe, as Catholics, that Jesus came to heal the whole person, the whole family, the whole Church, the whole world, and the whole universe.[7] While sin fragments our being, it is only God's love that restores us and makes us whole. We see this demonstrated in Jesus' many interactions with broken and sinful people. Some of my favorite Gospel passages involve stories of people once bound by sin and shame who are radically transformed through Jesus' love and truth. Some prime examples include the stories of Zacchaeus, the Samaritan woman, Matthew, Simon Peter, Mary Magdalene, and the woman caught in adultery.

---

[6] Benedict XVI, *Jesus of Nazareth*, p. 177.
[7] See chapter 5, "The Whole Person Perspective", in my book, *Be Healed* (Notre Dame, Ind.: Ave Maria Press, 2014).

In each of these encounters Jesus affirms the unrepeatable goodness of the unique person he beholds. He meets people exactly where they are in their brokenness, without reinforcing their shame. Instead he affirms their personal dignity, helps them face and overcome years of self-loathing, calls them to sin no more, and draws them out of darkness and into the light. Jesus restores their broken identity and thus enables people to live in the fullness for which they were created. His transforming love brings about an interior newness, the fruit of which is a capacity to live in intimate communion with the Father, through the Holy Spirit.

Transformation of Simon Peter

Simon Peter's process of healing and transformation is prototypical of this pattern in the Gospels, and a model for our personal transformations. When Jesus first meets Simon along the shores of the Sea of Galilee, he is working as a fisherman, alongside his father and brother. Jesus wastes little time pronouncing Peter's new identity: "So you are Simon the son of John? You shall be called Cephas" (Jn 1:42). Simon is renamed "Peter", which means "Rock". He will soon become the foundation stone of the Church (Mt 16:18); the fisherman will become a "fisher of men" (see Mt 4:19; Mk 1:17; Lk 5:10). In a similar way, Jesus sees our true identity long before we do.

Before any of this can be realized in Simon Peter's life, he must shed his old identity, by renouncing his pride and being delivered from his crippling shame. To accomplish this, Jesus will bring Simon through a series of trials over many years. In Luke's version of Peter's calling (Lk 5:1–11), Jesus confronts his pride almost immediately through a fishing miracle. Simon, the seasoned veteran, has been fishing all day without catching anything. When Jesus commands him to put his net in on the other side of the boat, he protests, but then catches an abundance. This is a lesson that will be reinforced later in Peter's journey: he cannot accomplish Jesus' mission through self-reliance. It is a lesson for each of us as well. We all need God, who alone can accomplish his mission in and through us, and must crucify our pride to do so.

In the face of God's glory, Simon reflexively recoils in shame because he fears his unworthiness will be exposed. Crying out to Jesus, he says: "Depart from me, for I am a sinful man" (Lk 5:8). Notice that Simon

Peter is not yet honestly facing his sin or shame, but running from it, just as we do when we hide behind our false identities. Notice also that Jesus does not press the issue, because he realizes that his disciple is not ready to face his brokenness. It will need to be unveiled gradually through many conversations and interactions with Jesus over the years. Not until Jesus' Passion, death, and Resurrection will Peter's shame be directly exposed.

Is there a more heart-gripping scene in the Gospels than the one where Simon Peter weeps bitterly after denying Jesus (Lk 22:54–62)? Coming face-to-face with his failure, he seems ready to give up his calling. But Jesus does not waiver. As I pray with this scene, I imagine Jesus gazing deeply into the eyes and heart of his beloved friend and follower with mercy, not disgust. From the entire context we see that Jesus neither rejects Peter nor denigrates his true identity. On the contrary, Jesus continues to entrust Peter with his mission as head of the Church (see Mt 16:18; Jn 21:15–17). One of my favorite quotations from Saint John Paul II expresses this moment poignantly, making it personal for each one of us: "*We are not the sum of our weaknesses and failures; we are the sum of the Father's love for us and our real capacity to become the image of his Son.*"[8]

Can we even fathom the amazement of Peter and the other disciples, when they discover that Jesus is alive and not still in the tomb, or their utter astonishment at witnessing Jesus walk into the room to speak these liberating words, "Peace [Shalom] be with you.... If you forgive the sins of any, they are forgiven" (Jn 20:21–23)? In his Gospel account, John reports that the disciples were elated, but I wonder whether Simon Peter fully entered into rejoicing with them. Was his peace totally restored? His calling was reaffirmed, but he must have felt intensely unworthy of it. I picture him still self-conscious, living from his old identity, trapped in the shame of his failures and weaknesses, much like we all do when we have not yet internalized Jesus' merciful love. In what transpired next (in Jn 21:15–17), I believe Jesus knew exactly what Peter was going through and prepared a personal and intimate encounter to restore him to wholeness. With brilliant insight, Jesus brings Peter back in touch

---

[8] "17th World Youth Day, Solemn Mass: Homily of the Holy Father John Paul II" (Toronto, July 28, 2002), no. 5, http://w2.vatican.va/content/john-paul-ii/en/homilies/2002/documents/hf_jp-ii_hom_20020728_xvii-wyd.html (emphasis in original).

with two painful and unresolved memories, where he was still bound by shame and self-reliance: first, the moment of Peter's calling three years earlier when he withdrew from Jesus rather than face his sin and weakness; and second, his recent triple denial of Jesus, where his sin and shame were fully exposed.

Repeating the fishing miracle from three years earlier, Jesus masterfully reaffirms Peter's calling, all the while reminding him that he cannot do it on his own. Jesus then patiently leads Peter to confess his love three times, essentially redeeming each denial, thus restoring Peter's dignity and capacity to love. Jesus demonstrates his trust in Peter as the chief shepherd for his lambs and sheep. Simon is finally free to be "who he is": Peter, the Rock. All that remains for Peter's complete transformation is Pentecost, where Peter will receive God's strength to aid him in his weakness. As we know from the Book of Acts and subsequent history, Peter did not end up defining himself by his weaknesses or failures. He became "the image of the Son", even dying as Jesus did by crucifixion. He no longer ran away or denied Jesus out of fear; he stood firm in the face of everything that challenged him.

Simon Peter's transformation, while personally tailored to him, is a model for each of our personal healing journeys, including for those who contend with unwanted same-sex attraction.

Transformation of Identity

Like Simon Peter, we all need our past reformed and our identities restored. It often takes years and decades to realize the new identities we received at Baptism, as the Father's beloved sons and daughters. We all have to overcome the effects of sin and shame in our lives, in order to shed the false identities we developed over a lifetime of being labeled by the world and ourselves. All these labels are contrary to who we really are. Before realizing our true identity in Christ, we must undergo this oftentimes painful process of restoration. Again Pope Francis describes this process with colorful language:

> Our resurrection begins here: when we decide to obey the commands of Jesus to come into the light, to life; when the masks fall from our faces—so many times we are masked by sin: the masks must fall!—and

we rediscover the courage of our original faces, created in the image and likeness of God.[9]

Regardless of our specific problems, we all need our identities restored in Christ so that our "original faces", made in the image and likeness of God, can be more fully revealed. The distorted labels we use to describe our problems may be unique, but they are still false identities. We all need the Divine Physician to heal our wounds and to dispel the core shame and identity lies that keeps us bound.

Each person and family contending with SSA has their own unrepeatable journey of wounding. Thus each has his or her unique healing process. Despite these distinctions, I have seen a remarkably common pattern emerge time and again. With that in mind, I offer the following story of one man's healing journey. It is uniquely his, but an illustration for all.

Case Example: Jim

I met Jim when he was in his late thirties. His struggle with same-sex attraction went back as far as he could remember. Although he experienced both heterosexual and homosexual attractions, his same-sex attractions were unwanted and caused a great deal of shame and self-loathing for him. After some time getting to know and trust each other, I asked him to describe his attractions and the imagery of his fantasy toward males.[10] After some hesitation, he eventually revealed that his attractions and fantasies focused primarily on pubescent boys around the age of twelve. Because he feared that he might be judged a pedophile, I reassured him that I was not here to label him, and that I believed these "disordered desires" were most likely a symptom of unhealed injuries in his development. He was greatly reassured by this possibility, having thought of himself as a "pervert" who would always be unworthy of love.

Within a relatively short time, the Holy Spirit revealed to him in prayer a connection between his attractions and his own sexual and

---

[9]"Pope Francis: There Is No Limit to the Divine Mercy", Vatican Radio, April 6, 2014, http://en.radiovaticana.va/storico/2014/04/06/pope_francis_there_is_no_limit_to_the _divine_mercy/en1-788316 (Pope Francis' commentary on the Gospel story of Lazarus, before he prayed the Angelus).

[10]I have found this question to be instrumental in identifying the underlying wounds in the person's life and the healthy desires of unmet needs.

physical abuse at the age of twelve. He began to realize that his fantasies were an unconscious attempt to reconnect with the lost part of himself at that age, where he lost his innocence. In my experience and study, I have found that this desire to reconnect with a lost part of one's masculinity or femininity is present in most if not all of those persons experiencing SSA, even when there is no sexual abuse present. SSA can be thought of as a kind of suppression or partial rejection of one's own gender identity and a desperate attempt to reconnect to one's lost or disowned sexuality.[11] This insight brought Jim even more relief. He soon recognized the utter futility of trying to hide his SSA and of depending only on his own power to control his compulsive desires. These had been his coping mechanisms for most of his life. As he faced the pain of his abuse in the light of Jesus' compassionate gaze, he (like Peter) began to weep bitterly. He grieved the deep and searing pain of his lost childhood and sexual innocence, as well as the ways in which his own sinful responses of masturbation, pornography, and fantasy had robbed him of self-respect and freedom over many years.

Letting go of pain and shame as he grieved, he realized he could no longer hold on to the destructive self-image that had been hovering over him like an ominous storm cloud. He decided to invest in the hard and painful work of addressing the underlying causes of his symptomatic desires. Like Peter, this man needed a healing of his identity, and to do this he needed to face his painful memories and to release the shame associated with them. This is often a challenging process, but when engaged in whole-heartedly with the guidance of the Holy Spirit, it bears great fruit. Many refer to this process as prayer for "inner healing" or "identity healing":

> In praying for inner healing we ask Jesus to walk back into our past.... It is having Jesus shine his divine light in all those dark places where Satan has hidden hurts and painful memories.... Every experience we have ever had has molded our personalities.... All of us need inner healing to some degree or another.[12]

---

[11] See Leanne Payne, *The Broken Image: Restoring Personal Wholeness through Healing Prayer* (Grand Rapids: Baker Books, 1995) and *Crisis in Masculinity* (Grand Rapids: Baker Books, 1995); and Alan Medinger, *Growth into Manhood* (Colorado Springs, Colo.: Waterbrook Press, 2000).

[12] Betty Tapscott and Robert DeGrandis, *Forgiveness and Inner Healing* (Carol Stream, Ill.: Tyndale, 1980), pp. 14–15.

When the identity lies [source of false identity] contained in those memory sources are identified and exposed to the light of Christ, freedom can
follow.[13]

As Jim's memories were brought to light, grieved, and then transformed by Jesus' love and truth, he was able to reclaim his "original
face". The lifelong shame that kept him hiding from others and hat-
ing himself dissipated. His countenance became bright and cheerful; his
compulsive fantasies eventually lost their appeal and disappeared; and his
attraction for young males transformed into a beautiful compassion for
himself as a boy, as well as for those who suffer in similar ways. He realized that he was neither "gay" nor a "pedophile". In place of these false
identities, which he had assumed for many years, he began to believe at
a heart level that the Father truly loved him and that he was lovable. His
masculine identity, which had been largely stolen from him, was finally
being restored and celebrated after years of suppression. As his sexual
desires became rightly ordered, he grew in chastity and in his capacity
for self-giving love. For most of his life he believed healing was impossible. But, through this experience, he encountered the crucified and risen
Jesus and was transformed much like Simon Peter. Jesus set them both
free and gave them each their true identity. This is something I believe
he desires for each one of us.

The Healing Process

Healing is the process of "reclaiming our original faces" by becoming
whole in Christ. I believe there are three primary phases involved in this
process of restoration:

1. Envisioning our wholeness in Christ
2. Shedding our false identity
3. Embracing our true identity in Christ

I believe these elements are essential in every person's healing process. In
the rest of this essay, I will lay out a framework for understanding each of

---

[13] Ed Smith, *Healing Life's Hurts* (Ventura, Calif.: Regal Books, 2002), p. 31.

these three phases, and then apply this framework to the healing of those who struggle with same-sex attraction.

Envisioning our Wholeness in Christ

The Catholic worldview encourages us to see beyond the brokenness that is inherent in a world fragmented by sin. We see reality from the vantage point of God's glory, both in light of creation and as a result of our redemption and glorification in Christ.[14] This vision allows us to see all things according to their true nature. This is not denial of present reality and brokenness, but seeing what is not yet visible, with faith, hope, and charity.

During a personal eight-day silent retreat, I received new insight into God's design for us in Christ, insights captured by the words "security", "maturity", and "purity". Later, in studying Saint Paul's Letter to the Ephesians, I discovered that these three words serve as a summary description of our path to holiness as we grow in wholeness in Christ.

> *Security*: Our identity is rooted and grounded in Christ's love (Eph 1–3).
> *Maturity*: We are called to grow into the fullness of Christlike love (Eph 4).
> *Purity*: In prayer we battle to live our vocations purely in Christ's love (Eph 5–6).

The following tree image shows how *purity* is the fruit of *maturity* and is rooted in *security*.[15]

From this revelation, I came to realize that wholeness in Christ is something we receive as a gift, in seed form, but must cultivate. It grows organically, like a firmly planted and well-nourished tree, which is "rooted and grounded" in Christ's love (Eph 3:17) and matures through years of healthy development and tender care. God's love brings us into perfection.

---

[14] See John Paul II, *Man and Woman He Created Them: A Theology of the Body*, trans. Michael Waldstu (Boston, Mass.: Pauline Books and Media, 2006).

[15] Bob Schuchts, "Security, Maturity, Purity: Foundations for a Chaste Celibacy", *Chaste Celibacy: Living Christ's Own Spousal Love*, Institute for Priestly Formation Journal and Symposium (March 2007): 71–81.

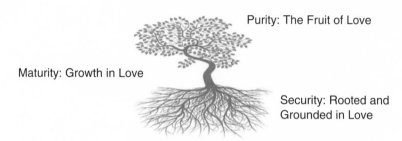

Purity: The Fruit of Love

Maturity: Growth in Love

Security: Rooted and Grounded in Love

Figure 1: Tree of Life: Wholeness in Christ

The only perfect example of this kind of love on earth is found in the Holy Family: "Mary was the first to enter into this realm, and she introduced her husband Joseph into it. They became the first models of the 'fairest love', which the church continually implores for young people, husbands and wives and families."[16] Immersed in the secure, mature, and pure love of the Holy Family, Jesus grew in wisdom and maturity. By God's design, each one of us is created to have the potential to develop in a similar way in our own families.

God's Design for Sexuality

God's intention from the beginning of creation is for us to grow as whole persons, united in body and soul. He created our sexuality to become a source of blessing for love and life (see *CCC* 2332). This is the integral vision of our humanity that Saint John Paul II referred to as the *Theology of the Body*. "Purity", he says, "is the glory of the human body before God. It is the glory of God in the human body, through which masculinity and femininity are manifested."[17]

From the beginning, Saint John Paul II contends, God created us as whole and integrated people, fully capable of sexual purity. His design, stamped into our bodies, is intended to unfold naturally as we grow and develop in an atmosphere of loving nurturance and protection in a healthy family. As we mature into whole men

---

[16]John Paul II, *Letters to Families*, February 2, 1994, no. 20, http://w2.vatican.va/content/john-paul-ii/en/letters/1994/documents/hf_jp-ii_let_02021994_families.html.

[17]John Paul II, *Man and Woman He Created Them*, 57:3, p. 353.

Table 1: Stages of Healthy Development

Stages of Psychological and Sexual Development	Ages	Development of Security, Maturity, and Purity
Attachment	0–2	Developing secure love bonds with mother/father
Identification	3–5	Identifying with same-sex parent
Peer-group belonging	5–12	Belonging with same-sex peer group
Sexual exploration	13–22	Learning how to develop opposite-sex relationships with self-mastery
Self-giving love	Adult	Sexual fidelity and fruitfulness

and women, we become capable of self-giving and chaste love with one another.

The above table highlights the stages of psychological and sexual development for boys and girls that occurs in a healthy family where a child's needs are met. The ages associated with each stage are not exact, but give a general framework for seeing how healthy development proceeds when love is present throughout.[18]

Healthy Human Development

This is how God designed the psychological and sexual development to proceed for those who are formed in love. Within the earliest stage of

---

[18] This table has developed over many years of teaching classes and giving conferences on personal development, family relations, sexuality, and healing, as well as years of working as a therapist and seeing how it naturally unfolds in the lives of individual people. There are many contributors over the years, among them are the following: Erik H. Erikson, *Identity and the Life Cycle* (New York: W. W. Norton, 1994); John Paul II, *Man and Woman He Created Them*; Mary Healy, *Men and Women Are from Eden* (Cincinnati, Ohio: Servant Books, 2005); Christopher West, *Created and Redeemed*, CD set (Necedah, Wis: Catholic Word, 2004); Elizabeth R. Moberly, *Homosexuality: A New Christian Ethic* (Cambridge, England: James Clarke, 1983); Andrew Comiskey, *Pursuing Sexual Wholeness: How Jesus Heals the Homosexual* (Lake Mary, Fla.: Charisma House, 1989); Gordon Dalbey, *Sons of the Father: Healing the Father-Wound in Men Today* (Folsom, Calif.: Civitas Press, 2011) and *Healing the Masculine Soul* (Nashville, Tenn.: W Publishing, 2003); Medinger, *Growth into Manhood*.

attachment, we have the primary need for security with both mother and father. Healthy attachment enables us to receive and trust love, which gives us a firm foundation in our identity as "beloved". To the degree to which love is missing from one or the other parent, our attachments become insecure and our desires become disordered. When needs are grossly unmet during this stage, children become vulnerable to mental, emotional, and sexual disorders of various kinds that manifest later in life. Joseph Nicolosi and Leanne Payne, who have spent their lifetimes ministering to those with same-sex attraction, have confirmed time and again that attachment problems are often at the root of SSA.[19] This is one reason why most who suffer with SSA say they have recognized these desires all their lives.

When love bonds with both parents are secured, we then naturally desire to model after them in the next stage of *identification*. With a secure attachment, a boy will naturally model after his father (or father figure) and the girl after her mother (or mother figure). When this proceeds in a healthy manner, the child naturally accepts his sexuality and gender identity. When that attachment is disordered, children have difficulty identifying with their same-sex parent and in some cases disconnect their hearts from "unsafe" parents. Elizabeth Moberly, Andrew Comiskey, Leanne Payne, and others note that longings for same-sex love often begin to take root during this stage, when a child's defensive detachment cuts him off from receiving love from the parent of the same sex. This longing for unfulfilled masculine or feminine love is not yet sexualized (erotic desire), but comes from a suppression of one's own sexuality to some degree.[20]

Children who grow in relative wholeness through the first two stages find it easier to develop a sense of *belonging* with siblings and peers in this third developmental stage. During the school age years, a healthy sense of belonging allows boys and girls to receive affirmation, not only as persons but in their identity as a boy or girl. Children who are rejected, ostracized, or labelled in this stage can be deeply wounded in their sexual identity for years to come. Alan Medinger and Dr. Rick Fitzgibbons have noted that wounding in this stage of development often provides

---

[19]Joseph Nicolosi, *Shame and Attachment Loss: The Practical Work of Reparative Therapy* (Downers Grove, Ill.: InterVarsity Press, 2009); Payne, *The Broken Image* and *Crisis in Masculinity*.

[20]Moberly, *Homosexuality: A New Christian Ethic*; Payne, *Broken Image* and *Crisis in Masculinity*; Comiskey, *Pursuing Sexual Wholeness*.

critical reinforcement of a child's homosexual identification and tends to deepen his sense of shame.[21]

When a child develops and matures in a healthy way, he will naturally gravitate to opposite-sex attractions during the stage of *sexual exploration*. In normal development, the adolescent will mature physically, emotionally, and spiritually. He will learn a balanced self-mastery over sexual desires, even in times of heightened arousal and attraction. The maturing person will also develop an integrated social identity. Without healthy development during this stage, disordered desires are frequently expressed compulsively in fantasy, masturbation, pornography, sexual promiscuity, or isolation. Same-sex attraction, formed in earlier stages, is often manifested during this time, especially among adolescents with low confidence, negative body image, a history of sexual abuse, and unhealed identity wounds.[22]

In the process of healthy development, the emerging adult is learning the virtue of chastity in the stage of *self-giving love*. The secure and mature person, living in the wholeness of his sexual identity as God designed, is able to live in purity in whichever vocation is chosen. There is a capacity for both intimacy and generativity. As the *Catechism* notes: "Chastity includes an *apprenticeship in self-mastery* which is a training in human freedom" (*CCC* 2339; emphasis in original). Chastity "involves the *integrity of the person* and the *integrality of the gift*" (*CCC* 2337; emphasis added). Those who suffer with same-sex attraction, as well as many with opposite-sex attraction, often have developmental injuries that prevent them from fully entering into this stage of maturity and purity. Still seeking satisfaction of unmet basic personal needs for attachment, affirmation, and belonging, they can have an exaggerated focus on self and a lack of self-mastery, as well as a failure to see the gift of sexuality in its true meaning.[23]

Some might object that this picture of wholeness is an ideal that is beyond our reach in a broken world, since none of us are perfectly

---

[21] Medinger, *Growth into Manhood*; Rick Fitzgibbons, "The Origins and Healing of Homosexual Attractions and Behaviors", in *The Truth About Homosexuality*, ed. Father John Harvey (San Francisco, Ignatius Press, 1996).

[22] Payne, *Broken Image*; Catholic Medical Association, "Homosexuality and Hope: Questions and Answers about Same-Sex Attraction", pamphlet, December 14, 2010, http://www.cathmed.org/resources/position-papers/homosexuality-and-hope.

[23] Joseph J. Nicolosi, *Shame and Attachment Loss*; Payne, *Crisis in Masculinity*; Moberly, *Homosexuality: A New Christian Ethic.*

integrated and few understand the full meaning of sexuality as gift. In many ways I would agree. Because of original sin, we all have experienced levels of disintegration and a lack self-mastery. All of us have been falsely identified by our sin, wounds, and the negative labeling from the world. None of us grow up completely secure or in a perfectly loving family. None of us live with mature self-giving love, and none of us remain perfectly pure, aside from Jesus and his Blessed Mother. It is precisely for this reason that we need to have a vision of wholeness, before facing our brokenness. Unless we know what God intended from the beginning, we are left believing that our false identities are all we can ever become. Without a vision of wholeness, we will have no motivation to shed these false identities.

Shedding Our False Identity

Our false identity is primarily in distortions of self-image. It is based in pride and rooted in shame. Like Adam and Eve, we cover ourselves with various kinds of fig leaves, afraid that our nakedness and shame will be exposed (Gen 3:10–11). Father Jacques Philippe describes this with great insight in his book *Interior Freedom*:

> Here it is worth reflecting on the problem of pride. We are all born with a deep wound, experienced as a lack of being. We seek to compensate by constructing a self different from our real self. This artificial self requires large amounts of energy to maintain it; being fragile, it needs protecting. Woe to anyone who contradicts it, threatens it, questions it, or inhibits its expansion. When the Gospel says we must "die to ourselves", it means this artificial ego, this constructed self, must die, so that the real self, given us by God can emerge.[24]

Before we can be restored to our true identity in Christ, we must die to our false identity, which hides our "original faces". We must repent of our pride by bringing our sins and wounds into the light of Jesus' penetrating gaze, just as Peter did. Only then can we release our shame and face our pain. This is often difficult, but always deeply purifying. Joseph

---

[24]Jacques Philippe, *Interior Freedom*, trans. Helene Scott (New York: Scepter, 2007), p. 122.

Nicolosi compellingly demonstrates in his book *Shame and Attachment Loss* that SSA is rooted in deep shame and the unresolved pain of attachment loss (from the earliest years of life). My own experience confirms his point.

Shame and SSA

Shame seems to operate at two fundamental levels. The first constitutes a healthy shame, which is an awareness of our sin and deficiency. The second is a toxic shame, which is the belief that we are not good or worthy of love. The first kind of shame is based in truth. The second is based (at least partially) in falsehood, because it denies the mercy and goodness of God, and our own inherent goodness and worth. These two levels of shame are often deeply intertwined.

Jim, whom we discussed earlier, is a good example of how these two levels of shame can form the fabric of a false identity. Jim rightfully felt a sense of shame concerning his disordered sexual desires and acts, because he was violating the "integrality of the gift" of his sexuality. Pornography, sexual fantasy, and masturbation are sins of impurity in the eyes of Christ and his Church (see *CCC* 2351–54). Jim's shame over these thoughts and behaviors constituted a healthy shame. He was aware, at least some level, that God's glory was not being revealed through his personal body. He was not yet capable of self-mastery, so he felt ashamed over his lack of maturity. All of this constituted his awareness of shame based in truth.

Underlying this healthy shame was a toxic shame, based in a false identity and the resulting sin in his life. This shame came from Jim's deeply rooted beliefs that he was "deficient", "tarnished", "dirty", and "unlovable". This false shame was due, at least in part, to the sins of his father and brother who abused him physically and sexually. Their behavior toward him had kept him from developing secure same-sex relationships at an early age. The abuse left deep scars and a pervasive sense of unworthiness, which actually fueled Jim's sexual compulsions and promulgated his disordered attractions. Believing he was unlovable, Jim put on masks, just like we all do, to cover our shame. Even his self-identification as "gay" was a mask of pride to keep him from looking at his deeper shame and underlying pain.

Pride and Shame

Though intended to overcome shame, pride actually covers the deficiencies that drive the compulsions in the first place. Just as pride in all of us hides our shame, so-called gay pride hides the underlying shame that runs deep under the surface of every person and family member who faces the struggle with SSA. The ones I have accompanied on their healing journey (where SSA was an issue) had to overcome both kinds of shame before they could find freedom.

Tom, another man I accompanied on his healing journey, came for help after being publicly humiliated for looking at homosexual pornography. Up until then, he was generally well respected in his community. After being publicly exposed, he felt completely ostracized and unworthy of love. When he came to meet with me and related what had happened, his shame seemed almost palpable. Slumping over in his chair, he could not look me in the eye and could barely get his words out. Seeing that he needed help desperately, I asked if he would be open to prayer. When he consented, we simply asked Jesus to meet him in the place of his shame.

I wondered whether Tom had been sexually abused (like Jim), but was surprised to discover a completely different source of his toxic shame. Filled with anguish, Tom related an image of himself as a young boy about five years old, standing by himself in the living room of his childhood home. He felt very alone, even though his dad was in the next room. As he shared the story, he began to sob. I verbally asked the Holy Spirit to make it clear how this memory was related to Tom's shame. The answer came quickly and powerfully to Tom's mind and heart: "As a boy, I wanted my dad's love and when I didn't get it, I felt like something was wrong with me. I felt completely ashamed *of me* and *my masculinity*. The Holy Spirit is showing me this is the root of my attractions to men. I have rejected my own masculinity and therefore seek it in other males. I am still hungering for the love of a man because I didn't receive love and affirmation from my dad. Deep down in my heart, I believe I am not worthy of a man's love, so I have to grasp for it in pornography and fantasy."

With that insight from the Holy Spirit, everything became crystal clear to Tom. He became aware of the deep and pervasive shame that had governed his entire life. He felt deficient as a boy, and now as a man.

His lack of masculine confidence, which should have naturally developed from a close relationship with his father, left him always hungering for affirmation. Feeling powerless to get what he needed from his father, he vowed to meet his own needs (pride), which eventually led him into fantasy and pornography. Failing to satisfy his need, this only increased his sense of shame. He was caught in a hopeless cycle. In seeing all this, Tom was ready for change. So we again asked the Holy Spirit to guide him into freedom.

Moving back into prayer, Tom renounced the lies he believed about himself, such as: "I am not worthy of my father's love"; "I am not worth any man's love"; "I will never receive pure love from a man so I have to grasp for it through lust and pornography"—lies connected to his use of pornography, fantasies, and homosexual attractions. Tom stood in his authority and identity in Christ as a beloved son and renounced "perversion", "lust", "homosexuality", "hopelessness", "abandonment", and false ties with other men. Seeing how these had previously filled his empty heart, Tom turned to Jesus to fill the emptiness with God's love. We ended by asking the Father to bless Tom as a boy and as a man and to fill him with the Holy Spirit in all the places that were devoid of the Father's love.[25]

Tom left a different man than the one who came in. After giving thanks to God, he looked me in the eye and gave me a warm and confident hug. His healing was not complete, of course. Complete healing generally takes time, counseling, more prayer, and friendship. Following our meeting, Tom felt compelled by the Spirit to attend a men's retreat, which he later reported was the first time he felt like he belonged with other men. Since then, he has continued to grow in his relationship with men in a healthy rather than disordered way. He had years of false beliefs and injury to unwind, so it has certainly been a process. The last I heard he was planning on getting married. All of this was a necessary part of him shedding his false identity and beginning to embrace his true identity in Christ.

Tom's situation, while unique, has much in common with others who struggle with same-sex attraction as well as those with sexual

---

[25] For a more in-depth understanding of this process, see *The Five Keys*, in Neal Lozano's book *Unbound: A Practical Guide for Deliverance* (Grand Rapids, Mich.: Chosen Books, 2010), p. 57.

compulsions that are directed to the same sex.[26] I have come to discover that underneath every disordered desire, whether toward the same or opposite sex, there resides a healthy need that remains unmet. In the case of those with SSA, this unmet need usually involves some rejection of masculine or feminine *attachment, identification, and belonging*. Left dormant for too long these unmet needs eventually give way to lust's perversions and compulsions, leaving the sufferer further bound in sin and shame.

Sometimes, these compulsions are related to the avoidance of sex, such as when a woman is sexually or physically abused by men. She may inwardly hate men and see all masculinity as a threat. In response, she may turn to a woman for her emotional needs and comforts. Her compulsion is oriented toward the avoidance of sex with a man, rather than a compulsion for sex with a woman. With her homosexual lover, she may even become disinterested in sex all together, but enjoy the companionship. Each person who struggles with SSA is uniquely wounded in his sexuality, so it is unwise to make blanket generalizations.

No matter the underlying issues, these disordered desires do not define a person. Labeling oneself or another person as "gay" or "lesbian" only serves to reinforce a false identity. It may feel true, because it describes sexual attraction or other factors in the person's life, but it fails to see the person in his wholeness in Christ. These false identities need to be renounced. In order for Jesus' love to transform us, we need to humble ourselves and allow his love and truth to penetrate the deepest places of our shame and wounds, where the lies and false identity are rooted. We need to release this false identity in order to embrace our true identity in Christ.

When Tom and I were praying, we were not trying to get rid of his unwanted attractions or shame. We were intent on discovering and then, through prayer, beginning to heal the wounds that Tom experienced that led to his SSA. Certainly we want him to be free from his unwanted same-sex desires, but since his SSA was related to wounds, dealing with those wounds was a necessary part of any further healing he would eventually experience, which, again, might include various forms of counseling and psychotherapy, more prayer, and strong spiritual friendships.

[26] In my book *Be Healed*, I give a detailed account of this with a man who had a heterosexual compulsion due to early attachment wounds with his mother (see chapters 8 and 12).

Embracing Our True Identity in Christ

Our true identity is our "original face" made in the image and likeness of God. Jesus came for this express purpose: to redeem each one of us and to restore us to wholeness, according to his plan and purpose for love and life. When he ascended to the Father, Jesus did not leave us orphans. He gave us the Holy Spirit, established his Church on Peter and the other apostles, and thus provided an ever-present means of our redemption. The Church, living vibrantly the life of the Spirit, is called to be our new family in Christ (see Eph 2:19), and thereby completes what was lacking in our development within our families.

When practiced authentically and with faith, the sacraments of the Church are intended to be the means for us to reclaim our true identity. As the *Catechism* states: "The seven sacraments touch all the stages and all the important moments of Christian life: they give birth and increase, healing and mission to the Christians life of faith. There is thus a certain resemblance between the stages of natural life and the stages of the spiritual life" (*CCC* 1210). In practice, this means the Church needs to live what we claim to believe. Rather than judge or reject those who are broken or living from a false identity (which is every person to greater or lesser degrees), we are called to see people in their wholeness and truly believe that God's love can heal all who come. We need to appropriate the powerful presence of the Holy Spirit through the sacraments and in prayer, and assist people on their path of healing to become who they are.

Healing and Restoring Security

Healing is an expression of being rooted and grounded in Christ's love. Through healing we come to rediscover the security of being loved and loveable, which enables us to grow in maturity and purity. We have hardly even begun to appropriate the fullness of the graces available to us in the Church through the sacraments and prayer. Pope Francis is calling the entire Church to become a field hospital, which means appropriating these graces to heal wounds and restore all people to security and wholeness in Christ. Sadly, in many places we do not see the Church living her mission. Where the faith is being lived out authentically, lives are being transformed and people are coming into their true identity, as beloved sons and daughters of the Father.

One of my most vivid experiences of seeing the Church live her mission in this way came during a Steubenville Youth Conference years ago. Led by the local bishop, hundreds of priests, religious leaders, and lay leaders were gathered to minister to over five thousand youth. During adoration of the Blessed Sacrament, Jesus' healing presence filled the room, so that nearly all were profoundly impacted. I had the privilege of praying for healing for many youths that weekend, some very deeply wounded in a myriad of ways.

Among those was Ellen, a young girl of sixteen who attended the conference with her "lesbian" lover. In the presence of the Blessed Sacrament, Ellen felt overwhelmed by Jesus' love and convicted by the Holy Spirit to confess her sin. After she had gone to the Sacrament of Reconciliation, the priest encouraged her to seek prayer for healing of her deeper wounds. It was there that I met her. In prayer together, the Holy Spirit led us to uncover three roots to her disordered desires, which came in the form of three memories. First, Ellen's mother slapped her when she was four years old. She subsequently hated her mother and closed her heart to her in unforgiveness, thus disconnecting her heart from feminine nurture and identification. Second, Ellen, at the age of six, felt abandoned by her father and alone with her mother (whom she hated) when her parents divorced. Finally, she was seduced and molested by a female teacher at the age of eight. Although Ellen knew what the teacher was doing was wrong, there was part of her that loved the teacher and hungered for the disordered love and affection.

All of this together created an incredibly deep well of pain and shame in Ellen, as well as a fertile ground for lies about her deepest identity to take root. As Jesus administered his merciful love and truth to her wounded heart in each of these three memories, she experienced a new freedom, not only from her wounds but from her false identity that flowed from them. In those few minutes, Ellen was enabled by the Holy Spirit to forgive her mother and teacher, sever the unhealthy attachment with her teacher and girlfriend, and receive deep healing of her abandonment and rejection wounds. All of this released her to shed the false identity that she was "unlovable and alone" and "a lesbian", thus enabling her to begin to embrace her true identity as a young woman who was deeply loved by God the Father and cherished by her Blessed

Mother. From there, over time she would reengage with her youth leaders, priests, and mentors who could incarnate this love and help her grow in maturity.

Growing in Maturity

With new freedom and greater security, we can pursue the holiness to which we are each called. Jim, Tom, and Ellen would each say that their healing of deep wounds enabled them to release their false identity and to begin living from their true identity in Christ. Without any convincing on my or anyone else's part, all three naturally shed the self-identification that they were "gay" or "lesbian". They received this knowledge intimately in their hearts, directly from Jesus. They did not have to convince themselves or try to achieve anything through their own effort. The freedom came from a deep interior knowledge that came freely from the Holy Spirit communicating within their spirit. But even after these powerful healing encounters with Jesus, each of them had to mature and grow in purity, which would include ongoing healing and the cultivation of virtue in their lives, through prayer, the sacraments, community, and the development of chastity. In effect, each needed to find ways to restore the lost development and unmet needs that had led them on their path previously.[27] All of this became much easier after their healing experiences and their shift in the way they saw and identified themselves.

Alan Medinger, a former "gay activist", speaks of this process in his book, *Growth into Manhood*.[28] In it, he describes his own journey of identifying himself as a homosexual for many years, due to his self-perceived deficits in masculinity and his attraction to boys and men when he was growing up. Following some powerful and life-changing healing experiences, Alan began to see himself differently and eventually let go of his gay community and identity. But he still needed to learn how to live life as a man among men, and as a man among women. Injured in his relationships with boys around sports, Alan began putting himself in vulnerable positions with other men, in sports-related activities. Since

[27] See Table 1: Stages of Healthy Development, p. 510.
[28] Medinger, *Growth into Manhood*.

these had been sources of shame, he needed to overcome the shame and develop confidence in his ability to relate to his own body and to other males in this way. Later, he had to overcome his fear of rejection and inadequacy with women. Eventually, his maturation process led him to interact more freely with women, which eventually led him to marriage. Even after marriage the maturation process continued as he learned how to love his wife and become a good and loving father to his children. By the time I met Alan, he was a happily married family man and a leader in the church—a man in love with Jesus and comfortable with himself, able to relate well to men and women alike.

Like Alan, all of us are called to mature and to develop the capacity for self-giving love and purity. With those overcoming SSA, the process has its own particular challenges and triumphs.

Cultivating Purity

Purity is the fruit of the Holy Spirit and a manifestation of life lived in an abiding relationship with Jesus Christ. Father Raneiro Cantalamessa describes this well:

> The reason for Christian purity is precisely in consecration. We are not our own; we belong to the Lord. We cannot use our bodies for our own pleasure, for some personal satisfaction in itself. This is a defilement of the temple of God; it is desecration, the exact opposite of consecration. And how much defilement we see in the world today.[29]

To consecrate ourselves to the Lord is to grow in holiness. We glorify him with our bodies and souls. This requires the successful integration of our sexuality and the inner unity of body and spirit (see *CCC* 2337). When we call ourselves Christian, we no longer have the right to exercise our minds or bodies in the way the world does, selfishly and out of a desire to satisfy our lusts. Instead we are called to participate in Jesus' holy self-giving love, which is life-giving to all who receive it. This is not easy for any of us, whether attracted to members of the same sex

---

[29] Fr. Raneiro Cantalamessa, *Sober Intoxication of the Spirit: Filled with the Fullness of God*, trans. Marsha Daigle-Williamson (Cincinnati, Ohio: Servant, 2005), p. 90.

or the opposite sex, because it requires a certain renunciation and the humility to receive the gift. It requires purity, which Professor Mary Healy describes in this way:

> Purity is a virtue, an aptitude that we acquire through consistent "abstention from un-chastity." In this sense it demands a painful process of crucifying the flesh. But at the same time purity is a gift of the Holy Spirit, given only through redemption in Christ. Purity matures in the heart of the person who cultivates it, to the point that the person enjoys the fruits of the victory won over lust.[30]

Jim, Tom, and Ellen each conquered lust and had their chastity restored as a gift of the Holy Spirit, as their shift in identity gave them a renewed capacity to walk in purity. Jim and Tom were finally able to overcome years of unchastity in the form of pornography, fantasy, and masturbation and eventually reordered the disordered attractions they had toward other males. Ellen likewise experienced a radical shift in her relationship with her friend, after her experience of healing. She no longer felt compelled to sexualize the relationship, as the teacher had done with her. In all three of these situations, the individuals would still have to walk through a process of denying themselves, but the capacity to see themselves in wholeness and with a renewed innocence certainly helped them to choose virtuously and to embark upon a process of continued growth.

Choosing to die to our false self and to embrace our true identity in Christ is a redemptive suffering. In this world, there is no other way to wholeness or holiness. But it is deeply worth it for all who embark on the journey. The rewards are otherworldly, bearing the fruit of the Spirit in love, joy, peace—and self-control.

Summary

The healing process for those who struggle with unwanted same-sex attractions is remarkably similar to the healing process for all people who desire to live a life of holiness. Jesus, who sees us in our wholeness, loves us in our brokenness. He invites each of us to shed our false identity that

---

[30] Healy, *Men and Women Are from Eden*, pp. 48–49.

was gradually formed through sin, wounds, and identity lies. He calls us personally, like he did Simon Peter, and invites us to overcome our shame and pride so that our original faces can be revealed. Ultimately his call to purity requires that we find our security in the Father's love and affirmation, so that we can mature into the fullness for which we were designed. To illustrate this process of transformation, three stories were presented of people who struggle with SSA, who shed their old identities and embraced their true identities in Christ as beloved sons and daughters of the Father. The popular song from David Crowder sums up my message here well:

> Come out of sadness, from wherever you've been
> Come broken hearted, let rescue begin
> Come find your mercy, oh sinner come kneel
> Earth has no sorrow, that heaven can't heal
> So lay down your burdens, lay down your shame
> All who are broken, lift up your face.[31]

---

[31] David Crowder, "Come As You Are", MetroLyrics, http://www.metrolyrics.com/come-as-you-are-lyrics-david-crowder.html.

The Healing Role of Friendship in Aelred of Rievaulx's *De spiritali amicitia*

Dennis J. Billy, C.Ss.R.

Cistercian abbot Aelred of Rievaulx's *De spiritali amicitia*[1] numbers among the great works of Christian literature on friendship. Composed in a monastic setting over a number of years and completed sometime before Aelred's death in 1167, it offers a comprehensive vision of the nature of Christian friendship and some very practical advice about how such friendships should be developed and maintained over time. Using Cicero's famous dialogue, *De amicitia*,[2] for his inspiration and point of departure, and incorporating insights from Scripture, the Fathers of the Church (especially Augustine), and his own experience, Aelred provides his readers with some very profound insights into the healing role of friendship in a person's journey through life.[3]

This abbreviated version of the essay is reprinted with permission and appears in full as "The Healing Role of Friendship in Aelred of Rievaulx's *De spiritali amicitia*", *Studia moralia* 40 (2002): 63–84.

[1] The critical Latin edition of Aelred's *De spiritali amicitia* (hereafter referred to as DSA) appears in Corpus Christianòrum Continuatio Mediaevalis (hereafter referred to as CCCM) 1:279–350. The English translation (hereafter referred to as SF) comes from Aelred of Rievaulx, *Spiritual Friendship*, Cistercian Fathers Series, no. 5, trans. Mary Eugenia Laker, with an introduction by Douglass Roby (Kalamazoo, Mich.: Cistercian Publications, 1977).

[2] Cicero, *De senectute, De amicitia, De divinatione*, Loeb Classical Library (1923; repr., Cambridge, Mass.: Harvard University Press, 1979), pp. 100–211.

[3] For the sources of the *De spiritali amicitia*, see Douglass Roby, "Sources of the *Spiritual Friendship*", in SF 29–35. For the centrality of Scripture in Aelred's spirituality, see André Vauchez, *The Spirituality of the Medieval West: The Eighth to the Twelfth Century*, trans. Colette Friedlander, Cistercian Studies 145 (Kalamazoo, Mich.: Cistercian Publications, 1993), pp. 157–58. See also Etienne Gilson, *The Mystical Theology of St. Bernard*, trans. A.H.C. Downes (Kalamazoo, Mich.: Cistercian Publications, 1990), p. 6.

Theological Context: Creation, Fall, Redemption

Aelred provides some important theological parameters for understanding his teaching on the healing role of friendship. These parameters concern the Christian doctrines of creation, man's fall, and redemption in Christ.

1. *Creation*. In his discussion with Ivo in Book 1 about the nature and origin of friendship, Aelred states that God "has willed that peace encompass all his creatures and society unite them".[4] Every level of creation reveals some trace or vestige of that unity. A look at inanimate creation, for example, reveals that the earth produces not a single stone, but many, while forests contain not a single tree of a single kind, but a great number of different species. For Aelred, such variety reveals that a certain love of companionship has been imprinted into the very nature of the inanimate world.[5] Much the same can be said for animate life. Although they are irrational, by nature, a look at the way animals run, play, and enjoy each other's company almost makes one want to believe that they are acting with reason. Their enjoyment of one another's company is another sign that the love for companionship has been implanted in their natures.[6] Even immaterial beings such as angels delight in each other's company. God created not one but many of them, thus giving them the opportunity to live together in charity through a union of will and desire.[7] Finally, within this hierarchical ordering of creation, God united the animal and spiritual realms in the figure of Adam. Because God deemed that it was not good for man to be alone, however, a helper was made for him, one like unto himself (see Gen 2:20–23). In Aelred's mind, "It was from no similar, nor even from the same, material that divine Might formed this help mate, but as a clearer inspiration to charity and friendship he produced the woman from the very substance of the man."[8] Aelred goes on with a beautiful description of the equality of the sexes and the need for friendship as the basis of their existence and mutual relationship: "How beautiful it is that the second human being was taken from the side of the first, so that nature

---

[4]DSA 1:53 [CCCM 1:298 (300–302); SF 62].
[5]DSA 1:54 [CCCM 1:298 (305–10); SF 62].
[6]DSA 1:54–55 [CCCM 1:298 (310–18); SF 62–63].
[7]DSA 1:56 [CCCM 1:298 (318–24); SF 63].
[8]DSA 1:57 [CCCM 1:298 (327–30); SF 63].

might teach that human beings are equal and, as it were, collateral, and that there is in human affairs neither a superior nor an inferior, a characteristic of true friendship."[9] Aelred's point in all of this is that nature was created in such a way that, from the very beginning, the desire for friendship and charity was implanted in man's heart.

2. *The Fall.* Up until this point, Aelred's description of the orientation toward companionship and society implanted in creation by the divine will and the eternal reason does not take into full account the reality of sin. When the fall of Adam occurs, however, the original harmony within nature and in man's heart is radically disrupted. Since Aelred is primarily interested in spiritual friendship, he focuses on the repercussions of this fall for mankind. The main effect, for Aelred, has to do with a fundamental dissonance that enters into the relationship between charity and friendship. Prior to the sin of Adam, charity and friendship are coextensive; after it, however, they grow apart:

> After the fall of the first man, when with the cooling of charity concupiscence made secret inroads and caused private good to take precedence over the common weal, it corrupted the splendor of friendship and charity through avarice and envy, introducing contentions, emulations, hates and suspicions because the morals of men had been corrupted. From that time the good distinguished between charity and friendship, observing that love ought to be extended even to the hostile and perverse, while no union of will and ideas can exist between the good and wicked. And so friendship which, like charity, was first preserved among all by all, remained according to the natural law among the few good.[10]

This passage identifies the fall of Adam as the primary cause for disruption between charity and friendship. Prior to the fall, the intimate union between nature and grace allowed friendship and charity to exist in close relationship with one another and to share a certain "splendor". After the fall, however, this "splendor" was corrupted: friendship contracted in its extension and was limited to a very few; charity, in turn, remained limited in scope, but was possible only under the influence of grace. Elsewhere in the treatise, Aelred describes the relationship between charity and friendship in this manner: "Divine authority approves that

---

[9]DSA 1:57 [CCCM 1:298–99 (330–33); SF 63].
[10]DSA 1:58–59 [CCCM 1:299 (336–47); SF 63–64].

more are to be received into the bosom of charity than into the embrace of friendship. For we are compelled by the law of charity to receive in the embrace of love not only our friends but also our enemies. But only those do we call friends to whom we can fearlessly entrust our heart and all its secrets; those, too, who, in turn, are bound to us by the same law of faith and security."[11] For Aelred, the fall is also responsible for the different types of friendship in the world today. Since reason was not completely corrupted through the fall, the wicked experience an inclination toward companionship and society that often resembles friendship. After the fall, therefore, it is important to distinguish between true friendship and other relationships "of some slight resemblance".[12] Aelred's discussion of the differences between "carnal" and "spiritual" friendship presupposes and springs from this underlying theological premise.[13]

3. *Redemption.* Aelred's doctrine of the fall helps one to understand how the disharmony between charity and friendship crept into human affairs. Aelred recognizes its importance in this regard, but refuses to dwell on it. His theology of friendship is eminently positive, one that flows from the love of God who, through the death of Christ, enables a person once again to enjoy the friendship of God. In Aelred's mind, "Christ himself set up a definite goal for friendship when he said: 'Greater love than this no man hath, than a man lay down his life for his friends' [Jn 15:13]."[14] Through his redemptive suffering, a healing process begins that will eventually make them coextensive. In Jesus, charity and friendship once again exist in close harmony. Through him, original sin is overcome and its effects will eventually be completely wiped out:

> And so in friendship are joined honor and charm, truth and joy, sweetness and good-will, affection and action. And all these take their beginning from Christ, advance through Christ, and are perfected in Christ. Therefore, not too steep or unnatural does the ascent appear from Christ, as

---

[11] DSA 1:32 [CCCM 1:294 (183–89); SF 58]. Aelred develops his general theory of love in *De speculo caritatis* (CCCM 1:3–161). For an analysis of this work, see Amédée Hallier, *The Theology of Aelred of Rievaulx: An Experiential Theology*, Cistercian Studies 2 (Spencer, Mass.: Cistercian Publications, 1969). For a general treatment of Aelred's position on friendship, see Douglass, "Doctrine of *Spiritual Friendship*", in SF 15–35. See also Squire, *Aelred of Rievaulx: A Study* (Kalamazoo, Mich.: Cistercian Publications, 1981), pp. 98–111.

[12] DSA 1:60 [CCCM 1:299 (358–59); SF 64].

[13] See DSA 1:39–49 [CCCM 1:295–97 (220–79); SF 59–61].

[14] DSA 2:33 [CCCM 1:309 (238–39); SF 78].

the inspiration of the love by which we love our friend, to Christ giving himself to us as our Friend for us to love, so that charm may follow upon charm, sweetness upon sweetness and affection upon affection. And thus, friend cleaving to friend in the spirit of Christ, is made with Christ but one heart and one soul, and so mounting aloft through degrees of love to friendship with Christ, he is made one spirit with him in one kiss. Aspiring to this kiss the saintly soul cries out: "Let him kiss me with the kiss of his mouth."[15]

Friendship, for Aelred, is the "medicine of life", because it ultimately brings a person into relationship with Christ, who is "the way, and the truth, and the life" (Jn 14:6).[16] It plays a healing, even elevating, role in man's sojourn. By entering into a true "spiritual" (as opposed to "carnal") friendship with another individual, a person begins a process that will eventually enable him to share in the friendship of Christ. For Aelred, "friendship is a stage bordering upon that perfection which consists in the love and knowledge of God, so that man from being a friend of his fellowman becomes the friend of God, according to the words of the Savior in the Gospel: 'I will not now call you servants, but my friends' [Jn 15:15]."[17]

Applications

This general theological framework of creation, fall, and redemption helps one to interpret some of Aelred's better-known statements on spiritual friendship. Aelred himself insists that "friendship bears fruit in this life and in the next."[18] The phrase "in this life" implies that friends receive concrete benefits in the present even though they are still weighed down by the effects of original sin. The phrase "in the next" points to the time when, on account of Christ's redemption, they are completely free from the shackles of concupiscence and live in close

---

[15]DSA 2:20–21 [CCCM 1:306 (143–55); SF 74–75].

[16]The phrase "A faithful friend is the medicine of life" (*Amicus fidelis medicamentum vitae est*) comes from Sir 6:16. See *Biblica sacra iuxta vulgatam versionem*, vol. 2, ed. Robertus Weber (Stuttgart: Wüettenbergische Bibelanstalt, 1969), p. 1036. Aelred refers to it in DSA 2:12; 3:74, 97 [CCCM 1:304 (82–83), 332 (532), 339 (750); SF 72, 109, 117].

[17]DSA 2:14 [CCCM 1:305 (104–8); SF 73].

[18]DSA 2:9 [CCCM 1:304 (64–65); SF 71].

intimate union with God and the communion of saints. By keeping
the distinction between the fruits of friendship clear in one's mind, the
reader is better able to understand the significance of Aelred's teaching
on the meaning of the goodness, the three kisses, and the formation of
spiritual friendships.

Application One: The Meaning of "Goodness"

It may be surprising to learn that, for Aelred, friendship "can begin
among the good, progress among the better, and be consummated among
the perfect".[19] If this is so, one may wonder if anyone can be good
in a world where the effects of original sin influence man's activity so
strongly. Aelred, however, draws a strong distinction between goodness
as it exists in God and in one who is journeying to God. God, in Aelred's
mind, is "supremely powerful and supremely good, is sufficient good
unto himself, since his good, his joy, his glory, his happiness, is himself".[20] In God, there is no distinction between good, better, and best.
His goodness is his perfection—and vice versa. Man, by way of contrast,
is on a journey that hopefully involves a movement along a distinct series
of grades of spiritual and moral perfection.

When Aelred says that spiritual friendship begins with the good, he
does not mean that two people must be good in the same way that
God is good. Nor does he mean that they are good in the same sense as
those who have already passed through death and experience God in an
immediate way in the beatific vision. Nor does he mean that they have
no experience of concupiscence in their lives as a result of the effects of
original sin. He merely intends to say that spiritual friendships in this life
are forged by those who struggle to move further along (as opposed to
away from) the journey of eventual intimacy with God. In answer to a
question by Gratian about friendship among those who are not good,
Aelred says:

> I am not cutting "good" so finely as do some who call no one "good"
> unless he is lacking no whit in perfection. We call a man "good" who,

---

[19]DSA 2:38 [CCCM 1:309 (252–53); SF 78–79].
[20]DSA 1:51 [CCCM 1:297 (290–91); SF 62].

according to the limits of our mortality, "living soberly and justly and godly in this world," is resolved neither to ask others to do wrong nor to do wrong himself at another's request. Among such, indeed, we have no doubt that friendship can spring up and that by such it can be perfected.[21]

As far as man is concerned, "goodness", for Aelred, resides in the firm resolution not to participate in wrongdoing of any kind. It does not mean that a person is perfect or that he has never committed sin or will not do so in the future. A "good person", for Aelred, is someone who intends not to sin and who takes appropriate measures to keep himself from being overcome by unruly passions.

Friendships among "good persons" of this type are not rare in this life. As Aelred reminds his readers:

> The Christian ought not to despair of acquiring any virtue since daily the divine voice from the Gospel re-echoes: "Ask and you shall receive...." It is no wonder, then, that pursuers of true virtue were rare among the pagans since they did not know the Lord, the Dispenser of virtue, of whom it is written: "The Lord of hosts, he is the King of glory." Indeed, through faith in him they were prepared to die for one another—I do not say three or four, but I offer you thousands of pairs of friends—although the ancients declared or imagined the devotion of Pylades and Orestes a great marvel. Were they not, according to the definition of Tullius, strong in the virtue of true friendship, of whom it is written: "And the multitude of believers had but one heart and one soul; neither did anyone say that aught was his own, but all things were common unto them?"[22]

The highest expression of Christian love is to lay down one's life for one's friend. Those who did so, the thousands of pairs mentioned by Aelred in the above passage, were weak individuals who, like everyone else in this fallen world, were hounded by doubts and temptations of various kinds. To enter into a spiritual friendship, one needs to be good—not perfect. It is the friendship itself that, rooted in Christ's grace, leads a person along the way of purgation, illumination, and ultimate union with God.

---

[21]DSA 2:43 [CCCM 1:310 (283–89); SF 80].

[22]DSA 1:27–28 [CCCM 1:293–94 (154–66); SF 56–57]. For the theology of the kiss in monastic theology, see Jean Leclercq, *The Love of Learning and the Desire for God*, trans. Catharine Misrahi (New York: Fordham University Press, 1982), pp. 226–28.

Application Two: The Three Kisses

Aelred uses the metaphor of a kiss to point out what the process of growth in friendship precisely entails: "In a kiss two breaths meet, and are mingled, and are united. As a result, a certain sweetness of mind is born, which rouses and binds together the affection of those who embrace."[23] He extends the metaphor to demonstrate the different types of friendship that can be forged: "There is, then, a corporeal kiss, a spiritual kiss, and an intellectual kiss. The corporeal kiss is made by the impression of the lips; the spiritual kiss by the union of spirits; the intellectual kiss through the Spirit of God, by the infusion of grace."[24]

Although the carnal kiss is supposed to be offered or received for definite and worthy reasons (e.g., as a sign of reconciliation or a mark of peace), Aelred points out that it can be misused for perverse and lustful ends.[25] The spiritual kiss, by way of contrast, is "the kiss of friends who are bound by one law of friendship; for it is not made by contact with the mouth but by the affection of the heart".[26] According to Aelred, Christ is already present in this friendship. His presence is not directly experienced, however, but mediated through another person: "I would call this the kiss of Christ, yet he himself does not offer it from his own mouth, but from the mouth of another, breathing upon his lovers that most sacred affection so that there seems to them to be, as it were, one spirit in many bodies."[27] As the soul becomes accustomed to this kind of friendship, it tastes the sweetness that comes from Christ and eventually yearns for something more than a mediated encounter and sighs for direct contact with Christ through the intellectual "kiss of grace".[28] When this happens, "all earthly affections have been tempered, and all thoughts and desires which savor of the world have been quieted, the soul takes delight in the kiss of Christ alone and rests in his embrace, exulting and exclaiming: 'His left hand is under my head and his right hand shall embrace me.'"[29]

---

[23] DSA 2:23 [CCCM 1:307 (162–65); SF 75].
[24] DSA 2:24 [CCCM 1:307 (165–68); SF 76].
[25] DSA 2:25 [CCCM 1:307 (177–85); SF 76].
[26] DSA 2:26 [CCCM 1:307 (185–87); SF 76].
[27] DSA 2:26 [CCCM 1:307–8 (190–94); SF 76].
[28] DSA 2:27 [CCCM 1:308 (198); SF 77].
[29] DSA 2:27 [CCCM 1:308 (199–203); SF 77].

Friendship, for Aelred, is the "medicine of life" because it moves two people along this wide spectrum of relationships and enables them eventually to meet Christ face-to-face. It calms their disordered passions, enables their spirits to mingle, and eventually brings them to an intimate relationship with the Spirit of Christ. All of this is possible because of Christ's redemptive suffering. By laying down his life for his friends, Jesus gives mankind the chance once again to become the friends of God. Because of Christ, charity and friendship are slowly coming back into harmony with one another. If they presently appear to still be in dissonance with each other, it is simply because the full effects of Christ's redemption are not yet manifest. When they become so, "this friendship, to which here we admit but few, will be outpoured upon all and by all outpoured upon God, and God shall be all in all."[30]

Application Three: Practical Advice

Aelred's interest in providing concrete measures to help others establish and develop strong friendships in Christ stems from his consciousness of the great caution and care that needs to be taken in an imperfect world still under the sway of the effects of Adam's fall. Even though he firmly believes in the victory won for mankind by Christ's suffering and death, he is still very conscious of the struggle with temptation and the tendency to sin that even good people must deal with in their daily lives. Indeed, there would be no need for him to give such advice if the rages of concupiscence no longer had any hold over man's heart.

It is for this reason that Aelred offers some very concrete and practical advice to his readers about forming spiritual friendships. In his mind, there are "four stages by which one climbs to the perfection of friendship: the first is selection, the second probation, the third admission, and the fourth perfect harmony in matters human and divine with charity and benevolence."[31] In the selection process, Aelred instructs his readers of the types of person who should (and should not) be chosen for friendship. He advises them to avoid strong ties with those who have a difficult time restraining the passions that lead a person to quarreling,

[30]DSA 3:134 [CCCM 1:350 (1116–18); SF 132].
[31]DSA 3:8 [CCCM 1:319 (64–68); SF 93].

anger, fickleness, suspicion, and talkativeness.[32] Friendships with those
who can give love and affection, security and happiness, by way of contrast, should be actively pursued.[33] If one has already begun a friendship
with someone who cannot withstand these tendencies, he reminds his
readers that they are still bound by the law of charity and should unstitch
the bond "little by little" rather than breaking it off immediately.[34] As
far as the period of probation is concerned, Aelred says that a potential
friend should be given a trial period where the qualities of loyalty, right
intention, discretion, and patience are tested.[35] Once these qualities have
been carefully examined in a potential friend, that person can be admitted to be one's closest confidant, where a union of spirits will eventually
take place and where one will discover "how good and how pleasant it
is for brethren to dwell together in unity".[36] Aelred himself provides his
reader with an example from his own experience of the gradual process
whereby a person is admitted into the intimacy of spiritual friendship:
"All this in a most wondrous way had bound him to me by the most
intimate bounds, and so had brought him into my affection, that from an
inferior I made him my companion, from a companion a friend, from a
friend my most cherished of friends."[37]

The need for all of this practical advice arises out of Aelred's keen
awareness of the various pitfalls before anyone who seeks to enter into
a friendship with another person that is rooted in Christ. It is also why
Book 3 (where this practical advice occurs) is the longest part of the
treatise and generally the most widely read.

Observations

Given the above literary and theological contexts—as well as accompanying applications to Aelred's understanding of goodness, the kiss of
friendship, and the need for practical advice about entering into and
sustaining such a bond—a number of observations are in order.

[32]DSA 3:55 [CCCM 1:328 (379–82); SF 104].
[33]DSA 3:51 [CCCM 1:327 (346–47); SF 103].
[34]DSA 3:41 [CCCM 1:325 (281–85); SF 101].
[35]DSA 3:61 [CCCM 1:329 (418–19); SF 105].
[36]DSA 3:131[CCCM 1:349 (1090–91); SF 131].
[37]DSA 3:122 [CCCM 1:346 (1001–4); SF 127].

1. To begin with, Aelred's teaching on friendship and his lively conversation with Ivo, Walter, and Gratian encourage the reader to examine the quality of his own personal relationships. Aelred adapts the dialogue form to suit his practical, experiential concerns for entering into the friendship of Christ. He does so by presenting his readers with a number of possibilities regarding the range of spiritual friendships available to them and by urging them, at least implicitly, to be aware of their own potential for entering into and maintaining such relationships. By engaging his own active imagination and helping the other characters of dialogue to do the same, Aelred raises questions, makes suggestions, and opens possibilities that may inspire the reader to embark on a similar process of reflection.

2. When going through the treatise, one gets the strong sense that the written conversation reflects a conversation going on in Aelred's mind that, in turn, has its roots in actual conversations with his friends. Aelred's dialogue, in other words, is the fruit, not only of his real-life friendships with Ivo, Walter, and Gratian, but also of his reflection on the meaning of spiritual friendship with them in his mind. As such, it reminds readers that their thought processes are influenced by their relationships with others—and greatly depend on them. When going through the treatise, they should try to be aware as much as possible of the various influences on their own thought processes. The origin of the various questions and concerns that help to shape one's convictions should be very helpful in this respect.

3. Aelred is not only the author of the treatise, but also the principal character in the dialogue. Although it would be nice to imagine that the two are one and the same, careful reflection should lead the reader to conclude that they are not. In all probability, the "Aelred of the dialogue" is a "persona" projected onto the page by "Aelred the writer". That is not to say that there are no continuities between the two; more continuities probably exist than discontinuities. Still, "Aelred the writer" is making only a selective representation of himself when he portrays himself in words for others to see. However small the gap between the "author" and his "persona", it is important for readers to keep the discrepancy in mind as they go through the text. Reading the dialogue should encourage them to be aware of discrepancies in their own lives between the people they are and the "personae" they project for others to see.

4. The dialogue form brings to the fore the dialogical dimension of spiritual friendship: the closer the friendship, the more intimate the dialogue. This holds true for one's relationship with others—both living and dead—and especially with Christ. Aelred's dialogue encourages his readers to be conscious of the quality of the dialogue that they have with their friends and also of the quality of their prayer. The depth of these conversations provides them with a good gauge for determining the strength of the bonds that tie them. In his dialogue, Aelred feels free not only to discuss a serious subject with his friends, but also to root that discussion in his own experience. By presenting this dialogue to a wider audience, he is inviting those who read his words to do the same.

5. For Aelred, the doctrine of creation provides his teaching with a focal point of paradisal innocence. He uses it to show that all creatures—inanimate, animate, human, and angelic—have an innate orientation to some kind of companionship and life in society. His beautiful description of the collateral relationship between man and woman, moreover, contrasts sharply with the predominant hierarchical view of the day. Aelred considers friendship before the fall to be coextensive with the life of charity. In this state, it is the "medicine of life", not in the sense of healing (since there is no need of it), but in the sense of bringing ongoing strength and sustenance to one's life. Aelred uses the doctrine of creation to point to an original compatibility of the dual love of friendship (*amicitia*) and charity (*caritas*). Even today, this usage causes its readers to reflect upon the origins of these loves, the reasons for their present dissonance, and the orientation they have toward the future.

6. Although Aelred does not devote a great deal of space to it in his treatise, the doctrine of the fall plays a significant role in his understanding of friendship as the "medicine of life". The fall of Adam disrupts the original relationship of harmony between charity and friendship within mankind. This fall from grace results in a corresponding disruption in the relationship between God and mankind and unleashes the powerful force of concupiscence in the heart of every individual. The doctrine of the fall provides an important part of the theological rationale for Aelred's teaching on friendship. Deeply wounded by Adam's fall, man's nature is in desperate need of healing. Even after Christ's redemptive action, mankind still suffers from the horrible effects of original sin. Spiritual friendship helps people to experience in their lives the concrete fruits

of Christ's redemption. Its curative powers tame the unruly emotions of the heart and enable people to live in unity with one another—and with God.

7. The healing of man's wound, of course, comes primarily through the redemptive suffering of Christ, which reestablishes a basis for friendship between the human and the divine. Spiritual friendship is again made possible only because Jesus, out of loving obedience to the Father, has laid down his life for his friends (cf. Jn 15:13). Without this gratuitous act of self-offering, the harmony between charity and friendship would never be able to be brought back into harmony. For Aelred, the doctrine of the redemption creates the possibility for a renewed relationship of friendship between God and mankind. It is this renewed relationship with Jesus that heals mankind of its deadly wounds and gives it a new lease on life. In this respect, a person's friendship with Christ is the true "medicine of life". All other spiritual friendships are of a participatory nature. Their curative powers flow from Christ and ultimately lead back to him.

8. This participatory nature of spiritual friendships in Christ provides an important context for Aelred's understanding of goodness. In God, goodness is a transcendental perfection (e.g., the One, the True, the Good, the Beautiful) and possesses all the characteristics typically associated with it. In mankind, however, goodness is merely participatory and can never achieve the transcendental status reserved only to the divine. The distinction between the divine and the human, between the Creator and the created, must always be strictly maintained. For Aelred, moreover, the participatory nature of man's goodness differs greatly depending on which particular mode of man's nature one is talking about at the time. Mankind's participated goodness before the fall, for example, differs from what it is like after the fall and also after Christ's redemption has reached its full effect. Aelred's practical concerns about the formation of spiritual friendship reflect this qualified understanding of the participatory nature of man's goodness.

9. The qualified participatory nature of man's goodness allows Aelred to treat the healing of man's nature as an ongoing process. Rooted in an allegorical interpretation of Song of Solomon 1:2 (the only such interpretation in the entire treatise),[38] his metaphor of the three

---

[38] Song 1:2 reads, "O that you would kiss me with the kisses of your mouth!"

kisses—carnal, spiritual, and intellectual—allows him to describe spiritual friendship as a mingling of spirits that mediates one's relationship with Christ and eventually leads to a direct mingling of one's spirit with the Spirit of Christ. Spiritual friendship is likened to the exchange of breath that takes place in a kiss. Just as breathing is necessary for life, so too is friendship necessary for spiritual life. This necessity, however, comes not from the bond of friendship itself, but from the grace of Christ, who makes it possible and to whom the spiritual friendship ultimately leads. The medicinal powers of spiritual friendship, in other words, derive from their "graced capacity" to mediate Christ's presence and to lead a person into an intimate relationship with Christ himself.

10. All of the practical advice on spiritual friendship given in Book 3, the longest in the treatise, stems from Aelred's sensitivity to the precarious nature of mankind's present earthly existence. Even though Christ's redemptive suffering has made it possible for mankind to enter once again into fellowship with God, the effects of original sin still influence man's heart and can easily get in the way. Concerned more with experience than with abstract doctrines, Aelred provides his readers with concrete suggestions about the precautions they should take when entering into spiritual friendships. It is for this reason that Aelred goes to great lengths to describe the various steps involved in the fourfold process of selection, probation, admission, and union. This practical advice helps to ensure that genuine spiritual friendships can actually be established and bear fruit. Without it, the reader would be at a loss concerning the concrete ways of developing these important bonds.

Conclusion

Spiritual friendship, for Aelred, has an important role to play in a person's journey to God. The various literary and theological contexts of his treatise highlight this firm conviction. One might go so far as to say that Aelred's use of the dialogue form and of the Christian doctrines of creation, fall, and redemption give shape to his teaching and cannot be separated from it without drastically changing it. To do so would be to overlook some of his most basic presuppositions about the present state of man's nature and the remedies given by God for facilitating a person's growth in holiness.

In describing spiritual friendship as the "medicine of life", Aelred highlights mankind's present need for healing and strengthening. The literary form in which he casts his teachings reminds the reader of the various types of spiritual friendships possible and that dialogue itself is an essential element for the establishment and ongoing development of such relationships. The theological background of his teaching offers some helpful insights into his qualified understanding of participated goodness, his presentation of spiritual friendship as a process of growth reaching its perfection in intimate union with Christ, and his penchant for giving very concrete, practical advice about their care and maintenance.

Aelred's primary interest in his *De spiritali amicitia* is to help his readers to foster intimate friendships among themselves and with Christ. One does not journey long into the treatise, however, before discovering that the two kinds of relationships are intimately related—and in a circular way. Spiritual friendships lead those involved into an intimate relationship with Christ. Christ, in turn, makes such relationships possible and orients them from the very beginning toward himself. Spiritual friendships, in other words, "begin in Christ, continue in Christ, and are perfected in Christ".[39] They lie at the heart of Aelred's spiritual doctrine and have much to offer those who enter into a critical yet constructive dialogue with their underlying literary and theological premises. Only by examining these contexts will the reader discover the influence that Aelred's own monastic background had on the shaping of his teaching. Only then will he or she be ready to begin to make appropriate adaptations of this teaching to the present day.

[39] DSA 1:10 [CCCM 1:29 (171–73); SF 53].

At the Heart of the Matter:
Lived Experience in Saint John Paul II's
Integral Account of the Person

Deborah Savage, Ph.D.

It would be an understatement to point out that the issues under consideration in this volume are a matter of furious debate in contemporary discourse—and, further, that they are of urgent concern. It seems clear that both the self-evident and natural order of things is under attack and that the future of our civilization may well depend on mounting an adequate response. But though this certainly forms the backdrop for these reflections, we need not enter into the broader contours of that debate in this essay. Our aim here is fairly narrow: to provide insight into the anthropological framework that could inform the pastoral care of our brothers and sisters in the Lord who experience same-sex attraction (SSA). In other words, our question here is *not* whether or not persons are free to ignore the natural order, but how to minister to those who wish to engage in the struggle to conform themselves to it. And, while circumstances may differ, it should be acknowledged at the outset that conforming to the natural order is a struggle to which all are called.

The immediate context for these proceedings is the *Lineamenta* issued by the extraordinary synod on the family in October 2014, convened by Pope Francis to prepare an agenda for the ordinary synod scheduled for October 2015. The document includes a *Relatio Synodi*, as well as a set of questions intended to "prompt a faithful and bold response from the Pastors and the People of God in a renewed proclamation of the Gospel of the Family".[1] In light of our purpose here, I would like to point

---

[1] Synod of Bishops, XIV Ordinary General Assembly, *Lineamenta*, "The Vocation and Mission of the Family in the Church and Contemporary World", December 2014, Part 2, opening paragraph, http://www.vatican.va/roman_curia/synod/documents/rc_synod_doc_20141209_lineamenta-xiv-assembly_en.html.

to the section entitled "The Importance of Affectivity in Life" as the place in the document that gives us a way of entering most directly into our topic.[2]

In two brief paragraphs, the Synod Fathers put our questions here into the wider context of the family itself and offer an insightful conclusion: that the breakdown of the family, that is, of what would otherwise be the locus of love and care for one another, in combination with the rampant and toxic individualism characteristic of our culture, is resulting in the widespread phenomena of persons seeking to care for themselves emotionally and otherwise in ways that do not always promote their emotional and spiritual health. This often results in an affective immaturity that compromises the capacity of individual persons to make and keep the commitments necessary to stable, lifelong marriage. It seems logical to conclude that SSA is included in this description.

The Synod Fathers further state that "cultural tendencies in today's world seem to set no limits on a person's affectivity in which every aspect needs to be explored, even those which are highly complex."[3] For those who experience SSA, this undeniable feature of contemporary culture represents something of real significance. In some cases, because they did not find properly ordered love in the family, or even more frequently, find themselves in a social context in which these attractions are not understood in light of the full truth about the human person, such complex emotional needs can be mistaken—indeed, often are mistaken—for perfectly "natural" desires.[4] Aspirations that would otherwise quite naturally "lead to a desire to put greater effort into building relationships of self-giving and creative reciprocity" are often stunted by the very real twin dangers of modern life: "individualism and a tendency to live only for oneself".[5] We will see that the pastoral care of those who experience SSA must begin with the recognition that, at their origin, such desires issue from a very natural impulse: the need for love and for friendship.

[2] Ibid., Part 1, nos. 8–9.

[3] Ibid., no. 9.

[4] I do not mean to imply that SSA is only the result of disordered family systems. Clearly such inclinations can be the result of complex factors. But because of the assumptions governing our culture, they are often considered just another manifestation of normal human desire. Please see Jean Lloyd, "The Girl in the Tuxedo: Two Variations on Sexual Orientation and Gender Identity", *Public Discourse*, February 5, 2015, http://www.thepublicdiscourse.com/2015/02/14388/.

[5] *Lineamenta*, Part 1, no. 8.

The question is how to acknowledge their experience while affirming and integrating it into the full truth about the human person.

We know that pastoral care, no matter how sensitively exercised, can never be divorced from the truth. Few would deny that we owe it to those whom we are called to serve to remain forever grounded in the full vision of the person and to point them toward it. But anyone who has actually engaged in this effort knows well that entering into the conversation often requires a starting place in experience; one usually does not begin with a summary of the metaphysical anthropology of Saint Thomas Aquinas. But what must be acknowledged is the perception that this starting place can bring with it certain risks. There may be a fear that acknowledging someone's experience, especially one we take to be disordered, will be mistaken for approval. Such fears, while not illegitimate, can be an obstacle to a full-throated pastoral engagement.

And here we come to what I believe to be at stake in this essay. These concerns may be valid. But we simply cannot cede the territory of experience to those for whom there is no objective moral order. If we allow that, we may not only lose the battle; we may lose the war—for it is the language of our times. It seems clear that unless we find a way to speak in the language of experience with those we seek to serve, we may find that we are unable to intervene, not only in *their* lives, but in what appears to be the inexorable movement of destructive cultural forces that are now forcing their way into *everyone's* lives. The future of the family, of our young people, and even of our political order is clearly at stake. We are in urgent need of an approach that will permit us to integrate personal experience into a fuller account of the human person. This is a matter of utmost urgency: What is the place of personal, subjective experience in that account? How can it be acknowledged without risking the inevitable slide into "subjectivism"?

It is the thesis of this essay that we will find the answers we need in the account of the person proposed by Saint John Paul II as the philosopher Karol Wojtyla. In a very real sense, the late Holy Father seems to have anticipated our difficulty and provided the route to its resolution. When one grasps the significance of John Paul II's teaching on this subject, one comes to realize that his intellectual contributions and pastoral witness, both as pope and as a philosopher, could only have been an act of Divine Providence. He has given us a way out of our dilemma.

John Paul's approach is a synthesis of two strands of philosophical thought: It invokes and affirms the received tradition on the meaning of the person (the Thomist account). And it affirms the centrality of "lived" (conscious) experience in grasping the full truth of the individual person (the phenomenological account). Indeed, his claim is that the arguably more abstract description found in the Thomist tradition, while absolutely valid as far as it goes, seems to leave out the reality of lived experience and the dynamism of the individual person *in act*.

Setting aside the question of whether or not this is a valid criticism of Aquinas' philosophical anthropology, we will see that John Paul's own approach permits us to acknowledge the experience of actual existing persons without compromising the more properly "ontological" framework that we know reveals the unchanging truth about personhood.[6] It will show us the route to the integration of the affective aspects of the person, aspects in the case of SSA felt as "natural desires" and misinterpreted as "natural desires"—but which really are not "natural" at all. Importantly, the late Holy Father's insights will illuminate the anthropological significance and meaning of the news from the "front lines" of this debate—namely, that those who experience SSA but who have opted for chastity or celibacy in the pursuit of holiness consistently report a new sense of vocation and, not surprisingly, of peace, of healing, and of wholeness.[7]

In what follows, we begin by calling into question a couple of the foundational assumptions silently governing the larger debate and which impinge on our purposes here. The first will be to confront the insidious dualist anthropological framework introduced into the Western intellectual tradition most explicitly by Rene Descartes. The pervasive

---

[6]It will not be possible to provide a fully elaborated account of this method and its results in this essay. For a fuller treatment please see Deborah Savage, "The Centrality of Lived Experience in Wojtyla's Account of the Person", *Philosophical Annals* 61 (December 2013): 4. And though I will reference the metaphysical anthropology of Aquinas, the presupposition here is that Aquinas' achievement is already grasped by the readers of this volume and that many aspects of it will be treated in other contributions. See also Janet Smith, "The Universality of Natural Law and the Irreducibility of Personalism", in the English edition of *Nova et Vetera* 11, no. 4 (2013): 1229–47.

[7]See Lloyd, "Girl in the Tuxedo"; Doug Mainwaring, "Hearts, Parts, and Minds: The Truth Comes Out", *Public Discourse*, March 9, 2015, http://www.thepublicdiscourse.com /2015/03/14510/. See also Eve Tushnet, *Gay and Catholic: Accepting My Sexuality, Finding Community, Living My Faith* (Notre Dame, Ind.: Ave Maria Press, 2014), p. 59.

influence of Descartes' thought has resulted in a persistent and wide-spread tendency to think of the body as merely an appendage, and of one's "identity" as something that resides in one's mind or conscious-ness. In my view, this is an essential but mostly unexamined flaw at the center of contemporary debates about sex and sexual identity. And, I would argue, it is the precise point at which the Catholic understanding of the union of the body and soul conflicts with cultural assumptions about personhood and sexuality.[8]

In a real sense, this dualist outlook made possible the second assump-tion we must confront, that is, the very legitimacy of even thinking in terms we now take for granted, that of dividing the human species into the categories "heterosexual" and "homosexual". We will see that the taxonomy of sexual orientation is flawed in its conception and its use has resulted in a fateful substitution: what is, in fact, a form of sexual *behavior* has come to constitute instead an actual sexual *identity*. This has led unquestionably to profound confusion on the nature of the person and the place that sexuality occupies in his identity. Uprooting such assumptions will clear the way for the fuller account of human person-hood we seek.

But let me say at the outset that the underlying premise of this essay is that our mission is to point all those we serve toward their true potential for intimacy, something that cannot be reduced to erotic desire. True and chaste friendship is not a lower-order good than marriage—it is the thing toward which all human relationships are ordered. Neglecting to call any person to this possibility, no matter what their difficulty or addiction, is to lower their dignity before God and, in the end, to define them according to their temptations and their sin. All persons, no matter what their struggles or desires, are called to holiness and to the work of conforming their lives and their very being to the revelation of God and the telos toward which all of mankind is ordered. More particularly and in light of our topic, all persons are called to chastity, all *unmarried* per-sons are called to celibacy, and *all* must be presumed to be both receptive of grace and possessed of the power to live out the commands of Christ. To treat certain persons as if they have no "choice" and thus no hope of

---

[8]In his February 2, 1994, *Letter to Families*, St. John Paul II refers to this phenomenon as one of the elements in the "New Manichaeanism" (see John Paul II, *Letter to Families*, no. 19, http://w2.vatican.va/content/john-paul-ii/en/letters/1994/documents/hf_jp-ii_let _02021994_families.html).

conversion or of healing is to treat them according to a different standard.[9] Faithful Christians are asking the Church, indeed pleading with her, to affirm the truth about the person and to help all of us to live in conformity with it.

We will see that, above all, the work of ministering to those experiencing and struggling with SSA calls for unwavering compassion and authentic *caritas in veritate* (truth in charity). For the truth we will uncover is that there really is no such thing as a "transgender" person or a "homosexual" person or, for that matter, a "heterosexual" person. While pastoral situations call us to acknowledge the pain of those who struggle with SSA and other sexual disorders, we are also called to affirm, no matter what the context, the truth that our bodies do matter. In union with the soul, they tell us who we are and, ultimately, who we are meant to be. It is the hypersexualization of our culture, arguably underway now for over 150 years, that has led us to confuse sexual impulses and desires with our identities as persons. The road to authentic personal freedom is not easy for anyone. It requires self-knowledge, prayer, and fasting and—above all—the gifts of mercy and forgiveness.

Dualism and Its Deadly Impact

In the early seventeenth century Rene Descartes attempted to put the pursuit of knowledge on an entirely new footing. He began by first doubting all that he knew in order to arrive at certainty about what might constitute first principles. And he famously arrived at the formulation that he was a "thinking thing" (the *res cogitans*) somehow united to an "extended thing", otherwise known as a body (the *res extensa*).[10] These two substances are united but only in a partial sense, for the body is, in fact, more properly a part of the material world, that is, the world of extended things, an objective world of pure externality without any interior life.[11] Utterly distinct from this world is man's soul, Descartes'

---

[9]Jean Lloyd, "Seven Things I Wish My Pastor Knew about My Homosexuality", *Public Discourse*, December 10, 2014, http://www.thepublicdiscourse.com/2014/12/14149/.

[10]Rene Descartes, *Meditations on First Philosophy*, Meditation 6. See also, Étienne Gilson, *Modern Philosophy* (New York: Random House, 1963), p. 69.

[11]Michael Waldstein, introduction to *Man and Woman He Created Them: A Theology of the Body*, by John Paul II (Boston: Pauline Books and Media, 2006), p. 42.

"thinking thing", whose only attribute is pure and rational consciousness (knowledge and free will), a world defined exclusively by interiority. In Descartes' account, this mind (*l'ame* or "soul" in French) is the substance that constitutes his identity and which therefore can exist without the body.[12]

Descartes' subsequent influence on the modern period is indisputable, and, it can be argued, the results for contemporary culture have been catastrophic. Saint John Paul II identifies some of these results in his 1994 *Letter to Families:*

> The separation of spirit and body in man has led to a growing tendency to consider the human body, not in accordance with the categories of its specific likeness to God, but rather on the basis of its similarity to all the other bodies present in the world of nature, bodies which man uses as raw material in his efforts to produce goods for consumption. But everyone can immediately realize what enormous dangers lurk behind the application of such criteria to man. When the human body, considered apart from spirit and thought, comes to be used as *raw material* in the same way that the bodies of animals are used—and this actually occurs for example in experimentation on embryos and fetuses—we will inevitably arrive at a dreadful ethical defeat.[13]

Saint John Paul goes on to point out that this same anthropological perspective has contributed to what he calls a "New Manichaeanism" in which body and spirit are seen not as united but "in radical opposition". In this account, the "body does not receive life from the spirit and the spirit does not give life to the body. Man thus *ceases to live as a person and a subject. . . .* He becomes merely *an object.*"[14] It is this precise line of thought that has turned human sexuality into the arena for manipulation and exploitation it has clearly become.[15]

Perhaps I can be permitted one brief personal anecdote that will serve to illuminate the underlying assumption leading to this phenomenon. For several years I taught a seminar on Catholic identity to members of the university community. The seminar culminated in a leadership

---

[12]Descartes, *Meditations on First Philosophy*, Meditation 2.

[13]John Paul II, *Letter to Families*, no. 19.

[14]Ibid.; emphasis in original.

[15]For an extended analysis of the philosophical framework that undergirds St. John Paul's thinking on this, see Waldstein, introduction to *Theology of the Body*, esp. pp. 34–44.

retreat at which, among other things, we considered the Church's teaching on human sexuality. During one somewhat painful discussion, a faculty member, a fine, Lutheran gentleman with no particular hostility to the university's Catholic identity, stated with a measure of impatience: "I don't understand what the fuss is all about; after all, it's *only bodies*." A more precise formulation of the problem would be hard to articulate.

On the Church's account, of course, it is never "only bodies". Foundational to the Catholic understanding of the human person is the hylomorphic union of the body and soul; this is the fundamental starting place for grasping the radical unity of the person.[16] According to this understanding, the soul is everywhere in the body, permeating it and informing it as its principle of life, the source of all its potency and capacity for action. The soul, in union with the body, is what makes man who he is. Thus, one's identity is a reflection of that unity, and every action one takes implicates the whole of that identity, both body and soul.

Questions of Identity Must Include the Body

But this is not the basis upon which human identity is understood in contemporary discourse. Instead, current controversies concerning sexual identity are grounded in the assumption that my "identity" (what the Catholic tradition might refer to as "my nature" or essence) is a function of my consciousness; it is completely up to "me", and my body has nothing to do with it. The body is merely an appendage, a "carrier" perhaps of my consciousness, of what I call "myself", an instrument at my disposal that I am free to use for pleasure or for whatever I choose. Thus, if I have a male body, but feel myself to be a woman, I am perfectly justified in assuming that the physical reality of my body is irrelevant to the identity I wish to claim as my own. After all, my identity resides in my consciousness; it is a reality distinct from that of the body, merely a matter of personal discernment or choice. Further, as is now maintained, at least for political purposes, this is a completely malleable reality; on any given day, or in any given situation, I may identify with a different persona that resides in my consciousness. Thus I may claim

---

[16]See Vatican II, Pastoral Constitution on the Church in the Modern World, *Gaudium et spes*, December 7, 1965, no. 12.

to be any "gender" I wish, and it is a sensibility that may change. My identity is up to "me".[17]

In contrast to this view, the Catholic vision of the person begins with the self-evident and timeless proposition that *human* beings are born with an expressly *human* nature, something shared by all of mankind, past, present, and future. This fact is a reflection of the truth observable in all of creation, that is, that all creatures have natures that are discernable because they are revealed through their ways of being in the world, their acts. All living things are composites of body and soul (matter and form), and their natures manifest in both the potencies and acts that characterize them.

The human person occupies a particular place in the created order because he possesses a rational soul, one that equips him in a special way to share in the responsibility for the stewardship of that order. He is made in the image of God and possesses intellect and free will, faculties that, when consistently ordered toward the good, permit each of us to become who God *means* us to be through the exercise of authentic freedom. Our movement toward fullness cannot be actualized without the body, for we are not pure spirits. To claim that the body is irrelevant to human identity is to tear the person asunder. Inevitably, it will either put him in conflict with the desires of his body or make him a slave to them.

To make the implications of this analysis clear and explicit, on this account, what defines the person is most definitely not his "sexual orientation", sexual desire, or even the capacity to procreate. What is definitive of the person is his capacity for reason, self-determination, and self-giving. These are the defining characteristics of the essence or nature of man. And our capacities, desires, and actions, including our sexuality, must be guided by all of these characteristics. As John Paul states in his *Letter to Families*: "Revelation leads us to discover in *human sexuality* a *treasure proper to the person*, who finds true fulfillment in the family but who can likewise express his profound calling in virginity and in celibacy for the sake of the Kingdom of God."[18]

Our sexuality exists more for the sake of others than for ourselves. It exists to reveal to us that we are meant to live lives of self-giving. It exists to enable us to join our lives exclusively and indissolubly in a giving and receiving way with a spouse, with whom we can participate in the

---

[17] Recent legislation has been enacted in several states (California and Minnesota, just to name a couple) in which high school students are free to use whichever restroom they determine reflects their particular gender identity on any given day.

[18] John Paul II, *Letter to Families*, no. 19; emphasis in original.

co-creation with God of new life. For those who are called to lives of chaste celibacy, sexuality is also to be integrated into a life of complete self-giving; priests and religious, the consecrated, and those who are single must also make of themselves a total gift—both body and soul—to God and to his Church. This calling may seem more diffuse than marital self-giving, but it still calls for a recognition of the radical unity that characterizes the human person. It is with our souls *and* our bodies, with the *whole* of ourselves, that we live lives of service to others.

Heterosexual, Homosexual?

The use of differentiated gender categories in describing sexual identity and its ever-multiplying permutations has become such a normal feature of our culture that we no longer even question it. It can be a surprise to realize that the use of terms such as "heterosexual" and "homosexual" were introduced into our lexicon as recently as the late nineteenth century and did not enter into everyday parlance until the 1930s.[19] Prior to that time, such categories had never been used; before then, pretty much no one who had ever lived had any kind of "sexual identity" per se. There were no "heterosexuals" because there were no "homosexuals". These terms only make sense in reference to each other; they "are like fraternal twins; they may not look alike but they shared a common gestation."[20]

When they first appeared, both terms referred to medical conditions that were described as aberrant. They were labels relied on exclusively by the medical profession and the developing field of psychology.[21] At first, even "heterosexual" referred to one of "several 'abnormal manifestations of the sexual appetite.' "[22] The heterosexual was someone for whom sex had no conscious connection to reproduction. His desires

---

[19] Williams Paris, *The End of Sexual Identity* (Downers Grove, Ill.: IVP Books, 2011), p. 39. Here Paris relies on the first edition of the work *The Invention of Heterosexuality*, by Jonathan Ned Katz (New York: Dutton, 1995).

[20] Paris, *End of Sexual Identity*, p. 41.

[21] Jonathan Ned Katz, *The Invention of Heterosexuality* (Chicago: University of Chicago Press, 2007), pp. 28–29.

[22] Ibid., p. 28. Katz is referring to an article by Dr. James G. Kiernan, "Responsibility in Sexual Perversion", published in the *Chicago Medical Recorder* 3 (May 1892): 185–210. Katz marks this as the earliest known use of the words "heterosexual" and "homosexual" in the United States. Dr. Kiernan himself is relying on the work (misused, according to Katz) of Dr. Richard von Krafft-Ebing of Vienna.

were essentially erotic and, in an age when marriage was the norm and procreation was assumed to be its overarching purpose, this was deemed deviant. But though, in a sense, reproduction as the natural end of sexual intimacy retained its normative status, as cultural norms changed and pleasure began to find its place alongside reproduction as an accepted feature of what governed intimate relationships, "heterosexuality" subsequently lost its connotation as a sexual aberration. It began to represent what constituted normal sexual behavior: sex—that could result in a child—was primarily for pleasure. In contrast, homosexuality signified a same-sex, pleasure-seeking desire that continued to be defined as pathological because it was, by definition, nonreproductive.[23]

For many of those concerned to make an argument about what constitutes normal—and therefore moral—sexual behavior, this language may all seem just fine. And perhaps it would be just fine, if the terms were being meant and heard in the context of a natural law that makes reference to the natural telos of things. But there is a very real though perhaps hidden danger in subscribing to these categories—because heterosexuality was offered as the "regulating ideal", not through reference to the natural law or as the result of moral reasoning based in eternal *verities*; it was considered normative because, at the time, *science* pronounced it as "natural". It was an important moment in the progression we are concerned with here: "scientific" arguments replaced moral reasoning—grounded in an adequate account of the human person—as the source of understanding ourselves and our sexuality.

The cultural norms governing sexual relationships at the time still required sanctions against sodomy and other sexual aberrations. But as the pleasure principle began to take actual precedence over the procreative power of the sexual act and in the way people thought about the purposes of sexual activity, it became harder, if not impossible, to maintain the usual social prohibitions against what were widely accepted as sexual aberrations; there was a risk that such sanctions would lose their power to control sexual behavior. The culture actually needed the scientific and medical community to establish "heterosexuality" as normative in order to provide continued sanctions.[24] Of course, in our contemporary

---

[23] Ibid., p. 29.

[24] Michael Hannon, "Against Heterosexuality", *First Things*, March 2014, p. 28. In addition to other sources, Hannon relies on what he refers to as an "unexpected ally": Michel Foucault, whose work *The History of Sexuality*, volumes 1, 2, 3 (New York: Vintage Books, 1990) provides additional documentation and analysis of these developments. For a more thorough

context—and especially since the advent of the birth control pill—the pleasure principle *alone* is thought to govern sexual activity, and as a result, we are approaching a moment when there will be no such thing as a "sexual aberration". If it "feels good, do it" is on its way to becoming not only a cultural norm, but a politically and legally sanctioned norm.

The "scientific" definitions of these terms have shifted many times since the late nineteenth century. Undoubtedly the most dramatic example is found in the theories of Alfred Kinsey. Kinsey's studies in the mid-twentieth century, mostly discredited now, were widely influential at the time and served to provide the scientific basis for the launch of the sexual revolution. His theories have been used for the past fifty years to "sway court decisions, pass legislation, introduce sex education into our schools, and even push for a redefinition of marriage".[25] Kinsey argued that human sexuality should be conceived of as a continuum rather than discreet categories.[26] And he estimated the homosexual population to be upwards of 10 percent, a figure known now to be very inaccurate. (Studies now indicate that those who identify as homosexual constitute about 2.3 percent of the population).[27]

That this sets the stage for current debates should be patently obvious: we face the widespread assumption that it is only a matter of time until the search for proof that homosexuality is genetic and therefore natural, inevitable, and innate is finally successful. In fact, it can be argued that our federal government, most of the media, the cultural elite, and many ordinary citizens simply operate on the assumption that "homosexuality" and its various permutations is the equivalent of "heterosexuality", that is, a naturally occurring phenomenon, innate to the person in question, and inevitable in its expression. Ironically, since we have come to believe one's sexual identity is not evident from the body one is born

---

and truly excellent analysis of the historical accounts of both Foucault and Katz, see David S. Crawford, "Liberal Androgyny: 'Gay Marriage' and the Meaning of Sexuality in Our Time", *Communio* 33 (Summer, 2006).

[25] Sue Ellen Browder, "Kinsey's Secret: The Phony Science of the Sexual Revolution", *Crisis Magazine*, May 28, 2012, http://www.crisismagazine.com/2012/kinseys-secret-the -phony-science-of-the-sexual-revolution.

[26] Paris, *End of Sexual Identity*, p. 44.

[27] Center for Disease Control and Prevention, National Health Statistics Reports, "Sexual Orientation and Health Among U.S. Adults: National Health Interview Survey", 2013. "Based on the 2013 NHIS data [collected in 2013 from 34,557 adults aged 18 and over], 96.6% of adults identified as straight, 1.6% identified as gay or lesbian, and 0.7% identified as bisexual. The remaining 1.1% of adults identified as 'something else,' stated 'I don't know the answer,' or refused to provide an answer" (ibid.)

with, but, as we have just seen, a feature of consciousness, scientific evidence is, in the end, unnecessary anyway.

But in truth, the taxonomy of sexual orientation is flawed in its origins and dishonest about its identity. Homosexuality and heterosexuality "masquerade as natural categories ... claiming to be not simply an accidental nineteenth-century invention but a timeless truth about human sexual nature".[28] As we have seen, both of these identities are man-made inventions; they are, in fact, completely "socially constructed", to borrow a particularly apt term from our postmodern colleagues. Again, ironically, these terms purport to designate two (or more?) naturally occurring, innate sexual orientations that have now assumed the mantle of personal identities. Their use has resulted in a fateful substitution: what is in reality simply sexual *behavior* has morphed into the presumption that it constitutes distinct sexual *identities*.

It is this very substitution that leads to the now commonplace (and dreaded) accusations of racism, bigotry, and homophobia whenever anyone suggests that same-sex sexual behavior is in some sense disordered. Despite the fact that, for the most part, the entire created order is sustained via the complementarity inherent in all species and confirmed in the obvious design of the human body—that is, despite the self-evident fact that it takes a man and a woman to "make" a baby—any alternative way of looking at the situation is suspect from the start. We are to deny the evidence of our senses and are precluded from relying on the very thing that makes us human—our reason—to unpack any of the arguments supporting the gay lifestyle. Why? Because to question someone's "identity" is a very different thing than to question his behavior, even when one is careful to distinguish the two. As philosopher Charles Taylor quite correctly points out, to refuse to acknowledge someone's identity is an act of violence against him.[29] Advocates of the "gay agenda" simply assume that those opposed to it can have no reasonable arguments to support their point of view and thus conclude that any claims to the contrary automatically fall into the category of hate speech. It must be said that this is not simply an affront to religious liberty. It is an attempt to force our children to live in a world in which they cannot believe the

---

[28] Hannon, "Against Heterosexuality", p. 27.

[29] Charles Taylor, *Multiculturalism and the Politics of Recognition* (Princeton, N.J.: Princeton University Press, 1994), p. 26.

evidence of their senses; it is to ask them to live in a world that doesn't make sense.

But the problem is broader than just the debate concerning the gay lifestyle. This terminology has, in fact, led also to a reduction of all persons to their sexual identity. We are all now forced to specify with which sexual orientation we *do* identify, whether that be "heterosexual" or any number of other identities slowly making their way into formal recognition in both the legal system and cyberspace.[30] This is not only profoundly confusing for our young people; when unquestioned, it becomes unspoken and therefore assumed. And, if allowed to stand, it will be fatal to our mission to lead all souls to Christ.

There are those with SSA who think the challenge they face is to live as a "homosexual" Christian.[31] This theory blinds us to the very real fact that so-called heterosexuals also do not find it easy to conform their desires to the natural law and the moral demands it makes on all of us. We are all struggling—or should be—with disordered desires. Though my particular appetites may manifest differently, when they drive my choices without regard for the good, it is the very same struggle as the person who struggles with SSA. These categories are not only utterly foreign to the meaning and telos of our faith; they are inadequate for justifying sexual norms, and antithetical to a coherent philosophical anthropology.[32] Their use has diverted our attention from the real issue: how individuals understand and value the virtue of chastity and the meaning of authentic friendship.

We need not convince persons with SSA that they are heterosexual; we need only to remind them that they are *human* and, as such, cannot be reduced to their desires, sexual or otherwise. The persons we seek to serve are, without exception, beings composed of both body and soul and possessed of intellect, will, and freedom. They each are called to the beauty of life in Christ. This gift is the unique privilege of mankind— and our unique destiny. To think—or act—otherwise is to bind the person who identifies as homosexual or transgender to appetites that will

---

[30] Facebook now permits subscribers to select from over fifty different sexual-orientation categories.

[31] See Tushnet, *Gay and Catholic*, and Ron Belgau, "Ontology vs. Phenomenology in the Gay Christian Debate", *First Things*, January 28, 2014, http://www.firstthings.com/blogs /firstthoughts/2014/01/ontology-vs-phenomenology-in-the-gay-christian-debate.

[32] Hannon, "Against Heterosexuality", p. 34.

preclude his entry into full participation in that life. It is to normalize sin. And it is the worst form of bigotry—the assumption that someone is somehow not fully human.

Toward a Christian Anthropology: Human Nature and Lived Experience

In an interview in *America Magazine* published last summer, Pope Francis reflected on a moment when he was asked if he approved of homosexuality. His reply echoes a now familiar theme often heard in the public declarations of this eminently pastoral pope:

> Tell me: when God looks at a gay person, does he endorse the existence of this person with love, or reject and condemn this person? We must always consider the person. Here we enter into the mystery of the human being. In life, God accompanies persons, and we must accompany them, starting from their situation. It is necessary to accompany them with mercy.[33]

Francis' approach, especially his comment that we must start from the personal situation of those we accompany, has been taken to heart by many in the Catholic community. Some of those in what is coming to be known as the "Spiritual Friendship" approach to SSA, and its basic assumptions concerning the need for what amounts to lifelong celibacy, believe he has identified an important point of entry into the discussion.[34] They point to Pope Francis' starting place as support for their own argument: that an account of the human person intended to illuminate the nature of SSA must begin with a description of the *experience* of what it means to be human (including the diverse experiences associated with same-sex attraction), rather than with a prior and more properly "ontological" treatment, such as that of Saint Thomas Aquinas—that is, a reasoned account of the true nature of the person and the place of sexuality in that nature. Though this "Spiritual Friendship" group does not seem to deny that, ultimately,

---

[33] Antonio Spadaro, S.J., "A Big Heart Open to God: The Exclusive Interview with Pope Francis", *America Magazine*, September 30, 2014, http://americamagazine.org/pope-interview. Quoted also in Belgau, "Ontology vs. Phenomenology".

[34] See Belgau, "Ontology vs. Phenomenology".

only an ontological account will equip us with a complete understanding of the full mystery of what it means to be a person, they hold that only a starting place in experience will permit us to engage the person in a consideration of the "whole"—which ultimately will include one's foundational identity as well as one's own personal experience.[35]

It could be said that posing the question in this way presents us with a false dichotomy between the two approaches. After all, the metaphysical anthropology of Aquinas finds its own starting place in contact with the world around us; it is wrong to think his philosophy is not rooted in man's experience. The philosophical framework that provides the scaffolding for the Church's teachings is grounded in the conviction that knowledge begins in the senses and therefore, by extension, in experience. We are presented with a false choice. But that is another issue. What we want to establish here is that the anthropology advanced by Saint John Paul II and his method for arriving at it are uniquely suited to bring together the two approaches. As stated in the introduction to this essay, a fuller consideration of his proposal will set the stage for an exploration of what might constitute an adequate approach to Christian anthropology under the present circumstances.

The papal corpus of Saint John Paul II is certainly grounded in his earlier philosophical work. And he states quite explicitly that "the category of lived experience must have a place in anthropology and ethics— and somehow be at the *center* of their respective interpretations."[36] He is adamant that fears about where it might lead must not prevent us from investigating human experience or from investigating the interior life of particular persons. For if our account of personhood is to be complete, he argues, it cannot leave out the elements of human experience and personal "subjectivity". That is, the full truth about man must also include not only the recognition that each person is a member of the species "human", possessing a human nature and all the properties and potencies that accompany that nature.[37] It must also include the recognition that each person is a concrete and particular instantiation of the species "human", a personal "subject" who is an actor in his own life, not the abstraction referred to as "human", but a unique expression of

---

[35] Ibid.

[36] Karol Wojtyla, "Subjectivity and the Irreducible in the Human Being", in *Person and Community* (New York: Peter Lang, 1993), p. 213; emphasis added.

[37] Ibid.

that human nature, which reflects both inner intentionality and things which merely "happen". All of this—that is, both his objective human nature and that which makes him a personal subject—can be said to constitute his "subjectivity". And further, Wojtyla insists that a focus on human experience is not only possible but essential, if we are to account for the reality of moral goodness, which is itself a real perfection of an actual existing subject.

Now, though the "turn to the subject" begun by Descartes and advanced by Kant preserved a sense that truth could be found, in the hands of Nietzsche and other philosophers since, this possibility came more and more to be denied. Acknowledgment of the importance of what goes on in the interior of man, itself a legitimate and proper object of philosophical reflection, has turned into a conviction that objective truth is not only inaccessible but nonexistent. To the modern, interest in human "subjectivity" is attributed many contemporary maladies, including subjectivism and its well-known twin, relativism, as well as the pride of place now given to any individual point of view, no matter how ill informed. All this has resulted in the widespread view that the only "truth" that exists is the "truth" of one's own experience. Claims about the existence of universal truth or an objective moral order often cannot find a foothold when confronted with the argument that such realities do not resonate with a particular individual's personal "experience". The priority given to subjective personal experience in determining what constitutes right thinking and moral behavior, assuming that question is even asked, is well documented; sadly, in disputes on moral questions, personal preference has taken the place of sound reasoning from self-evident first principles.[38] This is a reality confronted daily by persons in all circumstances, no matter what their philosophical persuasion. It is a position advanced by our culture and encountered in the media, in education, in our political discourse, and—perhaps most disturbing—even in academia.

We all know that this is a fact and that it is unquestionably a source of genuine concern. It can seem impossible to combat. And yet, combat it we must. I do not think it is putting it too starkly to say that we cannot refuse to speak to our children, our friends, our students, and our

---

[38] See Alistair MacIntyre, *After Virtue* (Notre Dame, Ind.: University of Notre Dame Press, 1984), esp. chap. 1.

parishioners in the language of experience, for it is the vernacular of our age. We must learn to speak that language in a new key. We cannot cede the territory of human experience to those who refuse to recognize that all human activity takes place within an objective moral context or who deny the movement of self-transcendence that, as Wojtyla will argue, exists at its core.

Wojtyla clearly grasps the problem and its meaning for us; he knows that we fear that if we put lived experience at the center of our interpretation of the person and then, further, allow that to inform our interactions with those we encounter, we will fall into subjectivism as an almost inevitable step.[39] It will force us to affirm behaviors that we take to be fundamentally disordered—and this we cannot, in all conscience, allow. On the other hand, despite what the culture wants to insist on, we could not claim to suspend the act of judgment entirely, even if we wanted to. The person is, at his core, a seeker of truth, and his capacity to make judgments about the truth or falsehood of particular claims, moral or otherwise, is a defining characteristic of his nature. We not only *possess* the faculty of judgment; it is this faculty that gives us the natural right and the responsibility to make distinctions and arrive at judgments concerning what we are ready to conclude is true and good. We operate this way in our everyday lives, in raising our children, while at work, in our political and social contexts—anyplace we strive to participate in or make a contribution to the common good. In a very literal sense, it would be impossible and disastrous for any of us to cease making judgments. And all this Wojtyla, both as a philosopher and as pastor to the universal Church, would affirm.[40] How then do we go about this?

First, Wojtyla argues that we are not "doomed to subjectivism", provided we always maintain a connection to the *integral* experience of the human being.[41] The key is to remember that the experience of constituting a specific phenomenon in ourselves *must always* be referred to the *whole* of which it is only a *part*. In other words, no discrete or single human experience can be said to define the person, but must always be interpreted in light of the whole that constitutes the person in total.

[39] Wojtyla, "Subjectivity and the Irreducible", p. 213.

[40] Indeed, there is probably no clearer statement of these principles in the contemporary period than St. John Paul II's 1993 encyclical *Veritatis Splendor*.

[41] Wojtyla, "Subjectivity and the Irreducible", p. 213.

This is relatively easy to see if we are considering things such as a single encounter with a particular aspect of the external world, a strongly held belief, or even the desire for friendship. Clearly, such things are only one element in our experience of ourselves and of the world. But the point of significance here is that SSA is also this kind of experience; it is obviously delimited by other experiences, even when a part of a pattern. It simply cannot be said to constitute that person's identity. One's sexual desires, whether referred to as "heterosexual", "homosexual", "bisexual", or "asexual", by *definition*, cannot and do not constitute an identity, no matter what the medical community wishes to claim. The (apparently) somewhat ephemeral impulses (though deeply felt as unchangeable at times) of the "transgender" person certainly cannot claim it. In point of fact, it should be noted that such a claim is actually beyond the purview and the expertise of medical science, especially in the absence of any medical or biological evidence to support it. Only philosophy (one grounded in contact with the natural world and the created order) is qualified to consider such questions. In any case, the experience of SSA can *never* under any circumstances, just like the others mentioned, be said to be the whole of the person. To claim that it is is to reduce the human person to a single aspect of his experience; it is to deny the full reality of who he is—a creature made in the image of God, endowed with intellect, will, and freedom, and ordered toward the true and the good.

In light of this, Wojtyla's specific proposal takes on special significance. He proposes a particular method, one that he argues allows us adequately to consider and to interpret the person in the context of his personal subjectivity. We can do that without leaving the ontological framework just referenced, well established as a foundation of the Church's understanding of the person. He refers to this method as "*pausing at the irreducible*".[42] His argument is that, in front of the concretely existing person, the actual "subject" of existence, we are face-to-face with a reality that, again, cannot be defined as merely a member of the species "human". Certainly each person is that, and his dignity and his value are a reflection of his very humanity. But in Wojtyla's account, each person is at the same time unique and unrepeatable—a *someone*, not a *something*.

---

[42] Ibid.

Pausing before the irreducibility of the person in this way allows us to consider him in his entirety. We can recall that he is an instantiation of an objective reality, what the philosophers call "man per se", and holds a particular place in the created order. As such, we can assume that he possesses features known to be common to all persons: intellect, will, and freedom; passions, appetites, and instincts. But it also frees us to regard the individual person as a concrete self, a self-experiencing subject; we are able to introduce the aspect of *consciousness* into the account. We are not severing the person from his objective nature; we are pausing before his particularity and attempting to go more deeply into it through an analysis of a real, concretely existing, particular person as a subject who not only exists, but also experiences his own dynamism, his acts and inner happenings, and with them his own subjectivity—that is, his own personhood.[43] When we turn toward the person in his entirety, the *integral* experience of who he is comes within the orbit of consciousness and reveals both aspects of his being, as well as the demands they place on him to move toward wholeness.

Wojtyla states that this dynamism is captured in two distinct and observable dimensions of human experience that "cut across the phenomenological field of experience, but ... join and unite together in the metaphysical field".[44] These are the fundamental experiential phenomena that provide the basis for his analysis of human action: the experience of "*I* act", that is, of "man-acts", and that of "something-happens-in-man". Both of these phenomena are given in experience; their common root is the being of the person who experiences them. Taken together, they constitute the totality of the concrete manifestation of the dynamism proper to man; they are themselves a universally occurring phenomenon.[45]

It is only in the experience of "man-acts", when the person experiences himself as the efficient cause of his actions, that an authentically human act, an *actus personae*, can be said to take place.[46] In this moment, the person experiences his own intentionality; he recognizes

---

[43] Ibid.

[44] Ibid.

[45] Karol Wojtyla, *The Acting Person* (Boston: D. Reidel Publishing, 1979), p. 65.

[46] Perhaps not surprisingly, Wojtyla argues that *actus personae* is more precise and meaningful than the traditional *actus humanae*. He does use this latter term when speaking more globally, but we find more frequent references in his papal writings to *actus personae*.

himself as "the actor". This experience "discriminates man's acting from everything that merely happens in him".[47] It is here that *lived* experience enters the picture and consciousness reveals to him the reality of his own subjectivity. It will reveal what Wojtyla proposes constitutes the threefold structure of human subjectivity: self-possession, self-governance, and self-determination, ordered ultimately toward self-gift. And, importantly, since these aspects of experience are certainly a shared human reality, we can arrive at the conclusion that the subjectivity of the person is itself an actual, objective reality, one that can be studied and understood.

In Wojtyla's account, subjectivity is a term that both proclaims the irreducibility of the person and is a synonym for it. Subjectivity refers to the person in both his metaphysical and immutable essence *and* his personal experience of himself in relation to the world he encounters. It is the element of consciousness that provides the link between these two dimensions of selfhood. Conscious reflection will certainly lead to a recognition of the faculties of the intellect and free will that we know are naturally ordered toward the true and the good. But Wojtyla wishes to emphasize that these realities are *not* only known through the metaphysical deduction of a philosopher; in the first place, they are known through human experience.[48] The human person exists *permanently* within a moral context; there is never a time when his actions take place outside of it. The sense of right and wrong is written on the human heart because it is a form of reality, an esse, given in experience.[49]

In the pastoral context of interest to us here, we are inviting the person into a conscious reflection on the totality of his experience, one that will reveal the distinction between things that merely "happen" and those decisions and choices that reflect an authentically personal act. We are inviting him to consider discrete experiences (such as SSA) in light of the wholeness of his being and to reconcile those elements with the integral experience he has of himself.

It will help to spell out the implications of this analysis for our topic and offer an example.[50] First, the sexual impulse at its origin is

---

[47] Wojtyla, *Acting Person*, p. 66.
[48] Wojtyla, "The Problem of Experience in Ethics", in *Person and Community*, pp. 107–27.
[49] Ibid., pp. 116–17.
[50] I am indebted to Professor Janet E. Smith for her insights in this section.

something that "happens" in man. In *Love and Responsibility*,[51] Wojtyla speaks of the sexual urge that draws male and female to each other as ordered toward authentic human love that leads ultimately to children. However, we know that this impulse, when the person is not in full possession of himself and able to govern himself, can and often does lead him to use the other, to treat the other as an object.[52] But there is another possibility: those who are conscious of their own personhood in its totality realize that the sexual urge is something that "happens to them" and that it is up to them to exercise control over such "happenings", and further, that they are capable of doing so through the proper use of their intellect and will. They may reflect on the fact that the other to whom they are drawn is also a person; they may find themselves thinking they should not use a person, since persons are free and should never be used—and act according to the dictates of their conscience in that moment. Man is *not* at the mercy of his sexual urges; only nonrational animals have sex without thinking about it. And in exercising mastery over himself, the person both transcends himself and determines who he will become.

SSA lends itself to the same analysis and hope. The testimonies of many of those who experience SSA, who have been drawn into SSA sexual relationships, but who have discovered the truth of the person and of Christ, testify that they were greatly aided by John Paul II's insight that a starting place in a particular experience can in fact lead one to consider it in light of the more comprehensive (integral) experience they have of themselves. These testimonies seem to confirm the possibility that those who become conscious of the nature of the person as one who should never be used but always be loved, then come to the realization that their real desire is to learn how to conform their sexual urge to that truth. They long for the wholeness that being in relationship with another brings; they find they are willing to submit to the demands of love. And the demands of love call them to live in accord with reality— not in a subjectivist world of one's own making—but in one that reflects the truth about who they are. The person is conscious that he *is* a *person*, a creature who can know the truth and who is obliged to live in accord with the truth—the whole truth about the person.

---

[51] Karol Wojtyla, *Love and Responsibility* (San Francisco: Ignatius Press, 1993), pp. 45–54.

[52] See also Janet E. Smith, "Conscious Parenthood", in the English edition of *Nova et Vetera* 6, no. 4 (2008): 927–50.

Wojtyla is suggesting that the entry point into the person is not just any experience, but *lived* experience—that is, experience that falls within the orbit of consciousness. And when this is the case, the person discovers that he denies his very self when he pretends that any one experience constitutes the whole of who he is. If he pauses before the fullness of his personhood in a conscious act of reflection, he will encounter the whole of himself, a reality that includes the experience of those same ontic structures others have derived from metaphysical reflection. And he will have to acknowledge that this whole includes not only the sexual impulse, but the faculties of reason and will, the passions and appetites, the experience of freedom, the desire for happiness, love, and truth, a movement toward self-possession and self-governance that makes possible real acts of self-determination, and the recognition of a tendency toward self-transcendence and self-realization, finally only fully expressed in the act of making of himself—his whole self, body and soul—a gift to another.[53]

These are reflections of the totality of man—but not one of them can be said to capture the identity of what it means to be human. For who I am is, in fact, irreducible. I am not heterosexual. I am human—and in virtue of the body to which my soul is united, it was given to me to be either a woman or a man, with a distinct way of being in the world. It is my mission here on earth to become that person, to actualize the potency that is unique to me, to prepare myself to live out the vocation that is mine alone.[54]

Here we can return to the questions confronting the synod on the family with which we began and the very real concern about the "affective immaturity" that seems to characterize many in our culture. As I highlighted in my introduction, in the *Relatio Synodi*, the bishops refer to "cultural tendencies" that seem to set "no limits" on the exploration of any and every aspect of a person's affectivity, even the most complex. My argument here has been that Wojtyla's method provides us with a route to helping those we serve to integrate these complex aspects of

---

[53] See Wojtyla, *Acting Person*, esp. chaps. 3–4.

[54] The best place to find a treatment of the question of gender in Aquinas is in the *Summa Contra Gentiles*, Book 2, q. 80–81. For a fuller account of gender and complementarity, see my paper "The Nature of Woman in Relation to Man: Genesis 1 and 2 through the Lens of the Metaphysical Anthropology of Thomas Aquinas", *Logos: A Journal of Catholic Thought and Culture* 18, no. 1 (Winter 2015).

human experience, not by denying them, but by helping such persons to understand that they undoubtedly issue from a deeper impulse that can only be grasped correctly when seen in light of the whole of who they are. Persons who experience SSA deserve our pastoral care, our compassion. But above all, they deserve the truth, for pastoral care itself—though it may be expressed in ways that begin, not with "doctrine", but with an acknowledgment of experience—can *never* be divorced from the truth. Saint Thomas argued that to love was to will the good of another. We express authentic Christian love to the person experiencing SSA only when we will his or her authentic good.

Conclusion: The Real Meaning of Christian Friendship

As we said at the beginning, the pastoral care of those who experience SSA begins with the recognition that, at their origin, such desires issue from a very natural one, the normal human aspiration for love and for friendship. In our very essence, we are made for relationship; true and authentic friendship is therefore essential to our happiness. But in contemporary culture, this desire for intimacy has taken on what seems to be an almost inevitable erotic cast. Our culture's obsession with sex has obscured the true meaning of friendship; pervasive assumptions about the irresistibility of sexual desire have caused us to forget that there is a possibility of intimacy that does not involve sex or sexual attraction. For all intents and purposes, the kind of friendship traditionally referred to as "platonic" has been left behind in our culture; to say that two people are "just friends" is to relegate their relationship to an ambiguous state of suspension while they wait for the "right" person—that is, someone to whom they are sexually attracted—to come along. We have forgotten that love need not be sexual to be complete, and that friendship itself has its own inherent meaning and value. The Christian tradition has consistently maintained that happiness is not possible without friendship. For creatures meant to love and be loved, friendship provides opportunities to live out our destiny.

But it has also been firmly established that what is necessary for happiness and for friendship is virtue. Both Aristotle and Saint Thomas Aquinas, who echoes and builds on Aristotle's analysis, argue that true friendships are impossible without virtue; they are the result of virtue because they are based on a reciprocal recognition of the goodness in oneself and another, an objective goodness worthy of love. In Aristotle's classic account of the taxonomy of friendship, he considers the three reasons why one might wish to be friends with someone: because someone is good, useful, or pleasant.[55] Authentic friendships cannot be based on the utility a person has for another, or even on the pleasure one finds in his company because of his pleasant demeanor.[56] The only basis for real friendship is the virtue one encounters in another person and the realization that his virtuous acts call one to a life of virtue as well. There seems to be no lack of friendships based on utility in our culture. But there most certainly is a true dearth of friendships grounded in virtue.

For Aquinas, true friendship is based on unselfish love for another person, the "constant, effective desire to do good to another."[57] But ultimately, Aquinas puts human friendship into the context of friendship with God, and when God becomes the object of one's friendship we call it *charity*. All friendships, including our love of ourselves, issue from this singular, primary relationship. We are able to love because we have first been loved and have developed the habit of charity made possible by our relationship with its source. This is what makes it possible to give our neighbors the same supernatural love.[58]

Thus, we see that true and chaste friendship is not a lower-order good than marriage; nor is it an ambiguous state where one waits for a potential spouse. Rather, it is the thing toward which all relationships are ordered. The good proper to Christian friends, that which unites them as friends and that toward which their friendship by its nature inclines, cannot be just sexual intimacy or even the family, but God himself.[59]

[55] Aristotle, *Nicomachean Ethics*, Books VIII–IX. As is well known, Aristotle considers the three reasons why one might like someone: because he is good, because he is useful, or because he is pleasant.

[56] Here we see the long history that grounds Wojtyla's notion of the personalistic norm: that one can never consider another person as a means but only regard him as an end in himself.

[57] Walter Farrell, O.P., *A Companion to the Summa*, vol. 3 (New York: Sheed and Ward, 1940), p. 61.

[58] Ibid., p. 79.

[59] Michael Hannon, "Against Obsessive Sexuality", *First Things*, August 13, 2014. I am indebted to Mr. Hannon for his insights on friendship found in this essay. He points us all toward a mostly forgotten treasure of the Christian tradition, St. Aelred of Rievaulx's *Spiritual Friendship*.

In the mostly overlooked twelfth-century classic *Spiritual Friendship* by Saint Aelred of Rievaulx, we find a profound account of friendship's divinely ordered meaning. Here Saint Aelred's vision of the importance of authentic friendship is expressed in clear and unambiguous language: "In human life nothing holier can be desired, nothing more useful sought after, nothing is harder to find, nothing sweeter to experience, nothing more fruitful to possess than friendship."[60] Saint Aelred's teaching begins with what Jesus tells us about it: that there is no greater love than to lay down one's life for one's friends (Jn 15:13), pointing out that friendship is grounded in a love that both relies on and leads to the moral life. For immoral actions are really a kind of hatred; they cannot constitute friendship—or sustain it.[61]

Neither Aristotle nor Aquinas nor Rievaulx would consider an erotic interest in another person a good foundation for a friendship of virtue or a spiritual friendship directed toward holiness. Erotic attraction is a feeling appropriate to male/female relationships, and properly confined to marriage. Those drawn to others with the hope of finding a virtuous friend or a friend with whom they might realize virtue in themselves would want to avoid relationships that have the possibility of temptation to sin written right into it. Though they may claim that their experience suggests to them that chaste, erotically charged friendships have been good for them, or could be good for them, they would find little support in the wisdom of the ages about the nature of the person. After all, we all pray for the grace to avoid the near occasion of sin; it is one of the conditions of true repentance and reconciliation.

Thus our task is clearly to help those we serve to grasp their potential for true intimacy. To neglect to invite individuals into the possibility of authentic friendship, no matter what their difficulty or addiction, is to lower their dignity before God and, in the end, to define them according to their temptations and their sin. There are any number of disordered appetites—emotional, sensual, even intellectual—that can interfere with our movement toward authentic happiness. And everyone is called to struggle with particular temptations and overcome them where possible. But no one should identify such difficulties with who he is or let that

[60] St. Aelred of Rievaulx, *Spiritual Friendship* (Washington: Cistercian Publications, 1974), Book 2:8, p. 71.

[61] Ibid., Introduction, p. 24.

struggle define or consume his life—or allow those difficulties to be the basis of the friendships formed. Freedom and happiness would remain elusive, true friendship beyond one's grasp. This would be the real sin—for freedom, happiness, and the joy of friendship are God's gifts to all of his children.

No matter what one thinks about the questions we face in this volume, one cannot help but be moved by the search for healing so evident in the writings of those for whom this is not a theoretical problem. Their search is documented and readily accessible in electronic media, the blogosphere, and other publications. Yes, there are controversies. Those that claim that their identity is to be both "gay" and Catholic are perhaps the most touching, since they have already decided that they are incapable of the fuller appropriation of their nature called for by God; their journey toward wholeness is thus cut short. But there are many who have found their way to a deeper contact with who they are and have found happiness and peace. We have seen that this is no accident; it is a demonstration of Saint John Paul II's claim that all personal experiences must be integrated into the whole that, in truth, constitutes the human person.

Finding the Water in the Desert:
The Conversational Use of
Natural Law in the Context
of Same-Sex Attraction

J. Budziszewski, Ph.D.

A New Public Philosophy

The ability to speak clearly, honestly, and intelligently about sexuality is rare in our culture. Some people say we need "a new public philosophy". What would that mean? In its finest sense, "philosophy" is love of wisdom, so a "public" philosophy would be a way to speak in that love to the people. It would have to be wise or it wouldn't be philosophy; it would have to be plain or it wouldn't be public—and it would have to be transparent in its love. In what sense would it be "new"? The foundational truths of man's nature do not change, but they do meet new challenges, and we always need new ways to explain them.

Some people try to speak wisely in the public square by quoting from the Bible. I am a Catholic; I believe that the Holy Scriptures are authentic divine revelation. But I have noticed something strange about this approach. Though it claims to be "biblical", the Bible is actually against this approach. Although the Scriptures recommend themselves supremely, nowhere do they recommend beginning conversations with the unconvinced by hurling passages of Scripture at them. The scriptural model of conversation is to begin with such truth as people know and believe already. When Saint Paul spoke with his fellow Jews, who believed in the Scriptures, then, yes, he began with them. But in every case in which he spoke with gentiles, he set Scripture aside. For example, on the famous occasion when he spoke in

Athens, he quoted to his pagan listeners what some of their own poets had said about God.[1]

A theologian would say that when Paul adopted this way of speaking to the pagans, he was appealing to "general" revelation. The Bible is "special" revelation—what God has made known to the community of faith. By contrast, general revelation is what he has made known to everyone—Jews, Christians, Muslims, Hindus, pagans—yes, even contemporary secularists. How has he made it known to everyone? By giving human nature an understandable pattern; by fashioning the human mind in such a way that it spontaneously recognizes certain first principles as true; and by situating us in creation in a way that allows this mind to draw further true conclusions. The purpose of this chapter is to explain how all of this works.

Philosophers call the moral part of general revelation the *natural law*. We may think of natural law as the most basic of all moral principles, principles that are not only right for all but at some dim level even known to all, principles that we can violate or deny but which we literally *can't not know*—together with their various corollaries and implications, both near and remote. Deep down, even the murderer knows the wrong of murder. Even the adulterer knows that he ought to be faithful to his spouse. Even the God mocker knows that God deserves honor, not mockery.

Such knowledge doesn't come merely from childhood socialization. The only reason we can be socialized at all is that the ability to recognize the truth of what our parents tell us is latent within us already and blooms when we reach the age of reason. I can be taught that two and two make four—but only because, once the fact is called to my attention, I can see for myself that they make four. I can be taught the Golden Rule—but only because when Mama commands, "Don't pull your sister's hair. How would you like it if she pulled your hair?" I can see for myself that I shouldn't treat my sister differently than I would want to be treated myself.

I am not saying that we already know the remote implications of these moral basics; we have to work them out. And I am not saying that we cannot lie to ourselves about these basics, pretending that we don't know what we really do; we certainly can. But we can *only* lie to

[1] See Acts 17:28.

ourselves about them. We cannot be genuinely ignorant. Someone who says he thinks adultery is permissible, for example, is not morally ignorant; he is merely in denial. That is a very different thing.

The Wrong and Right Way to Use Natural Law

Although I am a scholar of natural law, I can't help noticing that quoting the *academic theory* of natural law does not get us much further than quoting Scripture. Though it is true, its intellectual apparatus is abstract and academic. To most people it seems more like particle physics than like real life. It's hard to unpack, easy to challenge, and hard to defend in a few words. Allow me to offer several examples of what can happen when your conversation in the public square is too academic.

Perhaps you suggest that intercourse with persons of the same sex is "contrary to natural law". Someone will object, saying, "But I believe in a *different* natural law that upholds the right to choose." (This was the basis of then-senator Joseph Biden's notorious defense of abortion.)

Perhaps you avoid the theoretical expression "natural law" and just say, with Saint Paul, that intercourse with persons of the same sex is against nature.[2] The next thing you know, someone will suggest to you that "same-sex attraction is as natural for some people as opposite-sex attraction is for others."

Perhaps you avoid both the expressions "law" and "nature", simply pointing out, as natural law thinkers do, that the sexual powers have two inbuilt purposes—the procreation of children and the union of the procreative partners—and that intercourse with persons of the same sex frustrates both of these purposes. Now you're really in trouble. One fellow doesn't agree about the purposes—he says the purpose of sex is just pleasure. Another likes the idea of union, but protests, "How dare you say persons of the same sex can't be united?" A third one accuses you of hypocrisy, saying that if sex is about forming families, then infertile couples shouldn't be allowed to marry either.

Don't misunderstand me—there are good and convincing answers to each of these objections. The problem is that the objection takes five seconds, the reply takes a hundred and fifty, the attention of the

[2] See Rom 1:26–27.

audience lasts only twenty, and the sound bite lasts only ten. Whose point do you think is remembered? Whose point do you think is understood? And by the way, whose point do you think gets into the evening news?

The mistake in this approach to public philosophy is that it confuses conversing with people about natural law with appealing to the academic theory of natural law, with its terminology and intellectual apparatus.

All people experience the things that gravitational theorists talk about—things like force, weight, and mass—but few understand the theory of gravity. Similarly, all people experience the things that natural law philosophers speak about—things like deep conscience, the teleology of the body, and the complementarity of the sexes—but few understand natural law philosophy. Fortunately, we don't have to teach people gravitational theory to caution them against standing underneath a falling piano, and we don't have to teach them natural law philosophy to explain the problem with same-sex attraction. In both cases, we can appeal to common sense.

I don't say this is easy. Although the plain person has common moral sense, he holds it in a confused and disordered state. He knows many more things than he is aware of knowing. His latent understanding of things is like a very large connect-the-dots picture in which not all of the dots are connected, and some of them are connected wrong. He may even be afraid of connecting the dots correctly, because there are certain true conclusions that he would rather not reach. The upshot is that his common sense needs to be elevated, purified, elaborated, and purged of denials and inconsistencies. A wise conversationalist reminds people of what they know that they know, for example, the sweetness of bringing children into the world. He elicits things they don't realize they know, for example, that a true union between spouses requires the difference of man and woman, because otherwise people are adoring mirrored images of themselves. And he looks for opportunities to blow away smokescreens and disperse self-deceptions.

The sine qua non of such conversation is to know the design of the heart. This introduces a paradox. We must speak to our friends in the language of common sense rather than the language of natural law philosophy; yet, in order to appeal to their common sense effectively, we ourselves must know something of natural law philosophy.

Yet, I suggest that this is what it means to speak wisely to the people; this is what a proper public philosophy is all about.

What, Deep Down, Does the Unconvinced Person Know?

The reality of general moral revelation, of this confused common moral sense, of this natural knowledge of moral basics, raises two questions. First, what, deep down, does the unconvinced person know? We can't make contact with the latent, disorganized, and suppressed knowledge in the unconvinced person's mind unless we understand what is down there. Second, how can we connect with that deep-down knowledge?

As to the first question, the Bible itself mentions a number of extrabiblical ways in which God has made his basic moral requirements known. Moved by Saint Paul's remark in the city of Lystra that God has not left himself without witness even among the pagan nations,[3] I like to call these ways "witnesses".

The Witness of Deep Conscience

The first such witness is the witness of deep conscience.[4] What I mean by "deep" conscience is the natural tendency of the mind to be aware of the foundational moral truths, even apart from how we have been taught. Deep conscience is an aspect of how the mind is made. It doesn't make moral teaching unnecessary; rather, it is the thing that makes moral teaching possible. It is the soil in which the seeds of good teaching are planted.

Saint Paul speaks of deep conscience in his Letter to the Romans, where he says that even the pagans, who have never heard of the biblical commandments, know God's basic moral requirements because they are "written on their hearts, while their conscience also bears witness".[5]

The fact that this knowledge is written on our hearts doesn't mean that we can't pretend to ourselves that we don't know what we really do know. We can. The problem is that each such act of self-deception leads to another. Is this surprising? It shouldn't be. Didn't we all discover in childhood that in order to cover up one lie we had to tell another? "I hear a rattling noise," says Mom. "Are you in the kitchen raiding the

---

[3] See Acts 14:15–17.

[4] The technical term is "synderesis", not to be confused with *conscientiae*, or surface conscience, the actualization of synderesis in day-to-day judgments.

[5] Rom 2:15.

cookie jar just before dinner?" "No," I say, "that was the dog rattling his supper dish." "But the dog is in here with me." "Then it must have been the cat." "We don't have a cat." "Then it must have been the neighbor's cat." And so it goes.

It is the same when we lie to ourselves. Eventually our self-deceptions metastasize; they become so manifold and complex that we can hardly keep track of them all. They take on a life of their own.[6]

The natural tendency of suppressed moral knowledge is to rise back into present awareness, and a fearsome expenditure of energy is necessary to try not to think the thoughts we are trying to avoid. This is universal. Count on it. I don't mean that everyone who is at odds with the moral basics has guilty feelings; feelings come and go. But even when the feelings of guilt are absent, the knowledge is still present at some level. The weight of the burden of this knowledge is so great that even if the soul refuses the relief of repentance and the mercy of God, it seeks futile, substitute reliefs that may even drive it further into harm's way.

Just as people do not allow probing fingers to come near their wounds, so they do not want hard words to come near their wounded consciences. Yet, there are times when they are so desperate that they may listen to gentle words.

The *meaningfulness* of conscience depends on the perception of meaning and design in creation in general—to which we now turn.

The Witness of the Designedness of Things

The second witness is the designedness of things. The heavens proclaim the glory of God,[7] and so do our own minds and bodies. Both the outer world and the inner world strike us as things of pattern and inbuilt meaning. Even apart from specific knowledge of this meaning, the sheer recognition that there is a meaning is overwhelming. No wonder the pagans had an altar "[t]o an unknown god".[8]

What does this have to do with morality? First, it spares us from a confusion concerning the previous witness: deep conscience. If we didn't

---

[6] St. Paul remarks in Romans 118–27 that "suppressing" the knowledge of God (v. 18) "darkens" (v. 21) even our reasoning about the created sexual order (vv. 24–27).

[7] See Ps 19:1.

[8] Acts 17:23.

recognize the Creator, we might have thought—as the neo-Darwinian paleontologist George Gaylord Simpson wrote—that "man is the result of a meaningless and purposeless process that did not have us in mind."[9] In that case, *so what* if we have deep conscience? It may seem to speak with the authority of God, but those are just selfish genes talking. But since we do recognize the Creator, we know better. Saint Paul remarks in Romans I that even the pagans are aware of the true God; they are not ignorant of him, but suppress their knowledge of him.[10]

A corollary of the designedness of things is that every desire in us is *for* something. Thirst is directed toward drink and is satisfied by drink; hunger is directed toward nourishment and is satisfied by nourishment. Yet, strangely, we have one longing that can be satisfied by nothing in the created order. C. S. Lewis called it "that unnameable something, desire for which pierces us like a rapier at the smell of a bonfire, the sound of wild ducks flying overhead, the title of The Well at the World's End, the opening lines of Kubla Khan, the morning cobwebs in late summer, or the noise of falling wave".[11] If it is really true that "nature makes nothing in vain",[12] then this strange longing too must be *for* something. Its purpose is to direct us *beyond* the created order to the Creator. Nature points beyond herself; she has a face, and it looks up.

If we refuse to look where she is pointing, then we may lavish on her all the loving looks that she wants us to bestow somewhere else. We give to created things the worship that is due to the Creator. Created things like what? Like sexuality. One would think that the idolatry of sex would always be about sexual love. Amazingly, no. It is possible to make an idol not only of sexual relationship, but even of the absence of relationship. The writer David Loovis describes anonymous intercourse as "an irresistible experience of beauty in the person of the stranger ... one of the most mysterious and awe-inspiring in the entire homosexual galaxy of experience."[13] He is thinking primarily of male homosexual intercourse, and of course this particular idolatry is

---

[9] George Gaylord Simpson, *The Meaning of Evolution*, rev. ed. (New Haven: Yale University Press, 1967), pp. 344–45.

[10] See Rom 1:18–21.

[11] C. S. Lewis, preface to *The Pilgrim's Regress*, 3rd ed. (New York: Bantam, 1986), p. xii.

[12] Aristotle, *De Caelo*, bk. 1, chap. 4; *Politics*, bk. 1, chap. 2.

[13] David Loovis, *Straight Answers about Homosexuality for Straight Readers* (Englewood Cliffs, N.J.: Prentice-Hall, 1977), pp. 130–31.

found among male heterosexuals, too. It is a distorted exaggeration of the specific character of male sexuality, to which I will return.

Idolatry is so tiring. Even the idolater must sometimes rest from the toil of denial. His friends must be patient. They must not badger him. They must stand ready for the moments when he relaxes his mental censors, ready to listen, perchance even to speak.

I mentioned the specific character of male sexuality. This turns our attention from designedness in general to the *details* of our design—so let us go on to that.

The Witness of the Details of the Design

The entire fabric of man's experience, extending through all its dimensions, physical, emotional, intellectual, and spiritual, speaks to us of inbuilt purposes and meanings.

Interestingly, at the only place in the Bible where those so-hard-to-hear expressions "natural" and "unnatural" are used, they're used in reference to one of the figures in this fabric. When Paul calls intercourse with persons of the same sex "contrary to nature" (*para phusein*),[14] he's not banking on the fact that his readers have studied natural law; he's banking on the fact that our very bodies sing of the complementarity of the male and the female, and our spirits sing along in polyphony.

For God could have made only one sex. He might have arranged that we reproduce asexually, for instance, by budding. But he didn't. Instead he made two different kinds of us, each of which, by itself, is unbalanced and incomplete.

The male is created with a potentiality for biological or spiritual fatherhood, the woman with a potentiality for biological or spiritual motherhood. Certain soft chords in her nature resonate more powerfully in his. Certain pale hues in his nature glow more luminously in hers.

Paradoxically, we are not *less* because of this incompleteness. We are *more*. There is more melody, more color, more laughter in the world because there are two kinds of us. A husband and wife uniting in love in the hope of having children is a more splendid thing than meiosis or parthogenesis, for it makes possible a kind of love that would otherwise not exist: a love which in turn can also give rise to new life.

[14] See Rom 1:26.

We do not all need to marry and enjoy sexual love, but we do all need to recognize that the pattern of sexual love is shaped by the polarity of the sexes and is designed for the relationship of matrimony. A man and a woman are necessary not only to conceive the child but to bring the child to birth, because the woman incubates him and the man protects them both. A man and a woman are necessary not only to bring the child to birth but to raise him, because mothers and fathers are not the same: the child needs a mom and a dad. The procreative vocation of the spouses continues even after they have passed the age of childbearing and their children are grown, for then they are needed as grandparents.

Same-sex intercourse is not only intrinsically nonprocreative, incapable of forming new life, but also intrinsically nonunitive, because two men, or two women, cannot balance each other in the utterly distinctive way that a woman and a man do. Friendship between two persons of the same sex is a gift, but the *sexualization* of such friendship works *against* balance. One of the forms such imbalance takes place in some men is explosive promiscuity. One of the forms it takes in some women is implosive emotional demands. This difference is due to the specific difference between male and female sexuality. The sexuality of a woman is characteristically directed inward, toward being wooed, and later toward nurturing the relationships around the hearth. But that of a man is characteristically directed outward, toward wooing a woman, and later toward protecting the hearth against dangers. The joining of a man's and a woman's sexuality can bring them into equilibrium; the joining of the sexuality of two men or two women pushes them out of equilibrium.

We see then that to sing against the harmonies of our creational design is to produce discord in ourselves. Even if our aim is to *reduce* this discord by singing in the key of our desires, we cannot succeed, because we are still out of key with our design—for the reality of being male and female is something that we *are*, not just something that we want. A man who is sexually attracted to other men *is a man* who suffers desires that cut across the grain of what he truly is. A woman who is sexually attracted to other women *is a woman* whose longings are out of alignment with what she truly is. These facts subsist at a level deeper than ideology, deeper than choice, deeper than desire. They can be overwritten, but they can never be erased.

By speaking of what brings about discord, I have hinted at the final witness. Let us turn to it now.

The Witness of Natural Consequences

The fourth witness—in some ways the easiest to talk about, but in other ways the most difficult—is the witness of natural consequences. Whatever we do has results, and some of these connections result from the way we are made. Because of our physical nature, if we cut ourselves, then we bleed. Because of our social nature, if we betray our friends, then we lose them, and if we lose our friends, we are lonely. Because of our intellectual nature, if we try to keep ourselves from thinking straight about some things, we will have difficulty thinking straight about a lot of other things, too. As Saint Paul puts it, we reap what we sow.[15]

It isn't just physical consequences like bodily disease that make the hedonism of what is called the gay lifestyle like the merriment of a *danse macabre*. A hundred notes of sorrow tell the tale. For example, desperate to find a way to make empty sex seem meaningful, some young male homosexuals are more *consequential* by deliberately seeking out men with deadly infections as partners; this is called "bug chasing".[16]

Unless one is a physician or counselor whose business it is to heal the sundry hurts of flesh or spirit, it is not usually helpful to say too much about such dreadful things, because the shock of hearing of them is so great that in order to defend themselves against it, listeners tend to "shoot the messenger". Suffice it to say that the literature of the movements of disordered sexuality talks about them more frankly than I can here. We don't have to tell people about the witness of natural consequences; they know it only too well. The very expression "safe sex" is an inadvertent confession of dangers from which one needs protection.

How Can We Make Contact with This Deep-Down Knowledge?

The discussion of the four witnesses has shown how, in a certain sense, our unconvinced friends are more on our side than they think, for they

---

[15] See Gal 6:7; cf. Prov 1:31; Jer 17:10; Hos 10:12.

[16] See Gregory A. Freeman, "Bug Chasers: The Men Who Long to Be HIV+", *Rolling Stone*, February 6, 2003, p. 915.

know a great deal more than they are aware of knowing, or perhaps more than they *want* to be aware of knowing. They can suppress deep conscience, but cannot erase it. They can deny the designedness of things, but they cannot stop perceiving it. They can try to sing along with their desires, but they cannot rewrite the melody of their design. And even if they ignore these first three witnesses, the natural consequences of their mode of life catches up with them.

For these reasons, effective conversation is not so much about pumping water into the well as about drawing up the water that is already there.

Instead of arguing about the Bible, we must follow its example; we must begin with what people dimly know already. Instead of speaking in the language of the academic theory of natural law, we must allow its insights to guide our use of the language of common sense. Instead of being defensive, we must be confident that the deepest, most general principles of the natural law can never be blotted out from the human heart. Instead of being apologetic, we must be loving, which is not the same thing. We do not desire to hurt people; we desire to end their hurt.

Possible Conversations

When possible, one-to-one conversations are best. Honesty is difficult to achieve in group conversations or in conversations before an audience, because people are eager to score debating points and are afraid to lose face. My counterpart in a debate about same-sex attraction spoke about the hatred that he said had killed Matthew Shepard.[17] I replied, "Surely you know I don't hate you. I love you. I want to spend eternity with you in heaven." On camera, he gave no ground. But after the debate was over, he smiled and thanked me, saying that he could tell I did love him. He added that many people don't, which I know is quite true.

Perhaps the hardest part of conversation is giving a gentle and truthful answer to challenges that emerge from pain and anger. There is no guarantee of success, because when people are deep in denial, they may

---

[17]Matthew Shepard was a homosexual man who was beaten and left to die in Laramie, Wyoming, in 1998, after being picked up by men who purported to be interested in sex.

even regard gentleness as a provocation. But it can be done, for the four witnesses are in the background, whispering encouragement.

A male friend who experiences same-sex attraction might say, "You reject me because I'm different from you." But he is not different; he is a man, like me, who suffers temptations, like me, even if somewhat different temptations than mine. I must affirm his masculinity. If I think he is able to hear me, I might mildly ask whether it could be that he is the one who rejects the challenge of the Other—the complementary sex.

He might say, "You are demeaning my dignity." I must insist on his dignity. But I must also make clear that we are working from two different understandings of what upholding his dignity requires. Though I want to uplift it, I think he is harming it.

He might say, "You don't respect my love for my partner." I must honor all love and friendship. The issue is not whether two people of the same sex can be loving friends; the issue is whether sexual intercourse improves every kind of love. Does it improve the love of a teacher and student, a father and daughter, a mother and son? Of course not; rather, it introduces an alien and distorting element into those relationships. In the same way, it introduces an alien and distorting element into the love of two men or two women.

He may say that "gay is just as natural for some people as straight is for others." But the meaning of natural inclination is not what I *happen* to desire; it is what I am *made* to desire. Each sex is *made* for its polar counterpart.

He may say, "I was born this way." Certain behavioral predispositions really are latent from birth. For example, it is fairly well established that some people suffer the misfortune of a genetic predisposition to the abuse of alcohol. But this wouldn't make drunkenness *naturally good* for them. It merely means they will have to work harder than other people to resist the temptation.

In each of the previous examples, the conversational partner has been a person who experiences same-sex attraction. But most of our unconvinced friends will be heterosexual, and most of the difficulties of conversing with them arise not from sheer logical puzzles, or from lack of familiarity with academic natural law theory, but from the fact that so many are either leading sexually disordered lives themselves or confusedly trying to defend friends and relatives who lead them. They may be reluctant to concede that any form of sexuality could be problematic, just because then they would be forced to face up to what is wrong with the other things they think they must shield.

One way the discomfort of heterosexuals about their own behavior manifests itself is fear of not being "compassionate". They may exercise so little restraint in their own sexual lives that they consider it cruel to expect restraint from anyone else. Perhaps it is sufficient to point out that compassion is good, but there is a difference between true compassion, which is a permanent commitment to the true good of others, and false compassion, which is a temptation to allow them whatever they desire.

Another way heterosexual discomfort manifests itself is a desire not to "discriminate". For example, people may say that changing the laws of marriage "doesn't hurt anyone"—so why not change them? I answer this question with a question. Why are there marriage laws in the first place? After all, the law doesn't take an interest in my love for my fishing buddy. Marriage is about turning the wheel of the generations. It is the only institution that can give a child a fighting chance of being raised by a mom and a dad. To proclaim that two men or two women can be legally "married" is to proclaim that henceforth family law should be based not on the well-being of children, but on the sexual convenience of grown-ups. "It doesn't hurt anyone"—really?

Finally, the uneasiness of heterosexuals about their own conduct frequently manifests itself as a desire not to be "hypocritical". After all, they say, we don't hear many complaints about heterosexual sins. There is only one possible reply: We ought to!

We would not be so confused about homosexuality if we had not already allowed ourselves to become so confused about heterosexuality. God the Giver has made the polarity of the sexes the vaulted arch into three great goods: the generation of new life, the union of the procreative partners, and, for those of faith, the sacramental participation in the same love that binds Christ with the Church. Once these goods have been sullied by adultery, divorce, masturbation, hooking up, cohabitation, abortion, pornography, and the contraceptive mentality, the celebration of same-sex attraction comes almost as a thing expected.

Perhaps my readers will consider the analogy I am about to offer farfetched. But I am convinced that just as President Abraham Lincoln urged the North and South to join in binding the wounds they had inflicted on their nation, so the Church should be urging those who do and do not suffer from same-sex attractions to join in binding the wounds we have all inflicted on chastity.

We dare not hold purity in contempt; we dare not dispense with marriage; and we dare not tamper with its creational design. Too much good is at stake to treat these things lightly, too much power and danger to waste it on selfish games. From the best gifts come the worst miseries, if we are too foolish to follow directions—the directions built into our nature.

Homosexual Inclination as an "Objective Disorder": Reflections of Theological Anthropology

Monsignor Livio Melina, Ph.D., S.T.L.

The issues relating to the difference between the sexes are not trivial ones, but indicate epochal shifts in culture and the spiritual history of mankind.

One of the most significant changes made by the Corrigenda in the official Latin edition of the *Catechism of the Catholic Church*[1] with respect to the 1992 vernacular version[2] concerns the *Catechism*'s treatment of homosexuality. The first commentaries, which focused on other moral issues such as the death penalty, self-defense, and organ transplants, somewhat neglected this modification, which is nonetheless of great importance. Paragraph 2358 of the original text spoke of "innate homosexual tendencies" in a considerable number of men and women, who, it said, had not "chosen" this condition. The revised text, by contrast, limits itself to calling these tendencies "deep-seated", without saying that they are innate or that they are not chosen. It does, on the other hand, state that "this inclination . . . is objectively disordered". The *Catechism* thereby better harmonizes its formulations with the "Letter to the Bishops of the Catholic Church on the Pastoral Care of Homosexual Persons" (cf. no. 3), published by the Congregation for the Doctrine of the Faith on October 1, 1986.

This article first appeared in *Communio* 25 (Spring 1998). © 1998 by *Communio: International Catholic Review*. It was translated by Adrian Walker.

[1] *Catechism of the Catholic Church* (Vatican City: Libreria Editrice Vaticana; Washington, D.C.: United States Catholic Conference, 2000).

[2] *Catechism of the Catholic Church* (Vatican City: Libreria Editrice Vaticana; Liguori, Mo.: Liguori Publications, 1992).

What is the significance of this statement? Without entering into the moral issues,[3] I would like to offer a few reflections on the level of theological anthropology in order better to understand precisely what is meant by calling homosexual inclinations an "objective disorder".

1. Homosexual Inclination as "Objectively Disordered"

An adequate description of the Catholic Church's teaching on homosexuality must say more than that homosexual acts are intrinsically disordered, inasmuch as they lack their essential and indispensable finality,[4] and that we must always treat homosexual persons with respect, compassion, and tact and must avoid any unfair discrimination.[5] Rather, it is also necessary to say that the inclination to homosexuality, "though not in itself a sin", is "objectively disordered" in itself.[6] If we fail to make this last point, compassion and respect can become ambiguous. An acceptance that makes no judgment about homosexual orientation, and that supposes it to be "natural", or at least "unchangeable", if not actually "part of personal identity", can slide into toleration of the acts that follow from the orientation. At the same time, there would be no good reason for calling homosexuals to chastity: to do so would be tantamount to imposing an extrinsic limit on an orientation that is deemed to be natural, innate, and constitutive of personal identity and that has no legitimate outlets. It thus seems that whoever denies that homosexual inclination is an objective disorder faces the following dilemma: toleration and approval of homosexual activity or despair.[7]

However, the ordinary Magisterium's affirmation that homosexual inclination is objectively disordered immediately provokes an objection,

---

[3] On this point, I take the liberty of referring to my article "Criteri morali per la valutazione dell'omosessualità", in *Antropologia cristiana e omosessualità*, Quaderni de *L'Osservatore Romano* 38 (Vatican City, 1997): 103–10; and to G. Grisez's response entitled "May a Parent Condone a Son's Homosexual Activity?", in *The Way of the Lord Jesus*, vol. 3, *Difficult Moral Questions* (Quincy, Ill.: Franciscan Press, 1997), pp. 103–12.

[4] See Congregation for the Doctrine of the Faith, Declaration *Persona humana*, December 29, 1975, no. 8.

[5] See *Catechism of the Catholic Church*, no. 2358.

[6] See Congregation for the Doctrine of the Faith, "Letter to the Bishops", no. 3.

[7] Methods for sound therapy and pastoral initiative have been sketched, for example, by the following: G. van den Aardweg, *Homosexuality and Hope: A Psychologist Talks about Treatment and Changes* (Ann Arbor, Mich.: Servant, 1995), and J. F. Harvey, *The Homosexual Person: New Thinking in Pastoral Care* (San Francisco: Ignatius Press, 1987).

which appears to be decisive. How can we define something as morally wrong if it is not the result of a free choice? Catholic teaching has made use of the distinction between "homosexual condition" and "homosexual acts" with the document *Persona humana*. This distinction implicitly acknowledges that homosexual orientation, insofar as it is not the fruit of deliberate choices, is not per se a moral wrong for which persons are to be held responsible. According to Saint Thomas Aquinas and the entire tradition of Catholic moral theology, we can speak of moral good and evil only in relation to what falls within the sphere of free will (*voluntarium*).[8] Tendencies that are merely "suffered" (*passiones*) are morally relevant only insofar as they are subject to the control of reason and will.

Nevertheless, what precedes our freedom, the basic predisposition that conditions our free choices, is of great significance for morality. It can therefore be assigned a moral quality analogically, insofar as it favors a certain orientation. After all, man's freedom is a "merely human"—that is, nonabsolute—freedom: a real, but finite, situated, and conditioned freedom, which rests on, and develops from, motivations, contingencies, and bodily determinations.[9] Concern for these prior conditionings, judgment of them with reference to the behavior toward which they incline, and the attempt to correct them are all part of the inescapable task of a sound, objective, and realistic moral teaching.

The very language that has become entrenched and that we are obliged to use in speaking of homosexuality carries with it a second difficulty and a dangerous ambiguity, for it seems to imply that "sexuality" is an abstract and neutral term, to which two apparently symmetrical versions are added only later: "hetero-" and "homo-" sexuality. In this way, normal sexuality is redefined as a later specification and is implicitly placed on the same level as abnormal behavior. The ideological and manipulative character of this contrived system of language must not escape us. The apparent symmetry is in reality false: sexuality is constitutively relative to the gender difference and is thus in and of itself "normally" heterosexual.

[8] See *Summa Theologiae* I–II, q. 24: "de bono et malo in animae passionibus" (concerning the good and evil passions of the soul); in particular, see *Summa Theologiae* I–II, q. 24, a. 3, ad 1. On this point, see S. Manero, "Sobre las mútuas influencias de las pasiones y del voluntario libre", *Revista de Filosofía* 30 (1949): 401–32.

[9] This is what, in analyzing the structure of man's voluntary action, we can call its "archeology". See P. Ricoeur, *La sémantique de l'action. Première partie: Le discours de l'action* (Paris: Ed CNRS, 1977); A. Léonard, *Le fondement de la morale: Essai d'éthique philosophique* (Paris: Cerf, 1991), pp. 33–100.

Nevertheless, what is not normal for the common condition can appear to be "natural" to the individual because of the disordered disposition of his being. Saint Thomas points this out in relation to unnatural pleasures: "What is contrary to the nature of the species becomes natural to this individual per accidens."[10] In the case of homosexuality, as in other cases, the complaint "that's the way I am" expresses many things: the frustrating realization that one cannot change, a way of blaming nature and perhaps God for one's condition, even the unwillingness to reconsider one's attitude toward reality.

The psychoanalysts point out that sexuality is not only a "natural" faculty or capacity but also the subject's articulated response to the world around him. Sexuality, then, is inclusive of a "stance". In any case, our focus here is not on the psychological aspects of homosexuality, but rather on the anthropological meaning of homosexuality in terms of what the Church calls a "disordered tendency".

2. The Meaning of the Expression "Objective Disorder"

To speak of sexuality as a "stance" or a "disposition" is to speak of a plurality of elements and factors in the personality that are meant to make up a unified tendency upon which the subject constructs his own sexual identity and recognizes his place in relation with others and the surrounding world. The concept of "order" and, correlatively, of "disorder" seems to apply precisely to this kind of stance or disposition.

Augustine defines order as "an arrangement of equal and unequal that gives each its place":[11] an appropriate disposition of differentiated, indeed, complementary elements such that each finds its proper place within the harmony of the whole. Thomas Aquinas offers a definition that makes more of the dynamic aspect of order. According to this definition, the formal principle of order lies in orientation to an end: "Now, an inclination to an end, or to action, or to something of this sort follows upon form; because each thing, insofar as it is an act, acts and tends towards what befits it according to its form. And this pertains to weight

---

[10] *Summa Theologiae* I–II, q. 31, a. 7, cited in G. Zuanazzi, "La condizione omosessuale: Atteggiamenti strutturali e considerazioni conclusive", *Antropologia cristiana e omosessualità, Quaderni de L'Osservatore Romana* 28 (Vatican City, 1997): 64.

[11] St. Augustine, *De Civitate Dei* 19, 13, 1.

and order."[12] Thomas' relating of order to an end also allows him to integrate the dynamism of personal freedom into the striving for perfection that permeates the whole universe and animates its movements.

For Aquinas, then, order is an expression of wisdom: "*sapientis est ordinare*" (it belongs to the wise person to order). It is precisely in establishing ends that God's provident wisdom orders the world. And by recognizing the goals preestablished in God's plan, the wise person is enabled to order his actions and dispositions.

We can thus understand more precisely what is meant by the expression "objectively disordered inclinations". Such inclinations are tendencies wherein the elements of the personality are disposed in such a way that they do not orient the subject toward the attainment of the end that God's plan assigns to sexuality. The Council of Trent spoke in an analogous sense of the disorder of concupiscence.[13] As a result of sin, the sense powers are no longer subject to reason in accord with their original ordering, but resist and rebel against it, thus pushing men to actions contrary to the moral order. In itself concupiscence is not a sin in the strict sense, but it is called "sin" by the apostle Paul insofar as it derives from sin and inclines to it (see Rom 7:22–23).

From the moral point of view, Catholic doctrine defines homosexual acts as intrinsically disordered, inasmuch as they activate the sexual dynamism of persons without (1) that unitive meaning of total self-gift to the other, which can be realized only in the matrimonial union of man and woman, and (2) openness to the procreative meaning whereby human sexuality is further ordered to the good of the child. But the criteria for ethical evaluation are rooted in a theological anthropology of human sexuality. It is only in the light of this anthropology that we can see, by way of contrast, the disorder inherent in homosexual inclination.

3. The Order of Human Sexuality in the Wise Design of God

As is the case with every other fundamental dimension of man's existence, we can understand human sexuality theologically only to the

---

[12] *Summa Theologiae* I, q. 5, a. 5.
[13] See Conc. Tridentinum, Session 5, June 17, 1647, *Decretum de peccato originali* (DS 1515).

extent that we relate it to Christ.[14] God's wise plan is recapitulated in him as its final point. The universe, in fact, was created in him and through him: he is the firstborn of every creature (see Col 1:15–20). In him we too have been "predestined" according to the plan established by God the Father before the creation of the world, in order to be the praise of his glory (see Eph 1:3–14). The mystery of human sexuality, which is part of the divine plan, is therefore the mystery of our likeness to Christ, of our call in Christ to express the wealth of Trinitarian Love, whose created image we bear.

In the perspective of a Christocentric and dramatic anthropology, and following the cue of Genesis 1:27,[15] we see that human sexuality, marked by the duality of male and female "genders", is a constitutive part of the *imago Dei*, which the Creator impressed on man at the moment of creation.[16] The difference between the sexes is a reminder of the original love, of the divine source of man's being, which is a whole composed of body and spirit. At the same time, it invites each person to a vocation of self-giving and welcoming the other in love.

The difference between the sexes is the sign of the creaturely and finite condition of human nature: "No individual human being is ever capable of exhausting by himself the whole of man: the other mode of being man (in respect to his own) is always before him."[17] At the same time this difference is an invitation to encounter and to communion, and thus constitutes, in the proper sense of the word, a vocation. As John Paul II has said in his catechesis on love in the divine plan, "Sex expresses an ever new surpassing of the limit of man's solitude which lies within the makeup of his body and determines its original meaning."[18] The body, then, is the place where both a limit and a vocation are

---

[14]See P. M. Quay, *The Christian Meaning of Human Sexuality* (San Francisco: Ignatius Press, 1985), pp. 9ff.

[15]"God created man in his own image, in the image of God he created him; male and female he created them."

[16]See Hans Urs von Balthasar, *Theo-Drama: Theological Dramatic Theory*, vol. 2, *Dramatis Personae: Man in God* (San Francisco: Ignatius Press, 1990), pp. 365–82; cf. A. Scola, *Hans Urs von Balthasar: A Theological Style* (Grand Rapids: Wm. B. Eerdmans/Ressourcement, 1995), pp. 92–95.

[17]Scola, *Hans Urs von Balthasar*, p. 92.

[18]John Paul II, *Man and Woman He Created Them: A Theology of the Body*, trans. Michael Waldstein (Boston: Pauline Books, 2006), p. 167. Also see J.M. Granados Temes, "La ética esponsal de Juan Pablo II: Estudio de los fundamentos de la moral de la sexualidad en las Catequésis sobre teología del cuerpo" (unpublished dissertation, Pontifical John Paul II Institute for Studies on Marriage and Family, Rome, 1997).

revealed. The body, with its masculine and feminine specificity, is a real symbol of a call to transcend original solitude, in order to encounter the other, who is different from oneself, and to form with the other a unity in which the original likeness of God's love shines forth. The body has, as the pope said, a "spousal meaning";[19] it is made to express the person's gift of self to another person who is different from oneself.[20] Christ's eucharistic gift to his Church ("take this all of you and eat it, this is my body" [see Mt 26:26; Mk 14:22; Lk 22:19]) is the unsurpassable model of every gift of love, even in marriage, as well as the source of grace that makes this gift possible.

The difference between the sexes thus establishes a polarity between man and woman that orients them to a reciprocal relation, even though one can never absorb the other as such. This brings to light a new, fundamental characteristic of sexuality. The reciprocity of the sexes is not an integral complementarity, but always leaves open—and uncloseable—the wound of an asymmetry. This word is the witness and the trace of the ontological difference, which distinguishes contingent being from the Being in which it participates. The claim that we can overcome the difference can only be a tragic illusion.[21] We inexorably experience the pain of lack when we realize that we cannot lay our hands on the other and that the very structure of our being prevents us from overcoming our difference from him or her. Desire never rests in completely satisfied enjoyment.

Though there can be no pacifying and totally satisfying fusion with the other, this very impossibility sets in motion a new dynamism. It also gives sexuality a new openness, in that it orients the lovers to a completion lying beyond themselves. By its very nature love is oriented to produce a fruit that transcends it. In order to avoid self-absorption and self-consumption, love must open up to a further fruitfulness, whose most obvious dimension is procreation. The procreative meaning, then, is not added extrinsically or biologistically to the unitive dimension of sexuality. On the contrary, procreation is the completed form of union.[22] Children are the crown of conjugal love,[23] which is inconceivable apart

---

[19] John Paul II, *Theology of the Body*, p. 183.

[20] See ibid., pp. 185–86.

[21] See G. Zuanazzi, *Temi e simboli dell'eros* (Rome: Città Nuova, 1991), p. 76.

[22] See A. Scola, ed., *Quale vita? La bioetica in questione?* (Milan: Mondadori, 1998). For these observations on the connection between "sexual difference and procreation" I am greatly indebted to the essay by A. Scola in this volume.

[23] See Vatican Council II, Pastoral Constitution on the Church in the Modern World, *Gaudium et spes*, December 7, 1965, no. 48.

from ready openness to fruitfulness. Otherwise, conjugal love becomes self-absorbed and makes an illusory claim to self-fulfillment. The necessary transcendence of sexuality toward a mysterious third factor, and the presence of this third in sex, is represented by the child. So much so that von Balthasar regards conjugal love and its fruitfulness, two aspects that cannot be separated, as an image of the Trinity.[24]

The history of the "sexual revolution"[25] is a negative proof that the attempt to cancel the procreative dimension of sexuality leads ultimately to the abolition of the meaning of the sexual difference and to the loss of its symbolic significance. The search for joy (*godimento*) in the encounter with the other is replaced by the more immediate and superficial search for pleasure (*piacere*). The cultural trend which denies that procreation is coessential to union is of a piece with the elevation of homosexuality to equal status with heterosexuality. The desire for the infinite in the love between man and woman is kept open to something beyond the couple by the procreative dimension. The denial of procreation bends this desire back on itself, in a narcissism that seeks pleasure independently of joy in the other (*godimento*).

The elimination of openness to procreation uproots sexuality from its insertion in time and history through the succession of generations. Without the dimension of the past and the future, the sexual encounter is condemned to an aesthetic fixation on the timeless moment. This is even more necessarily true in the case of homosexuality, which A. Chapelle has rightly called a "pointilisme esthétique".[26] The only hope for a future in the homosexual encounter is the exhausting search for a beauty that is dreamed of but always pursued in vain.

The Italian philosopher Augusto del Noce has acutely observed that "today's nihilism is gay in two senses. First, it lacks restlessness (we might even define it as the suppression of the Augustinian *inquietum cor meum*). Second, its symbol is homosexuality (in fact, we could say that it always intends homosexual love, even when it retains the man–woman relation)."[27] A. Scola, commenting on this passage, notes that "gay nihilism,

---

[24]See Hans Urs von Balthasar, *Prayer* (San Francisco: Ignatius Press, 1986), p. 78.

[25]On this point I take the liberty of referring to some notes I developed in the following volume: J. Lafitte-L. Melina, *Amor conyugal y vocación a la santidad* (Santiago de Chile: Ed. Univ. Catolica de Chile, 1997), pp. 51–62.

[26]See A. Chapelle, *Sexualité et sainteté* (Brussels: IET, 1977), p. 147.

[27]A. del Noce, "Lettera a Rodolfo Quadrelli" (unpublished letter, 1984), cited in A. Scola, "Paternità e Libertà", *Anthropotes* 12, no. 2 (1996): 339. It is a suppression inasmuch as it seeks a series of superficial satisfactions in order to eliminate the drama of the human heart.

not 'seeing' [the] difference, including sexual difference, as a sign of the other, risks conceiving of love as a pure prolongation of the I (again, in a homosexual way)."[28]

The difference between the sexes, in other words, has a meaning that transcends mere physical being: it is ontological before it is physiological; it is in the soul before it is in the body.[29] The ultimate explanation of this difference is threefold. It lies in the creaturely logic of the relation between God and the world that comes from him, in Christ's spousal covenant with his Church, and in the analogy of the Trinitarian life within God himself.

The "uni-duality" of the nuptial communion between man and woman is, infinitely distant, an image of the "uni-Trinity" of the Divine Persons.[30] As John Paul II has affirmed in *Mulieris dignitatem*, "We read that man cannot exist 'alone' (cf. Gn 2:18); he can exist only as the 'unity of the two' and therefore in relation with another human person. It is a question here of a mutual relationship: man to woman and woman to man. Being a person in the image and likeness of God thus also involves existing in a relationship, in relation to the other 'I.' This is a prelude to the definitive self-revelation of the Triune God: a living unity in the communion of Father, Son and Holy Spirit."[31]

4. Homosexuality as a Disorder: The Theological Dimension

The difference between the sexes is part of the creaturely image of God in the human person. It must be understood as an analogical term situated within the relation to the Creator, and of the Church with Christ, as well as within the call to mirror the communion of the Divine Persons. If all this is true, it is normal to expect the disorder of homosexuality to have a paradigmatic theological significance in the history of salvation. The French theologian Gaston Fessard offers an illuminating

[28] Ibid.

[29] See D. Schindler, *Heart of the World, Center of the Church: Communio Ecclesiology, Liberalism, and Liberation* (Grand Rapids: Eerdmans; Edinburgh: T. and T. Clark, 1996), p. 259.

[30] See John Paul II, Encyclical Letter *Dominum et vivificantem*, May 18, 1986, no. 67, in *AAS* 78 (1986): 900.

[31] John Paul II, Apostolic Letter *Mulieris dignitatem*, August 15, 1988, no. 7, in *AAS* 80 (1988): 1664.

interpretation of this paradigmatic significance in a commentary on the
first chapter of Saint Paul's Letter to the Romans (vv. 20–29).[32]

In the text, the apostle connects the refusal to recognize God on
the part of pagan idolaters with the sexual perversions to which they
have abandoned themselves: "For this reason God gave them up to dishonorable passions. Their women exchanged natural relations for unnatural, and the men likewise gave up natural relations with women and
were consumed with passion for one another, men committing shame-
less acts with men and receiving in their own persons the due penalty
for their error" (Rom 1:26–27). But what is the meaning of this connection between godlessness and idolatry and homosexuality, between one's
religious attitude toward God and one's sexual behavior?

To be sure, to avoid invidious misunderstandings, we must recognize
at the outset that Saint Paul is not interested here in homosexuality as an
individual matter and even less in its material causes. His aim is rather to
understand its typical meaning and value for society, indeed, for world
history, in which pagan and Jew are opposed, in order to illustrate the
historical essence of idolatry. Fessard presents an original interpretation
of the text, drawing on the three polarities that define man's historicity: the man-woman couple (natural historicity), the master-slave couple
(man's historicity), and the Jew-pagan couple (supernatural historicity).

Moreover, for Saint Paul the primal origin of these attitudes is not
carnal or psychic, but rather "spiritual", or, to be precise, diabolical (see
Eph 6:12). Now, the starting point of Fessard's interpretation of the
text is the observation that the apostle, following numerous and well-
known passages from the Old Testament, bases his account of the relation between God and mankind on the analogy of the man-woman
relationship. Both in creation and in the history of salvation, God is a
man who freely offers his love to mankind, which is a woman in relation
to him. The pagan's idolatry flows precisely from the spiritual pride that
drives man to want to be "like God", not recognizing his Creator and
refusing to obey him as a servant obeys his Lord.

The result is a perversion of the creature's original attitude of feminine receptivity to the Creator.[33] Refusing God, the pagan claims

---

[32] See G. Fessard, *De l'actualité historique, I: A la recherche d'une méthode* (Paris: Desclée de
Brouwer, 1960), pp. 186–97.

[33] On the spiritual and active dimension of receptivity as the fundamental attitude of the
creature before the Creator, see Schindler, *Heart of the World*, pp. 237–74.

to exercise an arbitrary freedom and an exclusively virile power over creation. In Fessard's interpretation, sexual inversion is ultimately an expression of spiritual pride, the sign of an aspiration to an asexual angelism revealing the human spirit's refusal to adopt before the transcendent the feminine attitude characteristic of a creaturely being. At the heart of idolatry, homosexuality—not only as a deliberately chosen and consciously justified lifestyle, but above all as a paradigmatic spiritual attitude—is actually a sin against the Spirit that denies the order of nature and attempts to posit itself as the principle of a culture without transcendent points of reference.

Our anthropological reflection on the objective disorder inherent in the homosexual inclination has led us to a final and delicate threshold: to the spiritual dimensions of the creature's relation with its Creator. As A. Chapelle puts it, "Much more is involved in the drama of homosexuality than a sexual behavior."[34] When the objective disorder is not merely acted out, but crystallizes through free decision into a spiritual attitude and an ideology, homosexuality takes on a typological significance. To be sure, it must be stated unequivocally that what we have said concerning the typological value of homosexuality cannot be taken as a judgment on individual persons, who may suffer because of an unchosen disposition and may act out of weakness. We are dealing instead with a general spiritual physiognomy that informs a consciously chosen lifestyle, though its influence often reaches well beyond what individual persons are actually aware of, a "spirit" that we must resist and which manifests itself in many and varied ways.

The obligatory struggle against certain unjust discriminatory practices in society, solidarity with persons with homosexual tendencies, and pastoral effort to aid them to live chastity must not lead us to neglect the cultural, indeed, spiritual dimensions of the struggle for the truth and the authenticity of love. It would be a profound distortion if the homosexual option were elevated to the same level as the choice of a man and a woman to contract a marriage and to form a family in which to raise children, or if such a lifestyle were woven into the cultural and legislative fabric of society. As clarified by the Congregation for the Doctrine of the Faith, "Sexual tendency is not a quality comparable to race, ethnic origin, etc., with respect to non-discrimination.

---

[34] Chapelle, *Sexualité et sainteté*, p. 150.

Unlike these, homosexuality is an objective disorder and calls for moral concern."[35]

"This is a great mystery, and I mean in reference to Christ and the Church" (Eph 5:32). The mystery of Christian marriage fulfills human sexuality as a gift of self that is open to life. It is great insofar as it finds its place in the order of the wise plan of God, who in Christ loves the Church. The issues relating to the difference between the sexes are therefore not trivial ones, but indicate epochal shifts in culture and the spiritual history of mankind. The act of recognizing and reestablishing the order willed by God's wise plan is thus the basis of the path of truth and freedom, a path that begins with the humble recognition that we are creatures before the Creator.

[35] Congregation for the Doctrine of the Faith, "Some Considerations concerning the Response to Legislative Proposals on the Non-Discrimination of Homosexual Persons", no. 10, in *L'Osservatore Romano*, July 24, 1992, p. 4.

Testimony

The Curse of the Ouroboros:
Notes on Friendship

Joseph Prever

When I was young, I felt myself very much alone. This is to be expected for anyone who is an oddball, as I have always considered myself to be. But when one comes from a family of ten oddballs, it is less explicable. As an oddball even among oddballs, I was very much of the opinion that nobody really understood me, or wanted to. So I dreamed of a twin brother, my exact age, with my exact sense of humor. He would even have my exact body, so I wouldn't be able to be envious of how he looked.

It's a pretty narcissistic dream, even if it's probably a common one. But when I was twelve, I did find somebody like that, my best friend, Omar. When I say "best friend", I mean "somebody with whom you can spend hours making noises into a tape recorder, learning handstands, or skipping rocks, and not get sick of." We were endlessly entertaining to ourselves, and we were probably intolerable to everybody else within earshot. It wasn't that we consciously tried to exclude people outside of our two-man circle; it's just that we had so many inside jokes that our conversations might as well have been in code. That's why we spent so much time with each other, and relatively little time with anybody else. It's so much fun to be with somebody who understands you so perfectly! Why would you choose to spend time with somebody who didn't?

The age when we met is around the age when "friend" starts to mean something more than "people whose birthday parties you go to", which is what it means when you are ten or so, and something more than "people who don't hit you, or not very often", which is what it means when you are five or so. Omar was one of the first friends I ever had who wasn't just anybody. He was the first person to cause in me that unexpected but deep sense of recognition. Our backgrounds and personalities were totally different, but there was some mysterious element that was the same. It was as if two identical flowers had blossomed from two different species of trees. Something in him made something in me resonate; he knew my frequency without trying.

Using physics words like "resonance" and "frequency" seems to give things an erotic connotation, like talking about "magnetism" or "electricity". (Why do we frame eros, that lofty human love, in terms of blind natural forces? A question for another time.) I don't mean that being with Omar gave me any kind of electric thrill. It's just that we were in phase with each other, like two waves, crest to crest and trough to trough.

He wasn't the same as me (thank God), so it wasn't a perfect narcissistic fantasy, but our differences didn't cause me pain. He was more rough-and-tumble than I was, but for some reason this didn't make me feel inadequate. When he showed me how to do the kind of things he did for fun, it never felt like he was patronizing me. When we spent time doing things that should have been outside my comfort zone, it never felt like I had to be brave.

With nearly everybody else, it was different. I was already not fond of team sports—all right, I was terrified of them—and preferred to watch from the sidelines, chatting with the girls or congregating with my fellow sensitive males to share our derision of the proto-jocks. This discomfort was only partly because sports were masculine and I felt myself to be deficient in masculinity. It was also that everybody's instincts, whether on the field or in conversation, seemed to be different from mine. This friction caused me great distress; I was always misinterpreting and being misinterpreted. With Omar, that friction just didn't exist.

So in one sense my friendship with Omar was perfect, at least as far as I remember. In another sense, it was very far from being perfect—or maybe it was just not mature—since it required very little from me other than what I was naturally inclined to give. And it was a bit too insular to be a grown-up friendship, maybe: I had adjusted my isolation enough to have room for Omar, but I wasn't prepared to make the circle any larger than that. I can still remember the few times that this two-man island of ours was invaded. Once when we were out exploring streams (New Hampshire is utterly suited to Calvin-and-Hobbes-style exploration), we met two other boys doing the same thing we were, namely, peering into streams and looking for tadpoles. I watched Omar as he chatted with the others, talking easily and naturally. I wondered why I felt a terrible, breathless pressure in my chest. When I asked him if maybe it was time to head back to the house, I was filled with a shame I didn't understand and spoke in a strangled voice that was just about to spill over into tears. This must have been almost as mysterious to Omar as it was to me; talking to people was something he seemed to do naturally, so what was the big deal? But for me, the ease of interacting with Omar was a mark of the special bond we shared. How could he interact just as easily with these strangers? I secretly wondered whether, after all, they were not more of his own kind than I was. I would never have been out exploring by myself, without him to instigate it, and I never would have suggested it on my own. Maybe having found people more like himself, he would leave me behind.

I will protest a second time that I don't think this intense jealousy means that our friendship was erotic on my part (and it certainly wasn't erotic on his part). Sure, eros and jealousy go hand in hand, but it exists in the other loves, too. Wherever there is love, there is the temptation to let our love become grasping—the temptation to circumscribe the beloved, hem him in until he contains nothing that doesn't serve us somehow. But our island was not invaded very often. It was a very happy time, even if it was a short-lived one. Maybe because my self-ishness got the upper hand, or maybe just because people change, our friendship did not maintain the altitude it achieved during these two or three years. All the raw material for a mature friendship was there: we shared a sense of humor and any number of experiences. We were in our early teens, so there was no shortage of things we could have confided in each other about. But we didn't do that. For one thing, when I was fourteen, I discovered that the mysterious word "gay" applied to me. Meanwhile, Omar was discovering girls, which he tried to talk to me about, and which I tried to be interested in, but it fell flat. It was one thing we just didn't have in common. I was also discovering depression, which I didn't know how to talk about, and he was dealing with his family's own patterns of dysfunction, which he didn't know how to talk about. So it's not surprising that we slowly stopped being able to talk to each other about most other things, too.

This was around the time I left town to spend my last two years of high school at an out-of-state private school. When I came home, as I did most weekends, Omar and I both tried to keep up our old habit of friendship—but everything felt somehow strained and artificial, and artificiality was the one air our friendship couldn't breathe. So we drifted apart, the way people do. With Omar more or less gone, it would have been good if I had figured out what boys often figure out, or so I gather, around this age: how to run with the pack, how to find some place of belonging within the circle of other boys. That was something I longed for, but just couldn't get the hang of. Almost my whole experience of friendship was one-on-one, and with my best (and almost my only) friend gone, that hole was going to need filling.

That was the emotional atmosphere in which I entered college. Not that anyone needs a special reason to be miserable during college, but it does help to explain how the next four years went. In college, I became the closeted gay analogue of the frat-boy-on-the-make. Not that I was looking for a sexual partner; rather, I was looking for a new best friend. There is a certain kind of man, or a certain kind of man at a certain stage of life, who will make no secret about needing somebody (anybody!) to sleep with, but who has a harder time admitting, or even knowing, that he craves emotional intimacy. I, on the other hand, developed an intense craving for same-sex emotional intimacy, and this craving helped me avoid looking too hard at the same-sex sexual craving that was developing alongside it.

It was about this time that I read Father John Harvey's book, *The Homosexual Person*.[1] It's been fifteen years since I read the book, so I don't know how its psychology would strike me now. But it is there that I first encountered the idea that homosexuality was not, as I had assumed, an utter perversion, arising *ex nihilo* out of the hearts of certain men, for no other reason than that they were monstrously twisted on the inside. It was the first time I saw my desire for other men as something other than evil. I devoured the book. I made a paper cover for it, so I could read it in public without giving myself away. In fact, to be *extra* unsuspicious I labeled it "Book". (Nothing to see here!)

But then I made it suspicious again by drawing on it a picture of the ouroboros, the serpent swallowing its own tail. The serpent was supposed to be a symbol of me, or anyway of that part of me that I was desperate to unravel: my self-absorption; my self-consciousness; my inability to open up, to let things out or to let people in. The symbol

[1] John F. Harvey, *The Homosexual Person* (San Francisco: Ignatius Press, 1987).

seemed to sum up my personality wonderfully, while at the same time summing up everything that frustrated me about my life with other human beings.

Reading the book was a step in unknotting that knot. I had already heard, any number of times, that it was homosexual actions that were sinful, not homosexual desires. But this book, as I remember it, went further. Instead of just making a distinction between desire and activity, it made a distinction within the desire itself. It pointed out that even the desire was good; it was only the manner of the desire that was bad. The desire was a desire for love. More specifically, it was the desire for the love of a man, for intimacy with men. And this desire was good.

By the time I read the book, I had moved beyond the inchoate jealousies and confused anxieties of my early teens. I don't mean I stopped feeling jealous and anxious. I just mean the feelings became more definite, and more urgent. I understood that I wanted a man, or wanted men, or wanted manliness. I don't think it's an exaggeration to say that this desire was the central fact of my life at that time. But simultaneously, I had the apparently certain knowledge that the desire was by nature unobtainable—not only because I was a Catholic, but because of what I thought I understood about Catholic theology on the subject. In my mind, my desire for men was not a desire for something that existed but was difficult to obtain, or that existed but I had been arbitrarily banned from obtaining. It was worse than that. It was a desire for something that could never exist, a desire for a per se impossibility.

Romantic/sexual desire, I knew, was based on complementarity. But that complementarity, by definition, could not exist between men. What could my desire be but a kind of insanity—like wanting to eat dirt or breathe water? Before I read Father Harvey's book, I had believed that my homosexuality was a mark of some unspeakable twistedness in my nature—not a twistedness that I had chosen, of course, but something that was nevertheless inherent to the kind of creature I was, as if I had been made wrong by accident. If anything, that was worse. As Psyche says in C.S. Lewis' *Till We Have Faces*, "Don't you think the things people are most ashamed of are things they can't help?"[2]

So this idea of Father Harvey's was a kind of salvation to me. For one thing, it meant that the desire at my center was not perverse in its

[2] C.S. Lewis, *Till We Have Faces* (San Diego: Harcourt, 1980), p. 111.

object, but only in its manner. For another, it meant that feeling the desire didn't make me a monster, but just meant that I was a normal human being who wanted normal human things, albeit wanted them in a nonstandard way. And finally, it meant that the desire that I had always assumed was unfulfillable might be fulfillable after all.

Could friendship really quench that burning ache?

There was the hint of a promise, too. If homosexuality was really all about wanting intimacy with other men, and if intimacy with other men was something good and also something achievable, then maybe if I achieved that intimacy, the homosexual feelings would go away, and heterosexual feelings would take their place.

(Spoiler alert: this story doesn't end with me becoming straight.)

On the contrary, as I became more and more comfortable in friendship with other men, I discovered more and more that my own struggles weren't as odd as I had thought. Most of the men I talked to had experienced the same sense of inadequacy, of insecurity, of not belonging, as I had. I even found, to my shock, that there were any number of straight men who felt more excommunicated from manliness than I ever had.

Meanwhile, despite the unraveling of my plans for orientation change, I kept up the quest for male intimacy. There's a funny paradox here: what I wanted was to find male intimacy so I could stop being so gay. What I did was to form a series of friendships that were, at least on my part, intensely homoerotic. The most characteristic of these, and the most painful, was with Doug, whom I met during my junior year of college.

My friendship with Doug really got underway the first time we got drunk together, which was late in the fall, down by the reservoir. In retrospect, our weird little campus (I attended a Catholic liberal arts college with fewer than one hundred students) seems to me a regular colony of the lost, the melancholy, and the frustrated. But maybe that's just how college is. Regardless, we had between us such a rich collection of hang-ups that, when we drank together, everyone tended to get, as one of my friends put it, "a little revealy". That night at the reservoir, Doug let some pretty heavy stuff spill, and since I didn't really understand yet how alcohol worked for most people, I took this as a sign of his desire to be emotionally intimate with me. I leaned over his sprawled-out body next to the campfire, fond and concerned and, above all, glad to have found a context in which touching his big strong chest might be kind of okay, or at least might be put down to booziness instead of gayness. We stumbled back to campus in slurred conversation, divesting ourselves of burden after burden. When we reached our room I helped him throw up in the wastebasket, and then I dissolved into tears. I made it to the upper bunk and he collapsed into the lower; I reached my hand down and clasped his; we professed our friendship and drifted off.

I woke up with a rotten hangover but still bathed in the glow of newfound togetherness, the feeling of having bared my soul to a friend and having been welcomed for it. When Doug was awake, I asked him, "Do you remember what we talked about last night?" He looked embarrassed, cocked his head, and said, "I think you were crying?" That was all he remembered, or at least all he was willing to talk about sober. I remembered *everything*. It was the first time he broke my heart, but oh boy, it wasn't the last.

By November, he was an integral part of the weird little posse that I always think of when I remember college. Some time in November the posse went together to see P. T. Anderson's *Punch Drunk Love*. In one scene the protagonist, a lonely, damaged man-child played with surprising pathos by Adam Sandler, has just disrupted a family party by smashing three plate-glass windows in the dining room. In the aftermath, he quietly admits to his brother-in-law, "I sometimes cry a lot? For no reason?" And he suddenly bursts into tears. At this line, Doug threw his head back and howled with laughter. Next to him, in the dark, I cringed. I had never seen a movie that laid bare my own sense of isolation with such accuracy. I had never identified with someone as much as I identified with Adam Sandler's character. Was that how people like me looked to people like Doug? So neurotic and crazy, so far outside of what normal people thought of as human, that all he could do was laugh?

A week or two later, the scene was still in my head. One night I lay awake in the top bunk while Doug sank to sleep in the lower (I usually made my bedtimes coincide with his). I felt, as I had felt so many times before, that I was down at the bottom of a well, while life went on above me. I wanted badly to tell Doug about it, but I was terrified. After maybe fifteen minutes of indecision, and before it seemed to me that I had really decided, I opened my mouth and, with a physical sense of vertigo, I said, "Roommate?" "Yeah, roommate?" I was glad he used the nickname that we had settled on for each other. "Can I tell you something?"

I spilled as much of it as I could—not the gay stuff; I couldn't do that yet, but everything else: the feelings of isolation, depression, anxiety, the sensation of being a hopeless loser, the certitude that if anybody saw me as I really am, they'd be disgusted at how pathetic I was. How I was ashamed even to feel that way, let alone say it. I still remember his response. He said, "That's real pain, roommate." It was something that I didn't have to be ashamed to feel, he said, because it was as legitimate a hurt as anybody else had ever experienced. But it was not true, or anyway it was not how he saw me. That was the moment in our friendship that was most like friendship, and it was a huge step for me. If I really was an ouroboros, telling Doug how I really felt about myself (or how I really felt about anything!) was an unbending of that self-devouring circle. It was a decision to step away from mirrors and mirages and toward reality—away from the safety of controlling what Doug might think about me, and into the risk of letting Doug encounter me as I really was. It was, in short, an act of love. And, being an act of love, it invited an act of love on Doug's part, too. Love begets love.

I would like to say that, after that, we developed a real, healthy, solid relationship, were mutually supportive of and honest with each other, helped each other to grow in virtue, and so on. It didn't happen that way, though. I can't say much about what happened on his end, because I didn't understand it very well and still don't—I was too much concerned with my own problems to really empathize with his. The closeness we had was itself a good thing, and it really was a breakthrough as far as I was concerned. But I didn't understand how to be close with somebody without being exclusive with them, or how to value his friendship while maintaining my own identity. Maybe this was because my main experience with friendship had been the exclusivity that Omar and I had shared. Or maybe my sense of self was underdeveloped. Or maybe it was because, from the start, what I had in mind with Doug was some kind of hybrid between friendship and romance, with an emphasis on the romance.

Whatever the reason, I became more and more jealous. If he left campus without telling me, I would be in a panic till he returned, torturing myself by inventing treacherous reasons why he wouldn't have invited me to whatever he was doing, and unable to think of anything else. If I passed by him and he didn't smile, I would assume that I had done something wrong and had lost his friendship. If I saw him in a group laughing at somebody else's jokes, I would have to rush off somewhere private so I could burst into tears.

Meanwhile, Doug's private problems were threatening to drown him. When he swallowed a whole bottle of painkillers one night, I should have been upset and concerned and self-forgetful. Instead, I was anxious that I should be the one to drive him to the emergency room, so I could occupy the coveted seat of the friend who sat by him in difficult times. Doug left the school not long after that. I wasn't sad. It felt like cutting out a tumor.

Not long after college, I was home visiting my parents for Christmas. Like I always did, I spent some time with my spiritual director, Father T—the man to whom I had first confessed, at the age of fourteen, that I was gay, and who responded with those magical words: Do you want to talk about it? (More than a decade later, we still talk regularly.) I went to the rectory for Confession and stayed to share the bottle of scotch I had brought over. Two glasses in, I suddenly started talking about Omar. Omar and I weren't a regular part of each other's lives anymore, but I still tried to see him when I came into town. The visits were never easy. Every time I saw him, he seemed to have a different job, a different girlfriend, and occasionally, a new child. I had no idea how to deal with any of this. How could I be friends with him, I asked Father T, when our lives were so little alike? How could I talk to him, when our ideas of life had less and less in common? Why should I keep trying to make the friendship work, when it was so hard—for me?

Father T had helped me through crushes, friendships, love triangles, and everything in between. In the case of Doug, he had gently asked me questions that were designed to help me see that the relationship was not quite the David and Jonathan story I was making it out to be, and that there was nothing wrong with admiring somebody but that maybe I should ask myself if I wasn't making myself desperately unhappy for no good reason. That was always the question: Was I happy? This time was different, because Father T didn't ask me whether being friends with Omar would make me happy. For once, it wasn't about me healing my wounds, and it wasn't about me finally learning to break into the world of men, thus banishing my gayness forever.

Instead, he told me that maybe I should be a friend *to* Omar. That caught me by surprise, because I was used to thinking of myself as the wounded one, the one in need, the one perpetually on the hunt for love, the one on the ground waiting for somebody to pick me up. I wasn't used to thinking of myself as having anything to give. Besides, thinking of friendship as something you did, rather than something that happened to you, had never made sense to me. Wasn't friendship based on something inborn, that natural resonance?

You learn about friendship when you are young. You read about Winnie the Pooh helping Eeyore find his lost tail, because being a friend means helping. You learn about "being a good friend" to people, how when there's someone in the group that doesn't fit in, you reach out and include them. That idea of friendship made sense to me when I was very young, because I thought of everybody as a potential friend. It wasn't till Omar that I discovered another kind of friendship, the kind C.S. Lewis talks about when he says, "Friendship is born at that moment when one man says to another: 'What! You too? I thought that no one but myself ...' "[3] For friendship to exist, I thought, this resonance had to exist. This mindset is partly to blame for something I noticed about myself in college: that I could not seem to form casual friendships. It was all or nothing, either intense intimacy or none at all. Where resonance existed, intimacy was possible. Where resonance didn't exist, what could you do?

So when, during those days, Father T would talk about "choosing your friends", it made very little sense to me. That wasn't the kind of friendship I was familiar with, and it wasn't a kind that appealed to me. I couldn't even imagine calling such a thing "friendship". To me, if you weren't spending time with people that you had some kind of resonance with, you ran the risk of acting hypocritically, inauthentically. You were pretending to be something you weren't, or feel something you didn't. I didn't see how limiting that was, or how selfish. At the same time, I was deeply engaged in exactly the kind of hypocrisy that I wanted to avoid. Since I was determined to be Doug's friend, and since the only kind of friendship I believed in was the friendship of resonance, I did my best to manufacture this resonance by making myself more like Doug—taking on his tastes, his sense of humor, his style of clothes, even his laugh.

It's another paradox. On the one hand, this idea of friendship is narcissistic: the more like you the person is, the more you want to be friends with him. But in practice, it is self-abnegating, at least in a certain sense: the harder I tried to be friends with Doug, the less like myself I became. Of course, it was not self-abnegating in the Christian sense at all, since it was always for my own sake and not for his. In the end, this idea of friendship was the ouroboros all over again. Looking for a way out

[3] C.S. Lewis, *The Four Loves* (New York: Harcourt, Brace, 1960), p. 238.

of myself, I practically destroyed myself, chewing on my own tail until there was almost nothing left.

"The love of our neighbor is the only door out of the dungeon of self, where we mope and mow, striking sparks, and rubbing phosphorescences out of the walls, and blowing our own breath in our own nostrils, instead of issuing to the fair sunlight of God, the sweet winds of the universe."[4]

Maybe there are different kinds of friendship, some deliberate and some apparently inevitable, just as there are different kinds of marriage. I have seen good marriages between people who complement each other so well that they seem literally to have been made for each other, like two precisely interlocking machine parts. I have also seen good marriages where both people seem to be engaged in grinding each other down, to make the fit more precise. And I have seen good marriages where the two people seem simply to have been next to each other for so long that, no matter what they were when they started, now they have grown together like two moss-covered rocks.

Aquinas says of the angels that each is its own kind of substantial being, so that each angel is utterly different from every other angel, not only the way animals differ from each other, but the way men differ from animals.[5] Maybe friendships are like that. Generalizing only gets you so far. Whatever perfect friendship is, I have found some things it isn't. It is not only the instinctual coming together of those who resonate at the same frequency, like Omar and I did, even though this is good. If natural resonance is all that's there, the friendship will scorch and wither when the sun grows hot. It is also not an all-admiring, self-effacing desire for union—a desire so strong to be *with* the beloved that one wants to *become* the beloved, as I wanted to become Doug. Even romantic love is not like that, or shouldn't be. Love is gift of self, but I can't give myself to anybody else unless I have a self to give in the first place.

Looking at my friendships since that conversation with Father T, it seems to me that they have been different from what they were before. I think they have been wider, less intensely focused on one person at a time. I think they have been less self-seeking and more generous. I think I have entered into friendships more consciously, and with an eye to

---

[4] See George MacDonald, *God's Words to His Children* (Vancouver: Regent College Publishing, 2006), p. 66.
[5] See Thomas Aquinas, *Summa Theologica* Ia, q. 50.

what I can give as well as what I can receive. If I have changed in this way, it hasn't been due to any conscious decision on my part. I haven't learned to give the gift of friendship by my increased effort, my striving to be a giver rather than a taker. We don't learn love by gritting our teeth. On the contrary, I think the ability to give love is always born out of having received love from others. These others see a self in us, or the seed of a self, when we can't see it with our own eyes. They are patient with us while this seed grows. They shine on it with the sun of their compassion, and they water it with the water of their affection, until its roots become strong.

Or, even stranger, sometimes people love us without meaning to, not out of an excess of virtue or charity, but just because they happen to like us. When I told Doug about my pain, he was surprised, because he didn't see the half-human excommunicate that I saw when I looked at myself—and this not seeing of his made that part of me less real. That works, too. It doesn't matter much to the seedling whether the light it receives is from the sun or from a sun lamp. The important thing is that, having received the gift, we give it to others.

I met a man once, a celibate Opus Dei numerary named Roberto. He told me, in his thick Colombian accent, "I am like Gandalf." I asked him why he was like Gandalf. He said, "I am not married, so I do not need to stay in one place. So God can send me wherever he needs me to go." He grinned. "Like Gandalf." What impressed me about Roberto was that he didn't consider his celibacy as a negative attribute, but a positive one—as a freedom, rather than a restriction. The background to this thought is the assumption that his happiness, his joy, is intimately tied to his ability to give of himself. He saw self-fulfillment and self-donation as two names for the same path.

I think that the degree to which people discover this fact is the degree to which they are happy. Some people do not discover it at all, and go on seeking their own happiness and fulfillment in avenue after avenue, and wonder why their capacity for enjoying life seems to shrink faster and faster, when they are trying so hard to expand it. It is the curse of the ouroboros. Or to put it another way, it is the paradox of the Gospels: he who seeks to save his life will lose it. But he who loses his life, loses it for love and in love, will save it.[6]

---

[6] Cf. Mt 10:39; 16:25; Mk 8:35; Lk 9:24; 17:33; Jn 12:25.

Total Abandonment to Divine Providence and the Permissive Will of God

Daniel C. Mattson

The greatest question I have had to wrestle with in my life is the question of why God allowed me to be attracted to men. I didn't choose to be attracted to men, and I certainly didn't want to be. Throughout adolescence I often prayed to God that he would take away my same-sex attractions (SSA), or at least bring into my life a woman whom I could love and be loved by and desire enough to marry.

I clung in desperate hope to the promise of God in Jeremiah that I learned while I was still a Protestant in high school: "'For I know the plans I have for you,' declares the LORD, 'plans to prosper you and not to harm you, plans to give you hope and a future'" (Jer 29:11, NIV). But it was hard to see how God could love me as I trudged through an unhappy life, which sometimes I wished would end. How could he love me if he wouldn't take away these attractions? How could he love me if I was attracted to men, and yet couldn't act on those desires? I turned to pornography and phone sex as a drug to sate my pain, but this turned me into an addict. I was living a secret hellish life filled with loneliness, shame, and self-loathing. I would occasionally try to date women, but all I ever seemed to experience was pain and rejection. I concluded that women didn't find me desirable or view me as man enough to be worth dating. I became envious of other men, wishing to be like them. I hated myself and often thought, "If only God had made me this way, or that, then surely I would be happy." I thought of my relationship with God as if it was a contract. I believed that if I at least went to church, prayed to God, and avoided having sex before marriage, God's part of the bargain was to make me happy in the way I wanted to be happy.

The pain in my life made me wonder why a God who supposedly loved me would ever allow such suffering in my life. Saint John Paul II wrote in his Apostolic Letter on suffering, *Salvifici Doloris*, words that describe my experience:

> Within each form of suffering endured by man, and at the same time at the basis of the whole world of suffering, there inevitably arises *the question: why?* It is a question about the cause, the reason, and equally, about the purpose of suffering, and, in brief, a question about its meaning. Not only does it accompany human suffering, but it seems even to determine its human content, what makes suffering precisely human suffering.[1]

My cry echoed the cry of Christ on the cross: "My God, my God, why have you forsaken me?" (Mt 27:46; cf. Ps 22:1). After trying to follow God as best I could, thinking that God would eventually make me happy, I turned my back on him. The God I thought I loved had shown himself as untrustworthy. I was filled with rage toward him. If I could have gone back in time, I would have gladly scourged his back with whips. I would have spat upon him as he stumbled on his way to Calvary and relished nailing him to the cross. So like the Prodigal Son, I left my heavenly Father to live the life I thought would bring me happiness. I would fly my middle finger at the basilica near my home as an act of defiance to God nearly every time I drove by it. I finally fulfilled my desires to be with a man: I found a man to date and was happier than I had been in a long time.

Looking back on that time now, however, I see clearly that I was only as happy as I knew how to be. C. S. Lewis writes in his sermon *The Weight of Glory*, "We are half-hearted creatures, fooling about with drink and sex and ambition when infinite joy is offered us, like an ignorant child who wants to go on making mud pies in a slum because he cannot imagine what is meant by the offer of a holiday at the sea. We are far too easily pleased."[2] I didn't know what true happiness was. I was content playing in mud. God needed to bring suffering into my life to make me realize how mistaken I had been all of my life.

---

[1] John Paul II, Apostolic Letter *Salvifici Doloris*, On the Christian Meaning of Human Suffering, February 11, 1984, no. 9 (emphasis in original), http://www.vatican.va/roman_curia/pontifical_councils/hlthwork/documents/hf_jp-ii_apl_11021984_salvifici-doloris_en.html (hereafter cited as *SD*).

[2] C. S. Lewis, *The Weight of Glory and Other Addresses* (New York: Harper Collins, 2001), p. 26.

After a long valley of deep pain, chronicled in part in the documentary *Desire of the Everlasting Hills*,[3] God brought me to the threshold of true happiness. Through suffering, I learned that the only path to happiness on this earth is, submitting humbly before God, to realize that God looks at our entire lives and never allows anything to happen in our lives that is not ultimately for our good. All things are transformed and redeemed for our good and for our sanctification (cf. Rom 8:28; Eph 1:11). God used suffering to teach me that all of his "Thou shalt nots" are guides that really say to man, "Thou shalt live and flourish and be filled with joy." I understand now why King David could say, "It was good for me that I was afflicted, that I might learn thy statutes" (Ps 119:71). Through clarity that only comes through suffering, I've learned that what my dad said to me as a boy is true: "God says no to us, because he loves us."

Father John Harvey, the founder of the Courage Apostolate, always taught that one of the most difficult virtues to acquire is the willing acceptance of the permissive will of God. His wisdom has helped me see that the only answer that makes sense for why God allowed me to live with attractions to men is that he allowed it, for my good.

The man who first helped me to see this truth was a man born blind.

In a particularly painful season of my life, I found myself on Good Friday, feeling the pull of God. Even though I had turned my back on him he was always pursuing me. Good Friday weighed heavily on me, and though I didn't want to go to church, I felt the need to do something vaguely spiritual. Watching a movie fit the level of religious fervor I felt, so I turned to Netflix for spiritual inspiration. I avoided the *Passion of the Christ* since I feared it would convict me to change my ways. Instead I watched the film *Into Great Silence*, which chronicles the lives of Carthusian monks in France. At the end of the movie, an elderly, blind monk says the most profound words I've ever heard anyone ever say. He said,

> When God sees us, He always sees our entire life. And because He is an infinitely good being, He eternally seeks our well-being. Therefore, there is no cause for worry in any of the things which happen to us. I often thank God that he let me be blinded. I am sure he let this happen

[3] Erik Van Noorden and David Michael Phelps, *Desire of the Everlasting Hills* (2013), http://everlastinghills.org/.

for the good of my soul. One must [never] part from the principle that God is infinitely good, and that all of his actions are in our best interest. Because of this a Christian should always be happy, never unhappy. Because everything that happens is God's will, and it only happens for the well-being of our soul. Well, this is the most important. God is infinitely good, almighty, and he helps us. This is all one must do, and then one is happy.[4]

His words astounded me. I marveled at the faith of this man who could joyfully say that he often thanked God that he let him be blinded, because he was sure that God let it happen for the good of his soul. How could anyone say that about something as debilitating and painful as blindness?

I was baffled, but his words rang true. I couldn't get them out of my mind. Eventually, a question, unbidden, came into my thoughts. Could I ever look at the painful things that had happened in my life as something to be grateful for? Was it possible that part of God's plans to prosper me and not to harm me included the suffering that I had experienced in my life? Could I one day say that I often thanked God he allowed me to live with attractions to men, for this was allowed by him for the good of my soul?

This blind Carthusian's total trust and abandonment to the permissive will of God was pivotal in my journey back to God. As a result of his faith, and a long journey in trying to understand the question of suffering, my world turned upside down. But when everything was upside down, I realized that the world was finally right side up, for the first time in my life.

Isaiah 29:16 says, "You turn things upside down! Shall the potter be regarded as the clay; that the thing made should say of its maker, 'He did not make me'; Or the thing formed say of him who formed it, 'He has no understanding'?" When I was angry at God, I thought he knew nothing about what plans would prosper me, or what wouldn't harm me, but as a result of the pain in my life, I cried out a cosmic "Uncle!" to God and was finally ready to try and submit to his will. And so began a slow and steady return to the place of my spiritual birth and Baptism, the Catholic Church. I gradually realized that the most hopeful answer to suffering was the Catholic view of redemptive suffering, which shaped how I viewed my desires for men. During this time I

---

[4] *Into Great Silence*, directed by Philip Gröning (Germany: Zeitgeist Films, 2005), DVD.

began to see my attractions, not through the lens of sexuality, but rather through a lens that told me that the lessons I needed to learn were about suffering, abandonment to Divine Providence, and willing acceptance of the permissive will of God.

I came to view the suffering I experienced because of same-sex attraction in the way Blessed Columba Marmion wrote in a letter of spiritual direction:

> Your soul is in God's hands; He loves it, He looks upon it unceasingly and He makes it pass through the states that, in His Wisdom, He sees to be necessary for it.[5]

This has become my central conviction surrounding why God allows men and women to live with confusion about sexuality. To be seen correctly, SSA must always be viewed through the lens of suffering. It is allowed in the world as a tool and scalpel used by God to shape and transform those of us who live with SSA into becoming more and more like Christ. It must be viewed as connected with the cross of Christ, the cross that Christ calls us to pick up and carry daily.

Our Mother, the Church, wisely teaches this to people like me with SSA when she says in the *Catechism*, "These persons are called to fulfill God's will in their lives and, if they are Christians, to unite to the sacrifice of the Lord's Cross the difficulties they may encounter from their condition."[6] In *Salvifici Doloris*, Saint John Paul II writes:

> Man suffers on account of evil, which is a certain lack, limitation or distortion of good. We could say that man suffers *because of a good* in which he does not share, from which in a certain sense he is cut off, or of which he has deprived himself. He particularly suffers when he ought—in the normal order of things—to have a share in this good and does not have it.[7]

This explains what SSA is, at its core: SSA is not a different form of sexuality than our God-given sexual orientation toward our sexual

---

[5] Columba Marmion, *Union with God: Letters of Spiritual Direction by Blessed Columba Marmion*, ed. Raymond Thibaut, trans. Mary St. Thomas (Bethesda: Zaccheus Press, 2006), p. 104.

[6] *Catechism of the Catholic Church*, 2nd ed. (Washington, D.C.: Libreria Editrice Vaticana—United States Catholic Conference, 2000), no. 2358 (hereafter cited as *CCC*).

[7] *SD* 7 (emphasis in original).

complement, but is rather a privation of that good, replaced by a false distortion of that good. To see it in its true light, we must see SSA not as a thing in and of itself, but rather as the absence of that which should be present in man, but is not. In this sense, it is similar in some ways to the way blindness exists in the world. Blindness is something in the world only because it is a lack of something that is good—sight, which in the normal course of events should be present in man.

In *Love and Responsibility*, Saint John Paul II helps makes sense of this. He writes that "the orientation given to a person's existence by membership of one of the sexes does not only make itself felt internally, but at the same time turns outwards, and in *the normal course of things* (once again, we are not speaking of sicknesses or of perversion) manifests itself in a certain natural predilection for, a tendency to seek, the other sex." On the most basic level, he says, "This sexual orientation has as its object 'the other sex' as a complex of certain distinctive properties in the general psychological and physiological structure of human beings."[8] This is the good that those of us who live with SSA have been deprived of. We are meant to partake of this good, but in the course of our lives, something has set us on a course that leads us away from the natural order of progression in our sexual development. Thus, as the *Catechism* says, homosexuality has a "psychological genesis".[9]

All man-made sexual identities are marked by this same privation of good, replaced by a faulty distortion of the good of our true sexual nature and orientation. The person, for example, who considers himself transgendered and believes himself to be a female rather than a male as God made him suffers from experiencing the good of his true sexual identity on the level of his psyche. This is a particularly painful form of suffering. Sadly, there are some in the Church today who would support him in his confusion, but they do no good service to him by supporting him in his false understanding of himself. The path to peace for him must be total abandonment to Divine Providence. He must learn to trust that God knew what he was about when God created him a male. He needs to humble himself before God, as one who did not make himself, but was made, and accept himself as he truly is. He should be lovingly taught the joy that comes in willing acceptance of

---

[8] Karol Wojtyla, *Love and Responsibility* (San Francisco: Ignatius Press, 1993), pp. 47–48 (emphasis added).

[9] *CCC* 2357.

the permissive will of God and encouraged to see his particular form of suffering as a unique way in which he, and he alone, can unite that suffering with the suffering of Christ on the cross.

There are few men whom God has graced *in this particular way* to suffer for others, in order to "complete what is lacking in Christ's afflictions for the sake of his body, that is, the Church", as Saint Paul writes in Colossians 1:24. This man needs a reason to hope, and a vision for why God would allow this in his life that counters the prevailing culture that tells him to accept his subjective sense of himself. That vision is the self-sacrificial, selfless, life-giving example of the love Christ showed on the cross. That vision comes from the words of Christ: "Greater love has no man than this, that a man lay down his life for his friends" (Jn 15:13). There will be a great number of souls in heaven if a man who longs to be a woman humbly accepts and acknowledges himself as God made him, and then offers up the suffering he experiences on behalf of the salvation of all those souls like him who consider themselves transgendered. His reward in heaven will be great, and in the context of eternity he will view the pains and sufferings he lived with as precious invitations of God to enter into his salvific love for mankind. Such is the interior freedom and peace that comes through willingly accepting the permissive will of God.

Seeing Ourselves as We Truly Are

Like for the man who feels that he is more truly a woman than a man, total abandonment to Divine Providence requires all of us who live with SSA to see and accept ourselves as we truly are. We must view our sexuality within the context of the teaching of the Church, trusting that what Blessed Paul VI said is true: the Church is "expert in humanity".[10] This knowledge is imparted to the Church by Jesus Christ himself, who, Saint John says in his Gospel, "did not need anyone to testify about human nature. He himself understood it well" (Jn 2:25, NAB-RE).

The Church teaches us that "chastity means the successful integration of sexuality within the person and thus the inner unity of man in his

[10] "Address of the Holy Father Paul VI to the United Nations Organization", October 4, 1965, http://w2.vatican.va/content/paul-vi/en/speeches/1965/documents/hf_p-vi_spe_19651004_united-nations.html.

bodily and spiritual being."[11] To be truly chaste persons, we must humbly submit to objective reality, regardless of what our subjective feelings and experiences might suggest to us, or how the culture around us might suggest we should identify. *The Compendium of the Social Doctrine of the Church* makes this clear when it states:

> Faced with theories that consider gender identity as merely the cultural and social product of the interaction between the community and the individual, independent of personal sexual identity without any reference to the true meaning of sexuality, the Church does not tire of repeating her teaching: "Everyone, man and woman, should acknowledge and accept his sexual identity."[12]

This takes humility. We must not run from our true sexual orientation or be swayed by the winds of culture. The only sexual identities that are true are male or female. Each man is objectively sexually oriented toward women, and vice versa, regardless of one's subjective experience. There are many in the Church today who believe that true pastoral care must accommodate a cultural understanding of homosexuality. Some actively encourage people in "coming out" and view this as a positive change for the Church. Some who live with attractions toward the same sex choose to call themselves gay, lesbian, queer, or bisexual and seem to embrace the language of the world concerning sexual identity. They sadly have accepted the pernicious segmentation of society into either "straight" or any variety of "something not straight". Some say they do this in part out of a desire to be evangelizers and to give pastoral care to the "gay community". But this is a mistake, for as the 1986 *Letter to the Bishops of the Catholic Church on the Pastoral Care of Homosexual Persons* states, "Only what is true can ultimately be pastoral."[13]

The 1986 *Letter* teaches us what is true, thus providing the antidote to confusions that stem from gender theory:

---

[11] *CCC* 2337.

[12] *Compendium of the Social Doctrine of the Church* (Vatican City: Libreria Editrice Vaticana, 2004), no. 224.

[13] Congregation for the Doctrine of the Faith, *Letter to the Bishops of the Catholic Church on the Pastoral Care of Homosexual Persons*, October 1, 1986, no. 15, http://www.vatican.va/roman_curia/congregations/cfaith/documents/rc_con_cfaith_doc_19861001_homosexual-persons_en.html.

Today, the Church provides a badly needed context for the care of the human person when she refuses to consider the person as a "heterosexual" or a "homosexual" and insists that every person has a fundamental Identity: the creature of God, and by grace, his child and heir to eternal life.[14]

We are admonished by Saint Paul in his letter to the Romans, "Do not be conformed to this world but be transformed by the renewal of your mind, that you may prove what is the will of God, what is good and acceptable and perfect" (Rom 12:2). This is especially necessary in our culture today, which views sexual identity as something that can be chosen and manipulated according to one's whims, rather than inherent to what it means to be human.

In our pursuit of chastity, we must forget ourselves, and our own view of ourselves, and rely on the objective truth of who we are, as taught by the Church. "Male and female he created them" (Gen 1:27; 5:1) is at the root of chastity. If we do not accept our true sexual identity as being either a man made for a woman, or a woman made for a man, we will forever be a puzzle to ourselves and we will not be able to realize fully the virtue of chastity in our lives, for we will never see ourselves and our sexuality as they truly are. If we fail to accept our true sexual identity, our sexuality will never be completely integrated in our person, in its bodily and spiritual unity, and we will never live fully chaste lives.

A word is necessary here to speak of the intersexed, those who exhibit sexual features of both sexes. The existence of these individuals doesn't point to a "third sex", as many supporters of gender ideology propose. We do not look to a man born with an extra limb as revealing that man is the sort of creature who doesn't walk about on two legs. In the *City of God*, Saint Augustine writes, "We know that men are born with more than four fingers on their hands or toes on their feet ... but far from us be the folly of supposing that the Creator mistook the number of a man's fingers, though we cannot account for the difference."[15] In the same paragraph he writes of those we would call intersexed today: "As for the Androgyni, or Hermaphrodites, as they are called, though they are rare, yet from time to time there appears persons of sex so doubtful,

[14] Ibid., no. 16.
[15] St. Augustine, *St. Augustin's City of God and Christian Doctrine*, ed. Philip Schaff, trans. Marcus Dods (New York: Charles Scribner's Sons, 1907), p. 315.

that it remains uncertain from which sex they take their name."[16] This is surely a great cross to bear, and like all forms of suffering, this too must be accepted with great patience and humility before God. But the existence of the intersexed does not prove that man is a creature divided into three or more sexes. When we consider the existence of the intersexed, the Church must echo Saint Augustine and say, "Far be from us the folly that the Creator mistook the division of the sexes into male and female."

Speaking to the Roman Curia, Pope Benedict XVI said that what is necessary to "protect man from self-destruction" is "something like a human ecology, correctly understood". He adds

> if the Church speaks of the nature of the human being as man and woman, and demands that this order of creation be respected, this is not some an-tiquated metaphysics. What is involved here is faith in the Creator and a readiness to listen to the "language" of creation. To disregard this would be the self-destruction of man himself, and hence the destruction of God's own work.[17]

On the occasion of his address to the Bundestag in Germany in 2011, Benedict XVI again spoke of this ecology of man:

> Man too has a nature that he must respect and that he cannot manipulate at will. Man is not merely self-creating freedom. Man does not create himself. He is intellect and will, but he is also nature, and his will is rightly ordered if he respects his nature, listens to it and accepts himself for who he is, as one who did not create himself. In this way, and in no other, is true human freedom fulfilled.[18]

Thus, in order to have true freedom, men and women like me with desires for the same sex must accept ourselves and our nature as they

---

[16] Ibid.

[17] "Address of His Holiness Benedict XVI to the Members of the Roman Curia for the Traditional Exchange of Christmas Greetings", December 22, 2008, http://w2.vatican.va /content/benedict-xvi/en/speeches/2008/december/documents/hf_ben-xvi_spe_20081222 _curia-romana.html.

[18] "Address of His Holiness Benedict XVI: The Listening Heart, Reflections on the Foundations of Law", September 22, 2011, http://w2.vatican.va/content/benedict-xvi/en /speeches/2011/september/documents/hf_ben-xvi_spe_20110922_reichstag-berlin.html.

really are. No one is rightly called gay, lesbian, or any other letter in the alphabet soup of sexual identities. These labels stem from an impoverished and polluted view of human sexuality.

The Canadian bishops understood this, as reflected in their document *Pastoral Ministry to Young People with Same-Sex Attraction*, which states:

> The terms "gay" and "lesbian" are not used to define people in the Church's official teachings and documents. Although these words are common terms in current speech, and many people use them to describe themselves, they do not describe persons with the fullness and richness that the Church recognizes and respects in every man or woman. Instead, "gay" and "lesbian" are often cultural definitions for people and movements that have accepted homosexual acts and behaviours as morally good.[19]

In addition to proclaiming the importance of accepting our true sexual identities, the Church must be tireless in combating the faulty notion of "the closet" and that "coming out" is the path to true freedom and liberation. This is not a path to freedom, or a way to be honest with who we are, or honest about our sexuality with others, as it is so often portrayed. Rather it is a door that leads to the prison cell of our cultural confusion surrounding sexuality. The "closet" is a trap constructed by the "father of lies" (Jn 8:44), who from the beginning of time has delighted in telling lies to mankind that appear to point to freedom and truth, but whose doors always lead to slavery.

The USSCB understands the problem with "coming out" as seen in their 2006 document *Ministry to Persons with a Homosexual Inclination: Guidelines for Pastoral Care*.

> For some persons, revealing their homosexual tendencies to certain close friends, family members, a spiritual director, confessor, or members of a Church support group may provide some spiritual and emotional help and aid them in their growth in the Christian life. In the context of parish life, however, general public self-disclosures are not helpful and should not be encouraged.[20]

---

[19] *Pastoral Ministry to Young People with Same-Sex Attraction* (Ottawa: Episcopal Commission for Doctrine, Canadian Conference of Catholic Bishops, June 2011), no. 2.

[20] *Ministry to Persons with a Homosexual Inclination: Guidelines for Pastoral Care* (Washington, D.C.: United States Conference of Catholic Bishops, 2006).

In some quarters today, there is great resistance to this teaching, even among some authors who promote sexual continence. They choose to call themselves "gay chaste Catholics" and some even seem to believe that the bishops don't really understand homosexuality.[21] However, in this area, I believe that part of abandonment to Divine Providence for men and women who live with same-sex attraction, or who are tempted to come out as gay, lesbian, or something else, is to trust that God has given the bishops in charge of our care more wisdom on our sexual identity than we have ourselves. Our attitude to any Church teaching that intersects our lives as intimately as this should always be one of humility and docility rather than believing we have more understanding and wisdom than the heirs of the apostles do.

I have never followed the path of "coming out". Though I have been called by God to speak about chastity and SSA, I have done so against my own desires that no one ever know about this part of my life. But through much consultation with many spiritual advisors and priests, I became public in part to be a credible voice that can counter those voices in the Church who recommend for people like me to "come out" as gay, lesbian, queer, or bisexual in the Church. I made a decision long ago never to speak on the subject of SSA in my own parish and will only do so if my priest requests it of me. Certainly some people have discovered my attractions to men in an organic way as a result of stumbling on my writings, but I see this as an undesirable consequence of obeying God's call to speak publicly about the hope that lies within me (cf. 1 Pet 3:15). I have come to accept this as part of the permissive will of God in my life. I find the experience lamentable and humbling, for I wish to be known and understood as I truly am, not as a "gay man". But I know that I am called to unite those humiliations with the humiliations of Christ. This is a view that is in keeping with the wisdom that I have learned from the Church, wisdom that all men and women living with SSA would do well to follow.

---

[21] In *Gay and Catholic*, author Eve Tushnet characterizes the bishops' understanding of homosexuality this way: "The bishops put out some kind of statement on homosexuality, asymptotically approaching understanding with the speed of a dying snail" (p. 155). Elsewhere she writes of official Church documents on homosexuality, saying that "this is an area where the Church hierarchy's level of understanding and its ability to convey the truth clearly and humbly are changing fast. Future statements will likely be better than these" (p. 182). (Notre Dame: Ave Maria Press, 2014).

In this world gone mad with ever-growing sexual identities, the Church must be a sign of contradiction (cf. Lk 2:34) and help those who do not see themselves as they truly are, to love themselves with what Josef Pieper calls "Selfless Self-preservation". He tells us that "the purpose inherent in self-love as in all love [is] to preserve, to make real, to fulfill. This purpose is given only to selfless self-love, which seeks not itself blindly, but with open eyes endeavors to correspond to the true reality of God, the self, and the world."[22]

Abandonment to Divine Providence and Loneliness

I would like to turn now to the role that total abandonment to Divine Providence plays in particular areas of pastoral need.

In a letter to a woman named Mrs. McCaslin, C. S. Lewis wrote of loneliness in the same way I have come to view the loneliness I sometimes feel as a single man. He writes:

> Loneliness, I am pretty sure, is one of the ways by which we can grow spiritually. Until we are lonely we may easily think we have gone further than we really have in Christian love: our (natural and innocent, but merely natural, not heavenly) pleasure in *being loved*—in being, as you say, an object of interest to someone—can be mistaken for progress in love itself, the outgoing active love which is concerned with giving, not receiving. It is the latter which is the beginning of sanctity.[23]

These words have great significance for those with SSA, who all experience the natural desire to feel the pleasures of love, of being an object of interest to someone. For us, that desire is often misdirected. So what are we to do with the loneliness we feel? Too often loneliness causes men and women to despair, but through total abandonment to God, the loneliness we feel can be transformed into a precious gift. It takes time and pastoral direction to reach that point, however.

---

[22] Josef Pieper, *The Four Cardinal Virtues* (Notre Dame: University of Notre Dame Press, 2011), p. 149.

[23] Lewis to Mary Margaret McCaslin, August 2, 1954, in *The Collected Letters of C. S. Lewis, Volume 3: Narnia, Cambridge, and Joy 1950–1963*, ed. Walter Hooper (New York: Harper Collins, 2007), p. 501; emphasis in original.

No doubt the first step in pastoral care for men and women living with profound loneliness is to bring them comfort. As Pope Francis said, "I see the Church as a field hospital after battle."[24] It is no use to speak of growth in spiritual maturity while someone is suffering great pain from isolation and loneliness, all the while despairing of a future that they believe will always be lonely. For me, one of the great sources of comfort in confronting the loneliness I sometimes feel is to realize that I am not unique in my loneliness, simply because I live with attractions to men. I have found there is a great temptation to self-pity on the part of men and women who live with SSA and fear that loneliness will be their sole lot in life. This is helpfully countered when they learn that there are far more single men and women who desire to be married who will be forever single than there are same-sex-attracted men or women on the planet. I choose to feel solidarity with them, rather than bemoaning my state. This has been a necessary development in my spiritual growth.

A mature response to loneliness, which can only be reached with the passage of time and with the help of compassionate and wise priests or spiritual directors, is to accept that the permissive will of God sometimes brings loneliness into our lives. It is a part of the universal human condition, and there will always be times when we cannot remove it from our lives, no matter how many friends or loved ones we have. The key to happiness within the painful condition of loneliness is to discover how to transform our loneliness and our desire to be loved into the impetus for giving love to others and giving companionship to others who feel alone.

The desert of loneliness bears fruit when we can learn to adopt the attitude of Saint Francis of Assisi:

> O Divine Master,
> Grant that I may not so much seek
> To be consoled, as to console;
> To be understood, as to understand;
> To be loved as to love.

---

[24]Pope Francis, in "A Big Heart Open to God", *America: The National Catholic Review*, interview by Antonio Spadaro, S.J., September 30, 2013, http://americamagazine.org/pope-interview.

Saint John Paul II wrote, "If God permits suffering because of illness, loneliness or for any other reason, 'he always gives us the grace and strength to unite ourselves with greater love to the sacrifice of his Son and to share ever more fully in his plan of salvation'".[25] This, too, then becomes one of the great invitations of loneliness. Spiritual growth in the face of loneliness eventually leads to this question: Who do you love enough to carry this loneliness for? When one accepts loneliness as a way to bring about the salvation of a loved one, it no longer becomes bitter, but is something that we gladly will endure—especially if this person is someone who might have been a former lover who still has yet to know the love of Christ.

Finally, loneliness becomes a source of rich consolations, once we realize that God brings loneliness into our lives so that we will know that only he, and he alone, can satisfy us.

A young widow raising two young children alone recently wrote me about how she has come to view loneliness in her life. She wrote me saying that she has come to view loneliness as a love song from God to her. The Lover of her soul has used loneliness to woo her toward himself, and for this she is grateful.

This is one reason I have always found the novel view of chaste or vowed same-sex relationships as being opposed to the will of God. Those who promote this idea I believe are sincerely trying to ameliorate a deep pain. But the path to finding peace in the midst of loneliness associated with SSA isn't to somehow live in a pseudo-marriage or an eroticized or romanticized version of friendship, even if this relationship is sexually continent. Rather, through total abandonment to Divine Providence we should choose that which we wouldn't consent to, naturally on our own, as being the permissive will of God for our lives. Let us not run away from the cross our Lord has permitted for us by attempting to live out a novel understanding of spiritual friendship. God made a way to overcome loneliness. In Eden, he said, "It is not good that the man should be alone" (Gen 2:18) and then instituted marriage. But not all are called to marriage.

The intimacy of marriage is unique, and to seek it in other relationships is misguided. Those who think they cannot be happy without the

---

[25] "Message of John Paul II for the Brazil's Lenten 'Campaign of Fraternity 2003'", January 4, 2003, http://w2.vatican.va/content/john-paul-ii/en/speeches/2003/march/documents/hf_jp-ii_spe_20030304_brotherhood-brazil.html. Internal quotation is from his 1999 *Letter to the Elderly*, no. 13.

sort of physical, emotional, or spiritual intimacy that marriage makes possible (but certainly doesn't guarantee) is to make an idol out of an earthly reality. Marriage is a precursor to the only intimacy that can ever really satisfy: intimacy with God. All of us must seek that intimacy whether or not we marry. Many are called to live lives of complete self-giving in the religious life; others serve many through their family of origin, their careers, or volunteer work. If it is God's will that we don't share in the particular form of love and intimacy that is proper in marriage, we do well to accept this lack as a gift from him. Even if we are sexually continent, trying to find a semblance of the intimacy of marriage through a "chaste celibate gay relationship" is running away from that which God has deemed as good for our souls. But most importantly, by attempting to run from the pains of loneliness through such a relationship, we cheat ourselves from the great storehouse of riches that God in his Divine Providence desires to give us through the loneliness he permits us to feel. We are settling for far too little love from God if we choose a path away from the scalpel he desires to use to shape us into the image of his Son.

Abandonment in the Face of Addictions

I would like now to turn to one of the great temptations to despair for a person who lives with same-sex attraction, which is the battle for chastity. There is often a sexual compulsivity that accompanies the condition, particularly among men.

For people like me who have gone down the road of sexual sin, moving from unchastity to a life of chastity is very difficult. The body has a memory, patterns of behavior have been established, and for so many men and women caught in this behavior the shame and self-loathing that often accompanies sexual sins creates a vicious cycle. The drug that sates the shame one feels is another sexual experience. This becomes immensely discouraging for the person who is trying, perhaps for the first time in his life, to live chastely.

Father John Harvey always warned those in the Courage Apostolate to guard against what he called "white knuckle chastity".[26] Thomas

---

[26]John F. Harvey, "Homosexuality and the Courage to Be Chaste", *National Catholic Register*, April 27, 2003, http://www.ncregister.com/site/article/homosexuality_and_the _courage_to_be_chaste/.

Merton writes, "We become saints not by violently overcoming our own weakness, but by letting the Lord give us the strength and purity of his Spirit in exchange for our weakness and misery."[27] Impatience and frustration has often accompanied my progress in chastity. But I have learned that Christ is the victor, not me, and I have learned that God has allowed this weakness in my life so that I might know that without him I can do nothing. In my life, God has used my weakness in unchastity to help root out that most cancerous vice of the soul: pride. I have no room for judgment of anyone—God has used unchastity in my life to point to my weakness and selfish nature in ways that I suspect no other tool could have done so effectively.

C. S. Lewis could have been speaking of me when he wrote the following about suffering in the *The Problem of Pain*:

> The creature's illusion of self-sufficiency must, for the creature's sake, be shattered.... The dangers of apparent self-sufficiency explain why Our Lord regards the vices of the feckless and dissipated so much more leniently than the vices that lead to worldly success. Prostitutes are in no danger of finding their present life so satisfactory that they cannot turn to God: the proud, the avaricious, the self-righteous, are in that danger.[28]

Blessed Columba Marmion wrote invaluable words for me when I have looked at my difficulties with chastity:

> Do not let yourself be discouraged by your miseries; the Good God leaves you some miseries to convince you thoroughly that you can do nothing. He does not wish us to be able to attribute to ourselves whatever good we can accomplish. *Jesus is our holiness*; we must be very faithful and wait for Him to act in us.[29]

Far too many souls have left the Church in despair over their inability to live out lives of virtue, especially with regard to chastity and SSA. Those engaged in pastoral care should emphasize hope and patience above all things. There has been no greater gift given to me by the Church than to realize that Jesus is my holiness and the truth that chastity can only be won by God alone.

---

[27] Thomas Merton, *Life and Holiness* (New York: Image Books, 2014), p. 31.
[28] C. S. Lewis, *The Problem of Pain* (New York: Collier Books, 1962), pp. 97–98.
[29] Marmion, *Union with God*, p. 96.

Saint John Cassian said that, "while all progress in virtue and successful expulsion of vice is due to the grace of God, the specific aid and special gift of God is necessary for chastity."[30] God knows what he is about, and he brings chastity at the right time, and in the right way. The task of the person struggling with chastity is to continue to persevere, even in the face of repeated failures. We need to be encouraged by those involved in our care to rise up again, to run and cling to the mercy of God, and try again and trust that God will grant victory when the time is right. It is good for us to hear the words of Saint Paul that where sin is, grace abounds (see Rom 5:20), and that God looks at us when we fall in the same way an earthly father might look at a toddler just learning to walk who stumbles. Our Father in heaven is pleased with us that we are striving to walk along the path he sets before us, and the greater the fall, the more quickly he runs to pick us back up and set us on our way again. We must cling to hope and the promises of God that all things are possible through Christ who strengthens us (see Phil 4:13; cf. Mt 19:26; Mk 10:27). It is a great grace to realize our weakness and to glory in the fact that, in our battle for chastity, the victory is God's, and God's alone.

Parents and the Permissive Will of God

I would like to now turn to how willing acceptance of the permissive will of God helps bring peace to parents. Parents are often troubled when a child "comes out to them", especially if his announcement coincides with the choice to live out a life of active homosexuality.

Myriad questions arise for parents when a child comes out: Was this our fault? Is there a way we can fix our son? How will my child ever be happy? What will the rest of the family think? Is he going to go to hell? Should I support him in his choice? What if he gets AIDS? What if she decides to marry another woman? Will we never have grandchildren? Why would God let this happen to him and to us?

I have known situations where one child's "coming out" divides a family. Some of the siblings choose to support their brother or sister who

---

[30]John Cassian, *Institute 6, Conference 12*, trans. mod. L. Dysinger, O.S.B; based on Terrence Kardong, trans., *Cassian on Chastity: Institute 6, Conference 12, Conference 22* (Richardton, N.Dak.: Assumption Abbey Press, 1993) and *The Monastic Institutes*, trans. J. Bertram (London: St. Austin Press, 1999), http://www.ldysinger.com/@texts/0415_cassian/02_inst-06.htm.

has come out and openly reject the parents or other siblings who don't affirm the one who has come out. Some parents who cling to the truth of Church teaching are completely cut out of their child's life. Here, too, the only answer that brings peace is total abandonment to Divine Providence and accepting this as part of the permissive will of God.

Often the first step in finding a path forward is to accept that the salvation of their children is in God's hands, and God's hands alone. Though parents are called to educate their children in the faith, it is only by the grace of God and the work of the Holy Spirit that a child comes to salvation.

Growth in spirituality for parents tends to follow a common path. They start to realize that God wants them to be more concerned with their own personal spiritual growth than they are concerned about their child's spiritual state. As they grow spiritually, they begin to see that this has been allowed in their lives for their good and for their sanctification. It is common to hear from parents that they would have never come to a deeper relationship with Jesus if they hadn't experienced the pain and sorrow resulting from their child's choices. This is the great paradox which always surrounds suffering: God turns that which is painful to glorious gain for those who are willing to turn to him.

I find the story of Saint Dismas helpful in giving parents inspiration and hope. Saint Dismas has been called the "Good Thief", the one to whom Jesus said, "Truly, I say to you, today you will be with me in Paradise" (Lk 23:43). How could Saint Dismas or his parents know that the most important day in his life was the day he was crucified with Christ, and that it was the permissive will of God that led him there?

When I hear from heartbroken parents, I urge them to think of the tears and prayers of the mother of Saint Dismas. I imagine she often went to the temple, beseeching God for her son's salvation. She must have been like Saint Monica, weeping and praying for the salvation of her son, Saint Augustine.

Could the mother of Saint Dismas have known what Divine Providence had in store? The very source of her pain and sorrow became the vehicle by which salvation would come to her son. Little did she know that the path to her son's salvation was a literal cross, and that her son had a divine appointment with the incarnate Son of God. Today he is now in heaven, no doubt singing God's praises with his mother who shed so many tears for him and for his salvation. Today, I'm certain they rejoice at the throne of Jesus, who says, "Behold, I make all things new" (Rev 21:5).

Parents should take encouragement from the stories of the men and women in Courage. When I chose the path of the Prodigal Son, how could I have known that the first step toward truly living in my Father's house was the step I took when I left his house, seeking my own vision of happiness?

Not long ago I heard from a mother who was troubled by her son's choice to come out as a gay man and to pursue a relationship with a man. He was very angry at his parents and she suffered great pain because of this. I wrote her the following as a way to encourage her to trust in all things that God had not left her or her son.

> I've become convinced that the pain and sorrow that a family feels at the poor choices of a son or daughter is something that can be offered up on behalf of the redemption of their child. The greatest way you can help bring about the redemption of your son is to unite whatever sufferings you endure—as a result of his choices—on behalf of his redemption. I think that gives a purpose to the sorrow and pain that you feel right now. There must always be hope, and there must always be a way God redeems our suffering, and I now know that parents and their suffering play a vital role in the redemption of their child. The "further sorrow" you speak about, resulting from your son's current disposition of anger towards you, is allowed by God to be turned around and redeemed as part of the source of your son's redemption. I think this is the only way St. James's words in James 1:2 can make any sense: "Consider it all joy, my brethren, when you encounter various trials." Naturally, no joy will ever be felt when we suffer, but I'm convinced we can endure it if we find purpose and meaning behind suffering, and in the beautiful paradox that is always present in God's redemption, that which is most painful becomes that which is most powerfully redeemed by God—and surprisingly, the source of great joy. Thus, the pain caused by a child's poor choices becomes an opportunity to love the child producing the pain and sorrow, by uniting that pain to the suffering of Christ on the Cross, on behalf of the child. God's redemption is beautiful in that regard, and I'm confident that your son will be redeemed, certainly in large part by your willingness to "offer it up" on his behalf.
>
> The timing of God is always perfect too—Oscar Wilde reconciled with the Church on his deathbed, which was exactly the right time. (I pray and trust that this won't be the case with your son!) Perhaps the hardest thing in the redemption of a child is waiting on God to act. But then that

becomes an opportunity to grow in your faith in God. I think it's hard to wait for God in all of this, but I'm confident that God is in control, and He has his eye on your son and is pursuing him. I didn't come back to the Church until I was 38, eleven years hence for your son. Don't expect too much, too soon, I would caution, and be prepared to endure more pain and sorrow—but when it comes, always view it as an opportunity to love your son even more. The more angry he gets at you, the more pain you will feel, and therefore the more suffering you can unite with the Cross, on his behalf.

My note helped her find a way forward through the pain she felt, and it gave her hope that all was not lost. She accepted the cross set before her, and through the pain she feels from her son's choices, she is able to love her son more than ever before.

Thus, it all comes back to the cross. It is the cross that helps me to understand the answer I began with: Why did God allow me to be attracted to men? I now know that it was because he loved me. Through the grace of God I can now say as the blind Carthusian monk said of his blindness, "I often thank God that he let me live with attractions to men. I am sure he let this happen for the good of my soul." But it is more than that, too. I am invited to unite whatever painful trials I might encounter along the way with the cross of Christ, for the salvation of the world.

Same-sex attraction has helped me see the world for what it is: it's not home; it's a novitiate for heaven. It's how God wants to transform me into being more and more like his Son. Much of it is painful, but like Saint Teresa of Avila said, "In light of heaven, the worst suffering on earth, a life full of the most atrocious tortures on earth, will be seen to be no more serious than one night in an inconvenient hotel."[31] C. S. Lewis said it another way: "If you think of this world as a place intended simply for our happiness, you find it quite intolerable: think of it as a place of training and correction and it's not so bad."[32]

Father John Harvey had it right. Willing acceptance of the permissive will of God is the only path that brings peace to those of us who live with same-sex attraction, for it is the path all of the saints have walked, following in the footsteps of Jesus. I can now see my life through the lens that the Little Flower came to view her own life, and say that "all

[31] As quoted by Peter Kreeft in Lee Strobel, *The Case for Faith* (Grand Rapids, Mich.: Zonderven, 2000), p. 47.
[32] C. S. Lewis, *God in the Dock: Essays on Theology and Ethics*, ed. Walter Hooper (Grand Rapids: William B. Eerdmans Publishing, 1970), p. 52.

is grace".[33] I now understand Saint Paul when he said "to live is Christ, and to die is gain" (Phil 1:21). For men and women with SSA, "to live is Christ" is to follow the path of the love of the cross, "to unite to the sacrifice of the Lord's Cross the difficulties they may encounter from their condition."[34] I now understand that "to die is gain", for I now know I am a stranger, in a strange land (cf. Ex 2:22; 1 Pet 2:11). But the time of my homecoming is in the hands of God. In the meantime, because of what I've learned through the permissive will of God, I can say with firm conviction the words of Saint Julian of Norwich: "All shall be well, and all shall be well and all manner of things shall be well."[35]

[33] Conrad De Meester, OCD, *With Empty Hands: The Message of St. Therese* (Washington, D.C.: ICS Publications, 2002), p. 69.

[34] *CCC* 2358.

[35] Julian of Norwich, *Revelations of Divine Love*, ed. Grace Warrack (London: Methven, 1901), p. lxx.

Why Maintaining Biblical Language Matters

Robin Beck

There has developed a debate among Catholics concerning homosexuality. It seems there are certain folks in our ranks committed to chaste celibacy but who prefer to keep their gayness as part of their identity and consider their same-sex desire to be a source of giftedness. This has not gone over well with Catholics who contend that this position is unorthodox, to say the least. This position is profoundly strange to me, for it seems obvious to me that homosexuality is one of the sins that put the nails in Jesus' hands and feet. Honestly, what more needs to be said than this? Why all the back and forth with endless debating that for the most part leaves both sides more entrenched in their positions?

But after much thought it finally occurred to me that such folks must think that what they experience as gayness is not the same thing as biblical homosexuality. In other words the passages in both the Old and New Testaments that condemn homosexual behavior can't possibly be referring to the same-sex attraction that they experience, because God called same-sex behavior an abomination whereas they contend that their gayness is a gift. And after making a case for gayness being a gift, the next thing they also point out is that what Scripture is condemning is homosexual behavior whereas they are committed to sexual purity. So, they contend, scriptural teaching about homosexuality does not apply to them.

There is another group committed to chastity who find it consoling that Scripture condemns *only* homosexual *behavior*, not the desire itself (see discussion below regarding 1 Cor 6:9–10). They do not consider same-sex attraction a gift but accept it as a cross, as a disorder in their being that they are willing to live with. In other words, as long as they are living chastely, they believe they, too, are exempt from all the awful things the Lord has to say about homosexual relations. This view simply leads some of them to accept their disorder and not to make attempts to be free from it.

I want to stress that the huge difference between these two camps lies in the question of one's identity. The first group is opting to have their gayness as a part of their identity. For example, someone might say, "I'm a man, a doctor, a Catholic, and I'm gay." They freely own their gayness as part of who they are because they see it as an enriching part of their being. The second group sees same-sex attraction as more of a cross to bear and not so much a flag to fly; as mentioned, they consider their attractions and desires to be an affliction. Yet, for them, too, in some way, experiencing same-sex attraction (SSA) is a part of their "identity".

I must confess that when I walked away from my "ungay" life five and a half years ago, I had never even heard of the term "same-sex attraction". During my active years as a homosexual sinner (ages nineteen to fifty-four), I referred to myself as "gay". I considered myself as "gay" when I was in a relationship (twelve of them), and I was "gay" when between partners. I behaved as a homosexual, I thought like one, and my heart had homosexual desires (lots of them). So when I hit my knees on September 5, 2009, I repented of all of it: the behavior, desires, inclinations, daydreams, and fantasies. It all got nailed to the foot of the cross. My repentance was genuine and biblical. My mind completely changed concerning homosexuality. God was right; I was wrong. I owned up that I had been living a life of sin for thirty-five years. And you can bet your boots that my behavior changed. It changed immediately! I did a complete forsaking of every bit of it.

Probably the surest indicator that my repentance was for real is that I changed my life drastically. I got rid of my television as well as all of my secular CDs and any DVD that I had in my collection that glorified fornication. I took down all of my Disney pictures from my walls and replaced them with Bible verses I had typed up and framed. (My house went from looking like Disneyland to the local convent overnight.) I found a Christian radio station and began to listen to it from morning till night. And, of course, I walked away from my friends who were pro-gay, whether they themselves claimed to be or just happened to support those who were. Romans 12:2 states, "Do not be conformed to this world but be transformed by the renewal of your mind". The only way for this to become a reality for me was to detox my life of the things that reminded me of my sinful past. I am convinced this purging prepared me for the deep healing work God had in store for me.

In my naïveté (or maybe it was my Protestant upbringing) I assumed that it had all been sinful—not just the sexual acting out but the inner desires to find love and intimacy with another woman. I really and truly believed I had to be free from not only bodily sins but from those that were in my thoughts as well. Much later I found out that what was required most of me was to remain chaste; if I continued to be attracted to other women, this was just something to be expected, because for the most part SSA doesn't go away. Somehow I never got that memo, and I assumed that even emotional desires that crossed the line had to cease.

Many Catholics these days contend that relationships with former sexual partners can continue as long as all sexual interaction ceases and healthy boundaries are established. Even some of us who consider same-sex attraction a cross stemming from a disordered desire think these friendships can be good. The "gay as a gift" group even want to have "vowed" friendships where they make pledges to have "nonsexual-committed relationships". My last partner (number twelve) suggested we could be chaste and have a "romantic friendship". She claimed she heard it suggested by someone on a Catholic radio program. At the time I thought she must have heard wrong, because what sane Catholic would make such a crazy suggestion? I mean, really, that to me seemed pretty, well for lack of a better word, stupid. It would be like a recovering drug addict having the cocaine laid out on the coffee table and deciding just to look at it. But after interacting and dialoging with many Catholics the past five years on the subject of homosexuality and hearing time and time again that "being gay is fine", I had to admit that perhaps my partner had heard someone on Catholic radio after all proposing such a thing as romantic, nonsexual friendships. In case you're wondering, I don't believe such a relationship glorifies God. So as far as my last partner and I were concerned, we never took a stroll down Romantic Friendship Boulevard. Truth be told, we couldn't even pull off a nonsexual, nonromantic friendship. After a year of constant drama and emotional upheaval we ended all contact with each other.

From the moment I repented of homosexuality (the behavior and desire) I was confident that chastity was something that could be maintained. My days of playing a lesbian harlot—absolutely finished. Of that I was most certain. My life had been ravished by this sin, and there was no way I ever wanted to go back there. But how was I going to deal with homosexual desire? Interestingly enough, I didn't approach this part of the equation with the mindset of having now to cease all inappropriate thoughts and desires. Had I approached it from the negative (can't, mustn't, stop it now), I would have felt too defeated. My mind had been on automatic pilot when it came to longing for a woman to completely love me. I had been thinking these thoughts since age ten. Instead, I just admitted to God that I had no idea what a healthy relationship with another woman would even look like, but I sure wanted to find out so that one day I would be able to have some godly friendships. So admitting to the Lord and to myself that I was clueless as to how to rightly relate to members of my gender, I did the only thing I knew to do: I started to ask for help. And wouldn't you know it, the most amazing thing happened. I began to be directed to various healing ministries (all of them right within our very own Church!). God began to bring one person after another who told me where to go, and my response was always, "Okay, I'll do it." I think this is referred to as "cooperation with grace". This wonderful Church of ours is definitely a place of life-transforming, sanctifying grace, and it began to flood my life by washing over my sin-battered soul.

Being filled with much joy over what the Lord has done in my life, I have shared my story with many people these past few years. Sadly, far too often I have felt blown off and shunned. My heart's desire is to speak at parishes in hopes of getting people to think rightly on this issue that is tearing our families apart and putting our churches in moral darkness. But many doors have remained closed to me. Perhaps because I've continually said, "The Lord has healed me", people have conjured up thoughts of God waving his magic wand over me and saying, "Voilà! All better now!" Am I seen as an exception, kind of like someone who wins the Mega Millions Lottery? The truth is, there were specific things that the Holy Spirit directed me to do as I journeyed the pathway toward wholeness. I certainly don't see myself as any kind of special case. In my heart I believe restoration can be a reality for the vast majority of us. For some reason, though, not many folks are buying what I am desperately trying to proclaim.

On Labor Day 2009 I made an about-face. I turned around and ran right into the arms of my heavenly Father, who had been chasing me down for three and a half decades. I got my nose back into my Bible and began to read with a right understanding all the passages on homosexuality. As I mentioned earlier, I had no knowledge that there was such a thing as being "same-sex attracted". I thought of myself as a repentant homosexual, and with all my heart I wanted to view this sin as I thought God did. Leviticus 18:22 told me that God abhorred it ("it is an abomination"). Truth be told, I've come to feel the same way. My iniquity robbed me blind. I missed out on having children, and I grieve that loss often. Romans 1:26 said that my passions, which I once considered beautiful, were actually "dishonorable". And Romans 1:28 let me know that men and women who revel in this sin are given over to a "base" mind. I know this to be true. When I look back at the things I once thought and believed when I was in my "not so gay" days, I absolutely shudder. And 1 Corinthians 6:9–10 really laid it on the line in letting me know that I almost forfeited heaven:

> Do you not know that the unrighteous will not inherit the kingdom of God? Do not be deceived; neither the immoral, nor idolaters, nor adulterers, nor homosexuals,[1] nor thieves, nor the greedy, nor drunkards, nor revilers, nor robbers will inherit the kingdom of God.

Pretty dreadful stuff, but I diligently embraced God's indictment concerning my past sinful behavior. And even though I continued to hear (often from very learned scholars) that only the external behavior is condemned, I continued to conduct my affairs as if God held my mind and heart accountable. After all, hadn't Jesus himself said that "out of the heart come evil thoughts"? (Mt 15:19). And didn't our Lord make the case that if you looked upon someone in a lustful way, you had committed the act in your heart? (Mt 5:28). Until someone could show me where the line was (this much desire and not a drop more), I was playing it safe, doing everything I could think of to keep my heart and mind free from all things homosexual.

But this isn't where it ends for those on Saint Paul's list in 1 Corinthians 6:9–10, who weren't heading toward heaven and perhaps not even purgatory. He follows up this dreadful condemnation of homosexual sin

---

[1] A footnote for this phrase in RSV-2CE makes it clear that "the apostle condemns, not the inherent tendencies of such, but the indulgence of them."

(and the other sins) with a verse that makes me want to jump right out of my chair and start shouting:

> And such were some of you. But you were washed, you were sanctified, you were justified in the name of the Lord Jesus Christ and in the Spirit of our God. (1 Cor 6:11)

Hallelujah! Thanks be to God! Praise to you, Lord Jesus Christ! If that isn't wonderful news, I don't know what is! Those who were *practicing homosexuals* have been washed clean, set apart, and put in right standing with God. In other words, homosexuals can be changed and completely set free. So, for this homosexual sinner who got nailed five different places in the Bible (six if you want to throw in Sodom and Gomorrah), there's a very happy ending to the homosexual nightmare. Yahoo!

So what's my point in all of this? Here it is. I feel concerned that we have detached from biblical language. While I very much admire the people I know who are living chastely with same-sex attraction, I wish they weren't so accepting of their "condition". I wish they would accept the hope that Scripture gives to homosexuals. Scripture proclaims they have been delivered. I want to proclaim that truth again to "cross-bearing" homosexuals. The message I keep hearing from them is that, for some, same-sex attraction is an affliction that doesn't go away. Perhaps this is true (I hope it's not), but wouldn't it be better to claim the truth of 1 Corinthians 6:9 and be free from all of it—the behavior and the desire?

As we remove ourselves from biblical language, I fear we are also removing ourselves from the power of God to restore our lives to wholeness. Here is where the thinking of those who "embrace" their gayness as a being a source of good things, and then even as a good in itself, is particularly confusing. But if gayness is a good thing, why would the behavior that issues from it not be a good thing? Even when it is not directly stated, many Catholics have been misled into drawing this conclusion and are therefore actively engaging in homosexual relationships. Some continue to receive the Eucharist (too often with a blessing from their priests). If you asked them why they receive the Body and Blood of our Lord when they are committing a sin condemned in Scripture, they would probably reply that what they are doing is not the same thing as the sin of homosexuality that Scripture condemns. (Sound familiar?) How can they say something so outrageous? That's a discussion for another essay. This is a slippery slope we find ourselves on when we move away from biblical terminology and start redefining what God's Word clearly spells out.

As for me, I was a homosexual: I engaged in abominable behavior, and sinful thoughts and desires. But that's who I was; it's no longer who I am.

> Therefore, if any one is in Christ, he is a new creation; the old has passed away, behold, the new has come. (2 Cor 5:17)

In This Our Exile

Eve Tushnet

If there is one word that has shaped my life, and that names my deep longings, that word might be "home". My father says I'm the only person he's ever known who gets patriotic about Washington, D.C. I grew up—in D.C. the hometown, not Washington—and I'll defend the city's virtues, real and imaginary. I'm lucky enough that my parents still live in the house where I grew up, and when I return there I'm grateful for the flowers the walnut tree drops in the springtime, the florid wallpaper in the dining room, and the sickly, struggling dogwoods.

Catholics have this tic where we call the Church our home. I like this and I do it: I joke that Rome is the place where, when you go there, they have to take you in. When somebody tells me he's just been baptized, I say, "Welcome home!"

But Christians are never fully at home in this world. The closest we come is the Mass, where eternity breaks into time and we experience some foretaste of the wedding feast of the Lamb. Kneeling before the altar (or at the communion rail—bring these back!), I know that I'm in my place, or as close to it as I've ever been.

And then we're dismissed, and I go back out into the Church Militant (occasionally too militant), where I'm frequently reminded of the many ways I won't be fully at home anywhere in this life. I'm an adult convert, without the long-ingrained habits and the (often stressful) familial belonging of the cradle Catholic. I'm Jewish, which you would think would make me feel especially at home in the Church of Jesus and his family, but history had other plans. And, of course, I'm gay (or, if you find that word difficult, I am attracted to members of the same sex)—a cultural construct, but a powerful one that, like many other such constructs (nationality, race, and class), has structured my life in some ways whether I've wanted it to or not.

It's good not to feel too much at home, even in the Church. Feeling entirely at home might mean that we stopped longing for the beatific vision. There's a kind of attachment in feeling at home, an over-identification with our own warm feelings. Alienation teaches its own truths about life after the fall.

This essay will not be chiefly about the people and communities that have helped me to see that my home is, at last, in the Catholic Church. It will be about people who have provided havens for me, shelter on the way. I'm focusing on the people who have helped me to negotiate life as a gay Christian, since that's the area in which I had the fewest role models and (therefore) the most obvious alienation. These are people who have helped me hear God's call.

Family

My family is not Christian. I was raised in a mostly secular household, with some Jewish religious education and practice. Nonetheless, my family influenced my conversion in a few ways. They taught me that religious tradition and community were inescapable parts of my heritage, rich in beauty, and that communal prayer was something you could do when you really felt like you needed it. They encouraged my artsiness, which eventually helped me to see that beauty in the world was the fingerprint of its Creator. They offered me models of unstinting love: they modeled how to apologize and how to forgive.

When I came out about my homosexuality to them, around age thirteen (so, in about 1992), they were entirely accepting. It was hard for my parents to let go of some aspects of their expectations and hopes for my future, but they made it clear that they accepted me. I doubt they would be thrilled to hear this, but their acceptance of my sexual orientation made it much easier for me to enter the Catholic Church later.

I came to the Church without any baggage: without the pain that so many gay kids endure, without the scars left by bullying or parental rejection. I had never been mistreated by anyone who told me that they were doing it in the name of Christianity. I had never had well-meaning people tell me that I wasn't "really" gay, that God would heal me, or that I could be fixed through psychotherapy.[1] The more gay Christians I meet, the more I realize that my experience was extraordinarily rare. I came to the Church with my defenses down—because I had never needed to defend myself against Christians. For what it's worth, my parents were equally accepting—even though I think it challenged them more—when I "came out" to them about my plans to get baptized and become Catholic. They weren't able to love me only when they understood or agreed with my choices.

Riot Grrrl

Riot Grrrl was a feminist movement within the punk scene in the 1990s. It was often treated as a style more than a political statement: people noticed the ripped fishnets and howly music, but didn't ask what those angry girls were howling about.

I wore my share of ripped fishnets. But what I remember most about Riot Grrrl was the honesty and intimacy of the meetings with them. We would sit in a group house in northern Virginia, with the dusty August sunlight falling on the posters and flyers for bands with names like Bratmobile and Bikini Kill, and girls my own age would talk about their experiences concerning such things as rape, eating disorders, and abusive families. Or we would share our favorite music and comics, encourage one another, and create a haven where glitter and feathers could overcome every sorrow. It was part consciousness-raising group, part therapy, part sleepover. There was a moral component: many girls were identifying for the first time how a misogynist culture had pitted them against other women, and how their judgmental attitudes toward women made them complicit in a cruel culture and fed their own self-hatred.

For me, Riot Grrrl—like SMYAL (the Sexual Minority Youth Assistance League, a local LGBT youth group)—was morally salutary in a different way. Both groups offered humbling encounters with my own

---

[1] We need to discern the best way to discuss our desires in a way which fosters our vocations, and that won't always include contemporary identity categories like "gay" or "same-sex attracted". People's sexual desires do shift for a lot of reasons, sometimes including the Holy Spirit or psychological healing. But the way these concepts have been deployed by Christians toward gay people has often been clumsy and sometimes even cruel. We've been treated as problems to be fixed, not as ordinary Christians negotiating an unusually complex historical situation.

luck and privilege. I learned that I didn't always know much about where other people were coming from; I learned to listen more than I talked. (Those who knew me in college will recall that I swiftly forgot this lesson!)

I don't pretend that those girls would agree with where I'm at now. But Riot Grrrl was the first place where I experienced true solidarity with other women. It fed a deep need in me to love and serve other women, to identify with them and share our strengths with one another.

Most of them would be appalled at the place where I find that solidarity today. When I left college, as a relatively new Catholic, I started looking for ways I could serve women. I now recognize this as a process of vocational discernment: listening to hear where God was calling me. And he called me to volunteer at a crisis pregnancy center.

The center lacks some of the best features of Riot Grrrl: its anarchic equality, for example, and its attention to larger structural problems in society. Riot Grrrl was a group of and for young women; they didn't concern themselves with issues like legal liability, institutional longevity, or best practices. The pregnancy center can't ignore those things. Even so, when I meet with clients (even this word, "clients", suggests some of what's lost in the transition from consciousness-raising to service provision and counseling), we create a tiny women's community.

I conceive of my job as a counselor in terms of service to *women*. I also serve the next generation, of course. I'm grateful for the opportunity to "be fruitful" even though I have no children of my own. But the core of the call from God was to serve women. My experience in Riot Grrrl helped me to know what I longed for, and to rejoice when God called me back to that.

Some Women I Wanted to Impress

In college I met the first practicing Catholics I had ever gotten to know well. I was openly gay, of course, but they didn't focus on that. They didn't do the thing well-meaning Christians often force ourselves to do (I've definitely done variations on this), where we think we have a *duty* to tell other people what to care about—where we think we can diagnose, often on the basis of extremely brief acquaintance, the most important and troubled areas of other people's spiritual lives. Instead of telling me what Jesus thinks of gay people, my new Catholic friends talked about what their faith meant to them. Several were converts, and they described what had drawn them to the Church. They talked about the collision of justice and mercy on the cross; they talked about that curdled or infected impulse, where we yearn for what's hurtful and not for what's loving, and they told me that this is what Christians mean when they talk about "original sin".

Eventually I asked them about the Church's teaching on homosexuality. They never raised this subject with me, and I think they were right to hold back. They talked about the beauty and truth they found in the faith and trusted me to come to them when I wanted to know more, and I did. Their explanations for Church teaching on sexual ethics didn't really make sense to me, but my friends consistently assured me that God had created the beauty of the world and the body. I didn't understand why he would ask me to accept these specific rules about how I responded to beauty, but I did begin to look for evidence of his creating hand. (More on this below.)

When I entered the Church, I did so without feeling that I understood or could defend Catholic teaching on homosexuality in a debate. What I knew was that I needed the Eucharist. I needed the Body and Blood of Jesus. And since Jesus is the Way, I trusted the Church who gave me Jesus in the Eucharist to also hand on to me a way of life: an ethic, including a sexual ethic.

We're not called to be theologians or debaters. We're called to be followers of the Way. This much I could do.

While I was struggling with all these weighty existential questions, I was also experiencing all the hubris and hormonal excitement of your average undergraduate. At the same time that I was exploring these new intellectual waters, I was also meeting a lot of pretty girls. The story is more complex than this for many reasons, but one true thing about my entrance into the Catholic Church is that it was assisted by attraction to women. Some were Christian women; I spent a lot of time thinking about their arguments because I was impressed by them and wanted to impress them.

But the most important thing beautiful women did for my conversion was not to argue or even to witness but simply to exist. I had a few iconic images I returned to when I was thinking about the beauty of the world and wondering what it meant, what it might point to that was deeper than mere pleasure. I was sure that there *was* something more to beauty than the pleasure it gives us. One of the images that seemed to me most strongly to suggest that beauty pointed beyond itself to some deeper mystery was the image, glimpsed one night at a party, of a woman's face appearing from behind a pillar in a darkened room. She was a stained-glass window through whom light poured from somewhere else. (Yes, fair enough, I was probably a *little* bit drunk.)

My rapture on seeing her face wasn't sexual, at least not in any immediate way—closer to Dante glimpsing Beatrice at the window than to David glimpsing Bathsheba in the tub. But I don't think I would have responded this intensely to her face if I had not been a lesbian. I don't think it's an accident that one of the touchstone moments on the path toward my conversion involved the beauty of a *woman*. I could be wrong—another touchstone moment for me involved summer sunlight falling through a window, so my response to beauty is obviously not always colored by sexuality—but my intuition is that I was able to recognize this woman's God-created beauty in part because I'm a lesbian.

Some of these pretty women became my friends: friendships that started, on my side, with a heady mix of intellectual shock, personal admiration, and sexual attraction. I know that can be a painfully volatile mix (regardless of the sexes of the people involved), and I'm lucky that I've been able to maintain and deepen friendships that did not always start with motives that Saint Aelred would approve.

Over time the eros of these friendships has transformed, becoming basically a matter of recognition of and gratitude for beauty, rather than a matter of sexual desire. I'm lucky in that as well. As it happened, these women were straight, which meant that I never faced the question of what I would do if they had reciprocated my desires. But I would argue that even if sexual desire had persisted, these friendships could still be spiritually fruitful. They would be more challenging, but there's more to the spiritual life than chastity, and much more to chastity than avoiding temptation. These friendships served my overall vocation—they made me more forgiving, more considerate of others, quicker to admit my own faults and failures, and more open to God's call—even when they were colored with sexual desire.

I was not always good at "avoiding the near occasion of sin". I wish I had viewed chastity less as a game with rules (how far can you go?) and more as a practice that would help me preserve the intensity and beauty of that moment when my friend's face became a window to the divine. I'm glad I wasn't scrupulous, but I wish I had been a little less stupid. I wish I had known that chastity could help me learn the surrender of the ego that is the heart of devoted love. As I became better at practicing chastity in my friendships, the friendships themselves deepened.

So why do I discuss these friendships—and specifically the erotic charge they once held for me—in this essay? After all, this was a long time ago; many of the friendships that brought me into the Church, and most of my strongest friendships today, never included any physical attraction on my part. Why not let bygones be bygones?

First, I was asked to write about the relationships that helped me hear God's call, and it's simply true that pretty women are part of that story. But more importantly, I think I was able to avoid some of the stress, shame, and alienation from God and the Church that so many gay Christians experience in part because I've always acknowledged my attractions to women and sought to find the good fruit that they could bear.

In my conversations with other gay Christians I've learned that, for many of us, when we view our sexual attractions as terrifying and shameful, sullying not only ourselves but the objects of our attention, it's harder for us to trust God. It's harder for us to believe that we are created and sustained by his love. It's harder for us to believe that we are not defined by sin. Unsurprisingly, this mistrust and shame in turn makes it harder for us to surrender our minds, hearts, and bodies to God in chastity. We're stressed and scared, not at peace with ourselves and our God. This is a mindset conducive to lust—as stress relief, if nothing else—not chastity and self-gift.

I don't experience these anxieties with regard to my attractions to women (I do have my share of shame and self-hatred, but not around this specific issue), and I think this more relaxed, matter-of-fact approach to my attractions has made them *less* tempting and easier to sublimate. The more ashamed and anxious I am about my sexuality, the more I struggle with chastity. And I don't think I'm unique in this. Basically, I think many people find it easier to live chastely when they chill out.

That said, I would never hold myself up as a role model! We all have different situations, and the best way to handle your desires is something you'll need to discern for yourself, with the help of a trustworthy guide and confessor (if you can find one). I would never advise someone, "Okay, just go make friends with the people you find physically attractive—I see no way this can go wrong!"

But the questions I get from younger gay Christians are more like, "How can I find the kinds of intimate, enduring friendships you've found? And what should I do if I *do* find myself becoming attracted to my friend?"

As is often the case with giving advice, the most responsible answer is, "Talk to your spiritual director or some other wise adult." But in addition, here's what I do say: Seek to deepen the friendships you already have. Consider staying in one place, in one parish. Seek to serve others in your local community, especially in the most prosaic and material ways such as the corporal works of mercy. Seek to give—and to give yourself away. If you strive for a friendship that will fill an emotional *or spiritual* void, you are likely to lose friends rather than gain them. If you instead seek to pour yourself out for others, you *may* find that you also make lifelong friends. (This will come as no surprise to those who have read Jesus' promise to us in Matthew 16:25: "For whoever would save his life will lose it, and whoever loses his life for my sake will find it.")

And as for the second question, "And what should I do if I *do* find myself becoming attracted to my friend?" again, the answers will differ radically from person to person and friendship to friendship. I generally believe people in this situation need *somebody* they can talk to: a priest, perhaps, or often another friend. People will need to surrender their egos and their expectations for the friendship. Some people will need to take some time away from the friend. Some people will need to chill out, as I said above, and remember that they're not uniquely broken, that they're not *damaging* someone by having a crush on him, that this too shall pass. Some people will need to wait it out, hold still, refrain from freaking out, and let time transform their feelings into agape.

Since the best path forward will be different for different people, spiritual guidance must be compassionate, deeply grounded in orthodoxy and orthopraxy, and flexible. As you'll see in this next section, I've been exceptionally lucky in this area.

Two Priests

When I had been Catholic for about fourteen years, I finally started spiritual direction, something I should have done much earlier. I started direction because I knew I needed to quit drinking and had been unable to do so without outside help. Unsurprisingly, once I got used to the luxury of having a regular confessor, I didn't want to give it up! I have been sober for a little over three years but still gain so much from direction. It's a place where I can be known, welcomed, and shown mercy—another kind of foretaste of heaven.

Neither of my spiritual directors have focused on my sexual orientation. It comes up sometimes; I've talked with my first director about the stresses that come from being a public face of gay celibacy, for example. But I've been—yet again—so lucky that my directors have not viewed it as their job to change my orientation or persuade me to stop calling myself gay. They've focused primarily on my prayer life. They've listened to me, rather than viewing my own account of my sexuality, friendships, or vocation with suspicion. And they've trusted that if they help me to pray and worship, then God can do the rest.

Too often, the *only* area of gay people's spiritual life on which other Christians focus is our sexuality or chastity. "Sanctification" has been defined solely in terms of becoming more chaste—or even becoming heterosexual—with other areas like humility, honesty, and solidarity with the marginalized, or even love of Christ, being ignored. My own spiritual directors didn't make this mistake. Even when I brought to them problems with chastity, they didn't focus on my sexual orientation but asked about my overall vocation: How was I praying? How was I living? How did I view God? When I sinned or even when I was tempted, could I pray that my weakness would prompt deeper humility and help me be merciful toward others?

The old-school confession "box" has many virtues. One of its great virtues is that it makes manifest the spiritual reality that Confession creates an enclosed "space"—even on the battlefield, or the site of an accident, or a contemporary "reconciliation room"—in which the penitent encounters Jesus in the person of the priest. The offices of my spiritual directors, with their armchairs and knickknacks and the occasional semi-domesticated cat, became havens for me where I could meet Jesus. They were places of peace in the midst of the chaos of cultural controversy.

Gay Christians

I found my first spiritual director through one of his other directees, a friend of mine—another celibate gay Catholic. One of the many ways in which I've led a charmed life is that I live in a city with a tiny but real subcommunity of gay Catholics faithful to Church teaching. This community, and the broader community of gay Christians, has been a haven for me in so many ways.

"Gay Christians" is a shorthand, as inadequate as all the other possibilities I can think of. I can't say "celibate" because some of them are married (to members of the opposite sex). I can't say "Catholics" since some are Orthodox or Protestant. Even "gay" is a major oversimplification: some of these people prefer to identify as same-sex attracted, or as members of the LGBT community, although I don't think the particular people I'm describing will be upset by my use of the succinct-but-imprecise umbrella term "gay". All the people I'm thinking of accept the historic Christian teaching that sex is only moral between husband and wife. But they would still be in an important way part of "my community" if they rejected this teaching. We have walked together for a time, and our walk together, our support of one another as we journey through what often seems an unexplored wilderness, has bound us together.

These people have a wide variety of vocations, and they've helped me to see the diversity of ways in which gay, same-sex attracted, or LGBT Christians can pour out our lives in love. Some are married, as I mentioned; some live in intentional communities; some find their vocation in service to those in need, in devoted friendship, or in caring for their family of origin; some are in celibate partnerships; some are called to art or to teaching.

Through my friendships with other "gay Christians" (again, for want of a better short phrase), I've seen how brutally unwelcoming our churches can be. It's hard to find people in our community who *haven't* been treated as inherently suspect outsiders; rejected, fired, or otherwise discriminated against; told that they must have been abused even when they know they weren't (or, conversely, told that the abuse they suffered was their own fault for being gay); or in a hundred other ways told that they weren't welcome. And keep in mind that I'm talking here only about people who accept and do their best to live according to the Christian teaching on homosexual acts.[2] Part of the reason many of these people seek out other gay Christians is that they need a refuge from their larger church community.

---

[2] I can't say "the Christian sexual ethic", because obviously Protestants, Orthodox, and Catholics differ on features of sexual ethics unrelated to homosexuality.

And this is why, in a different but real sense, gay Christians who *don't* accept the Christian sexual ethic are my community, too: people like us have often been mistreated in the same ways. (I was at a retreat with a group of people of different sexual orientations, where many of the straight people were shocked to learn that *all* of the not-straight people had either been physically attacked for our orientation or had close friends who were attacked.) I went to the Gay Christian Network conference this year, and heard from so many people who had been deeply damaged by the way their churches addressed homosexuality and gay people. The churches have not treated homosexual acts as simply one form of sin among others. We have treated homosexuality as if it separates someone from God, and we have cast people out of the Church simply for experiencing same-sex attraction and trying to figure out what that means.

We will never be fully at home in this life, not even in the Church. Gay, straight, same-sex attracted—this is true for all of us. But Christians have made so many of our churches and institutions not havens for gay people, but hostile fortresses.

Good theology is important. But I don't think we will get good theology unless and until we view gay and same-sex-attracted people without especial suspicion; unless we form communities where vocations other than priesthood and marriage are recognized and honored; unless gay people view our churches as refuges, places where we have more opportunities to love and serve than we do in the secular world— not fewer.

The question that has shaped most of my writing is, how is God calling gay or same-sex attracted people to pour out our lives in love? But there is another question, equally pressing: How can we make our churches refuges for *all* the exiles?

Breaking Free

David Prosen

My family consisted of my father, mother, and my younger sister, Darlene. My mother and I always had a good relationship, but my father and I did not. He was an alcoholic and often physically abused me.

While growing up, my dad tried to teach me the things in life that he enjoyed, such as carpentry and landscaping. Sadly, it would always end with him losing his patience, screaming obscenities, and calling me names. My dad never taught me sports such as baseball or football. At school, when it was time to divide into teams, I was one of the last picked. The team that ended up having me loudly complained and made it clear that I was not like them.

Everything associated with masculinity brought me much panic. As a child, I didn't enjoy playing with cars and toy guns. Instead, I enjoyed role-playing games such as house and, yes, even dolls. For as long as I can remember, I had an attraction to the same gender. When I reached puberty, this attraction intensified and brought me much turmoil. This confirmed to me that my male peers were right: I was different.

At about age fifteen, an older male befriended me. I began to look up to him as an older brother. One night, this friendship was betrayed when he took advantage of me sexually. He played many mind games and emotionally abused me. I sank into a deep despair as this sinful behavior continued for three months. I then decided to give Jesus a chance. At first, I was on an emotional high, but despite my years of catechism classes, I didn't understand my faith or the sacraments. For example, I didn't recognize the sustaining power of the Real Presence of Jesus in

Reprinted with permission of Catholics United for the Faith, cuf.org. This article, "Breaking Free from Homosexuality—One Man's Journey to Life in Christ", originally appeared in the January/February 2005 edition of *Lay Witness Magazine*.

the Eucharist. When the emotional high left, I became very lonely and felt once again that I didn't fit in.

Numbing the Pain

I began using marijuana and alcohol to help numb the pain. Once I turned eighteen, I went to my first gay bar. At first it was exhilarating. I felt like I finally could be myself, but the emptiness only worsened and I relied even more heavily on substances to help deal with the pain. I had lived an active "gay" life for two years, but was given a special grace and realized how sinful I had been. From this point on I turned my life over to Christ several times but, again, still not understanding that conversion is an ongoing, daily process by which God's grace transforms us. I would always end up falling back into the bondage of sin and heading deeper into darkness. After one of these falls, I learned of places where one could go to have promiscuous sex. I so desperately wanted to be held and loved that I fell into a horrendous cycle of addiction. I would want to be held, fall into sin, feel worse, do it again to feel better, feel even worse, and on and on and on.

In the midst of all this pain, my sister, to whom I was very close, suddenly collapsed with a heart attack and died instantly at the age of twenty-one. Her death forced me to face my own mortality. I realized I needed to work seriously at building a strong foundation on Christ, instead of looking for the emotional highs that I had depended on in the past.

Light in the Darkness

I was chaste for five and half years by God's grace, and some awesome things started happening. I quit alcohol and drugs and completely dropped out of the "gay" scene. Also, God helped me forgive my dad, and the relationship between us improved.

But I wasn't able to see these amazing things God was doing, because every day was a living hell for me filled with shame. When I saw someone good-looking, I would experience biological reactions in my body such as sweaty palms, heart racing, or "butterflies" in my stomach. I experienced these many times daily, and every time I begged God for a cure, but the attraction never went away. Some people said, "You don't have enough faith." Others said, "You must be sinning in some other area of your life." These statements only added to my shame. One day, a friend of mine said, "David, maybe God isn't curing you because maybe there isn't anything wrong with being homosexual." After much thought, I decided she might be right.

Although I went back into living a gay lifestyle, I believe God used this imperfect situation to teach me some truths about what love really is. He never let go of me, even when I let go of him. One day, I felt God say to my heart, "Yes, you never chose this attraction, but you can choose whether or not you will act on it." I picked up the *Catechism of the Catholic Church* and learned that this was a trial, and that we all have our trials and crosses to carry. "Then Jesus told his disciples, 'If any man would come after me, let him deny himself and take up his cross and follow me'" (Mt 16:24). He gives us the graces to carry our crosses; all we have to do is ask him and be open to these graces. If it weren't for crosses such as Darlene's death, I am sure that I would be spiritually and physically dead.

Ongoing Healing

I enrolled at Franciscan University of Steubenville a few years later. I read Dr. Gerard J. M. van den Aardweg's book *The Battle for Normality: A Guide for (Self-) Therapy for Homosexuality*.[1] I learned that the attraction I had toward males was actually an admiration of those who had masculine or physical traits that I felt I lacked as a child. In puberty, this admiration became sexualized. In addition, I learned that when I was living the homosexual lifestyle, I was coveting what other men possessed. I was affirmed when men who were more masculine or attractive than me showed an interest in me.

God brought into my life Catholic male friends who spent time with me by showing me how to throw, catch, and hit a ball. That child inside of me was getting the affirmation he had so desperately sought. And this

---

[1] G. van den Aardweg, *The Battle for Normality: A Guide for (Self-) Therapy for Homosexuality* (San Francisco: Ignatius Press, 1997).

was only the beginning. The Lord took me further in healing. I stepped into my courage, facing fears and taking risks in developing close relationships with several men. When actively living the gay life, I desperately sought an intimate relationship with a man. Then, I never thought I could be this close to other men the way I am now, today. In these relationships, I express my fears and my anger, as well as my hopes and dreams—and these men truly accept me. We are authentic with each other and as a result are able to help each other grow in our journeys with Christ. When I receive a hug from one of these men, it is more pleasurable and more fulfilling than any of the sexual acts of emptiness I had done in the past. This is what I have been desiring all of my life: true, authentic brotherly love, and I am so grateful for this.

Prior to the healings from God, I never saw myself as a man. I knew I wasn't a woman, but I didn't believe I was a man. The Lord brought me profound healing when I was working with a life coach. I was terrified of the locker room due to painful memories in high school. I joined a local gym, and my life coach helped me work through this. When I first went, there was a part of me that (although irrational) believed that the men were going to yell at me and tell me that I did not belong there. This did not happen. In fact, men actually talked to me. I learned that, yes, I do belong to the world of men and that I am masculine. All of my life, masculinity scared me, and as a gay man I desperately attempted to obtain it through other men because I thought I lacked it. But now, God has shown me that I am a masculine man. I no longer run from it but instead accept it as a part of who I am.

And as a result of these healings, I came to feel things toward the opposite sex that I hadn't felt before. Do I still struggle with same-sex attraction? Yes, but the attractions are less intense. For me, it's really not about sex. When the eroticized attraction happens, it's because I start to isolate, think negatively about myself, doubt my abilities, or compare myself to other men. However, if I give myself a break and accept myself for who I am as a Catholic man of God who does have what it takes, then the sexual charge dissipates. I don't know what God's will is for me, but I want to remain open to it whether it is the chaste single life or even marriage.

Married and Same-Sex Attracted: Are We Hiding the Light of the Gospel under a Basket?

Douglas Mainwaring

Intellectual Honesty and the Irresistible Truth of Natural Law

After my divorce, I lived as a gay man for ten years and was an outspoken promoter of same-sex marriage. In fact, my first-ever op-ed, published in the pages of the *Washington Post* in 2009,[1] was very *pro*-same-sex marriage. After all, it only seemed fair to me that gays should be able to marry each other. I remained an advocate for genderless marriage until I began to seriously consider *why* I supported it. I surprised myself with my conclusion: marriage is an immutable term and cannot be redefined. My unexpected fit of intellectual honesty then led to many more surprises.

I began to think about what I was doing and where my life was headed. I eventually came to conclude that divorcing my wife and attempting to create a family with another man was a grave injustice to my kids. They deserved to be raised by both their mom and dad under the same roof. Who was I to deny them this most basic of children's rights? I became determined to find a way to bring our family back together for the sake of our kids as they finished out their high school years.

But once I began thinking, reasoning, and examining my life, an extraordinary thing happened: I couldn't stop. For instance, at first I was willing to own up to the fact that I had hurt our children through our divorce and concluded that I needed to repair that wrongdoing.

Portions of this essay are adapted from pieces previously published at *Public Discourse*. Reprinted with permission.

[1] Doug Mainwaring, "The Wrong Way to Win the Right to Marry", *Washington Post*, November 12, 2009.

But hadn't a grave injustice also been inflicted on my wife? Against our families and friends who had always supported us?

Where and when should I draw the line with reason? With examining my conscience? With looking at the facts and making decisions based not simply on what I want or what I think is good for me, but based on truths which are absolute? Ultimately I chose to lead a chaste life. In view of the facts, in view of the constant testimony of nature all around me, it was the only reasonable thing to do.

Reason lead me to acknowledge natural law, which led me to begin rejecting some of my former ways of thinking and acting. Reason alone was enough to lead me to make an about-face and change the direction of my life. Then quite amazingly, natural law and reason working together in turn led me to recognize and acknowledge God's existence. And once I acknowledged God's existence, again there was only one reasonable thing to do: I asked Jesus Christ to take the throne of my life, and I became determined to reject the emptiness of my self-centered ways and futile thinking.

In the end I returned to full communion with the Catholic Church, but my choice to remain ever faithful to my wife predated my embrace of faith by a full two years. And although I had only hoped for peaceful coexistence with my then ex-wife as we agreed to join forces for a few years for the sake of the kids, I was met with another wonderful surprise. We found our relationship repairing itself day by day, and our love rekindled. And while our kids are now long past high school age, there's no question about the future of our marriage: *'Til death do us part.*

Although as a young person I often felt very much alone dealing with same-sex attraction (SSA), I more and more found myself buoyed by God's grace. When I called out to God, he answered. Looking back, I marvel at the many ways the Holy Spirit led me to truth, sometimes enabling me to make an honest assessment of myself, but wonderfully, more often than not, about the nature of God and his amazing plan for mankind. Through the Holy Spirit I came to have a personal relationship with Jesus Christ, and this helped me to embrace and understand more fully God's love.

As a child, I often experienced the stirrings of SSA. By the time I was a teenager, the urges were full-throttled. Yet, even from a very young age, I inwardly sensed something was not quite right. I knew that somehow I was different and felt apart from others—the universal experience of almost every self-identified gay or lesbian.

Nowadays it's nearly unanimously agreed that this comes from societal pressure exerted to conform to heteronormativity—that exterior cultural pressures are what causes that sense of being "different" and not "fitting in" in same-sex attracted young people, resulting in depression or worse. It seems to me that the opposite is true: there was a powerful, innate *interior* recognition that I was different. It wasn't society teaching me this or accusing me, disenfranchising me in the process; no, I simply knew it deep within my own soul from a young age. My own conscience was speaking to me, leading me to self-understanding.

In retrospect, I don't think there were actually significant exterior forces acting upon my life to make me feel this way. I was judged by no one because no one knew. Why would they even suspect? I didn't fit TV's stereotypical profile of a gay guy. When I was old enough to work, I worked as a carpenter with a local homebuilder. By the time I was seventeen, I had earned my private pilot's license and was on my way to a prestigious East Coast university. One of the most beautiful girls in school was my prom date. Yet, still there was always that gnawing self-awareness within.

The world tells me and others who are same-sex attracted to blame others for any discomfort we feel—perhaps our parents, the Church, or society at large. But to do so I would have to deny what I know to be true. My self-understanding wasn't inflicted upon me; its source was my perfectly functioning faculties of reason and conscience.

Although I had never heard of the term "complementarity", I was well acquainted with the truth that was all around me. I was created male, and no matter my predilections, I could look beyond those to understand that I was created to give myself fully, not to another male, but to someone who would one day be my wife.

False Choices

In his book *Denial*,[2] gay marriage activist Jonathan Rauch has asserted that being fully accepted as gay, both by himself and by others, isn't what fulfilled his life. Only being able to call himself and his male partner "husband" is what has truly brought healing and wholeness. He has

[2]Jonathan Rauch, *Denial: My 25 Years without a Soul* (Washington, D.C.: Atlantic Books, 2013), Kindle edition, http://www.amazon.com/Denial-Years-Without-Kindle-Single-ebook/dp/B00CLJAMII.

argued that only access to the institution of marriage can make gays and lesbians whole. Anything short of this will deny happiness and fulfillment, already available to everyone who is not gay. This sort of view is now treated as conventional wisdom.

Rauch's story implies that the long arc of the moral universe bends not toward "gay rights" or "acceptance" but to same-sex marriage—that this is the one and only way that justice can be secured for gay men and lesbians. LGBT (lesbian, gay, bisexual, and transgender) activists often present this Hobson's choice to those who have experienced SSA, especially young people: "Either jump out of the closet, join the celebration, make being gay or lesbian the dominant characteristic of your life and the sole foundation of your identity, and join the same-sex marriage lobby—or remain 'closeted', deny yourself, choose a false identity, become depressed, and risk suicide." This tactic purposefully suppresses the truth that there are many other options available to those who are attracted to persons of the same sex.

Many of us who are same-sex attracted know intuitively—in the very core of our beings—that this Hobson's choice can't possibly be all that the world has to offer. Many of us reject this narrative, not because of self-loathing, as name-calling activists insist, but because we are able to make an adult judgment based on reason and nature. Many same-sex attracted men and women have found great joy and fulfillment in heterosexual marriage. Others find joy in close same-sex relationships that do not become sexual and are never meant to be carnal.

Whereas LGBT activists seek to limit the options of the same-sex attracted, new voices have appeared on the scene to open wide the door to diverse choices. Voice(s) of Hope,[3] a website created by same-sex-attracted members of the Church of Jesus Christ of Latter Day Saints, is one such effort. In short videos, often seated next to their (opposite-sex) spouses, same-sex-attracted men and women testify to the choices—choices that go against the script the LGBT lobby promotes—that have given them profound joy: accepting themselves, but directing their love toward different ends.

Voice(s) of Hope delivers a self-affirming message that many hunger to hear. Since its inception just two years ago, the site has had 540,000 page views and over 175,000 unique users. Same-sex attracted men and

---

[3] The website Voice(s) of Hope can be found at http://www.ldsvoicesofhope.org/.

women around the world are starving for the very message that many LGBT activists seek to suppress.

The Promise and Necessity of Gay Marriage: Battling Media Myth

Even within the self-identified gay community, same-sex marriage appears to hold neither universal appeal nor the ultimately satisfying answer that has been promised. Many who are same-sex attracted question the wisdom of changing the definition of marriage, especially with regard to its impact on children. And while most major media present same-sex marriage as the only option to promote the wholeness and happiness of gays and lesbians, there are in reality many options available that respect natural law in general and complementarity in particular.

Media reporting has always led the nation to believe that there is a huge, pent-up demand for same-sex marriage. This is a fabrication. For instance, heading into Sunday, July 24, 2011—the first day that same-sex couples could legally wed in New York City—officials projected that twenty-five hundred couples might show up to get married. So they devised a lottery system to handle what they thought would be an overwhelming demand for same-sex marriage ceremonies. In the end, only 823 couples signed up—less than one-third of the anticipated demand.[4]

I recently spearheaded the writing of an amicus brief for the United States Supreme Court concerning the Sixth Circuit Court of Appeals' consolidated same-sex marriage cases. Research reveals that "many self-identifying LGB do not choose same-sex romantic relationships at all."[5] Also, a significant number choose *opposite-sex* relationships. Gates' study of the NHIS reveals that, "[a]mong bisexual adults with children, 51% were married with a different-sex spouse, 11% had a different-sex

---

[4]Chris Hawley, "New York Gay Marriage: First Gay Couples Marry at Midnight", *Huffington Post*, July 24, 2011, http://www.huffingtonpost.com/2011/07/24/new-york-gay -marriage_n_907901.html.

[5]"Brief of Amici Curiae for Same-Sex Attracted Men and Their Wives in Support of Respondents and Affirmance", April 3, 2015, p. 24. *Obergefell v. Hodges*, S. Ct. No. 14-556 (2014), http://sblog.s3.amazonaws.com/wp-content/uploads/2015/04/14-556bsacSame-Sex AttractedMenandTheirWives.pdf.

unmarried partner, and [only] 4% had a same-sex spouse or partner."
Even "[a]mong adults who identified as gay or lesbian and were raising
children, 18% had a different-sex married spouse and 4% had a different-
sex unmarried partner."[6]

Why would almost two-thirds of bisexual adults with children and
more than a fifth of gay or lesbian adults with children elect man-
woman relationships, principally man-woman marriage? While in
times past such relationships were often the only legal and culturally
acceptable options, in today's welcoming climate, the decision of
same-sex-attracted men and women to marry and remain married to
opposite-sex spouses is a testament to the uniqueness of man-woman
marriage as a familial relationship.

There are also many who are in gay or lesbian relationships who
reject the notion that marriage should be redefined. While they are often
too intimidated to speak out for fear of rejection, the gay community
seems to have "voted with its feet" against same-sex marriage.

The William's Institute at UCLA, the nation's preeminent LGBT
think tank, provides some important statistics. The total LGBT population in the United States is about 9 million, or 3.5 percent,[7] and of
those, a little less than half (1.7 percent) identify as exclusively gay or lesbian. There are 690,000 same-sex couples in the United States, of whom
130,000 are now married couples.[8] This means that only a little less
than 3 percent of the LGBT community has chosen same-sex marriage.
Given that same-sex marriage is now available in thirty-seven states and
the District of Columbia, and has been available in some states for up to
eleven years, the number of same-sex marriages is rather small. It appears
that many gays and lesbians are not keen on gay marriage as anything
more than a claim of symbolic victory. Another way of looking at these
gay marriage statistics is that *more than 97 percent* of gays and lesbians *have*

---

[6] Ibid., p. 25. Quotations regarding the Gates' study of the NHIS are from Gary J. Gates,
"LBG Families and Relationships: Analyses of the 2013 National Health Interview Survey", Williams Institute, October 2014, http://williamsinstitute.law.ucla.edu/wp-content
/uploads/lgb-families-nhis-sep-2014.pdf.

[7] "How Many People Are Lesbian, Gay, Bisexual and Transgender?", Williams Institute,
April 2011, http://williamsinstitute.law.ucla.edu/research/census-lgbt-demographics-studies
/how-many-people-are-lesbian-gay-bisexual-and-transgender/.

[8] "LGB Families and Relationships: Analyses of the 2013 National Health Interview Survey", Williams Institute, October 2014, http://williamsinstitute.law.ucla.edu/wp-content
/uploads/lgb-families-nhis-sep-2014.pdf.

not chosen same-sex marriage. Demand for same-sex marriage among gays and lesbians appears to be anemic, appealing to just a very few.

The Message and Power of the Gospel Tower over Today's Conventional Wisdom Offered by the World

Those who are same-sex attracted often think they have been sentenced to a life of singlehood if they are to remain faithful to the gospel. For some, this may well be the perfect path to live a life in faithfulness to God. But the Church and her pastors must be careful not to buy into a message that is similar to the one the world promotes. SSA does not make one ineligible for marriage. Thoughts and ideas like this come from the devil, the "father of lies" (Jn 8:44), who uses SSA to dehumanize us and decouple us from the magnificence of complementarity and the fullness of our humanity.

Many same-sex-attracted men have found lifelong happiness and fulfillment through marriage to their opposite-sex spouses. Here is what a few have to say:

> I am 52 years old, a father to five awesome kids, and have been happily married to my wife, Colleen, for 20 years. I am an actor, writer, marathon runner, and I have SSA.
>
> I may not have chosen to have SSA, but I certainly can choose to deal with it according to the dictates of my own conscious, mind, and faith. I stand as a voice to an alternative choice: that a man with SSA can be fulfilled emotionally, physically, and sexually in a traditional relationship and marriage, as the provider of the family and the patriarch of the home.[9]

> In my twenties I would have thought it was impossible that I could ever marry a woman, and even less possible that I would be happy and fulfilled in every way in that marriage. Eleven years and counting now, and I am happier than ever. That includes sexually, relationally, and emotionally. I don't blame people who doubt me—if I hadn't experienced it myself, I would find it dubious myself, it's so counter to the dominant cultural narrative out there. People like me have always been around, but we

---

[9] Kory Koontz to Doug Mainwaring, March 23, 2015. Used with permission.

seldom have any reason to speak up. I choose to do so now not out of any desire to help myself, but to advocate for those who are in the position I was in in my twenties and early thirties, and even more, for the children whom I believe deserve (if at all possible) to be raised by their biological parents if at all possible.[10]

I don't remember ever being attracted to someone of the opposite sex since my earliest memories. As a boy, I kept my feelings to myself knowing I would not be accepted if anyone knew how I felt. I joined the United States Marine Corps to learn how to be a man and learn masculine characteristics I lacked. After 6 years of service, I fell in love with the only woman I have ever been attracted to and we were married. We've had the privilege of seeing our children grow to maturity in a loving home as husband and wife. My greatest happiness in life has come from the privilege and responsibility of raising my family in a way I have chosen according to my beliefs. Grandchildren now visit our home and our family remains close more than thirty years since our marriage.

Had I followed my own desires and impulses toward other men, my life would be very different today.... My children have been told many times by their friends from single parent homes, just how fortunate they are to have both a Mom and a Dad even with our reversed non-traditional roles (I do the cooking and I hate sports—totally opposite of my dear wife, and it's ok).[11]

Here's the thing: all of these testimonials are from members of the Church of Christ of Latter Day Saints. We Catholics are perhaps too discreet, keeping the good news of our victorious lives and fruit of the gospel to ourselves at the expense of the greater common good. In this darkening age, what new thing might the Holy Spirit call us to do for the sake of evangelizing the world?

The Church and the World Languish, Waiting for the Witness of the Sons and Daughters of God

The Christian witness of same-sex-attracted Catholics must speak more loudly and become a greater presence in the world. Currently, we are

---

[10] Jeff Bennion to Doug Mainwaring, March 27, 2015. Used with permission.
[11] Joseph Allen Stith to Doug Mainwaring, March 25, 2015. Used with permission.

mostly silent. Because of this we have little or no influence on the world or within the Church, yet there are literally tens of millions who desperately need to hear the solid message the Church has to offer. It's as if we barely exist, and as if Christ and the Church have no real provision for us. But Christ and the Church most certainly do!

I wish the Catholic Church had an online vehicle like Voice(s) of Hope. I have approached many married Catholics I know who have successfully dealt with SSA their entire lives, but they all decline to tell their stories to the public because they have not disclosed their interior struggle with spouses or family. On the one hand, this makes perfect sense—these men and women don't want to disrupt their families or undermine the security of their marriages in any way. I get that.

Having said that, we are hiding our light under a bushel basket, especially during these very dark—and ever darkening—times! As the practice of homosexuality has become normalized, especially among millennials and younger, and as the race to redefine marriage to include genderless marriage grips the world, the world needs the testimony of men and women who have led triumphant, not self-indulgent, lives. There are hosts of Catholic same-sex-attracted men and women who respect natural law—quietly living their lives either as singles or married, faithful to their spouses and families. They don't seek to draw attention to themselves. They are quiet, unsung heroes. And they are legion!

Those who face SSA on their own need to know that there is a trail that has been quietly blazed that they can follow. If they don't know that trail is there, how can same-sex-attracted young people find their way to hope, joy, peace, and fulfillment? How else will they escape the relentless message of the world, which presents its dismal Hobson's choice? And frankly, this is not an out-of-the-way, rustic trail; it is a multilane highway to a life of grace. By not putting this highway on the map, we force young people to stumble around to find it on their own, a task that grows increasingly more difficult as the message of the world grows louder and more strident. For those of us who are same-sex attracted, "The institution of man-woman marriage is not an insult; it is an ensign, beckoning to everyone—regardless of sexual orientation—that the union of a man and a woman is uniquely significant because it is endowed with procreative power and complementary capacity."[12]

---

[12] "Brief of Amici Curiae for Same-Sex Attracted Men in Support of Respondents and Affirmation", *Obergefell*, S. Ct. No. 14-556, p. 5.

I would love to see the Church find a way to draw married men and women who experience SSA out so that their light might shine! Otherwise, we end up inadvertently hiding the power of the gospel. Perhaps a word from the Pope would call more of us out to the public square so that our voices, our testimony to natural law and the power of the gospel, might be heard. And through all this we have to remember that we each need the Holy Spirit to lead us to truth and grace, to enlighten us, and to help us to entrust our lives to God. Then the light of the gospel can be accepted, embraced, more deeply understood, and displayed through our lives.

From Pain to Peace

Bob and Susan Cavera

Devastated is perhaps the best word to describe our emotional and mental state upon learning that our youngest son struggled with same-sex attraction (SSA) and later embraced the gay lifestyle. We were grief-stricken, ashamed, and heartbroken. How could this have happened to him? To us? What did we do to cause this? How can we "fix" it? Where do we go for help? These feelings and questions became a part of our daily routine. Our deepest concern was for his spiritual, physical, and emotional well-being. It remains so to this very day. At first we didn't handle the news from our son very well. We objected. "God didn't make you this way", is what we said. In retrospect, we should have said, "We love you; we will always love you"—and wrapped our arms around him. Absorbed with our own pain, we failed to recognize the pain our son was in and had been in through most of his life.

Our son's revelation, that SSA was a factor in his life, shattered our peace about twenty-four years ago. It started us on a journey that led to Father John Harvey, the founder of Courage and EnCourage, and to the apostolate that he so lovingly shared with grieving parents. Meeting Father Harvey and attending our first Courage conference was the beginning of a journey that would move us from pain to peace. This journey to peace is certainly not a straight line between two points nor one that is ever finally achieved. As we sought help, read books, attended conferences, enlisted prayer partners, and counseled with professionals, we discovered that, in moving from pain to peace, we frequently moved back to pain. Father Paul Check, director of Courage/EnCourage International, often refers to EnCourage as a "Ministry of Tears", because parents are grieving the loss of their children. It is a spiritual, relational, and moral loss that causes parents and loved ones to grieve. This grief, if the situation remains unresolved, can last for years. Mourning for someone who is still living is extremely painful.

We have heard from many parents who, like us, were devastated, heartbroken, and frightened about the future. One response common to many parents is the desire to immediately "fix" the problem. The son or daughter is "broken" and thus "fixable". This "I can fix you" response often occurs early in the revelation, usually from the father (but not exclusively), and may last for a time. Parents reason that if we can locate the source of the problem or find the "right" counselor, we can resolve the issue satisfactorily and get on with our lives. That approach usually doesn't work and can alienate the son or daughter.

The younger the son or daughter is when his or her "coming-out" occurs, the greater the potential for a positive outcome of any effort at intervention. Our son was in his late teens when this first came to light, but he soon left home and was on his own. Because of the influence of popular culture, it is not uncommon for children even in middle school to make this declaration to Mom and Dad. Public schools have clubs and counselors who offer support and encouragement for teenagers who "come out". We have heard from many parents who arrange for counseling for their teen only to find out that the counselor, sometimes from a Catholic agency, encourages same-sex relationships. We recall an incident when the parents of an eighteen-year-old daughter sought counsel from a local Catholic college. They were told that homosexuality is like being born left-handed. It may be a little bit different, but a person is born that way, and to change it would cause irreparable damage. "Your daughter can't help who she is", they were told. A popular opinion often expressed by so-called Catholic scholars is that someday the Church will change. How tragic for the parents—and even more tragic for the daughter.

Parents who themselves are committed to Catholic teaching, who seek counsel from a faithful Catholic or Christian therapist, and who diligently work together on their relationship with their child have the best opportunity for success.

Sons or daughters out of college, living away from home and thus frequently beyond parental control, are a greater challenge. They may very well have expressed the view that "this is who I am and who I want to be, so—lay off." It is very important that parents attempt to maintain a relationship with their children. Without a relationship, we will have little or no influence. This doesn't mean that we affirm this newly asserted identity. We clearly communicate the truth about SSA as outlined in the *Catechism of the Catholic Church*,[1] and then we work on maintaining a relationship with our children. We don't need to repeat Church teaching at every visit. Indeed, one statement of belief is enough, unless the son or daughter brings up the topic. It should be noted that the older the son or daughter is, the more dependent he or she is on the "gay" support system that offers comfort. To step away from this network is very difficult, for it means being rejected by the very people with whom one identifies. When a person intends to pursue chastity, it is not unusual for that "gay" support system to turn against him or her in a hurtful manner.

When our son revealed his struggle, we went to see our pastor. Thankfully our pastor was a faithful priest who did not send us into that entangled swamp of false teaching and enabling behavior that surrounds this issue. We remember our pastor saying that he knew little about the subject but was willing to learn with us. (Remember—this was twenty-four years ago.) How grateful we were! We have heard from several parents that when they approached their parish priest they were told that they, the parents, were the ones with the problem and *not* their son or daughter. Their priest recommended *PFLAG* (Parents and Friends of Lesbians and Gays) or *Dignity*, *Fortunate Families*, or *New Ways* Ministries. These pseudo-Catholic organizations believe it is possible to be loving without honoring truth, and thus deceive parents.

With the grace of God, along with a faithful pastor and a supportive bishop, we were permitted to introduce Courage and EnCourage into our diocese. We had always intended from the beginning to be under the authority of the Church, and this was, indeed, an answer to prayer.

Our own experience of starting our EnCourage group was, however, a bit rocky at first. We set the meeting times, sent out notices to the bulletin editors in the diocesan parishes, brought treats and resources, and waited for the deluge of parents and loved ones to come to the EnCourage meeting. No one came. We did this for three months. We dragged our books and resources back and forth, minus the treats (we ate those). We went to our pastor and suggested that we meet quarterly. It would save us a hassle and keep us from eating too much unhealthy food. "No," he said, "I want you to meet every month regardless of

---

[1] *Catechism of the Catholic Church*, 2nd ed. (Washington, D.C.: Libreria Editrice Vaticana—United States Conference of Catholic Bishops, 2000), nos. 2357–59.

attendance or lack thereof and use this time for prayer." We agreed. Sure enough, parents, siblings, and loved ones began to come.

Attending a meeting and having to admit that there is a problem is difficult for many. They haven't told anyone; they feel embarrassed, ashamed, grieved, and discouraged. Do the same parents or siblings come week after week? No. Some participants of our diocesan EnCourage group come regularly, some come for a while and then stop coming, and others come occasionally, often in response to a crisis. We do mail a monthly letter, either electronically or via regular mail, and we always include an informational or spiritual article. Many who don't attend or can't attend rely on our mailing for maintaining a connection. The feeling of being connected to the truth is important to many parents. Knowing the truth is there and that it can be accessed at any time gives comfort.

Parents and family members often come because this issue is so divisive. Our experience is that this divisiveness frequently depends on how the parents respond to their loved one. If every encounter with the son or daughter results in an argument, the relationship will suffer. Father Harvey would always remind us, "If you don't have a relationship, then you don't have any influence." Maintain the relationship, if at all possible, but not at all costs. Stop arguing and start loving, but not at the expense of truth. Yet, our communication must not be exclusively about same-sex attraction; in fact, that should be a topic seldom mentioned. Our loved ones know or should know what we believe regarding SSA, so we don't need to bring it up again and again. What is important is that we hug them, love them, listen to them, and, if possible, spend time with them. We persevere in patient hope, waiting for the opportunity to share God's healing truth in love, with encouragement.

It is not only the relationship with one's child that can suffer. Sadly, we have witnessed couples divorce over this issue and siblings and other family members who stop communicating. We have heard stories of family reunions that exclude those faithful to Church teaching and holidays that become tense and hostile instead of welcoming and joyful.

With gay "marriage" prominently in the news, many families struggle with how to respond to same-sex situations such as wedding invitations or social events. One parent was asked to help a "lesbian" daughter pick out a wedding dress; many are asked to participate as witnesses, and some are asked to pay for the event. Whether the ceremony is religious or civil, we do not recommend that parents attend it, nor should they attend the reception. The parents' presence at either event is an implicit witness to others, especially to younger siblings, and should be avoided. Unfortunately, the cost to parents for not cooperating is frequently separation and isolation.

If there are younger siblings in the family, the parents need to be concerned about the relationship of the younger sibling to the brother or sister who has made public his or her SSA. For example, a fourteen-year-old brother may try to explain to his friends and classmates that the brother he loves and idolizes is "marrying" his same-sex "partner". This can be very difficult. One couple shared how they called a family meeting to discuss how best to love a son with SSA without compromising the truth and, at the same time, allowing his nieces and nephews to maintain a relationship with their uncle. This works well if there is agreement, but often there is not.

Another situation that frequently presents itself to parents and siblings is the son coming home for an overnight visit and bringing his "partner". Parents should feel comfortable in setting house rules just as if a son were bringing his girlfriend home for an overnight visit. Be aware that parents who establish such boundaries may be accused of narrow-mindedness.

Some years ago, as we encountered so many parents trying to understand and relate to their same-sex-attracted loved ones, we discerned four principles that have helped us and others move from pain to peace.

Pray

Seek to deepen your relationship with our Lord Jesus Christ and his Blessed Mother. Surrender your loved one to the Lord, by placing him at the foot of the cross. Attend daily Mass if possible; pray the Rosary, the Divine Mercy Chaplet, or the Chaplet of the Precious Blood. Participate in eucharistic adoration. Saturate yourself in God's Word; pray the Liturgy of the Hours and other spiritual readings such as the *Magnificat*. Have a Mass said for the intention of your loved one on special days such as a birthday or saint's day. Add a sixth decade to your daily Rosary dedicated to the Immaculate Conception for her intercession for the gift of chastity. Divide the week into daily prayer intentions. For example, on Thursdays we pray for Courage and EnCourage and our SSA loved ones. If at all possible, pray daily with a supportive person, such as your spouse, a dear friend, or a trusted family member. Pray for a "hedge of protection" around all your children and grandchildren, that they will embrace the Church's teaching on chastity. Pray in reparation for the sins of same-sex behavior in the tradition of Saint Margaret Mary Alacoque. Seek the intercession of patron saints or special saints such as Saint Monica, Saint Joseph, or Saint Charles L'Wanga.

Prepare (Study)

Educate yourselves on this issue. Read Father John Harvey's books: *The Truth about Homosexuality* and *Homosexuality and the Catholic Church*. Acquire and share the DVD *Desire of the Everlasting Hills*. Numerous resources are available through Courage and EnCourage. You need to learn to answer such questions as the following: Aren't people born that way? Will counseling cause mental and emotional damage? Isn't Courage all about change? Aren't Courage and EnCourage hateful and mean-spirited? The answer to all these questions is no, but you need to learn not only that the answer is no but why it is.

Persevere in Prayer

Persevere in the face of disappointments and obstacles. Connect with friends and family members who are prayer warriors and who will maintain confidentiality. Do not isolate yourselves! Resist discouragement, and embrace the fellowship that participating in an EnCourage group affords you. Remember, what you have no control over, you have no responsibility for.

Proclaim

Don't just sit by; become proactive! Go to your pastor and share Courage and EnCourage with him. Chances are he doesn't know much about Courage or about current resources. Seek to become a resource.

It is very important that you discern how to share (or not share) with other family members. It is not unusual to find that we are at odds with other family members regarding this issue. We can encounter the "throw-the-bum-out" attitude, and that would be unfortunate, but more likely we will encounter family members who approve same-sex behavior and will seek to enable the behavior. These family members and friends may challenge our views and seek to promote total acceptance of the behavior. Our responsibility is to be prepared to proclaim the truth in love. Please remember: to share the truth without love is hurtful; to share love and compassion without the truth is deceitful.

When we introduced our pastor to the five goals of Courage—(1) chastity, (2) the pursuit of holiness through daily Mass and frequent reception of the Eucharist, (3) regular use of the Sacrament of Reconciliation, (4) the formation of chaste friendships, and (5) being a good example to others—he said: "This is the way we all should lead our lives, not just persons with same-sex attraction."

We recommend that pastors pray for Courage and for all persons with same-sex attraction to lead chaste and holy lives, as well as pray for their families and friends. We urge priests and deacons to speak the truth in a homily about the issue of same-sex marriage and other disordered behaviors. They should be able to recommend therapists who are faithful to Catholic teaching—men to counsel with men and women with women. They should publish the availability of the Courage/EnCourage meetings in the bulletin and include a parish or diocesan phone number and e-mail address. To ensure confidentiality, meeting locations should not be published. Brochures, DVDs, and books about same-sex issues should contain appropriate contact information. And finally, they should invite speakers to help parishioners understand the Church's teaching on same-sex issues and learn how to be loving to those who experience SSA.

Parents' interaction with loved ones can be very stressful to their relationship. This issue should not be the only focus of parents' lives; it will drain their energy. Encourage parents to look for opportunities to deepen their relationship with one another. Plan fun times together. Parents should also be made aware that viewing, reading, and listening to same-sex attraction materials can be emotionally upsetting, especially the "gay rights" materials.

Archbishop Charles Chaput observed,

> Léon Bloy, the French Catholic writer and convert from Judaism, once
> said, "Man has places in his heart which do not yet exist, and into them
> enters suffering, in order that they may have existence." Just about all of
> Christian scholarship on the nature of suffering can be reduced to these
> few simple words. Suffering can bend and break us. But it can also *break
> us open* to become the persons God intended us to be. It depends on what
> we do with the pain. If we offer it back to God, He will use it to do
> great things in us and through us, because suffering is fertile. It can grow
> new life.[2]

It is not easy to be a parent to a loved one who embraces homosexuality and the homosexual lifestyle. The cross is never easy. Embraced
rightly, it will be the source of great graces to you and others.

---

[2] Archbishop Charles Chaput, introduction to *Beyond Gay*, by David Morrison (Hunting-
ton, Ind.: Our Sunday Visitor, 1999), p. 11.

Pastoral

Do No Harm: Considerations in Supporting Youth with Same-Sex Attraction

Janelle Hallman, Ph.D.

One of the four basic ethical principles or values ascribed by all medical and mental health professionals is the mandate first "to *do no harm*". Associated with this is the principle of beneficence, which means that we, as ethical professionals, agree to always strive to act or work toward the patient's or client's benefit or best interests. Additional ethical values include honoring each individual's autonomy or right to self-determination. Made in the very image of God, all individuals have inherent dignity and therefore deserve our respect.

Whether one is a mental health professional, clergy, or nonprofessional, often these basic ethical principles become clouded or even forgotten when we are confronted with moral issues that confuse, frighten, or horrify us. Homosexuality is often one of those issues. When a young person begins to disclose that he or she is experiencing same-sex attraction (SSA), it is natural for us to want to save or rescue this young soul from what we believe may be dangerous, not only emotionally and physically, but spiritually. So when a fellow believer is pondering the pursuit of what we judge to be a clearly sinful and therefore hazardous path, it is not uncommon for us to believe that the most important value in the moment is to alert the individual of the potential sin or to attempt to turn him or her from sinful ways. The truth is, many of us have actually been taught that this is *always* the most superior (or urgent), godliest, or righteous response. However, if we are driven by the energy to moralize and help others to see their sinful ways, we might also inadvertently shame, guilt, manipulate, coerce, accuse, or even unconsciously threaten them with a refusal to continue in relationship. Instead of inviting the person in front of us to speak and share his or her story or struggle, we often do all the speaking, pontificating on such maxims as God's design or intent for sexuality and the consequences of sin. Worse, we might even blame this unsuspecting "sinner" for all of *our* tumultuous or negative emotions such as shock, confusion, fear, or our own guilt and shame.

Needless to say, after several decades of sitting with Christian men and women with SSA, I have rarely, if ever, found this approach to be beneficial, especially at the onset of their disclosure about their same-sex feelings. Sadly, more often than not, this approach does *do harm* to the recipient of our exhortation. Typically what the person was probably hoping for and needing was just a caring, listening ear. Rarely do discussions focused on morality and behavior provide the kind of support that these individuals need to sustain the arduous journey ahead. Neither do they bolster a person's internal sense of belovedness as God's precious child. This is especially true for youth who are experiencing SSA.

In highlighting the potential negative impact of responding to people with SSA from a fear-based or moralizing perspective, I do not intend to judge, shame, or guilt anyone. Rather, I want to lay the foundation for a different type of response and ongoing pastoral care that is rooted in unconditional love and consideration for a young person's greater developmental needs, since these can often overshadow the immediate presenting issue of SSA. In part 1 of this chapter, I will discuss the various cultural and psychological points that lead me to believe it is necessary to cultivate a deeply sensitive and heart-based style of responding to youth with SSA, while in part 2 I will provide practical ways of communicating with and relating to this special group of young people.

Part 1: Understanding the Need

I am deeply struck by the attitude and presence with which Jesus approached people confused about their sexual longings and trapped in social shame. When conversing with the woman at the well (which by the way is amazing in and of itself since she was considered unclean and therefore not approachable by "good" Jews), Jesus first granted her dignity by asking her for a favor (see Jn 4:1–42). As you know, this alone surprised the woman who was expecting to be ignored or avoided. Throughout their conversation, he spoke gently and respectfully, giving of himself, affirming her for her truthfulness, and validating her desire and passion to worship the one true God. I believe it was his

Personhood, or *who* Jesus was (how he treated her), that inspired her to share the good news of his "knowing about her but loving her at the same time". For this outcast, to be known for all that she had done and yet respected and loved felt great! She had to tell others! While she may have turned from her sinful ways immediately, that is not stated. What is clear is that she had a complex journey ahead of her as she contemplated her deeper longings for living water in contrast to how she had previously attempted to quench her thirst. Now she knew of at least one Person who understood her predicament yet offered her grace, mercy, and compassion. She was no longer alone.

This is what our youth need. No young person wakes up one day and decides to be gay. Same-sex feelings typically emerge within a young person's experience as confusing and unwelcomed sensations or emotions. They were not manufactured or intentionally cultivated. They are often as surprising to the young person as they might be to the unsuspecting parents who first learn about their child's homosexuality. It is important, therefore, for us as pastoral caregivers to understand the various dimensions of these feelings if we are to be a safe place for youth to process their experiences.

In the most basic sense, same-sex feelings consist of a longing or desire to be close to others of the same sex. For many, these longings are *not* sexualized and in fact represent a very healthy personal drive to befriend and bond with others of the same sex. It is within friendships with others of the same sex that many of us continue to explore our maleness and femaleness, to gain understanding, appreciation for, and identification with others who are like us. In fact, friendships with others of the same sex are an incredibly important facet of healthy growth and development in preadolescent youth. There is no shame in having these innocent and legitimate love needs or longings for these needs to be met.

But for some, these longings or desires do indeed become eroticized, especially at the onset of puberty. Why this happens for some and not others is the subject of intense debate and scientific research, but what is most important for us to understand is that these erotic feelings emerge or are discovered by a young person without prior invitation or some intentional conjuring-up exercise. Once the young person acknowledges to himself the presence of eroticized SSAs, these feelings and sensations naturally become a very real (and rather large) component of a young person's lived experience as he attempts to move forward in terms of his inner and outer psycho-social development.

One of the most important components of healthy personal growth and development, as suggested by many psychodynamic and developmental theorists, is loving relationships or secure attachment. Without secure attachment or loving relationships, we wither and will often come to identify with the negative aspects of our experiences or self that produce shame, rejection, or worthlessness. In order to offer sound practices of pastoral care (and parenting) for these youth, we must consider the young person's basic and ongoing need for mirroring relationships that reflect back to them their worth, value, and belovedness. It is within the environment of loving relationships that youth can fortify a solid and optimistic identity and positive sense of self, from which they will be able to make the difficult choices that commonly face young people in our contemporary culture, which is replete with constant and powerful temptations that excite their lust for pleasure without consequence. It is toward these ends that I direct the following discussions.

Even prior to disclosing their same-sex feelings to another, these young people are required to navigate their developmental journey toward becoming an adult with the added burden of making sense of their sexual feelings. Often this secret burden becomes unbearable. It is at this point that they may decide to disclose their feelings, usually in an attempt to gather support and reassure themselves of their belovedness and acceptability as a son or daughter. They do so, however, with much fear and trepidation. They know realistically that they may not receive the support desired but instead may be confronted with condemnation, judgment, hostility, and even rejection. It is an extremely vulnerable moment when they first speak the words "I think I might be gay." It is in this moment that we have a great opportunity to respond in a way that meets this young person's greatest need for love, grace, compassion, and committed relationship.

In an effort to cultivate compassion and provide practical knowledge of what life might look like for young people who "come out" as having SSA, I would like to share some disturbing statistics.[1] Even though

---

[1] See Joseph G. Kosciw et al., *The 2013 National School Climate Survey: The Experiences of Lesbian, Gay, Bisexual and Transgender Youth in Our Nation's Schools* (New York: Gay, Lesbian and Straight Education Network, 2013), http://www.glsen.org/sites/default/files/2013%20 National%20School%20Climate%20Survey%20Full%20Report_0.pdf. See also Sabra L. Katz-Wise and J.S. Hyde, "Victimization Experiences of Lesbian, Gay, and Bisexual Individuals: A Meta-Analysis", *Journal of Sex Research* 49 (2012): 142–67.

our contemporary culture appears to be gay-friendly, gay-accepting, and gay-affirming, based on popular media, the reality experienced by many gay youth and adult men and women with SSA is far from friendly. The negative attitudes and sentiments that many people with SSA encounter are also not necessarily arising out of religious circles. For example, recent research has found, within public school environments, 71 percent of students (ages thirteen through twenty-one) with SSA frequently hear the word "gay" used in negative ways. Of these students, 91 percent report feeling distressed by these types of references. Additionally, 65 percent of students with SSA frequently hear derogatory terms such as "dyke" or "fagot", while 56 percent hear negative remarks about their gender expression, such as being a sissy. Over half of students with SSA have been verbally harassed, 40 percent have been threatened, while at least a third report an actual experience of physical harassment or assault. Sadly, these youth also frequently hear extremely negative or homophobic remarks from their adult teachers and therefore do not report their experiences of harassment or assault to the school staff. Of students who did, 37 percent reported that the staff did nothing to intervene. Naturally, the majority of students with SSA feel unsafe or uncomfortable at school, and in an effort to avoid risk of verbal or physical abuse, they avoid many school functions. This then translates into social isolation for many of these youth—an extremely detrimental factor to their ongoing development and health.

Many adolescents who experience SSA, for fear of being the object of increased negative attitudes, verbal abuse, and, possibly, even physical abuse, will not disclose their sexual feelings, but will instead conceal their internal struggle, confusion, and possibly shame. This strategy is very common with youth who grow up within the Church. Many youth who are in the beginning stages of facing the reality that they have SSA may begin to internalize negative societal attitudes and beliefs such as "gay people are condemnable or somehow inherently bad". It is my firm conviction that we, within church communities, should be actively standing against such treatment and educating lay people and leadership in how to be open, respectful, and caring of adolescents who may be facing such conditions. As mentioned, adolescence is an extremely vulnerable time for a child's ultimate development and growth, and therefore mandates safe places for youth wherein they are provided support as they share, discuss, and question their feelings and thoughts as they relate to their sexuality.

Indeed, the decreased level of psychological well-being in youth with SSA is an extremely important topic for researchers and counselors alike. In general, youth with SSA report greater difficulty in parental relationships, friendships, and overall psychological functioning. These youth commonly report an increase in parental rejection and lack of support and worries about loss of friendships. Within this population, there are increased levels of isolation, alienation, fear of rejection, actual relational failures, and social marginalization. Many of these factors have in turn been related to an increase in depression, anxiety, suicidality, and lower self-esteem. Some researchers have suggested that actual or feared rejection from others, especially parents, is one of the most challenging factors developmentally for sexual minority youth.[2] Stressing the importance of safe and familiar places and unconditional love, these researchers sadly note that very few of these youth "receive the continuity of caregiving they need for a 'good enough' developmental experience, and many are [therefore] negatively impacted" as a result.[3]

For Christian youth who have been raised in a theological milieu that supports the notion that the sexual union of male and female serves as sacred symbol of Christ's (the Bridegroom) union with the Church (the Bride), there may be an even greater vulnerability to experience shame and stigmatization. To be stigmatized is to be not only "marked" as a person who deviates from some acceptable social standard,[4] such as biblical or Church prescripts, but to be "marked" in such a way that the entirety of one's self is assumed to be bad or wrong. It has been suggested that shame is a consequence of being stigmatized. It is not uncommon for Christian youth with SSA to receive condemning or threatening messages from their families, churches, and friends. Over the years, my clients have shared how they came to believe that they, as a person, were disgusting, sinful, immoral, unworthy, and rejectable before God and before others just because they had same-sex feelings. Many, if not most, had never even acted upon these feelings as adolescents or young adults.

---

[2]Deborah Tharinger and Greg Wells, "An Attachment Perspective on the Developmental Challenges of Gay and Lesbian Adolescents: The Need for Continuity of Caregiving from Family and Schools", *School Psychology Review* 29 (2000): 158–72.

[3]Ibid., p. 159.

[4]See Michael Lewis, "Shame and Stigma", in *Shame: Interpersonal Behavior, Psychopathology, and Culture,* edited by Paul Gilbert and Bernice Andrews (New York: Oxford University Press, 1998), pp. 126–40.

It is these internalized negative feelings of self-disgust, self-hatred, and stigma that can lead to unhealthy, addictive, and numbing behaviors, such as substance use, resulting in even more shame should the person engage in these behaviors. Further, if a stigmatized person, such as an adolescent growing up within the Church, is intentionally or unintentionally blamed by others for his stigmatized condition, and in this case it would be for his SSA, shame will heighten, increasing the chances of the adolescent or young adult taking on what has been called a shame-based identity.

There have been some studies that have suggested, therefore, that religious affiliation does not necessarily serve as a protective factor toward positive psychological functioning in youth with SSA. This is a very, very sad finding and should not be so. Instead of receiving nurturance, understanding, support, unconditional love, and grace, many Christian youth with SSA commonly feel stigmatized, misunderstood, rejected, and isolated, inadvertently believing that they are to blame for their feelings and are no longer acceptable or loved by God.

Over the years, it seems that several clichés with respect to homosexuality have been developed and regularly proclaimed by many Christians, such as "homosexuality is wrong" or "I don't agree with homosexuality." Unfortunately, I believe these types of statements are the very culprits that create an environment of stigma and shame for youth with SSA. What exactly do we mean by those statements? What is "homosexuality"? For people who experience SSA, there are multiple components to their sexuality (as is true for all people). There are sexual feelings, which are to be distinguished from sexual behavior, which both are to be distinguished from a sexual identity label: the name one might assign to one's self, such as gay, lesbian, or straight. All of these components must also be distinguished from the complex and abstract concept of sexual orientation.

When we make statements such as "homosexuality is wrong", we inadvertently "blanket" the entire person with our implicit judgment. Are we saying that the person with SSA is wrong? Or when we say, "I don't agree with homosexuality", are we stating that we don't agree with the fact that this person is, indeed, experiencing same-sex feelings (which will make you appear possibly stupid or in denial), or are we attempting to make a statement about the morality of same-sex sexual behavior? I can almost guarantee that a fifteen-year-old female who has recently started noticing that she is more drawn to her female friends than males is going to hear those statements as a blanket judgment against her personhood and, perhaps, value and worth as God's child. As clergy and lay who are committed to *do no harm*, we must exert effort to *think before we speak*.

We must also make the effort to take a step back and consider other common statements, such as "Homosexuality is not part of God's design or purpose", "You can't be a homosexual and a Christian", "The Bible says . . .", or, "I don't believe you are a homosexual", to ask if they are truly communicating love, understanding, and care for the young person who has SSA. On hearing these phrases, the young person might be left asking, "Am I not designed by God?" or "Am I not a Christian anymore?" Additionally, imagine what the parents of a fourteen-year-old male son who recently disclosed his same-sex feelings might feel when others make blanket statements that could potentially be condemning of their son. To make matters worse, the shame that the son may already be internalizing can potentially spread to the parents, especially when simplistic and therefore naïve statements such as "poor parenting causes homosexuality" are made. It is these types of experiences that have led many families who have been faithful Christians and churchgoers to confusedly detach or withdraw from their church community for fear of further shame, or, ultimately, rejection. The child and his family may then not only face estrangement from community but confusion and a possible sense of estrangement from God. This is untenable if we are going to strive to become the true Church or Body of Christ, which was and is to be given sacrificially and wholly to one another, treasuring, cherishing, and forgiving the beloved. It is imperative that we as people of faith begin to examine our words, actions, attitudes, and sentiments toward youth (and all people) who experience SSA.

I would like now to take a deeper look at how unsafe, condemning, or nonempathetic environments can ultimately affect, not only the well-being of Christian youth with SSA in general, but create a potential fragmentation of their internal sense of self. In this discussion, I rely on psychological theory and theology in framing my understanding of the internal dynamics of the development of a person's core sense of self as a valuable, unique, and worthy person (made in the image of God).

The basic tenets of certain psychological theories suggest that we fully develop or "become" our true selves (as created and destined by God) within relationships, but not just any relationship. A positive sense of self that is rooted in worth and value arises out of an attuned, empathic, supportive, and caring environment in which secure attachment to caregivers is established. This means, for example, that as a mother or father mirrors a child's worth and value by consistently caring for and attuning to a child's needs (which, by the way, demands sacrifice on the part of the parents) and empathizing with a baby's emotional world (like smiling when the baby is smiling), a baby or infant is able to internalize a sense of being ("I exist and it is okay to exist") and a sense of well-being ("I am well and have worth and value"). Through consistent attunement and caring, an infant is also being given the support to healthily develop emotional regulation. Sadly, breaches in attunement and care, such as inconsistency or unpredictability of parental response to the infant's cry or failure to provide regular eye contact or empathetic mirroring facial expressions, have severe negative consequences on a child's forming sense of self.

In order to develop a sense of wholeness and value as a person, we do not need absolute perfection from our relational mirrors, but what has been called a "good enough" parent or caregiver. No parent consistently attunes to, cares for, or accurately empathizes with every need or felt affective state of his or her child *all the time*. However, to the extent that the parent regularly repairs such failures with his or her child, the child is able to view his mother, for example, as an integrated whole. This is what is commonly known as a "good enough" mom.

Essentially, a "good enough" mom provides a child with enough consistent facial messages and caring gestures that communicate to the child his own worth. This also provides a model from which the child can begin to integrate a sense of self (knowing there is good with some bad) into a cohesive whole. If the mother exhibits severe inconsistency in attunement, empathy, or care of her child, or fails to repair these breaches, or is generally unresponsive, the child often forms a split image of his mother, so to speak. Mom is not a single cohesive object, but two: "bad mom" and "good mom". Mother is not whole and Mother is not predictable. Not only then is the child's mirror (mother) inconsistent and unpredictable; the child's emotional states become tumultuous and unpredictable, leaving the child's inner world split and chaotic. The child is left with the primal impression that to feel bad is to be bad. The core sense of self therefore forms around some impression of "badness". It is not uncommon then, that as the child grows, he begins to formulate what is referred to as an idealized false self. Instead of living out of the authentic truth of who he is, which according to the child's perception is "all bad", the child may begin to detach and deny aspects of his own personhood. For example, a child may unconsciously repress what he perceives as "badness" (such as his sensitivity or longing for closeness since these were the very things that seemed to cause him pain) and begin to fabricate and live out of a persona that he hopes will finally draw the loving attention and care from his primary mirrors. One common idealized false self is the "good boy" or "the perfectionist". On the other hand, some children will tend to repress their potential "goodness" (such as their true ability to care for others) and take on extremely negative false selves. These may be the kids that seem hell bent on gaining the title of "black sheep" within a family. Many of us spend a lifetime coming to terms with these false selves, letting go of our self-protective strategies and learning to trust God's truth about who we are as his children.

So, how does this apply to adolescents who are beginning to experience SSA? Within this discussion it is first important to note that we, as persons, develop across our lifespan. Therefore, the mirrors (or people) that ultimately help us to develop, understand who we are, and internalize our core value not only include parents but other relatives, friends, spiritual leaders, teachers, work associates, and even society at large. They all matter. So let's walk through a vignette involving a fourteen-year-old son. Let's assume that up until now, for the most part, he has felt loved, accepted, encouraged, and supported by his parents, his church community, friends, relatives, and all social networks. (During adolescence, not only do the parents continue to have an important part in their child's life, but friends and social communities also hold a pervasive sway in communicating to the adolescent worth, value, and identity.) But in the past year or so, this beloved son has become increasingly aware that he is strongly pulled to members of the same sex and is not experiencing the interest or energy around opposite-sex romantic attractions. He is confused, scared, and aware of being very alone as he attempts to understand and navigate these feelings. At some point, the pressure builds and he comes to the conclusion that he must tell someone about his struggle. He knows he's not going to make it on his own. However, he also reflects on his history with the important people in his life in an effort to determine who might be a safe confidante.

Listen to some thoughts shared by youth who were at the precipice of such a disclosure. One young woman notes, "My family makes a big deal out of anyone who is homosexual, they talk about it like it is a disease or something. This will make it very difficult to 'come out' ".[5] Another fifteen-year-old female says, "Telling my parents is out of the question. They think homosexuality is a perversion and liken it to paedophilia and things like that which angers me".[6] A sixteen-year-old son commented that "my parents aren't very accepting of homosexuals, not discriminatory, but they don't think it is 'normal', whatever normal is.... So I haven't talked to them".[7] Children's worst fear, no matter how old they are, is to be ultimately rejected and cut off from their parents. All children still need to know that they are loved and that they belong, *no matter what*. All children also need to be heard, understood, and cared for in their unique experiences and struggles.

Needless to say, when a young person finally musters up enough strength to take the risk of disclosure about his same-sex feelings to his parents or friends, he steps into extreme vulnerability. Imagine if his worst-case scenario is then experienced. In response to his timid statement, "Mom, Dad, . . . I think I'm gay" (which translated means "I have feelings that I don't understand, but based on what I know from media and my culture, they must mean I'm gay"), Mom implores, "How could you do this to me?" and Dad angrily declares, "You should know better; we raised you differently!" His friends boldly inquire, "Don't you know it's a sin?" or, "You can't be gay; it's wrong." The Church proclaims, "Homosexuality is an abomination", or, "Homosexual feelings are disordered desires." Not only are these statements dangerous in terms of how the young man will receive them (i.e., "I am a bad son, I am sin, I am wrong, I am an abomination"), but in one fell swoop, this son's existing mirrors of love, acceptance, and belonging have just turned very dark.

Based on my previous explanation of mirrors, the image of "good mom", in its fullest symbolic sense, has been completely shattered. For all intents and purposes, "good mom" no longer even exists. All the young man encounters is what we would define as "bad mom" or

---

[5] Lynne Hillier and Lyn Harrison, "Homophobia and the Production of Shame: Young People and Same Sex Attraction", *Culture, Health and Sexuality* 6 (2004): 83.

[6] Ibid.

[7] Ibid., p. 85.

mirrors that reflect back shame, disgust, fear, and guilt, with profound breaches in attunement and empathy of the son's feelings and concerns. Essentially, the young man has been utterly emotionally abandoned. This is especially poignant if these relational breaches are never repaired, in other words, if parents, friends, or broader communities remain paralyzed in their state of shock, anger, or condemnation. John O'Donohue describes this devastating phenomenon in *Eternal Echoes* by noting that, once you have disclosed a potentially shameful aspect of yourself, "everything about you is telescoped into the single view of this one shameful thing. Everything else is forgotten. A kind of psychological murdering is done. The mystery of your life is reduced to that one thing. You become a thing of shame. Shame dehumanizes a person."[8]

After years of working with men and women with SSA, I have come to see clearly this crisis of "becoming a thing of shame". I in no way want to minimize the shock or sadness of discovering that a child, friend, or parishioner has SSA or is identifying as gay or lesbian, but I do want to highlight the danger of forgetting who the child or friend is in the broadest sense of the person. So often, once a disclosure is made about same-sex feelings or a possible gay identity, the beloved is now only seen through the filter of "homosexuality". They have been "marked" with a large "H" that seems to cover all other aspects of their unique and special personhood. Everywhere the child looks, he faces cloudy and dark mirrors and, in so doing, experiences severe negative emotions and receives the messages that they are, as a whole, bad, wrong, or shameful.

If most of the caretakers and significant relationships within this youth's life continue to project negative, rejecting, insensitive sentiments toward this youth, "they will become even more entrenched in the negative cognitions about self—severely impacting their development and ability to healthfully function in relationship to self and others."[9] This process is poignantly described in a poem by William Yeats:

> How in the name of Heaven can he escape
> That defiling and disfigured shape
> The mirror of malicious eyes

---

[8] John O'Donohue, *Eternal Echoes: Celtic Reflections on Our Yearning to Belong* (New York: HarperCollins, 1999), p. 112.

[9] Gershen Kaufman, *The Psychology of Shame: Theory and Treatment of Shame-Based Syndromes* (New York: Springer, 1996), p. 108.

Casts upon his eyes until at last
He thinks that shape must be his shape?
("A Dialogue of Self and Soul", stanza 2)

No human being can endure an ongoing state of internalized badness, rejectability, or shame without incurring damage to his very soul. In an effort to survive, many young people, like this young man, may begin to cut off aspects of their own self that appear to be connected to their negative feelings and sense of badness. And in this case, it may be their identities (and possible characteristics and deep longings) that keep them tied to their families, friends, or churches. What a young person previously thought was good, such as his family identity as cherished son, his religious identity of being one who is loved by God, his relational identity as one who cares and has meaningful relationships, his composite identity of understanding himself as a unique and valuable self, now only cause pain or no longer matter and are therefore cut off from his awareness. But to balance this internal abdication and ostensive rejection from his former places of belonging, the young person must find a positive or idealized self and a new loving and accepting relational network. This step becomes essentially a "no brainer" for the young man. By identifying with his same-sex feelings and cultivating relationships with other youth who feel similar and, therefore, understand this youth's journey, the youth is able to find a community in which mirrors are once again reflecting care, acceptance, affirmation, and friendship.

Rosaria Champaign Butterfield described this process in her excellent book called *The Secret Thoughts of an Unlikely Convert*. While still living in a long-term lesbian relationship, Rosaria shared how Christians, back then, scared her.

> The lesbian community was home and home felt safe and secure; the people that I knew the best and cared about were in that community; and finally, the lesbian community was accepting and welcoming while the Christian community appeared (and too often is) exclusive, judgmental, scornful, and afraid of diversity.... Christians still scare me when they reduce Christianity to a lifestyle and claim that God is on the side of those who attend to the rules of the lifestyle they have invented or claim to find in the Bible.[10]

[10]Rosaria Champaign Butterfield, *The Secret Thoughts of an Unlikely Convert* (Pittsburgh: Crown and Covenant, 2012), p. 5.

As Rosaria highlighted, all people long for a sense of home. And if our prior sense of home has been shattered by rejection, blame, condemnation, criticism, devaluation, and even disowning, it will be natural to long for a replacement home that provides safety, acceptance, unconditional love, attunement, empathy, and commitment. And for many youth with SSA, this home is often found with other young people who are like them. And in finding a new home, the young person may also often assume an identity that aligns with his place of belonging, that is, a gay identity. This, by the way, does not immediately translate into same-sex behavior. Many young people carry a gay identity and yet still retain their Christian sexual values. However, in many cases this new identity might carry the power and pervasiveness of what I referred to earlier as an idealized sense of self. The adolescent's entire self becomes subsumed under this identity label, which then becomes the primary organizing force behind the young person's sense of self and relational network. Sadly, if left unchecked, the adolescent's broader developmental and personal identity formation processes may become sidelined or, at worst, arrested. Regardless how the young person ultimately decides to live with SSA, the cessation of healthy adolescent growth and development could nevertheless leave the child to face lifelong difficulties and struggles. I would suggest that if we, as the Christian community, would remain constant and consistent in our care, attunement, empathy, and *acceptance* of these young people, these type of outcomes could be substantially curtailed.

By sharing this vignette, I am not saying that our consistent love, acceptance, and care of a young person with SSA will guarantee he won't eventually identify as gay or continue to wrestle with his same-sex feelings. I am suggesting, however, that the young person won't necessarily feel *desperate* to find his *only* solace and acceptance among other kids with SSA. I am also not suggesting that friendship with other kids who have SSA is wrong or negative. As noted by Rosaria Butterfield, these friendships can be characterized by the authentic care, love, and support for which the adolescent longs and needs.

Allow me also to define what I mean by *acceptance*. Many psychologists have discussed the concept and impact of what has been termed "radical unconditional acceptance". This type of acceptance means that I will face reality head-on by not resisting it, trying to change it, or denying it. I will look at it squarely in the face, acknowledge it, and radically unconditionally accept it—as it is. To accept that our youth have same-sex feelings (and therefore will most likely be on a long journey of figuring out how to live with these feelings) is not the same as saying, "I now celebrate these feelings." It is saying, "Yes, I know that you have same-sex feelings." It is essentially stepping into the young person's lived experience by communicating, "I can handle this part of your life, and my love for you has not wavered in the least." Remember, it is our job to provide an ongoing sense of home for these young people.

As we contemplate our pastoral and parental responsibility to these youth, I would suggest that what is at stake is not necessarily the direct moral implications of a child's experience of SSA, but his ongoing formational and developmental processes aimed at establishing a stable and positive sense of self and personal identity shaped by loving, attuned, sensitive, and respectful relationships. I believe these stakes are very high. What follows, therefore, are some practical guidelines in terms of creating safe places that could provide adolescents with an ongoing experience of love, care, and acceptance that will support their growth, development, and identity formation, not just as it relates to their sexuality (although this is still extremely important), but to their whole personhood as they continue to move toward God's purposes and destiny for their lives.

Part 2: Practical Tips for Pastoral Care

Affirm the Value and Dignity of the Youth

Guideline 1: Show delight.

Brené Brown, in *Daring Greatly*, talks about a moment when author Toni Morrison was being interviewed by Oprah and gave the following advice to parents: "Let your face speak what's in your heart."[11] She shared that, in the past, whenever she saw her kids she immediately concerned herself with whether "they had buckled their trousers" or combed their hair. They saw a critical face. But now when she sees them she allows her face to light up and say, "I'm glad to see you. I'm just so happy to be with you." Youth with SSA need to see faces light

[11] Brené Brown, *Daring Greatly* (New York: Gotham, 2012), p. 223.

up again in their presence. Made in the image of God, these young men and women should be *celebrated* for their unique and special giftings and blessedness that comprise their true self. I regularly coach parents to make a list of all of their child's incredible characteristics, talents, interests, passions, or abilities so that they can be continually prepared to create opportune moments to bless their child or express how special their child is. We can also do this as religious leaders and friends.

Guideline 2: Become their student.

If you do not have SSA, then you will never fully know what it is like to be in the shoes of a person who does. It is not the same as having a temptation to eat too much food or drink too much alcohol. It is not, in fact, all about temptation. It is about who an individual believes he is or who he feels drawn to or longs to deeply love. Allow these young people to teach us about this personal experience by asking them questions about their lives. What is their world like? Internally and externally? When did they first notice that they had SSA? What was that like for them? What are their fears and concerns? What do they need? How can we help or be a support? What do they experience at school? What have they heard people say about gays and lesbians? What do they like about their gay or lesbian friends? What are their beliefs about God? What do they struggle with? In allowing these young people to tell us about their lives and to teach us what it's like to have SSA, we restore their dignity, just as Jesus did when he asked the woman at the well for a drink of water. He allowed her to serve him!

Guideline 3: Stop speaking carelessly.

I've already mentioned a few phrases that I believe should be eliminated from our speech, but more important is the need to take the time to stand within the shoes of our young people and ask *how they will hear* or understand our words or comments. Be careful about telling youth that they "can't be gay", "can't identify as gay", "can't call themselves gay", "can't marry unless it is someone of the opposite sex", or "can't tell anyone about their SSA". These imperatives, as would most imperatives spoken in this way to adolescent youth, could backfire and result in hostility, defensiveness, and teen rebelliousness. To young people, we also might lose credibility since these words sound stupid or uninformed. But worst, they may create a sense of despair within young people struggling with SSA. It is hard enough to attempt to understand and navigate their same-sex feelings let alone be given a long list of things that they "can't" do while they are on this very difficult journey.

If our words could be misconstrued as judgmental, insensitive, or unloving, then we are not ready to speak. Attunement is the actual state in which I momentarily *feel* what the other person is feeling. To remain attuned to these youth and protective of their vulnerable developing sense of self, we must speak less, listen more, and exercise reflectivity, caution, sacrifice, and deep sensitivity.

Guideline 4: Resign from being God's "moral cop".

"Do you suppose, O man, that when you judge those who do such things and yet do them yourself, you will escape the judgment of God? Or do you presume upon the riches of his kindness and forbearance and patience? Do you not know that God's kindness is meant to lead you to repentance?" (Rom 2:3–4). Very few of us have reached a state of perfection that would justify our attention being more focused on another's struggle with sin rather than our own. We must "first take the log out of [our] own eye" (Mt 7:5). By striving to remove the "log out of [our] own eye", the virtue of humility is cultivated and we come into a deep experiential understanding of God's grace and mercy. It is this virtue and understanding that constitutes the platform from which we are to move sensitively into the life of another person.

This does not mean that we should not entertain discussions with young people about God's purpose for the union of male and female or the sanctity of full sexual expression having its place within the covenant of marriage. It means, though, that these types of discussions should not be the central focus or hallmark of our discipleship or ongoing relationship with the youth. Further, when these discussions are undertaken, they should be conducted from a stance of openness and dialogue. Young people must be given the space to wrestle with their beliefs, ask questions, or disagree. To simply lecture the youth about what is right or wrong, or to demand that they believe the same as you, will not afford them the respect they deserve let alone the opportunity to integrate and take full ownership of their sexual ethics. Further, their wrestling and questioning related to their sexuality and its meaning before God will also not end after a few years of deliberation. For many, the inquiry will not appear as a task that from time to time requires their attention, but will become a lifestyle. Frankly, we would all spiritually benefit from remaining committed to an ongoing process of wrestling deeply with existential questions such as our meaning, purpose, sexuality, and faithfulness to God.

Guideline 5: Become a person who can offer empathy and mercy.

In her book *I Thought It Was Just Me*, Brené Brown offers a great list of the many attributes of empathy:

1. To be able to see the world as others see it
2. To be nonjudgmental
3. To understand another person's feelings (feel them)
4. To communicate your understanding of their feelings[12]

It is not uncommon for many Christians to experience what has been called an empathy gap. It can be stated as those not directly experiencing the social pain of being a Christian with SSA consistently underestimating the pain and therefore not adequately responding to the needs of the person experiencing the social pain. This takes us back to the need of becoming a student of people with SSA. For a more in-depth look at how I offer empathy and attunement to my clients, you might want to refer to chapters 6 and 7 of my book entitled *The Heart of Female Same-Sex Attraction*.[13] Let us follow the example of the Samaritan who, rather than focus on his own safety, sense of morality, or cleanness, had compassion and mercy and helped to mend a man's broken body and soul (see Lk 10:25–37).

---

[12] Brené Brown, *I Thought It Was Just Me* (New York: Gotham, 2007).
[13] Janelle Hallman, *The Heart of Female Same-Sex Attraction: A Comprehensive Counseling Resource* (Downers Grove, Ill.: InterVarsity Press, 2008).

Guideline 6: Refresh your understanding of love.

When told to "just love", many people recoil, believing that "loving" someone who has SSA or is gay identified would give the message that they, the lover, condone the sin of same-sex behavior. It's almost as if "love" is viewed as this mushy, passive, weakened state in which the lover necessarily must lose himself or all of his belief systems and values that may differ from those held by the beloved. If this were the case, I suspect that we would not be commanded by Jesus to "love [our] enemies" (Mt 5:44; Lk 6:27). Nor would God be able to love us.

Love is neither passive nor weak. On the contrary, it is extremely powerful. Love, in its essential and godlike substance, will never fail the beloved. Love does not deny sin but covers a multitude of sin. Love redeems, heals, restores, delivers, and constitutes new life. All love is God's love. And praise be to God, we are able to love because we *are* loved. He launched the dance of love by loving us first—even when we were dead in our sins. Our love should never be conditioned on the state of the beloved.

In reflecting on the passage that says "perfect love casts out fear" (1 Jn 4:18), I used to believe that it was referencing the power of love in terms of the beloved. When the beloved is truly loved, the beloved will no longer fear. However, I'm now wondering if it doesn't also reference those of us who are trying to become the lover. The entire verse reads, "There is no fear in love. But perfect love casts out fear. For fear has to do with punishment, and he *who fears is not perfected in love*" (emphasis added). Is it possible that we fear "loving" because we still fear punishment for doing something wrong such as condoning someone's homosexuality? Is it possible that *we*, as fearful lovers, have not been made perfect in love? Perhaps we still need to sit under the fountain of God's radical unconditional love, grace, and mercy while acknowledging *our* ongoing struggle with sin, confusion, and need to be cleansed. Perhaps when we come into a deeper experience of the lavish love of Christ, we can freely and recklessly offer it to others. It is time that we begin to trust that love *will* accomplish its completing and redemptive purpose.

There is no circumstance in which we are not to love. We are even called to love, bless, pray for, do good unto, and give generously to our enemies! How much more are we called to love our own

children—just as they are? It is worth taking the time, therefore, to
remind ourselves about the specific attitudes and postures that seem to
constitute love. First Corinthians chapter 13 tells us that love is patient
and kind. It does not envy or boast. It is not proud or rude or self-
seeking. It is not easily angered and keeps no record of wrongs. It does
not delight in evil but rejoices with the truth. It always protects, trusts,
hopes, and perseveres. Therefore, within all of our relationships we
should aim to demonstrate love, joy, peace, patience, kindness, goodness, faithfulness, gentleness, and self-control. "[A]gainst such there is
no law" (Gal 5:23). Titus 3:1-2 further sums up our call to "be ready
for any honest work, to speak evil of no one, to avoid quarreling, to
be gentle, and to show perfect courtesy toward *all* men" (emphasis
added). There are no exceptions.

The ultimate sign of love is to lay our lives down for another. "Therefore be imitators of God, as beloved children. And walk in love, as
Christ loved us and gave himself up for us" (Eph 5:1-2). Is it possible
then that in these ultimate acts of love toward those with SSA they may
begin to see or awaken to the image of Christ and thereby arise as the
bride, longing for her bridegroom, opening to Christ's penetrating and
all-consuming love and life? Isn't this our mission? To not simply change
the minds of men and women, but to invite them to partake in the wedding feast that has been prepared for them since the beginning of time?
In the end, love will prevail.

Challenge Your Beliefs

When we are confronted with another's experience of SSA or his
announcement that he is gay, we often assume that our beliefs in this
regard are fully expressed within the moral framework of God's purposes for male and female. It is important, therefore, to explore and
notice the many other corollary beliefs that may be imperceptibly
related to the complexity of the lived experience of SSA. For example, do we believe that a young man has a choice about these feelings? If we do, we may inadvertently shame him. For a young person
to be able to sort through the complexity of his life, he needs us to
bring clarity to his journey, feelings, and experiences. There are many
aspects of this young man's *life* that we must normalize, but to do so,

we must start with a solid belief or conviction that it is *not* "his fault" or *shameful* that he has

- Same-sex feelings. He didn't create or ask for them.
- Deficits in same-sex socialization. He may not have had good same-sex peer friendships throughout childhood.
- Longings to be close to someone of the same-sex. These longings in and of themselves are healthy and normal.
- Feelings of identification with the opposite-sex. Some boys may identify more with their mothers than their fathers. This is also true for some girls in terms of identifying more with their fathers.
- A history of trauma. Many youth are confused about their sexuality because of past sexual trauma.

There are many aspects of a young man's or woman's *personhood* that we must normalize. It is often these aspects that leave the young person feeling different or on the outside. We therefore must start with a solid conviction that it is *not* "his or her fault" or *shameful to have*

- A sensitive temperament
- A high IQ and deep reflectivity
- An uncommon body appearance, shape, or size
- Strengths or interests that are gender-nonconforming or, in other words, not typical of people of his or her same gender

These factors are part of his or her unique design made in the image of God.

There are many aspects of a young man's or woman's *internal subjective experience* that we must also normalize. We therefore must start with a solid conviction that it is *not* "his or her fault" to have experienced

- Feeling different
- Not knowing how to fit in
- Not knowing who he or she is
- Being a victim of bullying
- Overt condemnation and rejection from parents, friends, or a church
- The loss of friends because of his or her same-sex feelings or gender-nonconforming mannerisms or interests

Establish a Healing Relationship

Guideline 7: Exchange fear-based relating with heart-focused connection.

I love Brené Brown's definition of connection in her book entitled *The Gifts of Imperfection*.[14] She describes connection as "the energy that exists between people when they feel seen, heard, and valued; when they can give and receive without judgment; and when they derive sustenance and strength from the relationship".[15] This type of a connection clearly defines what I call heart-based connection, which stands in contrast to fear-based relating. We, as caregivers, might relate out of fear to young people with SSA for several reasons, many of which I've already discussed. We may be afraid for their safety, fearful about their future choices, fearful that they may sin (which then might reflect on us somehow), afraid that we might do or say something wrong, and on and on. But typically, when we are filled with fear, we tend to operate out of an energy of control. If we believe that we can control reality in a way that our fear will not be realized, we will naturally feel better. Often it is out of fear that an overly moralizing (or worse, a desperate) "need to fix it" attitude may arise. If we clamp down in an attempt to control a young person, though, we are no longer connecting but building an unhealthy bond based on fear. We will more often than not deny the adolescent's autonomy, which, at this point in his or her development, is of utmost importance to attain. Without a sense of autonomy and competency (which is often learned through trial and error), a young person becomes paralyzed in his or her capacity to make good choices and important decisions or to exercise appropriate levels of self-assertion. Over the years I have observed many young people who were well into their twenties and still resentfully dependent on their mom and dad to tell them what was right or wrong. This is most pronounced in family systems with parents that tend to operate as "helicopter or hovering" parents. By attempting to control and manage their children or overprotect them, they have unintentionally blocked the child's developmental progression. Furthermore, this type of engagement often leads to resentment within the child, creating distance or relational cutoffs.

---

[14] Brené Brown, *The Gifts of Imperfection* (Center City, Minn.: Hazeldon, 2010).
[15] Ibid., p. 19.

Heart-based connection arises more out of an energy of faith and believing that God is the one in control and has the best interests of the young person in mind. Instead of trying to protect the child from the evil world, the caregiver will build an alliance with the young person so that they may face all the difficulties and ups and downs of life together. The adolescent is granted respect and allowed to fail (within reason) based on the belief that such experiences can be valuable and important for maturity and growth. This type of supportive relationship instills a strong sense of autonomy, responsibility, and, ultimately, a solid sense of competency to live life well and to its fullest. In the end, the relationship or connection forms a solidarity between caregiver and child, securing an attachment that will weather the upheavals of life. Above all else, our young people need this type of connection. If they do not find it with us, they will find it somewhere else.

Guideline 8. Be different.

Prepare by reflecting and surmising what the young man might fear or gingerly expect in terms of your response to his disclosures and ongoing experience of SSA. Then, do the opposite. Let him be pleasantly surprised by your gentleness, openness to understanding, unconditional radical acceptance, ongoing love, compassion, mercy, and grace. Be like Jesus in befriending the woman at the well. It is these types of responses that will begin to lay a foundation of wholeness and strength within his own forming self.

Guideline 9: Be courageous and persevering in compassion and grace.

Due to the surrounding social milieu of hate and violence commonly experienced by young people with SSA, it is not uncommon that many of them struggle with trust. Your relationship with these youth may consequently become the staging ground for the emergence of their internal splitting (between what they perceive to be their "bad" versus "good" self) or their burgeoning and global mistrust. At times, they may shut down or push you away as a means of protecting themselves from rejection or further pain. They may flaunt their sexual minority identity to see if you are truly committed to them for their sake. You must be willing to be vulnerable, deal with your own feelings of hurt or rejection, face internal turmoil, and yet remain committed for the long haul—even when the going gets rough. Let us follow the example of the father of the Prodigal Son who never wavered in his hope, love, and acceptance of the son of his loins (see Lk 15:11–32).

Conclusion

I hope that it has now become clear that *how* we interact and treat this special population of believers (and nonbelievers) is far more significant to their ongoing journey than the *content* of our moral belief systems about homosexuality. Believe me, on this hot topic we must earn the right to speak into their moral development by first showing our commitment to and care for their entire personhood and ongoing process of formation as developing adolescents and young adults. This means that we must place the young person's deepest developmental and relational needs at the forefront of all interactions rather than our personal moral beliefs. I am still so struck by how matter-of-fact Jesus was about the woman at the well's multiple husbands and lovers. By essentially acknowledging and accepting this reality about her life, he entered into an intense and clearly meaningful dialogue about this woman's true heart, her longings, and her deep desire to worship the one and only true God. In doing so, Jesus affirmed her dignity and invited her to live in a way that was consistent with her dignity, value, and worth.

In order to relate to the diversity of young people who experience SSA, we must also identify and correct our preconceived notions about "homosexuality" and "homosexuals". It is important that we educate ourselves on this topic by allowing the youth and adults with SSA to educate us on their experiences, feelings, and needs when it comes to supportive relationships. When I started counseling women with SSA over twenty years ago, I did not know (really, I didn't have a clue!) what I know now. Yet, somehow I intuitively sensed that if I was going to develop an environment of safety that would foster a trusting relationship between my clients and myself, I would first have to become their student. And that I did. I have learned by sitting with and befriending many men and women with SSA. By doing so, I have come to appreciate the vast diversity, distinctiveness, and specialness of these folks. I have also learned that while I may have some framework for understanding people with SSA, I must still slow down my assumptions so that I can fully encounter the unique person that is presently in my midst. They deserve my full attention and openness to their special life.

Because many youth with SSA do in fact face threats to their safety emotionally, physically, and spiritually, I believe we must also be willing to advocate for them within the Church and within society as a whole, especially when it comes to discrimination and violence. It is so important that these young people have a place to share their difficulties or perceived threats at school or work. Similarly, it is important that we, as leaders, become familiar with the journey faced by parents of children with SSA. Often they are the forgotten ones within our parishes and communities. We need to understand their common fears, anxieties, frustrations, potential guilt and shame surrounding the belief that they failed as a parent, or concerns about their child's present and eternal future. But most of all, we should radically and unconditionally accept and love these parents, just as we do their children. For it is only as individuals solidify around an identity consistent with their belovedness in Christ that they can internalize the courage and power needed to make the difficult choices that may be required to walk with consistency and long-suffering in response to God's purpose and call on their life. May we together regularly recite Paul's prayer in Ephesians 3:14–21 on behalf of all youth with SSA and their families:

> For this reason I bow my knees before the Father, from whom every family in heaven and on earth is named, that according to the riches of his glory he may grant you to be strengthened with might through his Spirit in the inner man, and that Christ may dwell in your hearts through faith; that you, being rooted and grounded in love, may have power to comprehend with all the saints what is the breadth and length and height and depth, and to know the love of Christ which surpasses knowledge, that you may be filled with all the fulness of God. Now to him who by the power at work within us is able to do far more abundantly than all that we ask or think, to him be glory in the Church and in Christ Jesus to all generations, for ever and ever. Amen.

Same-Sex Attractions as a Symptom of a Broken Heart: Psychological Science Deepens Respect, Compassion, and Sensitivity

Timothy G. Lock, Ph.D.

There are four goals for this essay: (1) to increase respect, compassion, and sensitivity for persons with same-sex attractions (SSA) and their families;[1] (2) to correct several common misconceptions regarding the topic of SSA; (3) to provide those who offer pastoral care to persons with SSA and their families a greater understanding of many issues related to this topic; and (4) to encourage those who offer pastoral care to reach out to these individuals who feel particularly marginalized by the Church. My remarks are addressed generally to anyone who counsels those with SSA, but particularly to priests.

Drawing on the secular empirical research and the insights of mental health clinicians who adopt a Catholic anthropology, the application of this information will examine how this research can be used to support various aspects of pastoral care. This essay is not intended to be an exhaustive critical evaluation of the research literature, nor is it intended to provide a commentary on the various research methodologies. When appropriate, the information and research cited in this essay will be referenced, and near the end of the essay there are recommended readings for the individual who desires to learn more about these areas of study (see the section titled "Good Reading and Education on the Topic of SSA").

I. Proper Terminology

When discussing this topic, we must be clear on the terminology that is being used. Homosexuality is the condition whereby an individual

---

[1] Cf. *Catechism of the Catholic Church*, 2nd ed. (Washington, D.C.: Libreria Editrice Vaticana—United States Catholic Conference, 2000), no. 2358.

experiences sexual attractions toward an individual of the same sex. In the medical literature, such persons would be referred to as "MSM" for "men who have sex with men", or "WSW" for "women who have sex with women". Culturally the more common way to reference an individual with SSA or a MSM is to refer to him "gay". This term is to be avoided because it is a loaded term and carries more baggage than necessary. Psychotherapist Jeffrey Beane explains his perspective on the use of the word "gay": "The word 'gay' has come to connote an attitude of positive self-acceptance, which includes emotions, affection, life-style, and political perspectives as well as sexual orientation."[2] Using the term "a person with SSA" is much longer and more cumbersome than simply saying "a gay person", but the term SSA avoids the notion that sexual attractions are a core element of one's identity. It moves away from the socio-political atmosphere of the "gay identity" and moves toward using words that provide a description of something that an individual experiences. When the term "gay" is used in this essay, it is to refer to individuals who embrace and celebrate same-sex sexual contact and that lifestyle.

In the Catholic world, there has been interest in the term "gay Catholic" as a way for individuals to both accept and to integrate their SSA and their Catholic faith. The term "gay Catholic" is sometimes associated with the notion that being "gay" is a condition blessed by God and that the person's "gayness" is a gift to the Church because "gays" can offer new and exciting ideas for the Church. The term "gay Catholic" should be avoided for several reasons. First, the United States Conference of Catholic Bishops (USCCB) clearly notes this point in the 2006 document titled "Ministry to Persons with a Homosexual Inclination: Guidelines and Pastoral Care": "Persons with a homosexual inclination should not be encouraged to define themselves primarily in terms of their sexual inclination."[3] An individual should avoid having his sexual attractions, or anything else for that matter, supersede his identity as a child of God. Saint John Paul II speaking at the 2002 World Youth Day

[2] J. Beane, "'I'd Rather Be Dead Than Gay': Counseling Gay Men Who Are Coming Out", *The Personnel and Guidance Journal* 60, no. 12 (1981): 222.

[3] United States Conference of Catholic Bishops, "Ministry to Persons with a Homosexual Inclination: Guidelines for Pastoral Care", November 14, 2006, http://www.usccb.org/issues-and-action/human-life-and-dignity/homosexuality/upload/minstry-persons-homosexual-inclination-2006.pdf.

in Toronto said, "We are not the sum of our weaknesses and failures. We are the sum of the Father's love for us and of our real capacity to become the image of Jesus."[4] Holding our identity as a child of God encapsulates our entire being, not just our attractions or feelings. Second, that the "gay movement" has been attempting to use the individual's identity as a platform for social change should veer Catholics away from supporting such an ideology.[5] Finally, the *Catechism of the Catholic Church* (no. 2358) states that the same-sex inclination is "objectively disordered"; thus to describe one's self by that term signals a rejection of the notion that SSA is disordered. Note that the Church makes a distinction between person, inclination, and behavior. The Church would argue that the person is always good, the inclination is disordered, and the behavior is sinful.[6]

But why is it that Catholics who are committed to living chaste lives want to continue to refer to themselves as "gay"? I believe that the term "gay Catholic" is an attempt to resolve the cognitive dissonance of accepting that one has SSA. To experience SSA and to embrace the notion that these attractions are "disordered" creates a conflict whereby the person has to make sense of this experience. Using the term "gay Catholic" suggests that the person is good, the inclination is good, and only the behavior is sinful. It is easy to reason that because an inclination comes from the person, a person who appears to be good, the inclination also must be good. However, the human experience includes many examples of the presence of inclinations that are "disordered", such as a tendency to eat excessive food or unhealthy food (especially an overabundance of desserts), or a tendency or attraction to drink alcohol in excess. Here, perhaps, it is easier to separate the feeling or disordered inclination from the person who is inherently good. Nevertheless, the same application could be made in regard to sexual feelings or inclinations. The person, who is good, could have a sexual feeling or inclination that is "disordered". This does not make the

[4]"Homily of the Holy Father John Paul II at the Solemn Mass of the 17th World Youth Day" (Downsview Park, Toronto, July 28, 2002), http://w2.vatican.va/content/john-paul-ii/en/homilies/2002/documents/hf_jp-ii_hom_20020728_xvii-wyd.html.

[5]Cf. D. Altman, *The Homosexualization of America: The Americanization of the Homosexual* (New York: St. Marin Press, 1981).

[6]P.N. Check, "True Compassion: On Topics from Adultery to Homosexuality, Church Teaching Is Consistent", *Catholic Answers Magazine*, July-August 2013, pp. 22–27.

person "disordered"; it only identifies the inclination as "disordered". The separation of our personhood from our feelings is a common struggle today, and the ability to make this separation indicates psychological maturity and mental health.[7]

II. Origins of SSA

A. Born That Way?

The origins of SSA are a question of importance. The prevailing assumption in our culture is that these attractions are inborn, inherited, or genetically transmitted. When examining this assumption, researchers in a variety of disciplines have attempted to identify various biological indicators to support the notion that individuals with SSA are "born that way". Genetic, brain anatomical, hormonal, and behavioral genetic research have attempted to show the undisputable inheritability of SSA. The support from the research is less than overwhelming.[8] For example, many lay people are surprised to learn that there is no "gay gene", and that in the most recent and comprehensive study of male identical twins, only in seven of seventy-one (9.9%) of the twins did both twins experience SSA.[9] If SSA were the result of an inborn genetic trait, one would expect much higher rates of concordance. The American Psychological Association initially published a pamphlet about SSA that emphasized the genetic contribution to SSA, in which they wrote, "There is also considerable recent evidence to suggest that biology, including genetic or inborn hormonal factors, play a significant role in a person's sexuality."[10] However, since the data does not support that position, they have revised their understanding of this issue and have

[7] Cf. M. Linehan, *Cognitive Behavioral Treatment of Borderline Personality Disorder* (New York: Guilford Press, 1993).

[8] For review see S. L. Jones and A. W. Kwee, "Scientific Research, Homosexuality, and the Church's Moral Debate: An Update", *Journal of Psychology and Christianity* 24 (2005): 304–16.

[9] N. Långström et al., "Genetic and Environmental Effects on Same-Sex Sexual Behavior: A Population Study of Twins in Sweden", *Archives of Sexual Behavior* 39 (2010): 75–80.

[10] A. Dean Byrd, "APA's New Pamphlet on Homosexuality De-Emphasizes the Biological Argument, Supports a Client's Right to Self-Determination", NARTH, March 6, 2008, http://www.narth.org/docs/deemphasizes.html.

deemphasized the inborn or genetic contributions. Their revised pamphlet notes, "There is no consensus among scientists about the exact reasons that an individual develops a heterosexual, bisexual, gay, or lesbian orientation. Although much research has examined the possible genetic, hormonal, developmental, social, and cultural influences on sexual orientation, no findings have emerged that permit scientists to conclude that sexual orientation is determined by any particular factor or factors. Many think that nature and nurture both play complex roles."[11] Researchers now think that there may be a series of genetic components for traits (such as gender nonconformity) that could manifest as a tendency to develop SSA; however, the genetic origin of these traits has yet to be understood. If a genetic component is identified, it would likely note a predisposition to develop SSA, not a predetermination to develop SSA. A predisposition means that the individual is disposed to develop traits that could prompt an individual to behave in certain ways, whereas a predetermination means that it has been determined that the individual will develop SSA.

It is of utmost importance to remember that this data could change. At some point in the future, researchers could find that there is a clear genetic predisposition connected with the development of SSA. This possibility is not alarming for two reasons. First, Catholic moral teaching is based on a philosophical anthropology that has been developed and refined over thousands of years. The Church's declaration of a behavior as moral or immoral has little to do with scientific findings, although science often affirms the soundness associated with the Church's moral teachings. Therefore, if research emerged indicating a genetic link to SSA, those findings would not affect the Catholic understanding of SSA. Second, the issue of the heritability of SSA is really a nonissue because not all genetic conditions promote the health and well-being of an individual. For example, the research indicates that alcoholism is influenced by a genetic component or predisposition. Based on this finding, it is wrong to conclude that alcoholism is a normal expression of liquid consumption or that it is right to support alcoholics as they drink themselves to death. The loving response

---

[11] *Answers to Your Questions for a Better Understanding of Sexual Orientation and Homosexuality* (Washington, D.C.: American Psychological Association, 2008), http://www.apa.org/topics/lgbt/orientation.pdf.

would include hope and prayer that the alcoholic would eventually see the self-destructive effects of alcohol on his emotional, physical, and spiritual health; sometimes even an intervention or confrontation would be appropriate. Again, the fact that the propensity to alcohol addiction is inherited does not then make the damaging behavior good or honorable.

Another example could be the issue of obesity. The medical sciences label obesity as a medical condition that is associated with a number of additional medical problems, including reduced life expectancy. Researchers know that there is a genetic predisposition within some people to put on weight. However, it makes no sense to say that obesity is normal and healthy. The genetic predisposition to gain weight is moderated by a number of different environmental influences. There are family influences, related to the family's level of activity, self-care, and food preparation. There are social influences, such as the activities of one's friends or social group. There are cultural influences, related to the types of food eaten and the way those foods are prepared. There is the influence of situational stressors. There is the factor of virtue as it is expressed in an ability to exercise self-control. There may be individuals who have absolutely no genetic predisposition to become obese, but who are influenced by a combination of environmental factors that cause them to gain excessive weight. Being at risk for obesity does not lead to the conclusion that one is not responsible for taking action to address his potential obesity and subsequent health issues.

B. Psychological Genesis

The *Catechism* states: "[Homosexuality's] psychological genesis remains largely unexplained" (no. 2357). This statement offers us a few points of interest. The *Catechism* notes that this is not an area where there is clear understanding. This reflects the slow, careful, and wise method by which the Church absorbs scientific facts into her understanding of the human person and the human condition. There is not a consensus in the psychological literature regarding the topic of SSA, and the Church in her wisdom will wait until one is reached and examined in the light of her understanding of the individual person. However, simply noticing the acknowledgment in the *Catechism* that there is a

psychological genesis, albeit not well understood, invites investigation
into the environmental influences that may impact the development
of SSA.

C. Common Childhood Issues

To explore the psychological genesis of SSA, the following topics will
be reviewed: first, particular childhood issues that are disproportionately
experienced by individuals with SSA compared with individuals with
opposite-sex attractions (OSA); second, patterns of family relationships
that commonly occur during the childhood of an individual with SSA;
third, a developmental model (i.e., a schematic that describes growth
from birth to puberty) that ties together these observations with other
clinical observations to produce a heuristic that can prepare the clergy-
man for the types of life events that he may hear in those who come to
him with pastoral needs.

Several psychotherapists have observed that a variety of childhood
issues are experienced more frequently by individuals with SSA.[12] The
clinicians have observed that men and women with SSA, compared with
men and women with OSA, both experience problems in a variety of
areas including mother conflict, father conflict, peer rejection wounds,
poor body image, and abuse (including physical abuse, sexual abuse,
and neglect). Men with SSA, compared with men with OSA, report
experiencing a failure in parents to encourage same-sex identification
and experiencing the loss of a parent. Women with SSA, compared with
women with OSA, report experiencing male betrayal and extreme loneliness. These findings simply suggest that there is an increased prevalence
of these issues in individuals with SSA; they do not provide support that
these childhood events cause SSA.

---

[12] *Homosexuality and Hope* (Bala Cynwyd, Penn.: Catholic Medical Association, forthcom-
ing), www.cathmed.org. S. Bradley, *Affect Regulation and the Development of Psychopathology*
(New York: Guilford Press, 2000); R. Fitzgibbons, "The Origins and Therapy of Same-Sex
Attraction Disorder", in C. Wolfe, *Homosexuality and American Public Life* (Washington, D.C.:
Spence Publishing, 1999), pp. 85–97; Janelle Hallman, *The Heart of Female Same-Sex Attrac-
tion: A Comprehensive Counseling Resource* (Downers Grove, Ill.: InterVarsity Press, 2008); J.J.
Nicolosi, *Reparative Therapy of Male Homosexuality: A New Clinical Approach* (Northvale, N.J.:
Jason Aronson, 1997); J.J. Nicolosi, *Shame and Attachment Loss: The Practical Work of Reparative
Therapy* (Downers Grove, Ill.: InterVarsity Press, 2009); G. van den Aardweg, *The Battle for
Normality: A Guide for (Self-)Therapy for Homosexuality* (San Francisco: Ignatius Press, 1997).

D. Abuse

The topic of abuse will be briefly expanded, since it is very important because of the notably high prevalence of childhood abuse in individuals with SSA. Men with SSA report having experienced childhood sexual abuse seven times more frequently than men with OSA (15.4% SSA; 2.2% OSA), and women with SSA report having experienced childhood sexual abuse three times more frequently than women with OSA (34.7% SSA; 10.3% OSA). Likewise, men with SSA report having experienced childhood physical abuse one and a half times more frequently than men with OSA (5.3% SSA; 3.0% OSA), and women with SSA report having experienced childhood physical abuse three times more frequently than women with OSA (11.3% SSA; 3.8% OSA). Men with SSA report having experienced childhood neglect four times more frequently than men with OSA (11.6% SSA; 2.5% OSA), and women with SSA report having experienced childhood neglect three times more frequently than women with OSA (12.4% SSA; 3.4% OSA).[13] As noted above, the presence of abuse is not necessarily a cause of the development of SSA; there are many individuals with SSA who have never experienced abuse, and there are many individuals with OSA who have experienced abuse. However, knowledge of this high rate of childhood abuse is very important for those who provide pastoral care because, for example, when a teenager reports feelings of SSA, the counselor must consider the possibility that this teen is a victim of abuse.

E. Family Dynamics

In addition to those experiences listed above, individuals with SSA report a greater frequency in difficulties related to family dynamics, particularly the quality of interactions between the mother, the father, and the child. The dynamic that will be described has been repeatedly noted over the past one hundred years by various mental health practitioners and has been particularly associated with the development of male SSA.[14] The clinician will frequently hear a description of this dynamic from his

---

[13] T. Hughes et al., "Victimization and Substance Use Disorders in a National Sample of Heterosexual and Sexual Minority Women and Men", *Addiction* 105 (2010): 2130–40.

[14] For a review, see Nicolosi, *Shame and Attachment Loss*.

clients, and the clinician can even observe the dynamic firsthand if the individual with SSA invites his parents to a psychotherapy session. The following description is not meant to be a caricature, nor is it meant to be a template by which the counselor should place an individual's experiences. It is easiest to describe this dynamic by first offering an explanation of the three personalities involved. The wife typically presents with a strong and dominant personality. The husband typically presents as quiet, withdrawn, or with a hostile personality. The son typically presents with a quiet, timid, and creative personality. Imagine the father being quiet and withdrawn, and possibly hostile, interacting with his dominant and demonstrative wife. The communication between the two, one could easily imagine, would be poor, since the wife would approach and the husband would avoid. The wife, with her communications needs unmet, naturally seeks an outlet to talk and finds a timid and creative and emotionally present individual with whom to communicate: the child. Therefore, a "special relationship" can develop between the mother and the son. Meanwhile, the son is quiet and the father is quiet (or hostile), and this creates a divide between the father and the son, especially when there are no shared activities of interest. While the idea of a "special relationship" may appear to be appealing, individuals with SSA will often describe this relationship as "too close", and they report that the relationship was unhealthy. Therefore, the dynamic yields the following results: the mother and father have poor communication and therefore a weak relationship, the mother has excellent communication with the son and a strong relationship, and the father has poor communication with the son and a weak relationship with him. Individuals with SSA will often report that some elements of this dynamic persist into adulthood. This description explains the relationships within the family, but does directly show how these relationships impact the development of SSA.

III. Developmental Stages

In examining the developmental issues experienced by individuals with SSA, it is helpful to review the stages of development chronologically to see where various experiences may have affected the development of psychosexual erotic attractions. When looking at the lifespan of an individual, developmental psychologists divide the years into stages or steps in an attempt to describe some of the significant events or challenges that are experienced during a particular developmental period. The model presented below is an amalgamation of various theories and ideas from a number of developmental, social, and clinical psychologists, as well as many in the medical profession. While this model has not yet been subjected to intensive empirical investigation, this model plays out frequently in the therapeutic office. This model is proposed as a heuristic or a way to think about the struggles of an individual with SSA, but it is not proposed as a template into which all individuals must fit.

Clearly, individuals are very different, and one person's experience is always different from another's. As the counselor encounters individuals with SSA, parts of the model will resound with the life experience of individuals with SSA, but parts will also not resound. There will certainly be individuals who, when explaining their development, will not have any of the experiences indicated in this model. Nevertheless, the proposed heuristic allows the counselor to understand some of the challenges that the individual with SSA may have experienced, and it allows the counselor to be prepared to hear some life experiences in men and women with SSA. The stages important in the development of sexual attractions will be described, followed by a description of healthy development, and then the development of SSA will be reviewed. This model is based heavily on the work of clinical psychologist Dr. Joseph Nicolosi, the founder and director of the Thomas Aquinas Psychological Clinic,[15] and draws on the work of many others.[16] This model is presented for the development of male SSA; however, many aspects of this model, although in a very incomplete manner, also relate to women. For a sophisticated yet

---

[15] Ibid.; Nicolosi, *Reparative Therapy*; J.J. Nicolosi and L.A. Nicolosi, *A Parent's Guide to Preventing Homosexuality* (Downers Grove, Ill.: InterVarsity Press, 2002).

[16] Conrad W. Baars, *I Will Give Them a New Heart: Reflections on the Priesthood and the Renewal of the Church*, ed. Suzanne M. Baars and Bonnie N. Shayne (Staten Island, N.Y.: Society of St. Paul / Alba House, 2008) (see www.stpauls.us); D.J. Bem, "Exotic Becomes Erotic: A Developmental Theory of Sexual Orientation", *Psychological Review* 103 (1996): 320–35; D.J. Bem, "Exotic Becomes Erotic: Explaining the Enigma of Sexual Orientation" (address presented at the annual meeting of the American Psychological Association, Chicago, August 1997); Fitzgibbons, "Origins and Healing of Homosexual Attractions"; Fitzgibbons, "Origins and Therapy of Same-Sex Attraction Disorder"; R. Green, *The "Sissy Boy Syndrome" and the Development of Homosexuality* (New Haven: Yale University Press, 1997); Hallman, *Heart of Female Same-Sex Attraction*; E. Moberly, *Homosexuality: A New Christian Ethic* (Cambridge, England: James Clarke, 1983); van den Aardweg, *Battle for Normality*.

easy-to-read review of the development of female SSA, see Dr. Janelle Hallman's book *The Heart of Female Same-Sex Attraction: A Comprehensive Counseling Resource.*

A. Overview of Development

During the first year of life, a child's personality is developed through an interaction of his temperament and his attachment style. From approximately age 1 to age 3, the child begins a new adventure in life: intentional locomotion; he also enters a period of development called the separation/individuation stage. From approximately age 3 to age 5, the child's relationship with his father assists him in entering the "male world" and in developing his sense of masculinity, and this period is called the gender identity stage. From age 5 to age 9, the child's relationships with his peers become the primary influence on his masculine development, and this period is called the peer integration stage. From age 10 to age 13, the child's sexuality rapidly develops. Included in this development is the emergence of his sexual attractions. This period is called puberty. Drawing on this brief summary, the development of opposite-sex attractions (OSA) will be reviewed.

B. Development of OSA

1. The First Year of Life

During the first year of life, a child's personality is developed through an interaction of his temperament and his attachment style. Temperament is a group of traits, identified within the first few months of life, which has an impact on the individual throughout the course of his life. Temperament researchers are not unanimous in their understanding of this concept, but many accept the notion that there are nine dimensions of temperament including physical activity, regularity, adaptability, intensity, and sensitivity.[17] It is worth noting that the term "temperament" is

---

[17] H. I. Kaplan, B. J. Sadock, and J. A. Grebb, *Kaplan and Sadock's Synopsis of Psychiatry: Behavioral Sciences, Clinical Psychiatry*, 7th ed. (Baltimore: Williams and Wilkins, 1994).

not referring to the "four temperaments" originally described by Hippo-crates, which refer to personality styles in adult behavior.

Attachment style refers to the quality of the social and emotional relationship between the infant and the mother as objectively measured at age 12 months. Attachment theorists categorize the quality of the rela-tionship as either a healthy attachment, specifically referred to as a secure attachment, or as an unhealthy attachment, which manifests itself in two types specifically referred to as an anxious/ambivalent attachment or an avoidant attachment. A secure attachment is achieved by a mother who was warm, consistent, and sensitively attuned.[18] Attunement, within attachment theory, is the action whereby the mother matches the baby's emotions and understands the baby's emotional needs.[19] "Goodness of fit" refers to the mother's ability to become attuned to her child and to meet the needs of the child.[20]

In the development of OSA, the most important factor considering these early traits is the goodness of fit between the mother and the infant. The attuned mother is able to discern the various needs of the child, meet the needs of the child, and if she cannot meet the child's needs, she is able to provide comfort to the child. It should be noted that the mother is not required to meet each and every one of the child's needs or to be the source of all comfort for the child; rather, the term that is used by developmental theorists is "good enough" mothering.[21] The "good enough" mother provides enough care to meet an acceptable amount of the child's needs; she is not perfect in meeting all of the child's needs, but she is not inattentive by ignoring the child's significant needs.

2. Ages 1 to 3

From approximately age 1 to age 3, the child begins a new adventure in life, intentional locomotion, and thus begins the next period of develop-ment called the separation/individuation stage. This stage is comprised

[18] R. Karen, *Becoming Attached: First Relationships and How They Shape Our Capacity to Love* (New York: Oxford University Press, 1998).

[19] J. Bowlby, *A Secure Base: Parent-Child Attachment and Healthy Human Development* (New York: Basic Books, 1988).

[20] Kaplan et al., *Synopsis of Psychiatry*.

[21] Ibid.

of two parts: separation and individuation. Separation is the process by which the infant realizes that he is actually separate from his mother. If you think of a baby in utero, he is surrounded by warmth and comfort, and all of his needs are taken care of. This baby in utero experiences a certain unity with his surroundings since everything appears to be in harmony. Once the baby leaves the womb, this sense of harmony is challenged, although he still experiences the benefit of the presence of his mother: the sound of her voice is calming; the beating of her heart is calming; the food that she provides is calming; the love that she provides is calming. Whenever he cries, within a relatively short amount of time there is a quick response to meet his needs, and this perpetuates the sense that there is a certain harmony and oneness between him and his mother. When the child begins intentional locomotion, and more so when he begins to walk and begins fast intentional locomotion, he begins to realize that he can go in his own direction to explore beyond the realm of his mother. This separation is both exciting and scary, as the child now lacks the constant protection of his mother and the constant care that she provides. After he understands that he is separate from his mother, he begins to realize that he is his own individual with his own individual desires and intentions. Language emerges with the infamous "no" and "mine", and this is a healthy manifestation of the little person's developing individuality.

In the development of OSA, the boy is allowed to separate. This can take place in two different ways. Most typically, the mother simply allows the boy to separate. Alternatively, if the mother has significant difficulty allowing the boy to separate, the father will step in and help the boy separate; the presence of the father's assistance is helpful to relieve this mother's anxiety associated with this separation.

For the mother who is able to allow the boy to separate, this unfolds steadily. While it can be exciting and scary for the infant when he motors beyond the immediate presence of his mother, it can be even more frightening for a mother to become aware that she does not always know the location of her son. The question "Where are you?" can be asked in a playful tone; however, it can also be asked in a panicky tone. The healthy mother learns to regulate her own emotions and use this question as an opportunity to connect with the child rather than terrify or smother the child.

For the mother who is not able initially to allow the boy to separate, this process requires the assistance of the father. Initially, some mothers have difficulty "letting go" and do not allow or do not encourage this separation. When this happens in a healthy family, the father, at peace with the mother, steps in to activate and guide the boy to separate. That is, without any tension between the parents, the father encourages this separation in a playful, strong, and confident way in which the boy learns that separation is good and favorable. An example of this could be when a father plays peek-a-boo and eventually hide-and-seek. Observing this interaction between father and son, one hears squeals of laughter and enjoyment in the boy and also observes the father delighting in his son.

It is important to highlight this example because it is a demonstration of a phenomenon called "shared delight". As just noted in the example above, moments of "shared delight" between a father and a son occur when the two are involved in an activity together and the son is delighting in the father, and the father is delighting in the son. Healthy development is seasoned with the regular occurrence of these moments of "shared delight". These moments are very formative in the boy's confidence, self-esteem, and masculinity.

Further, in the development of OSA, once the child has separated, he begins to learn that he is not only separate from the mother, but he is different from her. He realizes that he is his own individual person. In healthy development, the mother allows this development to flourish and reinforces the notion that the little one is his own person. This is often observed as the mother gives the child choices for various activities, and where the child is allowed to play with a variety of toys. Individuation is celebrated rather than stifled.

3. Ages 3 to 5

From approximately age 3 to age 5, the child enters the gender identity stage, where his relationship with his father assists him in entering the "male world" and in developing his sense of masculinity. Psychologists who write about the topic of masculinity emphasize that masculinity is a trait that is acquired, not something that "just happens".[22] As the infant learns he is separate from the mother and that he is his own individual,

---

[22] J. A. Vandello and J. K. Bosson, "Hard Won and Easy Lost: A Review and Synthesis of Theory and Research on Precarious Manhood", *Psychology of Men and Masculinity* 14 (2013): 101–13.

he also learns that he is male and that he is more like his father than his mother. Then it takes a degree of effort and risk tolerance to navigate away from the world of the feminine, but with his father as a guide, the boy grows in his confidence to make this paradigm shift. This identification with the father is assisted by the father's personality, particularly if he presents as strong and kind. As the boy grows through the gender identity stage, he grows in his identification with men, he experiences the benefits of being a man, and he embraces his own masculinity.

4. Ages 5 to 9

From age 5 to age 9, the child enters the peer integration stage, where his relationship with his same-sex peers becomes the primary influence on his masculine development. Early in this stage, the move from parallel play into cooperative play allows for boys to work together and to negotiate social relationships. If a boy has achieved a sense of masculinity during the gender identity stage, he is comfortable with boys, both individually and as a group. As his socialization with boys progresses, he "feels" like one of the boys, and one can observe the "pack mentality" as boys of this age interact with one another.

5. Ages 10 to 13

From age 10 to age 13, the child begins puberty, and it is in this stage that sexual attractions emerge. Before this period, the boy has developed his masculinity first with his father, then with his same-sex peers. During puberty, the boy continues to develop his masculinity, this time with his opposite-sex peers, particularly with the development of his sexual interest and attractions. With the surge in hormones observed during this period, there is the development of sexual attractions.

a. The Exotic Becomes Erotic

Psychologist Daryl Bem described the process by which sexual attractions emerge. He explains that the exotic becomes erotic.[23] Bem's

---

[23] Bem, "Exotic Becomes Erotic: A Developmental Theory"; Bem, "Exotic Becomes Erotic: Explaining the Enigma".

theory can be easily seen in the context of the model proposed above. The infant boy realizes that he is separate from his mother and that he is his own individual. He also realizes that he is male and more like his father than his mother. Beginning at approximately age 3, the boy's father assists him in entering the male world and deepening his sense of masculinity. When he turns approximately 5 years old and his play becomes cooperative, the most important contributor to his masculinity shifts from his father and other men to his same-sex peers. As he enjoys this social development, he deepens his knowledge and experience of the "boy world" and grows in his comfort with his identity as "one of the boys". At the dawn of puberty, sexual attractions will develop toward the exotic sex. For the boy who has experienced healthy development, what is exotic is not boys; he has been accepted by his father and other men, he has become "one of the boys" with his male peers, and his individual sense of masculinity has matured. At the dawn of puberty, what is exotic to this healthy boy is the female. He understands boys, but does not understand girls. This class of individuals, girls, are exotic, and they become eroticized during puberty.

C. Development of SSA

1. The Sensitive Child (Ages 0 to 1)

We will now turn the discussion of this model to the development of SSA. As discussed above, during the first year of life, a child's personality is developed through an interaction between his temperament and his attachment style. In the development of SSA, the temperament that is most often present is one of sensitivity. In the development of SSA, the attachment style most typically present is the anxious/ambivalent attachment. A child with an anxious/ambivalent attachment does not cope well with separation from his mother. When mother and child are reunited, the child will be difficult to soothe; the child will be angry yet will simultaneously seek comfort. The baby is chronically anxious in relation to his mother, and this limits the baby's exploration.[24] Therefore, the temperament combined with the attachment style yields a child who is both anxious and sensitive.

---

[24] Karen, *Becoming Attached*, p. 444.

2. Separation Increases Anxiety (Ages 1 to 3)

As previously mentioned, from approximately age 1 to age 3, the child begins a new adventure in life, intentional locomotion, and thus begins the next stage of development called separation/individuation. As noted above under healthy development, the separation is both exciting and scary, as the child now lacks the constant protection of his mother and the constant care she provides. For the child with developing SSA, the anxiety associated with this separation is compounded by the internal anxiety already experienced from his attachment difficulties and his temperamental sensitivity. In the development of SSA, the sensitive and anxious child will show less of a proclivity to separate from his mother and, therefore, less of an inclination to individuate. In addition, when the child makes strides toward separating, it is thought that the mother's anxiety does not allow her to encourage this separation. The child's separation prompts the mother's anxiety, which leads her to keep the child close to her and inhibit the child's attempts to separate.

In a healthy family, this failure to "let go" would be met by the father's initiative to help the boy separate. In the child with developing SSA, the father does not intervene, or if he does, it is ineffective. Eventually, the separation process will take place, but for the child with developing SSA, the process is slow and labored. After he understands that he is separate from his mother, the infant begins to realize that he is his own individual and that he has own individual desires and intentions. This individuation process for the child with developing SSA, due to his sensitivities and his internal anxiety and his mother's anxiety, leads to a decreased inclination to individuate and an increased inclination to stay close to the mother and, therefore, the feminine.

3. Entering the "Male World" through the Father (Ages 3 to 5)

As discussed above, from approximately age 3 to age 5, the child enters the gender identity stage, where his relationship with his father assists him in entering the "male world" and in developing his sense of masculinity. The young boy with developing SSA enters this stage with heightened anxiety and an incomplete sense of his own individual self.

As he turns toward the male world, he is often greeted by his father, who is ineffective in two possible ways. First, the father may be hostile; his hostility does not offer a sense of welcome, nor does it offer a sense of enjoyment associated with being a male. A young boy with a hostile father may likely avoid his father's presence and all things masculine, and return to take refuge in the feminine (his mother). Another possibility is that the young boy may have a weak father who does not offer the strength or confidence needed for the boy to stay in the father's presence and with the masculine. These unhealthy dispositions of the father do not further the son's identification with the father and do not support the development of the boy's masculinity. Moments of "shared delight" are noticeably lacking. As the boy unsuccessfully travels through the gender identity stage, he fails to grow in his identification with men, he fails to experience the benefits of being a man, and his identification with his own masculinity is inhibited.

4. Peer Integration Stage (Ages 5 to 9)

From age 5 to age 9, as previously mentioned, the child enters the peer integration stage, where his relationship with his same-sex peers becomes the primary influence on his masculine development. Early in this stage, the move from parallel play into cooperative play allows for boys to work together and to negotiate the social relationships of one boy to another. If a boy has not achieved a sense of masculinity during the gender identity stage, he is uncomfortable with boys both individually and as a group. In his socialization with boys, he does not feel like he is "one of the boys", and he has difficulty entering into the "pack mentality" of the other boys. This internal difficulty is not just a private matter. The other boys detect the individual's sense that he feels different, and this could lead to his being ostracized and excluded. The boy could even be mocked and pejoratively labeled as "gay" because he is avoiding the "pack" of boys. A boy with developing SSA, who already feels ostracized, will seek a group with whom he can associate. Girls are often available and kind; therefore, the boy may seek refuge with girls and with femininity. Thus, the boy becomes very accustomed to the "girl world" and spends his time with opposite-sex peers.

5. Exotic to Erotic (Ages 10 to 13)

From age 10 to age 13, the child begins puberty, and it is at this time that sexual attractions emerge. Before this period, the boy with developing SSA has not developed his masculinity with his father, and then he failed to develop his masculinity with same-sex peers. Further, the boy with developing SSA spent more time with his opposite-sex peer group while avoiding same-sex peers with whom he felt ostracized. As described above, Bem explained the process by which the sexual attractions emerge: the exotic becomes erotic. At the dawn of puberty, the boy with developing SSA does not find girls to be exotic; he has spent a fair amount of time with his opposite-sex peers and is very familiar with the "girl world". What is exotic to this fellow is boys. He has never felt that he was accepted by his father or other men; he has not had the experience of becoming "one of the boys" with his male peers; and his individual sense of masculinity is muted. He understands girls better than boys. Consequently, boys are exotic and become eroticized with puberty, resulting in SSA.

IV. Confusions Overcome

While the model I have proposed offers a simple chain of events that produces the development of SSA, it is worthwhile to note that many young people who report same-sex behaviors or SSA in their teenage years do not maintain these attractions in adulthood. Three possible reasons that these changes may occur will be reviewed: first, the phenomenon referred to as "gender confusion"; second, the phenomenon referred to as "sexual fluidity"; and third, psychotherapy.

A. Gender Confusion

Gender confusion is a term that refers to the young child's failure to strongly identify his sexual attractions. To demonstrate, the identification of sexual attractions across development will be reviewed at three points in time: preteens, teen years, and adulthood. One study asked over thirty-six thousand adolescents if they were heterosexual or homosexual. Fully, 25.9% of the preteens reported, "I don't know".[25] If one considers the mindset of a 12-year-old, one could easily see that this is not a primary consideration in a preteen's mind; there is not distress associated with this agnosticism. By age 18, only 5% reported, "I don't know." Finally, in the general population, approximately 3.5% of adults report having SSA.[26] These trends suggest that gender confusion may be manifested in preteens as a lack of awareness of their sexual preference, but this confusion tends to resolve itself in opposite-sex attractions in adulthood.

B. Sexual Fluidity

Some individuals believe that they are attracted to the same sex, but later they find themselves sexually involved with members of the opposite sex. This phenomenon is referred to as "sexual fluidity". In 2008, Dr. Lisa Diamond of the University of Utah published a book titled *Sexual Fluidity* that documents this phenomenon in her research with women. Sexual fluidity is defined by Diamond as "situation-dependent flexibility in women's sexual responsiveness. This flexibility makes it possible for some women to experience desires for either men or women under certain circumstances, regardless of their overall sexual orientation".[27] While Diamond presents this as if it is a phenomenon exclusive to women, others have found empirical support to confirm that fluidity is also present in men.[28]

[25] G. Remafedi, M. Resnick, R. Blum, and L. Harris, "Demography of Sexual Orientation in Adolescents", *Pediatrics* 89, no. 4 (1992): 714–21.

[26] G.J. Gates, "How Many People Are Lesbian, Gay, Bisexual, and Transgender?", Williams Institute, UCLA School of Law, 2011, http://williamsinstitute.law.ucla.edu/wp-content/uploads/Gates-How-Many-People-LGBT-Apr-2011.pdf; G.J. Gates, "LGBT Demographics: Comparisons among Population-Based Surveys", Williams Institute, UCLA School of Law, 2014, http://williamsinstitute.law.ucla.edu/wp-content/uploads/lgbt-demogs-sep-2014.pdf.

[27] L.M. Diamond, *Sexual Fluidity: Understanding Women's Love and Desire* (Cambridge, Mass.: Harvard University Press, 2008), p. 3.

[28] S.L. Katz-Wise, "Sexual Fluidity in Young Adult Women and Men: Associations with Sexual Orientation and Sexual Identity Development", *Psychology and Sexuality* 6 (no. 2), 2014.

C. Psychotherapy

Another way that individuals may experience a change in their sexual attractions is through psychotherapy. Reparative therapy or conversion therapy is defined as psychotherapy aimed at helping individuals change from experiencing SSA to experiencing OSA. A number of recent studies have documented the fact that many individuals have successfully completed this type of therapy resulting in a change of their sexual attraction from same-sex to opposite-sex.[29] However, critics believe this type of therapy is harmful,[30] and laws have even been enacted in some states (e.g., California and New Jersey) to ban this type of therapy with adolescents. Ironically, psychiatrist Robert Spitzer, who was the lead psychiatrist in removal of the diagnosis of homosexuality from the *Diagnostic and Statistical Manual of Mental Disorders* (DSM) of the American Psychiatric Association, published a study examining a group of two hundred individuals who completed reparative therapy to see if they were damaged by this type of therapy. Spitzer concluded, "There was no evidence of harm. To the contrary, they [the individuals who underwent reparative therapy] reported that it was helpful in a variety of ways beyond changing sexual orientation itself".[31] Nine years later, Spitzer published an apology to the "gay community" for how his study was used.[32] Spitzer explained more about this apology in an article published in the *New York Times*, saying that there was not an error in the data, but there was an error in the way the data were

---

[29] See, for example, S. L. Jones and M. A. Yarhouse, *Ex-Gays? A Longitudinal Study of Religiously Mediated Change in Sexual Orientation* (Downers Grove, Ill.: InterVarsity Press, 2007); S. L. Jones and M. A. Yarhouse, "A Longitudinal Study of Attempted Religiously Mediated Sexual Orientation Change", *Journal of Sex and Marital Therapy* 37 (2011), 404–27; A. D. Byrd, J. Nicolosi, and R. W. Potts, "Clients' Perception of How Reorientation Therapy and Self-Help Can Promote Changes in Sexual Orientation", *Psychological Reports* 102 (2008): 3–28.

[30] *Report of the APA Task Force on Appropriate Therapeutic Responses to Sexual Orientation* (Washington, D.C.: American Psychological Association, 2009), http://www.apa.org/pi/lgbt/resources/therapeuticresponse.pdf.

[31] R. L. Spitzer, "Can Some Gay Men and Lesbians Change Their Sexual Orientation? 200 Participants Reporting a Change from Homosexual to Heterosexual Orientation", *Archives of Sexual Behavior* 32, no. 5 (2003), p. 414.

[32] R. L. Spitzer, "Spitzer Reassesses His 2003 Study of Reparative Therapy of Homosexuality", *Archives of Sexual Behavior* 41, no. 4 (2012), p. 757.

interpreted. Spitzer stated, "The data were all there but were totally misinterpreted".[33]

V. Emotional Wounds

Returning to the discussion of the development of SSA, one notes the failure of the boy to have his emotional needs met by his parents. From his mother, the child fails to experience the proper encouragement to tolerate the negative emotions (including his sensitivities and anxieties) of separation and individuation. Likewise, he suffers by experiencing his mother's anxieties, especially when he is away from her or when he is in a situation of risk. The father does not "rescue" the boy from the mother's anxiety, or, worse, the son has to endure the father's hostility. The boy fails to experience the strong and kind presence of a father who helps him grow in his masculinity by drawing him into a relationship of "shared delight". Further, both of the parents do not notice the son's separation from other boys or do not offer effective intervention in assisting the boy in becoming incorporated with same-sex peers. Noting these deficiencies in his upbringing, one may wonder if these issues create any long-term difficulties for the boy, besides the impact on his sexual attractions.

A. At Risk for Psychological Disorders

The data from many research studies are now clearly showing that individuals with SSA are at risk for experiencing a number of psychological disorders. It is important to note a few things about this data. First, we must always remember that we are discussing individuals. The data come from research that examines thousands of individuals, and each person has his own particular story. Looking at large quantities of data can sometimes lead to the dehumanization of a condition. This is not

[33] B. Carey, "Psychiatry Giant Sorry for Backing Gay 'Cure' ", New York Times, May 18, 2012, accessed March 11, 2015, http://www.nytimes.com/2012/05/19/health/dr-robert-l-spitzer-noted-psychiatrist-apologizes-for-study-on-gay-cure.html?_r=0.

the intention of the author; the current review of the data is intended to promote charity and compassion for those individuals who are struggling. Second, we have to remember that each individual who presents himself to a counselor has his own individual story. There is no universal template or theory that we want to force upon those who seek our help. It is often most important and beneficial to listen to an individual as he relates his experience. The data help us with awareness of common experiences, and the data may guide us in forming a response, but the particular concern that manifests itself in the life of an individual varies among individuals. The individual who presents himself to the counselor would benefit most from having his personal story heard.[34]

Many studies have been published in the past twenty years that show the same pattern of results as the excellent study reviewed below that is comprised of a nationally representative probability survey of 34,653 adults in the United States age 20 and above.[35] Table 1 presents the disorder on the left (depression, anxiety, suicidal attempts, and so on) and shows the percentage of males who experience each disorder with OSA, with SSA, and with both-sex attractions. The table continues by showing the percentages of females who experience each disorder with OSA, with SSA, and with both-sex attractions. Clearly, the presence of SSA is one of many issues in the life of the individual with same-sex and both-sex attractions.

The data clearly show that individuals with SSA report much higher rates of the listed disorders as evidenced by the percentage of individuals who experience these disorders. Another way of presenting the data is to report the increased frequency of the disorder among individuals with SSA or both-sex attractions. Compared to males with OSA, males with SSA report two times greater prevalence of mood disorders, two times greater prevalence of anxiety disorders, and two times great prevalence of cluster B personality disorders (i.e., borderline, histrionic, antisocial, and narcissistic personality disorders). There are three times greater prevalence of psychotic illnesses and four times greater

---

[34] Cf. "Ministering to Persons with Same-Sex Attraction: What Courage Members Would Like Clergy to Know", Courage International, accessed March 15, 2015, http://couragerc .org/wp-content/uploads/Ministering.pdf.

[35] S. L. Bolton and J. Sareen, "Sexual Orientation and Its Relation to Mental Disorders and Suicide Attempts: Findings from a Nationally Representative Sample", *Canadian Journal of Psychiatry* (2011): 56, no. 1, 35–43.

Table 1. 2011 USA Study by Bolton & Sareen—Psychopathology
Rates for Persons with SSA and OSA

	OSA Male	SSA Male	BSA Male	OSA Female	SSA Female	BSA Female
Any mood disorder	19.8%	42.3%	36.9%	30.5%	44.4%	58.7%
Any anxiety disorder	21.4%	45.8%	40.6%	36.3%	48.4%	66.2%
Any substance use disorders	50.0%	65.0%	55.8%	24.3%	60.8%	61.9%
Any Cluster A PD*	8.7%	13.5%	20.5%	8.9%	21.3%	21.9%
Any Cluster B PD*	15.4%	30.7%	25.7%	10.8%	19.8%	31.7%
Any Cluster C PD*	9.1%	12.3%	12.1%	9.6%	11.1%	17.1%
Psychotic illness	2.7%	9.3%	2.1%	3.4%	2.9%	9.2%
Suicide attempt	2.1%	9.8%	10.0%	4.2%	10.9%	24.4%

*Personality disorders (PD) are divided into three groups: cluster A, cluster B, and cluster C.

prevalence of suicide attempts among those with SSA. These data beg the following question: Why do individuals with SSA report such high rates of psychological issues?

B. Nonacceptance?

One answer that has been suggested is that individuals with SSA suffer because they are not accepted by the culture, which includes the potential experience of stigmatization and discrimination. Following this line of logic, in cultures accepting of individuals with SSA, the rates of psychological issues should be the same for both individuals with SSA and individuals with other-sex attractions. To explore this idea, let us look at the data from the Netherlands, a country with open acceptance of the gay culture. Amsterdam is considered the gay capital of Europe, and some consider it the gay capital of the world. The Netherlands decriminalized homosexuality in 1811,[36] and the first gay bar in the Netherlands was opened in 1927.[37] The Netherlands' tourism website endorses this ideology: "For decades Amsterdam was known as the world's 'Gay Capital', a place where gay and lesbian couples could kiss in public without worry, and where local homosexuals enjoyed levels of social acceptance and legal equality unimaginable elsewhere."[38]

The rates of psychological disorders in the Netherlands are roughly equivalent to the rates of psychological disorders in the United States of America (see Table 2).[39] These data fail to support the idea that a culture that openly accepts the "gay lifestyle" yields lower levels of psychological disorders in those with SSA. Further, these data suggest that it is not the cultural acceptance of the "gay lifestyle" but some other factor that is causing the increase in psychological issues in those with SSA.

C. Fidelity and Partner Abuse

The rap artists Macklemore and Ryan Lewis wrote a song titled "Same Love",[40] which received a 2012 Grammy nomination for Song of the Year. The music video of this song first depicts a woman giving birth to a baby and highlights many tender moments between a man and a woman. Then the images begin to change: a man is seen alone, then with another man, and then the two kiss. The song continues by conveying the message both in video and through the lyrics that the romantic love between two men is the same as the romantic love between a man and a woman; thus, it is the "same love". As of March 2015,

---

[36] S. Barclay, M. Bernstein, and A. M. Marshall, *Queer Mobilizations: LGBT Activists Confront the Law* (New York: New York University Press, 2009).

[37] "Gay Capital of Europe", Amsterdam.org, accessed April 16, 2015, amsterdam.org/en/gay-capital.php.

[38] "Amsterdam Seeks to Reclaim Gay Capital Crown", RNW, accessed April 16, 2015, http://www.rnw.nl/english/article/amsterdam-seeks-reclaim-gay-capital-crown.

[39] T. G. M. Sandfort, R. de Graaf, R. V. Bijl, and P. Schnabel, "Same-Sex Behavior and Psychiatric Disorder", *Archives of General Psychiatry* 58 (2001): 85–91.

[40] Macklemore and Ryan Lewis, "Same Love", https://youtube.com/watch?v=hlVBg7_08no.

Table 2. 2001 Netherlands Study by Sandfort and Colleagues—
Psychopathology Rates of Persons with SSA and OSA

	OSA Male	SSA Male	BSA Male	OSA Female	SSA Female	BSA Female
Any mood disorder	13.3%	39.0%	nd*	24.3%	48.8%	nd
Any anxiety disorder	13.2%	31.7%	nd	25.1%	25.6%	nd
Alcohol dependence	8.4%	13.4%	nd	1.8%	11.6%	nd
Drug dependence	1.8%	4.9%	nd	1.2%	9.3%	nd
Any substance use disorders	29.0%	30.5%	nd	7.1%	25.6%	nd

*nd = no data; no data were available for the personality disorders, psychotic illness, and suicide attempts.

the official video of this song on YouTube has been watched over 135 million times.

When examining the research on the quality of the same-sex sexual relationship, we will examine two factors: infidelity and partner abuse. We will find that the same-sex couple is not equivalent to the opposite-sex couple.

Infidelity has been clearly shown to be an issue among opposite-sex couples.[41] The research shows that approximately 22.7% of married men have extramarital affairs. Two studies have been completed that show that in male same-sex couples, 82% to 100% have been unfaithful.[42]

Looking at abuse within the relationship is another issue. Data presented here will examine emotional abuse, physical abuse, and sexual abuse. Men in opposite-sex relationships report the lowest levels of abuse from their female partners: 49% emotional abuse, 14% physical

---

[41] Wiederman, 2010.

[42] P. Blumstein and P. Schwartz, *American Couples* (New York, William Morrow, 1983), cited in L. T. Peplau and A. W. Fingerhut, "The Close Relationships of Lesbians and Gay Men", *Annual Review of Psychology* 58 (2007): 405–24; D. P. McWhirter, *The Male Couple: How Relationships Develop* (Englewood Cliffs, NJ: Prentice-Hall, 1984).

Table 3. 2000 & 2014 USA Studies Demonstrate
Partner Abuse in Persons with SSA and OSA

	OSA Male	SSA Male	OSA Female	SSA Female
Emotional abuse	49%	83%	48%	82%
Physical abuse	14%	44%	24%	56%
Sexual abuse	2%	13%	9%	13%

Sources: The source regarding data for male and female heterosexuals is Breiding, Chen and Black, "Intimate Partner Violence"; for male and female SSAs, the source is Turell, "A Descriptive Analysis of Same-Sex Relationship Violence".

abuse, and 2% sexual abuse.[43] Men in same-sex relationships report drastically higher levels of abuse from their male partners: 83% emotional abuse, 44% physical abuse, and 13% sexual abuse.[44] Likewise, women in opposite-sex relationships report levels of abuse from their male partners: 48% emotional abuse, 24% physical abuse, and 9% sexual abuse.[45] Women in same-sex relationships report levels of abuse from their female partners that are again drastically higher: 82% emotional abuse, 56% physical abuse, and 13% sexual abuse.[46] The data here show that emotional, physical, and sexual abuse are all more prevalent in same-sex partnerships. While the popular presentation of same-sex couples suggests that they are equivalent to opposite-sex couples, the data indicate that there are monumental differences.

VI. Informed Pastoral Care

When encountering an individual with same-sex attraction, the most important attitude to remember is that which is noted in the *Catechism*

---

[43] M.J. Breiding, J. Chen, and M.C. Black, "Intimate Partner Violence in the United States—2010" (Atlanta, GA: National Center for Injury Prevention and Control, Centers for Disease Control and Prevention, 2014), http://www.cdc.gov/violenceprevention/pdf/cdc_nisvs_ipv_report_2013_v17_single_a.pdf.

[44] S.C. Turell, "A Descriptive Analysis of Same-Sex Relationship Violence for a Diverse Sample", *Journal of Family Violence* 15, no. 3 (2000), 281–93.

[45] Breiding et al., "Intimate Partner Violence".

[46] Turell, "A Descriptive Analysis of Same-Sex Relationship Violence".

of the Catholic Church: the individual with SSA should be treated with respect, compassion, and sensitivity. Furthermore, all those counseling individuals with SSA within the context of the faith should convey the love of Christ and the sense that the individual with SSA is welcome in the Church. A better understanding of the difficulties experienced by individuals with SSA, including the experiences with abuse, will lead to increased compassion, respect, and sensitivity. Listed below are some concrete compassionate pastoral practices to aid in the integration and application of the information presented in this essay.

A. Experts in the Spiritual Life

Those who minister to the spiritual needs of those with SSA have many opportunities to provide very meaningful assistance. I am going to address my remarks here to priests, but I believe they are widely applicable to other spiritual ministers.

The life of a priest today demands that he learn a tremendous amount about topics on which he has minimal if any formal training during seminary, such as the administration of a parish, and the development of educational curriculums, the management of properties, the management of parking lots. The priest is approached as if he should be an expert in everything. Pope Benedict XVI, when speaking to a group of seminarians in Poland, commented on this topic and offered a perspective that decreases the pressure under which a priest is expected to fulfill his duties: "The priest is not asked to be an expert in economics, construction or politics. He is expected to be an expert in the spiritual life".[47] Individuals with SSA approach a priest for the sacraments as well as spiritual guidance or direction. They hope that the priest has knowledge of same-sex attraction and hope he will listen to their story with a desire that their particular struggle be met with mercy and compassion.[48] In this situation and others when the priest is confronted with situations beyond his scope of

---

[47]Benedict XVI, Address at the Meeting with the Clergy (Warsaw Cathedral, May 25, 2006), http://w2.vatican.va/content/benedict-xvi/en/speeches/2006/may/documents/hf _ben-xvi_spe_20060525_poland-clergy.html.

[48]Cf. "Ministering to Persons with Same-Sex Attraction", Courage International.

knowledge, he should seek helpful resources. The Courage Apostolate is the first place that he can look for additional information and guidance as well as for referrals to others who can be of assistance.

B. Be a Father to the Fatherless

Individuals with SSA often have a difficult relationship with their fathers that has resulted in a certain perceived deprivation of fatherly care. A counselor extending kindness to an individual with SSA can have a profound positive effect. Dr. Conrad Baars, a Catholic psychiatrist who developed an approach to psychology from a Thomistic perspective, explained the process of affirmation whereby one person extends unconditional love and emotional support toward another.[49] "The authentic care, concern, and love for the parishioner by the priest is communicated on an emotional level through the priest's eyes, facial expression, countenance and other nonverbal communication, as well as gentle words of acceptance and encouragement emanating naturally from the priest's heart. This affective presence allows the parishioner to feel loved and worthwhile instead of simply trying to believe it with his or her intellect based on the words of the cleric".[50] This ability to offer affirmation is highlighted in what is called "the three As": attention, affection, and approval. The offering of undivided focus on the parishioner is somewhat self-explanatory, but it is particularly poignant in an age when everyone is "busy" and cell phones often command more attention than real people. The priest offering affection can be understood as the priest having a spontaneous and natural experience of enjoyment when seeing and talking to the parishioner. The priest offering approval can be understood as an endorsement of the person's goodness as a child of God. This affirming attitude communicates more than any words spoken; it communicates a kindness that may have been a rare experience in the life of an individual with SSA,

---

[49] Conrad Baars, *Born Only Once: The Miracle of Affirmation*, 2nd ed. (Eugene, Oreg.: Wipf & Stock, 2012).

[50] S. Baars and B. Shayne, "Affirmation Therapy", 2003, accessed April 16, 2015, http://conradbaars.com/affirmation-therapy.htm. (Note: this was originally written for the therapeutic setting, and the original text substituted therapist instead of counselor, and client instead of parishioner.)

especially from another man. This encounter could take place after Sunday Mass as the priest greets parishioners, or it could take place in the confessional, or it could take place in the context of a longer conversation. If the encounter includes a discussion, the priest should focus his efforts on listening and being present to the individual. It should be noted that the affirming attitude is the foundation of the "shared delight" experience, which may even be experienced during conversation. During these encounters, there is often no imminent need to stress particular Church teachings or evaluate the morality of certain behaviors (although this may be necessary if the encounter is taking place in the Sacrament of Reconciliation). Allowing the individual to speak about the issues he is facing will often be very helpful, since a person with SSA often does not find that others in the Church want to enter into dialogue with him about this topic. Typically, after a relationship has been forged, then the specific disputed moral issues can be explored.

There is a phenomenon in the literature that is called "defensive detachment", and it is important for the counselor to have some sense of this issue. In healthy relationships, one person may "reach out" to connect with another and that "reaching out" is received by the other. In healthy relationships between men, one observes this phenomenon, and sometimes the "reaching out" is accomplished in the form of making jokes about each other; however, these jokes are not intended to hurt the other, but they are a way that men connect (i.e., almost as moments of "shared delight"). In 1983, Dr. Elizabeth Moberly explained a phenomenon that she observed whereby men with SSA portrayed a sort of emotional distance, sometimes with a hostile disposition, when interacting with other men, and this emotional distance prevented the men with SSA from connecting with and developing relationships with men with OSA. Moberly explained, "The defensive detachment from the same-sex parental love-source will be marked by hostility, whether overt or latent, toward parental figures and toward members of the same sex".[51] The male counselor may experience this defensive detachment in casual or prolonged conversation with men with SSA. He should know that this defensive detachment is not an attempt to discount the counselor or his efforts to connect. The man with SSA often feels a certain deprivation in

---

[51] Moberly, *Homosexuality*, p. 7.

regards to male connection, and this defensive detachment style can per-petuate a feeling of disconnection. The proper response of the counselor is to continue to reach out to the man with respect, compassion, and sensitivity. The defensive detachment can sometimes lessen over time, but for some individuals, it remains constant. The counselor should be fortified in the understanding that this is not a personal affront to the counselor and that he can and should continue to extend the love of Christ to the individual with SSA.

C. The Courage Apostolate

When an individual with SSA presents himself to a priest, either in the confessional or outside of the confessional, he is often feeling very alone; typically, the struggle with SSA has not been shared with others. The priest can provide encouragement and spiritual direction, as well as the sacraments; however, there are other resources that can be used. The Courage Apostolate's main activity is to provide a support group for individuals with SSA to assist them in living a chaste life. In the Courage group, always led by a clergy chaplain, individuals with SSA gather together to pray and talk, sharing their joys and sorrows. Very often healthy, non-sexual, same-sex relationships are forged in these groups, and the members experience strength in their common goal to live a chaste life. Courage also provides regional retreats, days of recollection, a sports camp, and an annual conference. It should be noted that the goal of Courage is to help individuals with SSA to live a life of chastity. The goal of Courage is *not* to help people change their sexual attractions. The majority of indi-viduals who attend Courage groups do not seek therapy to change their sexual attractions, and the apostolate does not promote that endeavor. If there is not a Courage group in your diocese, please contact the Courage office for resources to help in the formation of a new Courage group. The Courage website is www.CourageRC.org.

D. Chaste Fellowship

An individual with SSA experiences a certain isolation from others of the same sex, and often isolation within the Church. In addition to Courage groups, individuals with SSA would benefit greatly from other parish activities that promote chaste friendships. In particular, same-sex parish organizations (such as men's groups, the Knights of Columbus, the Ladies Guild) can provide opportunities for men to grow in chaste relationships with other men, and women to grow in chaste relationships with other women. A counselor can recommend these parish activities to those with SSA.

E. Good Reading and Education on the Topic of SSA

The counselor meeting with an individual with SSA will want to recommend that he begin to read some publications that support the goals of living the virtue of chastity. There is certainly a great deal of spiritual writings by the saints, such as Saint Alphonsus Ligouri's chapter on chastity in the book titled *The Twelve Steps to Holiness and Salvation*,[52] and spiritual writings from modern authors, such as Father Benedict Groeschel's book titled *Courage to Be Chaste*[53] or Father Jacques Philippe's book *Interior Freedom*.[54] In addition, there are publications by Father John Harvey, the cofounder of the Courage Apostolate, including *Homosexuality and the Catholic Church*,[55] *Same-Sex Attraction: A Parents' Guide*,[56] and *The Truth about Homosexuality*.[57] For a "self-help" guide for men with SSA interested in deepening self-knowledge and growing in chastity, a book by Dr. James Phelan may offer some useful exercises.[58] For a thorough academic review of the literature regarding SSA, the interested reader is referred to the recently updated pamphlet, *Homosexuality and Hope*, published by the Catholic Medical Association and available on their website.[59] In addition to printed material, there

---

[52] Alphonsus Ligouri, *The Twelve Steps to Holiness and Salvation* (Charlotte, N.C.: TAN, 1986).

[53] Benedict Groeschel, *Courage to Be Chaste* (Mahwah, N.J.: Paulist Press, 1998).

[54] Jacques Philippe, *Interior Freedom* (New York: Scepter, 2007).

[55] John F. Harvey, *Homosexuality and the Catholic Church* (West Chester, Pa.: Ascension Press, 2007).

[56] John F. Harvey and Gerard V. Bradely, ed., *Same-Sex Attraction: A Parents' Guide* (South Bend, Ind.: St. Augustine's Press, 2003).

[57] John F. Harvey, *The Truth about Homosexuality: The Cry of the Faithful* (San Francisco: Ignatius Press, 1996).

[58] James E. Phelan, *Practical Exercises for Men in Recovery from Same-Sex Attraction (SSA)* (Columbus, Ohio: Practical Application Network, 2011).

[59] *Homosexuality and Hope* (Bala Cynwyd, Pa.: Catholic Medical Association, 2015), www.cathmed.org.

are a number of excellent resources on the Internet such as the Courage Apostolate website (www.CourageRC.org), and blogs by individuals who have SSA and are striving to live a life of chastity (www.Letters ToChristopher.wordpress.com).

F. Identify Therapists

There will be times when an individual with SSA presents with an issue that is beyond the scope of the counselor, and the assistance of a mental health or medical professional is necessary. It is important that a professional be sought who offers therapy in full accord with the teachings of the Church. Without a proper anthropology, a mental health and medical practitioner may lead an individual with SSA toward immoral behavior rather than toward a life of virtue. The USCCB also highlights this issue: "Professionals providing counseling services for persons who experience same-sex attraction and the families to which they belong should be chosen carefully to ensure that they uphold the Church's understanding of the human person. Efforts should be made to identify and publicize those services that conduct their work in a manner that accords with Church teaching".[60]

Identifying psychotherapists who offer services in harmony with Church teaching is sometimes difficult. Resources such as Catholic Therapist.com and WellCatholic.com provide a list of therapists who are working in full accord with the teachings of the Church. There are many more mental health practitioners who are not on these websites who can commonly be identified through word of mouth in a local area. Unfortunately, not all the therapists who work for Catholic Charities mental health clinics hold a correct Catholic anthropology. Indeed, there is a dearth of suitable professionals. To assist with this need, the Courage Apostolate is providing trainings for therapists who wish to learn more about working with clients with SSA.

The type of therapy recommended for an individual with SSA depends upon the goals of the individual. The individual with SSA who desires to live a chaste life may be inhibited by a variety of factors.

---

[60] United States Conference of Catholic Bishops, "Ministry to Persons with a Homosexual Inclination", p. 23.

Chastity Focused Therapy (CFT) could help him work through various issues that impede people from living chastity (for more information, see ChastityFocusedTherapy.com). Individuals with a sexual addiction could benefit from CFT, but also from Sexaholics Anonymous and other related recovery groups. The individuals with SSA who desire to change their sexual attractions so that they are sexually attracted to individuals of the opposite sex may benefit from reparative therapy. More information on responsible and ethical reparative therapy is available through the International Federation for Therapeutic Choice (see http://www.narth.com/international /international-federation-for-therapeutic-choice/).

G. "Turn the Hearts of Fathers toward the Children"

Men and masculinity are often threatened today. The priest can, in homilies and at other times, encourage fathers to be good husbands and fathers. If the spousal relationship is peaceful, it is psychologically healthier for the children. The presence of the father is associated with positive mental health outcomes and greater successes in life. A father may need extra encouragement to spend time with his sons and daughters.

H. When Parents Hear Their Child Say, "Mom, Dad, I'm Gay."

Many Catholic parents today are wrestling with the experience of learning that their teen or adult child is identifying himself as "gay" and is seeking same-sex sexual relationships. This presents a hardship for the parents as the child rejects a part of his upbringing and Catholic faith, and the parents are often overwhelmed with surprise and shock. The branch of the Courage Apostolate called EnCourage is a support group for family and friends of those with SSA. Parents should be guided to devote extra time to their spiritual lives and to engage with spiritual writings such as Father Jacques Philippe's book *Searching For and Maintaining Peace: A Small Treatise on Peace of Heart*[61] (see also other spiritual

---

[61]Jacques Phillipe, *Searching For and Maintaining Peace: A Small Treatise on Peace of Heart* (Staten Island, N.Y.: Alba House, 2002).

writing recommendations in Section E above). The struggle these parents are facing may last a week, or it may last until the end of their lives. Parents should be encouraged to devote time to cultivate their relationship with their child with SSA. While the parents may disagree with the ideas expressed by the child who is reporting SSA, the relationship as parent to child should be fostered and strengthened. To read a more detailed guide for parents whose child has newly professed a "gay" identity, an important resource is the free eBook called, "*Mom . . . Dad, I'm Gay: How Should A Catholic Parent Respond*" written by Catholic psychotherapists David Prosen and Allison Ricciardi.[62] Also useful for parents is the book primarily written for those with young children, and it can be extremely educational for those with adult children, called, "A Parent's Guide to Preventing Homosexuality".[63]

I. Extraordinary Devotion

In closing, these comments by Saint Francis de Sales underscores the need for the psychological to be infused with an authentic Catholic spirituality to enliven extraordinary devotion.

> When fruits are whole and sound they can be preserved, some kinds in straw, others in sand, and still others in their own leaves. Once damaged, they are almost impossible to keep except when preserved in honey and sugar. In like manner, when chastity has not been harmed or violated it can be kept safe in various ways. Once broken, nothing can preserve it except extraordinary devotion, which is the true honey and sugar of the spirit.[64]

---

[62] David Prosen and Allison Ricciardi, *Mom . . . Dad, I'm Gay: How Should A Catholic Parent Respond*, The Raphael Remedy, http://theraphaelremedy.com/mom-dad-i-m-gay.

[63] Joseph J. Nicolosi and Linda A. Nicolosi, *A Parent's Guide to Preventing Homosexuality* (Downers Grove, Ill.: InterVarsity Press, 2002).

[64] Francis de Sales, *Introduction to the Devout Life*, trans. John K. Ryan (New York: Image, 1950), III.12.

HIV and Other Health Risks Associated with Men Who Have Sex with Men

Timothy P. Flanigan, M.D.

The rates of HIV in the United States continue to rise among gay and bisexual men despite extensive knowledge regarding the risks of HIV and sexual transmission.[1] Other sexually transmitted diseases (STDs), such as syphilis, gonorrhea, and chlamydia, are also very common among men who have sex with men. Diseases associated with the human papillomavirus (HPV), such as penile cancer, anal cancer, and cancers of the tongue, are on the increase.[2]

Mental illness, such as depression and anxiety, as well as suicidality, occurs much more frequently among men who have sex with men. Substance abuse, be it alcohol or tobacco use, as well as the use of drugs (such as methamphetamines, party drugs, and cocaine) associated with increased sexual activity, can intensify health risks, lead to riskier sexual activity, and greatly exacerbate mental illness.[3]

Gay and bisexual men are not necessarily at an increased risk for HIV, STDs, and HPV-associated cancers. The risk for these infections and their health consequences is directly related to the number of sexual partners as well as the increased risk of transmission associated with unprotected anal intercourse.[4] Many Internet sites and online apps, such

---

[1] See Richard J. Wolitski and Kevin A. Fenton, "Sexual Health, HIV, and Sexually Transmitted Infections among Gay, Bisexual, and Other Men Who Have Sex with Men in the United States", supplement, *AIDS and Behavior* 15, no. S1 (April 2011): S9–S17.

[2] Healthy People 2020, "Healthy People 2020 Gay Men's Health Fact Sheet", The Center SD, revised October 2010, http://www.thecentersd.org/pdf/health-advocacy/gay-mens-health-fact-sheet.pdf.

[3] Ibid.

[4] Centers for Disease Control and Prevention, "HIV/AIDS, HIV Transmission", last updated January 16, 2015, http://www.cdc.gov/hiv/basics/transmission.html.

as Grinder, Manhunt, Adam 4 Adam, and even Craig's List, have facilitated meeting sexual partners quickly and anonymously. The explosion of pornography on the Internet and the ease of networking have fueled sexual exploitation of many types. The results have been a dramatic increase in HIV and STDs that directly relates to multiple sexual partners with risky sexual encounters.[5]

Many health concerns that occur at higher rates among gay and bisexual men are dealt with one at a time in relative isolation.[6] Depression and anxiety disorders are common. Substance abuse, which is frequently with multiple different drugs such as alcohol, cocaine, methamphetamines and party drugs, is often mixed with unsafe sexual behaviors. Intimate partner violence, suicidal ideation, and suicide attempts are more common among men who have sex with men. Sexual behaviors that facilitate multiple anonymous partners lead to much higher risks of sexually transmitted infections, HIV, and hepatitis viruses. All of these health concerns and challenges interact together and lead to higher rates of riskier and destructive behaviors. The interaction of these co-occurring epidemics has been coined "syndemics" because these co-occurring epidemics are synergistic.[7] It is a mistake to deal with just one or another of these issues in isolation.

A person-centered response takes into account how all of these health challenges and risky behaviors interact with each other, and how they can lead to much higher rates of self-destructive behaviors. For instance, it is not enough that a person stay HIV negative through prevention efforts, but at the same time engage in destructive anonymous sexual relationships along with drug use—the result can be severe depression and suicide. The overall well-being of the individual has to be of paramount

---

[5] Ibid. (See the response to the question "How is HIV passed from one person to another?")

[6] Steven A. Safren et al., "Mental Health and HIV Risk in Men Who Have Sex with Men", in "The HIV Epidemic in the United States: A Time for Action", supplement, *Journal of Acquired Immune Deficiency Syndromes* 55, no. S2 (December 2010): S74–S77.

[7] Ibid.; Brian Mustanski et al., "Psychosocial Health Problems Increase Risk for HIV among Urban Young Men Who Have Sex with Men: Preliminary Evidence of a Syndemic in Need of Attention", *Annals of Behavioral Medicine* 34, no. 1 (August 2007): 37–45; James E. Egan et al., "Migration, Neighborhoods, and Networks: Approaches to Understanding How Urban Environmental Conditions Affect Syndemic Adverse Health Outcomes among Gay, Bisexual and Other Men Who Have Sex with Men", supplement, *AIDS and Behavior* 15, no. S1 (April 2011): S35–S50; Steven A. Safren, Aaron J. Blashill, and Conall M. O'Cleirigh, "Promoting the Sexual Health of MSM in the Context of Comorbid Mental Health Problems", *AIDS and Behavior* 15, no. S1 (April 2011): S30–S34.

importance, not just one specific issue or another. A young man, for example, who is sexually active and using Internet sites, and who is suffering from severe anxiety or depression, may not readily admit to methamphetamine or detrimental alcohol use. Yet, addictive behaviors are usually intertwined. It is hard to address a sexual addiction without addressing co-occurring alcohol use or party drugs. Screening and treatment for HIV and other STDs is an important first step to address health risks, but also may help a person understand the destructive nature of casual sex acts. Addressing the health risks, without addressing the emotional and spiritual consequences, does a disservice. It does make sense to meet people "where they are", but then to inquire with an open-ended and caring tone as to their physical, emotional, and spiritual well-being. A person-centered approach starts with the concern that is of highest priority to the person, but acknowledges, inquires, and proposes healthier approaches in other realms. This is in contrast to an approach that tends to address areas in isolation, that is, health risks alone (HIV and STDs), emotional consequences alone (depression or anxiety), or just spiritual isolation or alienation. This is a daunting and challenging task, but the first step is to show care and concern in an open, honest, and supportive fashion.

HIV

Men who have sex with men are at the highest risk for HIV in the United States. The rate of new HIV diagnoses among men who have sex with men in the United States is more than forty-four times that of other men.[8]

In 2010 more than 60 percent of new HIV diagnoses were among men who have sex with men, even though the Centers for Disease Control estimates that men who have sex with men account for approximately 4 percent of the U.S. male population.[9] Younger men who have sex with men are at the highest risk for new HIV infection.[10]

---

[8] Centers for Disease Control and Prevention, "CDC Fact Sheet: HIV among Gay and Bisexual Men", March 2015, http://www.cdc.gov/nchhstp/newsroom/docs/cdc-MSM-508.pdf.
[9] Ibid.
[10] Ibid.

Substance abuse, meeting sexual partners online, multiple sexual partners, and unprotected anal intercourse, as well as younger age of first sex, are all associated with higher rates of HIV infection. Early in the HIV epidemic, many gay men dramatically decreased their risk-taking behaviors because of fear of HIV. In the last decade, the pendulum has swung the other way. Many men who have sex with men are complacent regarding the risk of HIV. There are specific sites online that advertise opportunities for unprotected anal intercourse, which is the highest sexual risk behavior for HIV. Some men who have sex with men even consider it a badge of honor or "joining the club" to receive an HIV diagnosis.[11] The result has been a dramatic upswing in HIV infection among men who have sex with men.

Sexually Transmitted Diseases and Hepatitis Infection

Unprotected anal and oral intercourse with multiple partners facilitates the spread of multiple infections. Gonorrhea and chlamydia infections can occur specifically in both the oral and anal areas.[12] Multiple anonymous sexual partners who are often met online create sexual networks with these infections, which can ping-pong back and forth very easily. Often these infections go undetected and thus lead to further transmission. Hepatitis B and C are easily transmitted—particularly through anal intercourse. The breakdown of the mucosa within the anal area facilitates the transmission of these viruses.

The Centers for Disease Control estimates that men who have sex with men account for approximately 4 percent of the male population over the age of thirteen, yet 10 percent of new hepatitis A infections and 20 percent of new hepatitis B infections occur among men who have sex with men. New infections with hepatitis C are being reported in significant rates among men who have sex with men and who have unprotected anal intercourse.[13]

[11]Duncan A. MacKellar et al., "HIV/AIDS Complacency and HIV Infection among Young Men Who Have Sex with Men, and the Rate-Specific Influence of Underlying HAART Beliefs", *Sexually Transmitted Diseases* 38, no. 8 (August 2011): 755–63.

[12]Centers for Disease Control and Prevention, "Gay and Bisexual Men's Health: Sexually Transmitted Diseases", last updated July 2, 2014, http://www.cdc.gov/msmhealth/std.htm.

[13]Centers for Disease Control and Prevention, "Gay and Bisexual Men's Health: Viral Hepatitis", last updated July 2, 2014, www.cdc.gov/msmhealth/viral-hepatitis.htm.

Syphilis

Although syphilis was on the verge of elimination in the United States in 2000, rates of syphilis have doubled from 2000 to 2013. Rates of primary and secondary syphilis have continued to increase since 2011. Into 2013, over 90 percent of all cases of syphilis were among men.[14] Over 75 percent of the men with syphilis were men who had sex with men. Men between the ages of twenty and twenty-nine years old had the greatest increase.[15] Meeting men online has been facilitated by websites that provide access to easy, quick, and anonymous sex partners; these create sexual networks, which rapidly spread syphilis and other infections. Sex associated with alcohol, methamphetamines, cocaine, and other substance abuse dramatically increases the risk of sexually transmitted disease including syphilis.

Suicide Risk

Lesbian, gay, and bisexual youth experience more suicidal behavior than other youth in general. Suicidal ideation is more common, as well as suicide attempts. Consistently high rates of attempted suicides (in the range of 20 to 40 percent) have been found in eight peer-reviewed studies among volunteer samples of gay youth.[16] There are a number of well-accepted protective factors related to suicide risk, including family support as well as positive school and community environments. Depression, substance abuse, and family alienation are risk factors. Those individuals who are homeless or runaways or involved in the juvenile court system are at higher risk for suicide. These factors are all intertwined.

The risk of suicide among men who have sex with men that are older is also substantial. Not surprisingly the risk of suicide or attempted

---

[14]Laurie Barclay, "Syphilis Rates in US Doubled Since 2000, Still Rising", Medscape, May 8, 2014, www.medscape.com/viewarticle/824863.

[15]Centers for Disease Control and Prevention, "Syphilis: Syphilis and MSM (Men Who Have Sex with Men)", last updated December 16, 2014, http://www.cdc.gov/std/Syphilis/STDFact-MSM-Syphilis.htm.

[16]Suicide Prevention Resource Center, "Suicide Risk and Prevention for Lesbian, Gay, Bisexual, and Transgender Youth" (Newton, Mass.: Education Development Center, 2008), p. 5, http://www.sprc.org/sites/sprc.org/files/library/SPRC_LGBT_Youth.pdf.

suicide correlates closely with depression, anxiety, ongoing substance abuse, lack of social support, and hopelessness.

Cancer Prevalence

Many cancers, although relatively uncommon, occur at much higher rates among men who have sex with men. Anal cancer, penile cancer, and some cancers of the head and neck area such as tongue cancer are associated with infection from HPV.[17] This virus is sexually transmitted. The earlier the age an individual acquires HPV, as well as the number of different HPV infections, is associated with higher rates of cancer.

Anal cancer continues to increase annually. Men who have sex with men who are HIV negative have seventeen times the rate of anal cancer as heterosexual men.[18] HIV-infected men who have sex with men have forty times the rates of anal cancer.[19] It is very good news that the HPV vaccine is very effective at preventing HPV infection and thus holds the promise of decreasing these cancers over time.

Men who have sex with men have higher rates of smoking, which results in higher rates of lung cancer.[20] Many also use supplemental testosterone, which can increase the aggressiveness of underlying prostate cancer.[21] HIV-infected men who have sex with men have a higher incidence of lymphoma as well.[22]

Conclusion

Overall, the very high risks of HIV and sexually transmitted infections, including hepatitis viruses, as well as the higher rates of anxiety,

---

[17] Centers for Disease Control and Prevention, "HPV and Cancer: HPV-Associated Cancers Statistics", last updated September 2, 2014, http://www.cdc.gov/cancer/hpv/statistics/.

[18] Centers for Disease Control and Prevention, "Gay and Bisexual Men's Health".

[19] Savita V. Dandapani et al., "HIV-Positive Anal Cancer: An Update for the Clinician", *Journal of Gastrointestinal Oncology* 1, no. 1 (September 2010): 34–44.

[20] Healthy People 2020, "Gay Men's Health Fact Sheet".

[21] Franklin D. Gaylis et al., "Prostate Cancer in Men Using Testosterone Supplementation", *Journal of Urology* 174, no. 2 (August 2005): 534–38; discussion 538.

[22] "Cancer", AIDS.Gov, last revised June 1, 2012, https://www.aids.gov/hiv-aids-basics/staying-healthy-with-hiv-aids/potential-related-health-problems/cancer/.

depression, poly-substance abuse, and violence among gay and bisexual men, is daunting and of grave concern. A person-centered approach that takes into account the multiple health issues and syndemics among gay and bisexual youth and adults is needed. A greater awareness of the high health risks associated with the earlier age of sexual initiation and with the practice of having multiple sexual partners is urgently needed.

Understanding the Sexual Revolution

Jennifer Roback Morse, Ph.D.

This article gives a thirty-thousand-foot overview of the sexual revolution from the last seventy years or so. We will get a clearer view of the battlefield by understanding how we got here. And observing the persistent patterns in the strategies of the sexual revolutionaries will give us a clearer picture of how to respond. Moreover, our bird's-eye view will give us a clearer picture of where the sexual revolution will next go. Redefining marriage by removing the gender requirement will not be the end of the sexual revolutionary movement. We need to be prepared for what the next steps are likely to be.

By the end, I hope every reader will discern some way in which he can contribute something positive to healing our current cultural disorder. People from every field of endeavor can become a force for positive change. Everyone can do something to heal the wounds of the sexual revolution and prevent further damage.

What Is the Sexual Revolution?

The sexual revolution consists not primarily of actions but of ideas, as well as the policies that put those ideas into practice. There are two main ideas that define the sexual revolution. The first revolutionary idea is the separation of sex and childbearing from each other and the separation of both sex and babies from marriage. The second is that men and women are completely interchangeable, and that all social differences between men and women are evidence of injustice that must be rectified. Taken together, these ideas have pummeled the institution of marriage, created structural injustices to children, and brought misery to millions.

Contraception and Divorce

The contraceptive ideology is the idea that a good and decent society ought to separate sex and childbearing from each other, and from marriage, in the name of freedom and gender justice. Marriage is an oppressive institution based upon illegitimate gender stereotypes. Unwanted children are oppressive for women. Sexual activity that does not result in a baby is an entitlement. Many social practices associated with the sexual revolution can be understood as some form of this idea. Cohabitation, divorce, and, of course, nonmarital sex and childbearing are all particular instances of the general idea that sex and childbearing can be separated from each other and from marriage. All of these social practices appear to be "done deals". These practices are so deeply embedded into the fabric of society that everyone takes them for granted—everyone, that is, except those who follow the magisterial teaching of the Catholic Church.

This social revolution is sometimes attributed to the introduction of oral hormonal contraception. But the Pill is just an inert piece of technology. We had, and still have, decisions to make about what meaning to assign to this technology, what place to assign it in our individual lives, and how the overall social system ought to adapt to it. Thus, the availability of contraceptive technology is not the really revolutionary point. Various methods for spacing pregnancies have been known since time immemorial. In fact, the "First Demographic Transition", in which birth rates dropped in half, took place in response to urbanization and industrialization, well before the advent of modern hormonal contraception.[1] Yet, no one in those earlier eras thought it was possible or desirable to build a society around the concept that sex is a sterile activity. It is the *propagation of the contraceptive ideology* that is really revolutionary.

The claim that preventing pregnancy and sexually transmitted diseases is a necessary and sufficient condition for rendering the sexual act "safe" is not a scientific or factual claim. Neither is the claim that everyone old

---

[1] The concept of a demographic transition, in which birth rates decline after declines in death rates and infant mortality rates, was discovered by Warren Thompson in 1929, based on observations from the previous two hundred years. Obviously, this pattern had next to nothing to do with hormonal contraceptive technology (see "Demographic Transition", *Wikipedia*, last modified March 22, 2015, http://en.wikipedia.org/wiki/Demographic _transition#cite_note-marathon.uwc.edu-6).

enough to give meaningful consent is entitled to unlimited sexual activity without a live baby. *These are ideological claims.*

Plainly, any claims about "entitlements" to sexual activity are philosophical and moral claims. And the technological, scientific fact is that contraception simply reduces the probability of any particular sexual act resulting in a pregnancy. No reversible forms of contraception reduce the probability all the way to zero.[2] The Centers for Disease Control (hardly an anti-contraception organization) reports the failure rate for oral hormonal contraception to be around 9 percent, and the failure rate of the condom to be around 18 percent.[3]

More importantly, sexual activity can create other problems in a person's life besides pregnancy or sexually transmitted diseases: attachment to one's sex partner and sexual jealousy, for instance. Our society's single-minded ideological focus on avoiding pregnancy blinds us to these very personal consequences of sex. This same single-mindedness also hides a tacit moral argument: a responsible person ought to avoid pregnancy and STDs. But avoiding heartbreak and disloyalty are not serious enough to be even worth considering.

Many of us want desperately to believe that we can have unlimited sex without a live baby ever resulting or without doing ourselves or others any harm. But this is a mistaken belief; it is wishful thinking. We might even call it a superstition: a belief we hold in spite of the evidence, because we like the way the belief makes us feel.

We should note, if only in passing, the relationship between the contraceptive ideology and abortion. If the ideological demand were simply to reduce the probability of pregnancy, abortion would not seem so necessary to so many people. But in fact, the ideological demand is

---

[2] It is also instructive to note that contraceptive failure rates are correlated with socioeconomic status, age, and marital status. Contraception is most likely to fail for the young, the poor, and the unmarried. These groups are those to whom contraception is most heavily marketed. See the following: Lawrence B. Finer and Stanley K. Henshaw, "Disparities in Rates of Unintended Pregnancy in the U.S., 1994–2001", *Perspectives on Sexual and Reproductive Health* 38, no. 2 (2006); M. Macaluso et al., "Mechanical Failure of the Latex Condom in a Cohort of Women at High STD Risk", *Sexually Transmitted Diseases* 26, no. 8 (1999): 450–58; Haishan Fu et al., "Contraceptive Failure Rates in the US: New Estimates from the 1995 National Survey of Family Growth", *Family Planning Perspectives* 31, no. 2 (1999).

[3] Centers for Disease Control and Prevention, "Contraception", last reviewed and updated February 24, 2015, http://www.cdc.gov/reproductivehealth/unintendedpregnancy/contraception.htm.

much more than reducing the probability of pregnancy from any particular sexual act. The tacit demand is that the connection between sex and babies be completely severed. Since contraception sometimes fails, abortion is absolutely necessary to shore up the claim that sex doesn't make babies.

The United States Supreme Court even said as much in its decision in *Planned Parenthood v. Casey*:

> For two decades of economic and social developments, people have organized their intimate relationships and made choices that define their views of themselves and their places in society, in reliance on the availability of abortion in the event that contraception should fail. The ability of women to participate equally in the economic and social life of the Nation has been facilitated by their ability to control their reproductive lives.[4]

Understanding the place of abortion in shoring up the contraceptive ideology also helps us to understand many of the debates surrounding the regulation of abortion. One might think that providing women with information would be an unambiguous good. After all, if abortion really is "just another medical procedure" and contraception really is "health care", women should have access to all relevant information about side effects and success rates.

However, anyone with the slightest experience in the American political arena surrounding "reproductive health" realizes that this is not the case. The revolutionaries do not view these facts as neutral information allowing women to perform an accurate cost-benefit analysis. Providing these bits of information would challenge the whole concept that sex is normally and normatively a childless activity.

The Catholic Church (along with modern science!) teaches that sex makes babies. Hence, it is utterly irrational to ignore the possibility of a baby when planning one's sex life. The Church has a whole moral teaching about human sexuality that adequately takes account of this obvious fact.[5]

---

[4] *Planned Parenthood v. Casey*, 505 U.S. 833, 856 (1992), Justice Anthony Kennedy writing for the majority.

[5] I hasten to add that the Church's teaching does much more than this. However, taking account of the connection between sex and babies is a fairly minimal requirement that the revolutionaries cannot seem to manage. For a full treatment of the Church's moral teaching,

By contrast, the sexual revolution teaches that sex does not make babies; unprotected sex makes babies. Only if adults intend to make babies should sex be connected to making babies. The government of the United States is now controlled by people who are committed to this ideological, but illogical, position.

No-Fault Divorce and the Deconstruction of Marriage

Losing the Presumption of Permanence

No-fault divorce was the second, equally important structural blow to the nexus of sex, babies, and marriage. A more accurate description of this legal innovation would be "unilateral" divorce: a marriage lasts only as long as the least committed spouse wants it to last. The government will side with the party who wants the marriage the least. Any person can get a divorce for any reason or no reason and never have to offer an account of themselves.

This government policy seriously damages the interests of children. Every child has a legitimate interest in having a relationship with and care from both of his biological parents. Marriage protects that interest by bringing the parents together, hopefully before the child is conceived, in a union of love, for life. Each of the parents will be irreplaceable to the child; the identity of one's parents is an irreducible fact of a person's life. The parents make themselves irreplaceable to one another in the permanent marital bond, precisely because they will be irreplaceable to their child.[6] Removing the presumption of permanence through the introduction of no-fault divorce greatly damages this interest of the child. Marriage began to become something that serves the interests of adults, with the interests of children becoming secondary or even expendable.

---

see John Paul II, *Male and Female He Created Them: A Theology of the Body*, trans. Michael Waldstein (Boston: Pauline Books and Media, 2006). For an overview of Catholic teaching, see the *Catechism of the Catholic Church*, 2nd ed. (Washington, D.C.: Libreria Editrice Vaticana—United States Conference of Catholic Bishops, 2000), "The Sacrament of Matrimony", 1601–660; and "The Sixth Commandment", 2331–400.

[6] William May pioneered this language of spouses making themselves "irreplaceable" to each other and to their children. See William B. May, *Getting the Marriage Conversation Right: A Guide for Effective Dialogue* (Steubenville, Ohio: Emmaus Road Publishers, 2012).

Losing the Presumption of Sexual Exclusivity within Marriage

No-fault divorce also harms the nexus of sex, children, and marriage by removing the social and legal significance of adultery. Under a fault-based system, adultery was considered a marital fault and grounds for divorce in virtually every jurisdiction. By contrast today, an adulterous spouse can sever the marriage bond without penalty. This was a truly revolutionary innovation. Removing adultery from the list of marital faults conveys the unmistakable message that sex with someone other than one's spouse is socially and legally permissible.

The argument for removing adultery as a fault was based on the idea that gathering the necessary evidence was too demanding, judgmental, and onerous. There was an undercurrent of belief that sophisticated people should not be inquiring into such things. However, Professor Lynn Wardle has shown that the American Law Institute's *Principles of the Law of Family Dissolution* had some serious inconsistencies.[7] Their original concept of no-fault divorce allowed consideration of the dissipation of marital assets as a kind of economic marital fault. Likewise, allegations of sexual and physical abuse of the children or of the spouse could be taken into account in property settlements, child custody disputes, and the like.

So if economic faults still exist and abuse faults still exist, what does no-fault divorce actually amount to? It means that the principal fault that was removed was adultery or sexual infidelity. As Wardle says,

> Disregarding fault, may make the jobs of lawyers and judges simpler, but it makes dissolution law and legal proceedings surreal, less responsive to the key issues, and less connected to what is really happening in the parties' lives, and therefore it makes dissolution law less effective, less complete and less just.[8]

When we consider that adultery is consistently ranked as one of the highest causes of divorce, when we consider the pain that sexual betrayal causes, when we consider that all branches of Christianity and Judaism

---

[7] American Law Institute, *Principles of the Law of Family Dissolution* (Philadelphia, Pa.: American Law Institute: 2008).

[8] Lynn Wardle, "Beyond Fault and No-Fault in the Reform of Marital Dissolution Law", in *Reconceiving the Family: Critique on the American Law Institute's Principles of the Law of Family Dissolution*, edited by Robin Fretwell Wilson (New York: Cambridge University Press: 2006), pp. 9–27.

consider adultery a serious sin, writing adultery out of the law was a major step in redefining marriage.[9]

In short, the promotion of a lifestyle based on contraception and the culture of unilateral divorce are two major structural changes that broke the nexus of sex, babies, and marriage. These ideas and the policies that support them set aside the interests of children for the benefit of adults. The loss of the presumption of sexual exclusivity, as well as the loss of the presumption of permanence, harmed the interests of children. Both undermined the legal and social expectation that adults would sacrifice some of their desires for the long-term good of their children.

Likewise, the contraceptive revolution was supposed to make "every child a wanted child". But who can take that cliché seriously now? It may very well be that every child born to highly educated members of the leadership class are "wanted" in the sense of being planned for and prepared for. This is almost certainly because membership in the educated classes practically demands that a woman abort any "unplanned" pregnancies, where "unplanned" means "pregnancy that would interfere with educational or career plans".

By contrast, the percentage of children born to unmarried mothers has increased dramatically among the less educated classes. This increase took place precisely during the period of time in which both contraception and abortion were legally available and highly promoted. These facts should give us a clue that there is something dreadfully incomplete about the contraceptive ideology that claims to make "every child a wanted child".[10]

The Gender Ideology

The second significant idea of the sexual revolution has been the denial of the differences between men and women. Men and women are said to

[9] See Paul R. Amato and Denise Previti, "People's Reasons for Divorcing: Gender, Social Class, the Life Course, and Adjustment", *Journal of Family Issues* 24 no. 5 (July 2003): 602–26; see esp. Table 3, p. 615.

[10] For an explanation of the connection between the contraceptive culture and the rise of nonmarital childbearing, see George A. Akerlof, Janet L. Yellen, and Michael L. Katz, "An Analysis of Out-of-Wedlock Childbearing in the United States", *Quarterly Journal of Economics* 111, no. 2 (May 1996): 277–317. (Akerlof won the Nobel Prize in economics in 2001.) For an analysis of the differences in marital behavior among American social classes, see Kay Hymowitz et al., *Knot Yet: The Benefits and Costs of Delayed Marriage in America* (Charlottesville, Va.: National Marriage Project, 2013).

be completely interchangeable. Gender ideology goes far beyond the reasonable demand that men and women be treated with dignity and respect. It insists that social differences between men and women are evidence of injustice. All such differences are suspect, at least, and quite possibly worse.

Unlike contraception and no-fault divorce, the implementation of the gender ideology cannot be detected in one or two easily identifiable policies. A whole series of public policies and social practices have emerged that are based on the premise that all differences between men and women are ethically suspect. Correcting these differences is an ethical imperative. Examples of such policies include the following: Title IX requires equality between men and women in university sports programs;[11] laws limit the use of physical fitness requirements for law enforcement officers;[12] single-sex educational programs are regulated to ensure that they are not "stereo-typed";[13] and father/daughter dances are considered unlawful gender stereotyping and hence are banned in some places.[14]

But beyond the legal landscape, the cultural landscape has deteriorated to the point that saying, "Men and women are different", is considered a kind of social heresy. It takes genuine courage to say such a thing on a college campus, or in professional settings.

This, then, is what I mean when I use the term "sexual revolution". The idea that we can separate sex from childbearing and separate both from marriage and the idea that men and women are interchangeable are a revolutionary set of ideas. The ideas of the sexual revolution are extremely seductive. Having sex without the responsibilities involved with parenthood and the commitment involved with marriage have an obvious appeal. Yet, despite the superficial and widespread appeal, the ideas are deeply flawed and destructive.

---

[11]Eliza Beeney, "Women Wrestlers Go to the Mat for Equal Rights", ACLU (blog), August 8, 2011, https://www.aclu.org/blog/womens-rights/women-wrestlers-go-mat-equal -rights.

[12]"Physical Ability Tests for Police Departments and SWAT Teams: Know Your Rights in the Workplace", ACLU, fact sheet accessed April 25, 2014, https://www.aclu.org/sites /default/files/assets/kyr_physicalabilities-rel1.pdf.

[13]"Teach Kids, Not Stereotypes", ACLU fact sheet, accessed April 25, 2014, https://www .aclu.org/womens-rights/teach-kids-not-stereotypes.

[14]Rene Lynch, "Father Daughter Dances Banned in R.I. as 'gender discrimination'", *LA Times*, September 18, 2012, http://articles.latimes.com/2012/sep/18/nation/la-na-nn -father-daughter-dances-gender-discrimination-20120918. For my commentary on this issue, see the following: Jennifer Roback Morse, "Home Front", *National Review Online* (blog), September 25, 2012, http://www.nationalreview.com/home-front/328429/father-daughter -dance-banned/jennifer-roback-morse.

Likewise, the idea that men and women are interchangeable appeals to an abstract notion of equality. We think we are bringing about justice. But trying to implement this idea has placed us at war with our own bodies. We are still watching these ideas work their way through the institutions, laws, and practices of society. The ultimate end of this process is nowhere in sight.

Why the *Obergefell v. Hodges* Ruling
Is No Surprise

The earlier stages of the sexual revolution have brought us to the doorstep of genderless marriage, and all that will flow from it. Unilateral divorce makes marriage an adult-centered institution that leaves the interests of children behind. The contraceptive ideology insists that we can act as if sex is a sterile recreational activity. The gender ideology claims that men and women are completely interchangeable.

Society has accepted these claims and, to some extent, institutionalized them in law. It is no wonder that people believe that we can safely remove the gender requirement from marriage. People who have accepted these ideas have already mentally redefined marriage. They cannot understand why others believe marriage should only be between a man and a woman. Animus against same-sex attracted people is the only reason they can imagine.

In every stage of the sexual revolution, one group of people has always been out: children. Sexual revolutionaries claim that "kids are resilient". This justifies divorce on demand. Sexual revolutionaries claim that the unborn child is not truly a person. This justifies removing consideration of the child from the sexual act. Therefore, we should not be surprised to learn that this newest stage of the sexual revolution—namely, removing the gender requirement for marriage—will also be harmful to the interest of children.

What Is Owed to the Child? The Just Entitlements
of Children and Structural Injustices to Children

Unlike adults, a child does not need autonomy or independence. Rather, the child needs and is entitled to a relationship with and care from both of the people who brought him into being. Therefore, the child has a legitimate interest in the stability of his parents' union. According to Article 7 of the United Nations Convention on the Rights of the Child, "The child ... shall have the right from birth to a name, the right to acquire a nationality and as far as possible, the right to know and be cared for by his or her parents."[15]

The sexual revolution has already undermined the rights of the child to a relationship with both of his parents. The widespread legal and social acceptance of nonmarital childbearing almost always means that the child's relationship with his biological father is compromised. The widespread acceptance of unilateral divorce without cause quite frequently results in children being separated from one of their parents.

In addition, children in reconstituted households face a particular set of risks. When a woman has a child out of wedlock, the odds are high that her next child will be with a different man.[16] This phenomenon is so common that demographers have created a new term to describe it. They call it "multipartner fertility". This situation is similar in some respects to the situation of the child of divorce whose parents remarry. In either case, the child is in a compromised situation. He shares living arrangements with a couple (married or unmarried), one of whom is unrelated to him. That new couple may go on to have children together. If and when that occurs, the child from earlier relationship(s) is not entirely part of the new family. That child may feel like a leftover.

This complex set of feelings may account for the consistent results in the social-science literature about the unique difficulties that stepchildren face, whether their parent is married to the new partner or cohabiting without marriage.[17] In addition, the child living in a household with

---

[15] "Convention on the Rights of the Child: Adopted and Opened for Signature, Ratification and Accession by General Assembly resolution 44/25 of 20 November 1989", accessed March 12, 2015, http://www.ohchr.org/Documents/ProfessionalInterest/crc.pdf.

[16] According to the definitive Fragile Families study, low-income, unmarried mothers seldom marry the father of their first child. When an unmarried couple has a child, only 16 percent of them eventually get married to each other and are still married five years after the birth of their child (Sara McLanahan, "Fragile Families and the Reproduction of Poverty", *Annals of the American Academy of Political and Social Science* 621, no. 1 [January 2009]: 111–31, http://www.ncbi.nlm.nih.gov/pmc/articles/PMC2831755/).

[17] See Paul R. Amato and Fernando Rivera, "Parental Involvement and Children's Behavior Problems", *Journal of Marriage and the Family* 61, no. 2 (May 1999): 375–84.

an unrelated adult, including a stepfather or cohabiting boyfriend, is at elevated risk for child abuse.[18]

I call these situations "structural injustices to children". They are injustices for two reasons. First, they deprive children of something to which they are entitled—namely, a relationship with both of their parents. Second, these situations introduce inequalities among children that could be avoided by their parents' committing themselves to permanent relationships with each other.

Some children do not live with both of their biological parents. Some children feel like leftovers from a previous relationship. Some children are asked to change their lodgings every week. Some children may come back to one of their homes to find that their stepsiblings and half-siblings have moved, because the adults' relationship broke up.[19] Other children, those with continuously married parents, do not experience these disadvantages.

These are "structural" injustices because they are inherent in the structure of the family. The adults may be good, decent people with good parenting skills. The problem is not with the particular individuals, and may not be solvable by the particular individuals. Children have these experiences and feelings, in spite of the best intentions of the adults.

Removing the gender requirement from marriage, as the United States has just done in the *Obergefell* ruling, tacitly dismantles these structural rights of children. A genderless marriage system cannot attach children to their own mothers and fathers. A genderless marriage system replaces biological attachments with the intentions and desires of adults. Hence, a genderless marriage system will aggravate existing systematic structural injustices to children and create new sources of injustice.

Over the past fifty years or so, our society has been experimenting with a variety of family structures. We have accumulated data showing that children do need both their mothers and their fathers,[20] and

[18] See Robin Fretwell Wilson, "Undeserved Trust: Reflections on the ALI's Treatments of De Facto Parents", in *Reconceiving the Family*, pp. 90–120, esp. pp. 106–17.

[19] For a collection of divorce stories by children, see the following: Marriage Ecosystem, Ruth Institute, "Kids' Divorce Stories", accessed April 17, 2015, www.kidsdivorcestories.org.

[20] Among the many citations that could be given, the following summarizes some of the most important research: Institute for American Values, *Why Marriage Matters: 26 Conclusions from the Social Sciences* (New York: Institute for American Values, 2005).

that fathers make distinct contributions to the well-being of children.²¹ Researchers have shown that problems for children of divorce become more serious as the children grow older. According to Judith Wallerstein, author of *The Unexpected Legacy of Divorce: The 25 Year Landmark Study*:

> Contrary to what we long thought, the major impact of divorce does not occur during childhood or adolescence. Rather, it rises in adult-hood as serious romantic relationships move center stage. When it comes time to choose a life mate and build a new family, the effects of divorce crescendo.²²

We already know that every one of the alternative family forms poses real and lasting risks for children. It simply strains the imagination to think that same-sex couples will be able to achieve what no other alternative family structure has achieved.

One might ask, where are the rights of children to be found in our legal system? Beyond recognition on the part of the United Nations, these entitlements of children have been implicit in the common law. These rights were once implicitly understood by civil society and the customs of the people, including but not exclusively their religious customs. Implementing genderless marriage requires that the government redefine parenthood throughout the law and suppress the customs and practices of civil society that interfere with the new understanding of parenthood.

Persistent Strategic and Rhetorical Patterns of the Sexual Revolution

The current struggle over the proper definition of marriage did not spring out of nowhere. The groundwork for this latest round of social experimentation was laid years ago by earlier rounds of social experimentation.

---

²¹ For the general overview of the issue, see David Blankenhorn, *Fatherless America: Confronting Our Most Urgent Social Problem* (New York: Harper, 1996). In one study, for instance, father involvement with children was the biggest single predictor of children having fewer behavior problems, as important as higher parental education. See also Amato and Rivera, "Parental Involvement".

²² Judith S. Wallerstein, Julia M. Lewis, and Sandra Blackslee, *The Unexpected Legacy of Divorce: The 25 Year Landmark Study* (New York: Hyperion, 2000), p. xxxv.

The promotion of genderless marriage shares important characteristics with other stages of the sexual revolution: (1) Revolutionaries generally begin their campaign with a relatively modest and seemingly inoffensive objective. Once the principle is established in law, they expand the principle. The public would not have accepted the original concept, had they known where it would lead. (2) Revolutionaries then systematically suppress evidence of the harms of their policies. This suppression includes the silencing of the victims. (3) Next, revolutionaries overstate the benefits of their policies, with a steady campaign of propaganda to promote their ideas of what constitutes a "benefit" from the sexual revolution. (4) The revolutionary concept is promoted in the name of expanding either freedom or equality or both. Never mentioned is the fact that revolutionary policies end up creating less freedom and equality in other areas. (5) The revolutionaries marginalize institutions and individuals who express disagreement with their policies. Dissent cannot be tolerated.

Let us examine these one by one. I make no claim to make an exhaustive list. I am sure that the average American reader will be able to add to it.

1. The modest initial objective. This strategy has been used since the very first days of the sexual revolution. I call it the "all we want to do" strategy. All we want to do is, for instance, lower the cost of divorce to the handful of people whose marriages have irretrievably broken down, allow abortion for cases of rape and incest, or allow married couples to use contraception for serious health reasons.[23]

Never mentioned in any of these episodes is the fact that the purveyors of these "goods" want much more than they admit. To take just one example, the day that *Griswold v. Connecticut* was handed down, the attorneys and supporters of *Griswold* began talking about how the Court's argument could be used to obtain a right to abortion.[24]

In the lead-up to *Obergefell*, we heard, "All we want to do is allow two people of the same sex who love each other to get married." The

---

[23] See, generally, David J. Garrow, *Liberty and Sexuality: The Right to Privacy and the Making of* Roe v. Wade (New York: Macmillan Publishing, 1994).

[24] Ibid., pp. 258–59. *Griswold v. Connecticut* was the 1965 U.S. Supreme Court case that overturned all state-level regulations regarding access to and information about contraception. Six months after *Griswold*, the lead attorney in the case wrote a law review article making the point that the *Griswold* argument could be used to overturn abortion laws (see ibid., p. 260).

same principles that demand removing the gender requirement from marriage will lead to removing the limitation of only two partners to a marriage, removing the prohibition on incest, and lowering the age of consent. But when questioned, advocates deny this obvious point.

2. Suppressing evidence of harms. Sex makes babies. Men and women are different. Trying to build a whole society around the opposites of these propositions is sure to hurt people. The success of a revolutionary endeavor depends on keeping a lid on the harms that people endure.

The sexual revolutionaries typically present an approved "narrative". Individuals and families whose lived experience does not fit that official "narrative" are dismissed. For instance, one official abortion "narrative" is that abortion is a harmless medical procedure that benefits women. Therefore, women who experience regrets or side effects are dismissed by the public, their families, their boyfriends, their therapists, and sometimes even their pastors. The official "narrative" around divorce is that "kids are resilient". Even inside their own families, children's wounds from their parents' divorce are minimized. The social-science evidence that has accumulated over the past fifty years supports children's feelings that something is dreadfully wrong. But this evidence is explained away or dismissed or ignored.

A closely related tactic is to suggest that any problems that you and your family may experience from the sexual revolution are not due to the flawed ideology, but due to your personal failings. Here are some examples: "Contraception works fine, if you use it consistently and correctly." "Women who get depressed after their hook-ups were prone to depression to begin with." "Stepfamilies can work out just fine, as long as the stepparents treat the children as if they were their own, as long as the biological parents do not criticize each other, and as long as the biological parent allows the stepparent to act as a parent with respect to discipline." "Single parenthood can work just fine, as long as the mother has enough financial resources." "Sexual activity is the key to fulfillment if you are born gay. Any gay person who wants to stop being sexually active because it isn't making him happy has something wrong with him. He is insufficiently accepting and affirming of his gay identity."

3. Overstating benefits with propaganda. Minimizing the costs and overstating the benefits ensures that each new generation continues to accept the sexual revolution. In fact, it is impossible to overstate the amount and intensity of the propaganda necessary to prop up the sexual revolution.

The *Huffington Post* has an entire page devoted to divorce, called Huff Post Divorce. This page is almost entirely pro-divorce propaganda. They have a chipper feature called "Blended Family Friday", in which they interview people "to learn how they successfully blended their two families. Our hope is that by telling their stories, we'll bring you closer to blended family bliss in your own life!" [25] They featured a story called "18 Inspirational Tattoos That Celebrate Divorce". [26] And on it goes.

Marriage is said to be dangerous for women, since they might be trapped with an abusive husband. Never stated is the fact that for most women, cohabitation is the likely alternative to marriage. And domestic violence and child abuse are more likely in cohabiting relationships than in marriage.[27]

The propaganda around the health risks of hormonal contraception is appalling. A study showing that hormonal contraception doubles the risk of glaucoma concluded blandly that "doctors should advise women to get their eyes checked." [28] A study of 1.6 million Danish women showed that some forms of oral contraception nearly doubled the risks of strokes and heart attacks.[29] The *Boston Globe*'s headline reporting on this story (I'm not making this up!) was "Birth Control Pills Raise Risk of Heart Attacks and Strokes, But Only Slightly".[30]

Continual propaganda is necessary because the ideas of the sexual revolution are irrational and inhumane. Sex actually does make babies. Children really do need and long for their own mothers and fathers.

---

[25] For weekly stories, see the following HuffingtonPost.com website: http://www.huffing tonpost.com/2015/03/18/advice-for-blended-families_n_6897816.html?utm_hp_ref =divorce&ir=Divorce.

[26] Joelle Caputa, "18 Inspirational Tattoos That Celebrate Divorce", Huff Post Divorce, *Huffington Post*, March 23, 2015, http://www.huffingtonpost.com/joelle-caputa/18-inspirational -tattoos-that-celebrate-divorce_b_6911090.html?utm_hp_ref=divorce&ir=Divorce.

[27] See Wilson, "Undeserved Trust", in *Reconceiving the Family*, pp. 90–120, esp. pp. 106–17.

[28] "Long-Term Oral Contraceptive Users Are Twice As Likely to Have Serious Eye Disease", American Academy of Ophthalmology, OphthalmologyWeb, November 19, 2013, http://www.ophthalmologyweb.com/1315-News/150975-Long-Term-Oral-Contraceptive -Users-Are-Twice-As-Likely-To-Have-Serious-Eye-Disease/.

[29] See Øjvind Lidegaard et al., "Thrombotic Stroke and Myocardial Infarction with Hormonal Contraception", *New England Journal of Medicine* 366, no. 24 (June 14, 2012): 2257, http://www.nejm.org/doi/full/10.1056/NEJMoa1111840.

[30] Deborah Kotz, "Birth Control Pills Raise Risk of Heart Attacks and Strokes, But Only Slightly", *Boston Globe*, June 13, 2012, http://www.boston.com/dailydose/2012/06/13/birth -control-pills-raise-risk-heart-attacks-and-strokes-but-only-slightly/G3wQiKMFSVbc9 W7HKJeWqO/story.html.

Men and women are different. People encounter evidence in support of these facts, just in the natural course of events. The propaganda is designed to overwrite experience.

   4. *The battle cry of freedom and equality.* Out in front of all these "modest reform" campaigns is the battle cry of freedom: "All we want to do is allow people the opportunity and the freedom to make their own choices about their lives." But if people do not have access to the information that would allow meaningful choices, they are not really free. They are being manipulated by those who control information.

   In addition, breaking down the small society of the family frequently ends up increasing the power of the state to intervene in people's private lives. No-fault divorce appears to make people more free, because the divorcing spouse gets to do what he wants. But in reality, no-fault divorce has led to an increase in the power of the government over individual private lives. That is because unilateral divorce means one party wants a divorce against the wishes of the other, who wants to stay married. Therefore, the divorce has to be enforced. The coercive machinery of the state is wheeled into action to separate the reluctantly divorced party from the joint assets of the marriage, typically the home and the children.

   Family courts tell fathers how much money they must spend on their children, and how much time they get to spend with them. Courts tell mothers whether they can move away from their children's fathers. Courts rule on whether the father's attendance at a Little League game, a public event that anyone can attend, counts toward his visitation time. Courts rule on which parent gets to spend Christmas Day with the children, down to and including the precise time of day they must turn the child over to the other parent. Involving the family court in the minutiae of family life amounts to an unprecedented blurring of the boundaries between public and private life. People under the jurisdiction of the family courts can have virtually all of their private lives subject to its scrutiny. If the courts are influenced by ideology such as feminism, that ideology reaches into every bedroom and kitchen in America.[31]

   One man, one woman, for life, is the family form that most effectively keeps the government out of the family. Deviations from this

---

[31] See Stephen Baskerville, *Taken into Custody: The War against Fathers, Marriage and the Family* (Nashville, Tenn.: Cumberland House Publishing, 2007).

norm require intervention into the family, sometimes very personal and intense intervention, in order to meet the needs of the family members.

The Scope of Equality

Sometimes, as in the discussion leading up to *Obergefell*, the strongest appeal is to equality. But we must ask ourselves, does marriage equality for adults introduce or aggravate other forms of inequality into society? A 2011 example from the United Kingdom will illustrate the problem.

> A High Court judge issued a stark warning ... about the traumatic effects on children when complicated homosexual parenting arrangements unravel. In a case in which a gay man and his lover took the lesbian mother of his children and her partner to court for access rights, the judge expressed frustration.[32]

Here is the first inequality: some fathers have clear and defined "access rights" to their children and others do not. The father of these children was evidently a perfectly fit parent. No contrary allegation has been made. Yet, unlike most known fit fathers, the father of a child born inside a lesbian relationship must get judicial permission to see his own children.

In such situations, the adults treat their sexual relationships as primary: the two women are a couple and the two men are a couple. Their relationship with the child's other parent is secondary by design. When everyone is getting along, the primary status of the adult sexual relationships is not so apparent. But as soon as conflict arises among the adults (as it surely must in any relationship as long-term and intense as a shared parenting relationship), the primacy of the sexual relationship becomes highlighted.[33]

---

[32] Steve Doughty, "High Court Judge's Blast for Four Gay Parents Fighting over Two Little Sisters", *Daily Mail*, October 10, 2011, http://www.dailymail.co.uk/news/article-2047671/High-Court-judges-blast-gay-parents-fighting-little-sisters.html#ixzz3UTp8dzo3.

[33] The report on this very case states, "After the birth of the first child, the couples maintained friendly relations for several years, but 'it all went wrong' in 2008 when they fell into dispute over the children" (ibid.).

The judge is struggling because there is no just solution to this problem. The judge intuits that both biological parents ought to have parenting rights. The judge also intuits that the children have established relationships with their parents' sexual partners. Disrupting these relationships may be problematic for the children. As long as the adult sexual relationships are competing with the parental relationships, there is no resolution that is fair to all parties.

These adults were relatively mature, sophisticated people, in their forties and fifties. The problem is not with the individuals. The problem is with the structure of the family. The structure of the family creates a higher than average likelihood of conflict. And once that conflict arises, resolving the conflict in a way that does justice to all parties is nearly impossible.

These inequalities are not unique to this particular case, but are inherent in the use of third-party reproduction as a normative method for same-sex couples to become parents.[34] Men who provide sperm to lesbian couples are not treated equally with other fathers. Some excluded fathers will want a relationship with their children, which they will be legally denied.[35] A woman who gives birth to babies inside a same-sex union is not treated equally with other mothers. The law treats her legal relationship with another woman as tacit consent for her partner to become, in effect, the adoptive parent to any children she may give birth to over the life of their union. The implicit assumption is that this plan for sharing parenthood with another woman will be in all respects equivalent to making a lifelong plan to share parenthood with the child's other biological parent, namely, the child's father. Biology can be safely subordinated to the intentions and plans of the adults. The further

[34] The Williams Institute classifies approximately half of the children being raised in same-sex households as "biological" children. This almost certainly means the use of third-party reproduction. See Gary J. Gates, "LGBT Parenting in the United States", Williams Institute, February 2013, http://williamsinstitute.law.ucla.edu/wp-content/uploads/LGBT-Parenting .pdf.

[35] See, for instance, Donal Thornton, "Gay Irish Sperm Donor Wins Visiting Rights to Lesbian Couple's Child", Irish Central, December 11, 2009, http://www.irishcentral.com /news/Gay-Irish-sperm-donor-wins-visiting-right-to-lesbian-couples-child-79055562. html. The *In re M.C.* case arose in part because the biological father came forward to try to care for his daughter after the birth mother went to jail for accessory to attempted murder of her former partner. See Jennifer Roback Morse, "Why California's Three-Parent Bill Was Inevitable", *Public Discourse*, September 10, 2012, http://www.thepublic discourse.com/2012/09/6197/.

implicit assumption is that the biological mother has no special status in comparison with the "social mother". They are both equally the child's generic, nongendered "parents".

By contrast, all other mothers who make adoption plans for their children are permitted to change their minds once the baby is born. No state in the United States honors an adoption contract made before a child is born. How often do we hear new parents say things like "I had no idea how I would feel." Up until now, the law has recognized the strength and uniqueness of the maternal bond. It is only the woman who forms a legal union with another woman who cannot reconsider after her child is born.[36]

Let us now look at the distress created for the children by the case in 2011 in the United Kingdom, introduced above. The Justice said that at least one of the children had suffered significant emotional harm. "The four adults in this case regard the price paid by these two children as an acceptable price for the pursuit of their own adult disputes." The judgment quotes a social worker who said the older daughter was caught in "a horrendous tangle of emotion and conflict that exists between these adults. The girl is being made to carry the responsibility for the failure of the adults in this system to overcome the conflicts between them."[37]

The children created through third–party reproduction and adopted by same-sex couples have no legally recognized right to relationships with their biological parents. Their parents have a conflict between their shared parental relationship and their primary sexual relationship. So, "marriage equality" for adults introduces new inequalities in other relationships, including family structure inequalities for children.

5. *Marginalizing dissent.* Marginalizing dissent from individuals and institutions has been one of the hallmarks of the sexual revolution. The "feminist" movement made it socially impossible for anyone to disagree with their primary tenets. Professor Larry Summers lost his job as president of Harvard University because he dared to suggest that men and

---

[36]This is probably a factor in the drama in the background of the *In re M.C.* case. It is surely a factor in the celebrated Miller-Jenkins custody dispute. See John Curran, "FBI Arrests Tenn. Pastor in Vt.-VA Custody Case", *U-T San Diego*, April 22, 2011, http://www .utsandiego.com/news/2011/apr/22/fbi-arrests-tenn-pastor-in-vt-va-custody-case/. Also, see "Vermont: Ruling in Lesbian Custody Case", *New York Times*, January 22, 2010, http:// www.nytimes.com/2010/01/23/us/23brfs-RULINGINLESB_BRF.html.

[37]Doughty, "High Court Judge's Blast".

women might have different aptitudes for math and science. This was potentially an empirically testable claim, one that is almost certainly correct.[38] But even the suggestion of differences between men and women was enough for a very powerful and sophisticated man to lose his job.

Viewed in this context, the persecution of the children of same-sex parents is not surprising. Children of same-sex couples have reported feelings of loss;[39] they are now being vilified for speaking out[40] and have even had their livelihoods threatened.[41] The anti-child comments on some threads on the Internet actually demonstrate that the sexual revolutionary system is quite fragile and cannot withstand dissent.

There is one last point that previous steps of the sexual revolution share with the political struggles that led to the redefinition of marriage. In each case, the innovation is the product of elite culture, against the values of the middle and lower classes. Abolishing all restrictions on contraception in the 1960s was a project of the WASP elites of Connecticut, including members of the Yale Law School and Yale Medical School.[42]

Warren Buffett has spent over $1 billion promoting abortion.[43] Almost 10 percent of international human rights philanthropy, over $100 million annually, is spent on "reproductive rights". Much smaller amounts are spent on protecting other, arguably more serious, forms of human rights abuses: freedom from torture and degrading treatment, $16.9 million; freedom from slavery and trafficking, $15.2 million; freedom

---

[38] See Simon Baron-Cohen, *The Essential Difference: Men, Women and the Extreme Male Brain* (Oxford: Penguin Press Science, 2007).

[39] See Amicus Brief of Oscar Lopez, *Brenner v. Armstrong*, case no. 14-14061 (11th Cir. 2014) (Case Pending); available online at http://www.scribd.com/doc/251078014 /Robert-Oscar-Lopez-Amicus-Brief#scribd. See also Kirsten Andersen, "'Quartet of Truth': Adult Children of Gay Parents Testify against Same-Sex 'Marriage' at 5th Circuit", *LifesiteNews*, January 13, 2015, https://www.lifesitenews.com/news/quartet-of-truth-adult -children-of-gay-parents-testify-against-same-sex-mar.

[40] See "Christian Daughter Spits on Her Gay Parents", *Daily Kos*, March 19, 2015, http://www .dailykos.com/story/2015/03/19/1372065/-Christian-Daughter-Spits-on-Her-Gay-Parents#.

[41] See Rivka Edelman, "This Lesbian's Daughter Has Had Enough", *American Thinker*, October 20, 2014, http://www.americanthinker.com/articles/2014/10/this_lesbians_daughter _has_had_enough.html. See also Robert Oscar Lopez, "A Tale of Targeting", *First Things*, October 21, 2014, http://www.firstthings.com/web-exclusives/2014/10/a-tale-of-targeting.

[42] See Garrow, *Liberty and Sexuality*.

[43] Mike Ciandella and Katie Yoder, "Warren Buffett: The Billion-Dollar King of Abortion", Media Research Center, May 13, 2014, http://www.mrc.org/articles/warren -buffett-billion-dollar-king-abortion.

from genocide, crimes against humanity, and forced disappearance, $1.3 million.[44]

The support for redefining marriage and parenthood has largely been financed by a handful of wealthy people and foundations. Paul Singer,[45] Tim Gill,[46] and George Soros[47] finance the think tanks and other pro-gay advocacy organizations. The lawsuit to undermine Proposition 8 was financed by Hollywood millionaire Rob Reiner.[48]

Next Revolutionary Steps

Seeing the structure of the sexual revolution helps us to see what the next steps are likely to be. Instituting genderless marriage is likely to usher in many changes. Legalized genderless marriage will block meaningful reform of the "third-party reproduction industry". The children of third-party reproduction will experience all the problems as children of divorce and others as well. As adults, these children report longings for their missing biological parent, anxiety about meeting and inadvertently falling in love with a half-sibling, and anger about being partially bought and paid for.[49] Thus, further structural injustices to children will take place.

In addition, further deconstruction of marriage will occur, to the extent that marriage itself may be abolished. The principle that "love

---

[44] Steven Lawrence and Christen Dobson, *Advancing Human Rights: The State of Global Foundation Grantmaking* (Foundation Center, 2013), http://foundationcenter.org/gain knowledge/research/pdf/humanrights2013.pdf.

[45] Sean Sullivan, "Meet the Billionaire Hedge Fund Manager Quietly Shaping the GOP Marriage Debate", *Washington Post*, May 3, 2013, http://www.washingtonpost.com /blogs/the-fix/wp/2013/05/03/meet-the-billionaire-hedge-fund-manager-quietly-shaping -the-gop-gay-marriage-debate/.

[46] Lawrence and Dobson, *Advancing Human Rights*, p. 109, shows that the Gill Foundation gave $10 million to international human rights groups supporting LGBT rights.

[47] Soros' Open Society Foundation gave over $4 million to international human rights groups supporting LGBT rights (ibid.).

[48] Gregg Kilday, "How Rob Reiner Became Anti-Prop 8 Kingpin", *Hollywood Reporter*, August 5, 2010, http://www.hollywoodreporter.com/news/how-rob-reiner-became-anti -26362.

[49] See Elizabeth Marquardt, Norvell Glenn, and Karen Clark, *My Daddy's Name Is Donor: A Pathbreaking Study of Young Adults Conceived through Sperm Donation* (New York: Institute for American Values, 2010).

makes a family" will not be easily contained. Demands for multiparty marriages and incestuous marriages will be difficult if not impossible to resist. And, since genderless marriage eliminates the essential public purpose of marriage (namely, attaching mothers and fathers to their children and to one another), the argument for marriage itself will grow correspondingly weaker. When marriage becomes nothing but a government registry of friendships, who needs marriage? Further promotion of the gender ideology and further deconstruction of gender will take place. The active promotion of transgenderism will certainly follow.

Implications for Pastoral Practice

This analysis has implications for pastoral practice, and not only for same-sex attracted persons. Indeed, one of the most powerful implications is that the problems of the sexual revolution are common to all of its victims, and not just same-sex attracted persons. We need not single out anyone for special attention. In fact, we ought to acknowledge that we have failed to take appropriate pastoral care of the victims of earlier rounds of the sexual revolution: children of divorce, reluctantly divorced people, refugees from the hook-up culture, and many other groups of people. We have also failed to hold accountable those who have inflicted harms on innocent people.

Most importantly, we have not confronted the lies of the sexual revolution as forcefully and as consistently as we should have. The Catholic Church can take pride in the fact that she, and pretty much she alone, has seen that this would all end badly. Even so, she still has not done enough.

We can say with authority that earlier rounds of the sexual revolution have not worked out as promised. Divorce hasn't made people happy. Contraception hasn't made people happy. Single parenthood hasn't made people happy. The interests of children have been set aside every step of the way. The odds are against the claim that embracing a "gay" identity and acting on sexual desires for a person of the same sex will make people happy.

The campaign for redefining marriage has itself created problems. The campaign seeks to convince people that "Love Makes a Family". This is not a legal doctrine. It is a cliché. This cliché undermines marriage and entrenches in people's minds what social scientists call the "soulmate" view of marriage. Under this superficial view of love and marriage, the proper attitude to take toward marriage is to seek someone who makes you "feel good". And when the "love" fades? The partners feel justified in ending the marriage, much to the detriment of any children they may have had or adopted together.

Conclusion: Something Positive for Everyone

This overview of the sexual revolution may seem overwhelming, and, in some respects, it is. Its seductive ideology is deeply entrenched throughout society. Superficially attractive, the "use and be used" lifestyle is only appealing when viewed from the "user" end. Being the "use-ee" is not nearly so appealing. And with the possible exception of a handful of predatory alpha males, just about everyone has been used or knows someone who has.

However, the very pervasiveness of the ideology and the rapidity of its spread can give us reasons for hope. Those people who have been wounded can become the greatest advocates for positive change. Young people can often be talked into things that are not in their long-run interest. Yet, even many young people have been victimized by the sexual revolution: they have experienced their parents' divorces and those of their friends. These young people already know that the "kids are resilient" storyline is a lie, an excuse created to justify adult self-centeredness. Many people from the baby boomer generation know from experience that the sexual revolution is one set of empty promises after another.

All these people are potential advocates for positive change. Instead of seeing people with a past and a guilty conscience as enemies, we can see them as potential allies. They can speak about the sexual revolution directly from their personal experiences. Mary Magdalene can speak a truth the Virgin Mary knows nothing of.

This analysis also shows why speaking the truth in love is always good policy. The sexual revolution has proceeded and succeeded by suppressing the truth, both at the personal level and the public policy level. Many people's lives have been damaged by trying to do the impossible task of living according to revolutionary ideology. Those people are hungry for the truth. And everyone, no matter what their walk of life, skills, or talents, can help bring that truth to the people they encounter.

Those of us of the baby boomer generation, who have participated in the sexual revolution and survived, need to make a second career out of speaking the truth about our experiences. I know what I know. I cannot, will not, be talked out of it. I am certain I am not the only person in this situation.

The ultimate Truth is a Person. Each of us, no matter our situation, may be someone's only connection with Jesus Christ. We cannot heal all the victims of the sexual revolution. But he can. Our job is to keep the lines of communication open, keep speaking the truth in love, and keep out of the way of the Holy Spirit leading people closer to Jesus. That is enough for one lifetime.

Our Prophetic Moment

Peter Herbeck

The Supreme Court of the United States has determined that same-sex couples have a constitutional right to marry. The battle for same-sex marriage was fought on every front: in federal and state courts, legislatures across the country, city council meetings, schools from elementary to secondary, churches, neighborhoods and in families. It does seem the country was not really "ready" for the legalization of same-sex marriages, but it is a done deal now.

The battle for the redefinition of marriage and for the full embrace of the gay agenda has been so widespread, in part, because those who were driving it planned it that way. Their intent has been to bring the battle to every corner of society, to every institution, including—and especially—to the Church. The Church, particularly the Catholic Church, has been and remains a primary target.

Although the Supreme Court has decided that same-sex couples have a right to marry, this decision has only heightened the responsibility of the Church. (Here I will not speak to the religious liberty issues, which are of immense importance, but go beyond the scope of this essay. Here I will address the educational responsibilities of the Church.) And, of course, the Supreme Court decision means that it will be more and more difficult to make the case against same-sex marriage.

The thought of where it is all leading and what it will likely mean for the Church can be unsettling and discouraging. I've felt both of those emotions at one time or another during the past few years. But recently, I've begun to see this whole conflict as a moment of great opportunity for the Church. I see it fundamentally as a time of testing for the Church, and an opportunity to honor God and love our neighbor by witnessing to the truth.

Why do I put it that way? First, because at the heart of the battle are two competing world views. Redefining marriage is, in part, a rationalization about homosexual behavior, which is simply the latest expression of the fundamental rationalization at the heart of the sexual revolution:

> At stake in the rationalization of homosexual behavior is the notion that human beings are ordered to a purpose that is given by Nature. The understanding that things have an in-built purpose is being replaced by the idea that everything is subject to man's will and power, which is considered to be without limits. This is what the debate over homosexuality is really about—the Nature of reality itself.[1]

At the heart of the sexual revolution is a different understanding of the nature of sexuality, which, however sincere those who hold it may be, results in the suppression of the truth about the nature of sexuality. It's an ideology, a collective deception to deny the nuptial meaning of the body and the procreative and unitive purpose of marriage. What makes the current fight so opportune is the strong, very public, and growing opposition to the Church by political and cultural forces.

This is an opportunity for the Church to witness to love. The modern world has disconnected truth from love. Sexual love is defined by feelings, passions, and desires, by personal choice, without reference to the objective truth about the meaning and purpose of sexual love. At the canonization of Saint Teresa Benedicta of the Cross, Saint John Paul II reminded us of her wisdom, calling her the "martyr for love" who taught us that "love and truth have an intrinsic relationship", that "truth and love need each other". He said, "St Teresa Benedicta of the Cross says to us all: Do not accept anything as the truth if it lacks love. And do not accept anything as love which lacks truth! One without the other becomes a destructive lie."[2]

The separation of truth from the meaning of sexual love is "a destructive lie". We cannot accept it. The challenge before us now is to love, to love God by honoring and giving thanks for his creative design and

---

[1] Robert R. Reilly, *Making Gay Okay* (San Francisco: Ignatius Press, 2014), front-cover sleeve.

[2] "Homily of John Paul II for the Canonization of Edith Stein", October 11, 1998, http://w2.vatican.va/content/john-paul-ii/en/homilies/1998/documents/hf_jp-ii_hom_11101998_stein.html.

purpose in human sexuality, and to love our neighbor by giving public witness to that truth in love.

The question is, are we ready?

Meeting the Challenge

At the moment, it doesn't look like we are ready to help the culture realize the mistake it has made. If recent polls are any indication, Catholics' opinions about the redefinition of marriage and homoerotic sex have moved in the wrong direction. A recent study by the Public Religion Research Institute found the following:

> Nearly three-quarters of Catholics favor either allowing gay and lesbian people to marry (43 percent) or allowing them to form civil unions (31 percent). Only 22 percent of Catholics say there should be no legal recognition of a gay couple's relationship, in addition, 56 percent of Catholics now believe that sex between members of the same sex is not a sin.[3]

A shift in attitudes toward same-sex "marriage" among Catholic millennials (people born since 1980) is even more pronounced. A recent Pew Research study shows 70 percent of millennials in favor of same-sex "marriage". That's up from 51 percent in 2003.[4]

How did we get here so quickly? There are many reasons, but without question one of the most important reasons is what we're up against. The forces set against the Church on this issue are formidable; they're very well organized, well financed, and totally committed to their cause. What they've accomplished in just a few decades is impressive. It may be one of the most successful propaganda campaigns our country has ever seen. They set out to change the way America thinks about homosexuality, and they have succeeded.

Their success is the result, in part, of the work of a small group of smart, focused leaders who produced a game plan that gave direction, vision, and concrete strategy to those who wanted to produce lasting social change.

---

[3] Public Religion Research Institute, "Catholic Attitudes on Gay and Lesbian Issues: Comprehensive Report from Recent Research", March 22, 2011, www.publicreligion.org.

[4] Pew Research Center, May 6, 2013, www.pewresearch.org.

That game plan was laid out by Marshall Kirk and Hunter Madsen in a book called *After the Ball: How America Will Conquer Its Fear and Hatred of Gays in the '90s*. The authors are both Harvard-trained social scientists who set out to "convert" America on this issue: "We mean conversion of the average American's emotions, mind, and will, through a planned psychological attack, in the form of propaganda fed to the nation via media."[5]

The "psychological attack" followed a three-step strategy: desensitization, jamming, and conversion. The first step was to "desensitize people to gays and gayness" by "inundating them with a continuous flood of gay-related advertising".[6] The point here was to normalize "gayness" in order to begin to break down peoples' discomfort and to soften the immediate "physiological reasons" for their resistance to the lifestyle, and ultimately to create feelings and attitudes of indifference. A compelling example of this has been the funny, endearing, harmless, sensitive, disarming gay characters that have appeared in so many prime-time sitcoms during the past decade.

Step two was a form of "counterconditioning" that inserted an "incompatible emotional response" in a person in order to create an internal conflict or "emotional dissonance" that will "tend to result in the alteration of previous beliefs and feelings so as to resolve the conflict".[7] In other words, "jamming" is a way of removing or stopping the "reward" a person feels when he is opposing something he believes is morally wrong. The psychological reward reinforces the conviction that one is doing the right thing. Jamming seeks to literally "jam" that feeling of reward by associating it with an "incompatible emotional response". For example, those who oppose the gay agenda or gay marriage are depicted as bigots, haters, "crude loudmouths and a[—]holes".[8]

The ultimate effect is to "get the bigot into the position of feeling a conflicting twinge of shame, along with his reward, whenever his homo-hatred surfaces, so that this reward will be diluted and spoiled."[9] The constant labeling of those who disagree with the gay agenda as "intolerant bigots", "haters", and "mean-spirited people" and associating them

---

[5] Marshall Kirk and Hunter Madsen, *After the Ball: How America Will Conquer Its Fear and Hatred of Gays in the '90s* (New York: Doubleday, 1989), p. 153.

[6] Ibid., p. 149.

[7] Ibid., p. 150.

[8] Ibid., p. 151.

[9] Ibid.

with racists, Nazi skinheads, and the KKK are exercises in jamming. Jamming produces the desired effect without having to make a rational argument: "Our effect is achieved without reference to facts, logic or proof."[10] Nobody wants to be thought of in negative terms. Jamming has worked like a charm; it is a potent weapon that has reduced multitudes to silence and has paved the way for the tidal wave of "conversions" documented in recent polls.

The furor that arose over Indiana's Religious Freedom Restoration Act provides a clear case in point. The response by the opponents of the bill went according to plan: jamming through hysterical propaganda, making threats, and denouncing supporters of the act as "homophobic bigots". Despite the irrational hysteria and the obvious false and unjust characterization of the proponents of the bill and the nature of the bill itself, the only response the bishops of Indiana could muster was to propose "dialogue".

That is exactly the kind of response the opponents of the bill were looking for—a timid, conciliatory nonresponse. The Indiana case provided a moment of real opportunity for the bishops and for prominent lay leaders to stand up together against the bullying and propaganda with a measured, clear, and confident response. Instead, what we got was backpedaling, conflict avoidance, and confusion.

To the average viewer, our leaders looked intimidated, confused, and completely unprepared for what they were up against. The net effect is to make it look as if our leaders lack the conviction of their principles. And that in turn destabilizes the convictions of their followers who are also trying to navigate their way through the hysteria.

A particular strategy that our opponents have directed toward the Church goes one step further. They have sought to subvert Church teaching and to remove the "psychic reward" some Catholics feel when they oppose homosexuality and the redefinition of marriage by highlighting sympathetic voices of authority in the Church who cast doubt upon the veracity of biblical proscriptions against homosexuality. It takes courage to stand against the tide of popular culture on this issue. When a lay person stands up to defend the Church's position and is then confronted by the words of a bishop, priest, theologian, or biblical scholar to the contrary, it creates the same "emotional dissonance" and subverts the "psychic reward" they should be feeling for defending the faith. Instead, they get jammed and reduced to silence, undercut by the voice of "authority".

[10]Ibid., p. 153.

The final step in the game plan has been conversion. Conversion makes use of "Associative Conditioning" by presenting "bigots" with pictures of people they admire or members of "their crowd" associating with gays. "In Conversion, we mimic the natural process of stereotype-learning, with the following effect: we take the bigot's good feelings about all-right guys, and attach them to the label 'gay,' either weakening or, eventually, replacing his bad feelings toward the label and the prior stereotype."[11]

This effect is produced when prominent Catholic politicians, athletes, entertainers, academics, and even clergy are "in the picture". Conversions have happened. Catholic "converts" are popping up each day, from Catholic Supreme Court justices to Catholic high school kids. Ironically, many are becoming positively evangelical for the cause, zealous to help change the mind of other Catholics who remain in the dark, "bigots" who need conversion.

The rapid pace of change on this issue among Catholics and other Christians has been disturbing, but not surprising. The "planned psychological attack" succeeded in "converting" many of the baptized, because a significant percentage of them have yet to put on "the mind of Christ". That is, they are essentially unconverted. They are still "conformed to the passions of [their] former ignorance",[12] taking their cues from the world, which makes them easy prey to the propaganda. Archbishop Charles Chaput put his finger directly on the weak state of so many of the baptized when he said, "A kind of foggy worldliness has settled into the American Catholic soul. In effect, a great many Catholics keep the Catholic brand name, but they freelance what it means.... In fact, by our actions, many of us witness a kind of practical atheism: paying lip service to God, but living as if he didn't exist."[13]

Build the Church

Al Kresta, host of "Kresta in the Afternoon" on Ave Maria Radio, has a mantra that captures our primary mission: "Build the Church, Bless the Nation." His point is simple. Our job as disciples of Jesus is not to fix the world. Rather, we are to build the Kingdom of God. The Church,

[11] Ibid., p. 155.
[12] 1 Pet 1:14.
[13] Charles J. Chaput, *Render Unto Caesar: Serving the Nation by Living Our Catholic Beliefs in Political Life* (New York, N.Y.: Doubleday, 2008), pp. 181–82.

a living sign of the Kingdom of God, is meant to be a "light to the nations".[14] The only way she can be a blessing to the world is to be that light, to be a distinct counterculture whose way of life radically expresses fidelity to Christ.

To express fidelity to Christ, one must first know him. Therefore our starting point has to be a genuine response to the urgent plea of the recent popes for a new evangelization, the reevangelization of the de-Christianized. Saint John Paul II put it succinctly: "It is necessary to awaken again in believers a full relationship with Christ, mankind's only savior. Only from a personal relationship with Jesus can an effective evangelization develop."[15] Only from a living, personal relationship with Christ will believers find the courage to love their neighbors in the truth, and to stand against the aggressively secularizing tide of our culture.

The next step is to "strengthen the brethren". What is needed is clear, confident leadership within the Church, beginning with our bishops. We have been blessed to have so many bishops who are faithful to the teaching of the Church, and some who are willing to speak up and to take the lead in providing a compelling defense of marriage and the family. These are challenging times for our bishops. It is a very difficult time to lead. The pressure coming upon the Church falls upon them in a particular way. They bear a heavy burden, a burden that seems to increase daily. They cannot and are not meant to carry that burden of leadership on their own, but the leadership they do exercise has to be clear, bold, and decisive. More than ever, we will need shepherds who are models of "apostolic courage based on trust in the Spirit".[16]

Catholics need to see bishops who embody that apostolic courage, men who are ready to engage this spiritual battle head-on. They must be as Pope Francis calls each of us, "willing to put his or her whole life on the line, even to accepting martyrdom, in bearing witness to Jesus Christ".[17] Many bishops put out strong statements against the Supreme

[14] See Is 42:6; 49:6; cf. Lk 2:32; Acts 13:47; 26:23.

[15] John Paul II, speech to bishops of Southern Germany, December 4, 1992, *L'Osservatore Romano* (English ed.), December 23/30, 1992, pp. 5–6.

[16] John Paul II, *Redemptoris Missio*, December 7, 1990, no. 30, http://w2.vatican.va /content/john-paul-ii/en/encyclicals/documents/hf_jp-ii_enc_07121990_redemptoris -missio.html.

[17] Francis, Apostolic Exhortation *Evangelii Gaudium*, November 24, 2013, no. 24, http:// w2.vatican.va/content/francesco/en/apost_exhortations/documents/papa-francesco _esortazione-ap_20131124_evangelii-gaudium.html.

Court's decision on same-sex marriages but they need to continue to speak out on this issue. This is the time to "preach the word, be urgent in season and out of season, convince, rebuke and exhort, be unfailing in patience and in teaching."[18]

The temptation for many leaders, including our bishops, has been to seek accommodation with the culture, to avoid conflict, or as some have put it, to "duck-and-cover"[19] by proposing dialogue as our default response to confrontation. Dialogue is an important pathway in many cases, but it cannot be the only arrow our leaders carry in their quiver. We also need bishops and leaders who are modern day "apostles and prophets", courageous witnesses who rally and embolden the faithful to live the radical demands of the gospel and to give witness to the beauty, truth, and goodness of the biblical vision of human sexuality.

Catholics need to hear the truth confidently proclaimed. There has been a systematic, unrelenting attack on the Bible, the catechism, and the teaching of the Church since the beginning of the sexual revolution. A great deal of confusion has been sown about what the Bible actually says about God's plan and purpose for human sexuality. The teaching of the Church is clear; it just needs to be proclaimed with greater confidence, clarity, power, creativity, and consistency.

Getting the message right is crucial. Saint John Paul II's *Theology of the Body* is an important starting point. It can be a potent antidote to the errors of the culture. However, it must be presented in a way that is accessible to ordinary folks, discussed in small, well-facilitated groups and coupled with personal testimony by ordinary men and women who embody its teaching. That process has begun, but much more is needed to make the truth it contains more accessible to a broader audience. We need a clear plan to teach this systematically, with the dedication and commitment to unpacking all of its beauty to every age group in the Church.

Expect Opposition

As beautiful as this teaching is, the resistance to it will become even greater now that same-sex marriage has been legalized. Bishops and senior leaders must train others in leadership to expect it. Those who

[18] 2 Tim 4:2.
[19] R. R. Reno, "Duck and Cover Catholicism", *First Things*, April 2, 2015, http://www.firstthings.com/blogs/firstthoughts/2015/04/duck-and-cover-catholicism.

hold to the full counsel of God's Word about human sexuality are now a minority in this country. The pressure to suppress the truth about human sexuality is strong. Cultural and political forces invested in that suppression are creating a climate where open hostility to the Church's teaching is acceptable. As Professor Robert George recently said:

> The days of socially acceptable Christianity are over. The days of comfortable Catholicism are past. It is no longer easy to be a faithful Christian, a good Catholic, an authentic witness to the truths of the Gospel.... To be a witness of the Gospel today is to make oneself a marked man or woman. It is to expose oneself to scorn and reproach.[20]

None of us want to face scorn and reproach. But we all need to come to terms with it. In the days ahead, it will be unavoidable; fidelity to the teaching of Jesus and his Church provokes hostility. We all need to be reminded—indeed, to be trained—to expect opposition, not as something to be feared and avoided, but as a normal outcome for those who identify publicly with Jesus.

Jesus said, "Blessed are you when men revile you and persecute you and utter all kinds of evil against you falsely on my account. Rejoice and be glad, for your reward is great in heaven, for so men persecuted the prophets who were before you."[21] There is great temptation, in the face of such opposition, to avoid conflict by not addressing the problem. It is especially difficult knowing that a growing number of people in our dioceses and congregations no longer agree with the Church's teaching in this area. Catholics are becoming more vocal in their support of the LGBT agenda.

Clergy, in particular, must resist the temptation to repeat what happened in the case of contraception. Because so many Catholics oppose the Church's teaching on contraception, it is rarely mentioned. The silence encourages dissent. It communicates a lack of conviction and nerve on the part of leadership, and the belief that in the end it's no big deal. After all, if Father thought it was a big deal, he would say something, right?

[20] "Remarks of Robert P. George, National Catholic Prayer Breakfast, May 13, 2014", *The Joys of Being Catholic* (blog), May 17, 2014, http://thejoysofbeingcatholic.blogspot.com/2014/05/remarks-of-robert-p-george-national.html.
[21] Mt 5:11–12.

We cannot allow the preaching of the Church to be cowed into silence. "We too believe, and so we speak."[22] We need to pray, to beg the Lord to increase in us the virtues of courage and fear of the Lord. We need courageous leadership, men and women who are "prepared to suffer injury and, if need be, death for the truth and for the realization of justice".[23] The redefinition of marriage, the denial of sexual complementarity and the procreative and nuptial meaning of the body, is a lie. It is the denial of reality, and, ultimately, it is a refusal to do justice to God and neighbor.

The psalmist cries out, "Teach me your way, O LORD, that I may walk in your truth; unite my heart to fear your name."[24] The fear of the Lord is a lost virtue today. Few seem to understand what it means. To the modern ear it doesn't sound nice. We consciously need to cultivate this virtue among our people once again. "The fear of the LORD is the beginning of wisdom";[25] it protects us against folly of walking in "our truth" and helps us to be rightly ordered to reality, to living in God's truth.

Saint Paul said, "[K]nowing the fear of the Lord, we persuade men".[26] Fear of the Lord leads to courageous proclamation of the truth. The fear of men leads to cowardice, timidity, silence, and feeling ashamed of the gospel because it is rejected by those we seek to please. There is a great deal of "blushing at the gospel" among the baptized, especially the gospel truth about human sexuality. The fear of men reveals an inordinate love of self. We are afraid of the high cost of social rejection, so we remain silent or accommodate our views as a means of self-protection. We need leaders who can help us identify that temptation and overcome it.

Leaders should present the witness of the martyrs: "And they have conquered him by the blood of the Lamb and by the word of their testimony, for they loved not their lives even unto death."[27] Teach us not to love our lives in such a way that we will lose them. Don't caress, flatter, entertain, or pamper the sheep. Arm them for battle!

---

[22] 2 Cor 4:13.

[23] Josef Pieper, *A Brief Reader on the Virtues of the Human Heart* (San Francisco: Ignatius Press, 1991), p. 11.

[24] Ps 86:11.

[25] Prov 9:10.

[26] 2 Cor 5:11.

[27] Rev 12:11.

Take Action

In order to equip Catholics to face these challenges, we need unity of vision and purpose among our leaders, and in our institutions of formation.

Beginning with the diocesan staff, the bishop needs to sound a clarion call, to gather his key leaders around him, and to forge a clear strategy for united leadership throughout the diocese. The unity and vision needs to begin with the senior staff of the diocese. The bishop will need to be unequivocal about the importance and priority of fighting this battle together.

A united team will help to set an example for the whole diocese. Nothing undermines the Church's mission more than a mixed message from the diocesan leadership. A house divided against itself cannot stand. A leader in either open or silent disagreement with this fundamental issue should not remain in leadership. The opposition the Church is facing on these issues is strong and getting stronger. Our people have a right to the truth about what Jesus and his Church teach about human sexuality, marriage, and family. Silence, direct opposition, or even a muddled, accommodating message has a devastating impact in the current climate.

It is not enough to just "get the message out" and assume leaders who don't agree with it will get the message and move on. That rarely happens, and even when it does, it usually takes a long time. There is no time to waste; the battle is in full swing—time is of the essence. Instead, the bishop needs to be ready to speak personally with any leader who is not on board. And when necessary, he must take action to remove whoever it is, even if it is a friend, an old seminary buddy, a person of influence, or someone who has been on staff for a long time.

Gathering the Priests

As with the example of the central staff of the diocese, the bishop must communicate the same vision, priority, and sense of urgency to his priests. The priests need to know how important this issue is to the bishop and how he wants them to communicate it to their people. The pressure on parishioners to acquiesce to mounting societal pressure on this issue is going to make it very difficult for priests to teach and lead in this area. There will be opposition, pushback, and division. People will get angry, some will hold back their financial giving, and others will leave the parish. Again, one temptation will be to avoid the issue, to not rock the boat, in order to "maintain unity" or simply to avoid conflict.

Priests will need to know if the bishop is going to back them when they teach the faith without compromise, and when the going gets tough. What will the bishop do if a prominent member or members of the parish push back or withhold their money, or if an influential staff member expresses disagreement with the Church's teaching on same-sex marriage?

The cost of "hanging in there" with the Church on these issues is going to be too much for some, maybe even for many, of our people. Ultimately, many priests, especially young priests, wonder if they will end up standing alone in this fight, or if they will be thrown under the bus if things get messy. As one priest put it, "I have to know the bishop has my back on this."

Getting the message clear is crucial. Priests will need some coaching, bullet points for homilies, and clarity about what the Church and the Scriptures actually teach. They need direction on what to teach and how to teach it. It will be helpful to dedicate a full day or two at the annual priests' study conference to equip priests to preach effectively in this area, and to provide answers—accessible to both the priest and parishioners—to common objections to Church teaching. Not every priest or deacon is equipped to teach effectively in this area without help.

Parishioners need to hear a clear, positive, and bold presentation on the meaning of human sexuality, marriage, and family life. They also need to hear what the Bible and catechism teach about the consequences of refusing to live according to God's plan and purpose for human sexuality. The temptation, and the typical pattern here, is to present the positive picture without presenting the consequences of rejecting that picture. That is a bad strategy. People need to know what is truly at stake in rejecting God's plan for human sexuality. Indeed, they have a right to know, and those commissioned to preach have the duty to tell them. The stakes could not be higher; eternal destinies hang in the balance.

Finally, priests or deacons who contradict the Church's teaching in this area or who simply refuse to teach it must be addressed. The pattern of permitting "dissenting" priests to lead what often become "dissenting" parishes weakens the Church's voice. There is plenty of room for diversity of opinion on many issues the Church faces in her life and mission. The meaning of human sexuality, marriage, and family is not one of them. It is foundational and leaves no room for compromise or accommodation.

Equipping Our Schools

The controversy at Charlotte Catholic High School, in Charlotte, North Carolina, over the content of Sister Jane Dominic Laurel's presentation of Church teaching on human sexuality, marriage, and family, provided an important teaching moment and wake-up call for all of our Catholic schools.[28] Among other things, it exposed the division that exists among parents, students, teachers, and administrators on these issues and made it clear that many of our schools, from universities to elementary schools, are profoundly impacted by the values of the prevailing culture.

In this highly charged climate, even small missteps can lead to big problems. The bishop and school superintendent should meet with the principals to communicate a clear vision and to form concrete strategies that will help bring clarity, confidence, and a sense of peace about communicating the beauty and truth of the Church's teaching.

Again, the bishop needs to know that his superintendent and principals are on the same page and, where it is needed, to give one-on-one time with these leaders to hear their concerns, answer questions, and encourage them in their leadership. The principals need to know exactly what is expected of them and to know that they are not fighting this battle on their own. Principals who are not able or ready to lead with conviction on these issues will need additional support and training. If the principal for some reason cannot take the lead, efforts should be made to find a teacher with effective leadership and to give that teacher authority to ensure that a school undertakes the education programs needed.

One important service the diocese can provide for schools is to put together an experienced, gifted, and well-trained team of speakers who

---

[28]See Amy Cowman, "Nun's Message to Students on Gays Prompts Parents' Ire", *USA Today*, April 3, 2014, http://www.usatoday.com/story/news/nation/2014/04/03/catholic-nun-homosexuality-speech/7250825/.

can serve as a resource "from the outside" to supplement the ongoing teaching of the theology faculty and campus ministers. Gifted communicators who have the message well in hand, and have been vetted by the diocese, can provide much-needed support to the staff and teachers of the school. They can provide some of the much-needed "conversion" moments that help move individuals and at times the entire school community forward on these sensitive issues.

Creating an atmosphere of open dialogue with students, as well as places where they can ask honest questions, is a delicate but essential piece of an overall strategy for helping students process and navigate their way through the cultural confusion in which they live. Young people are bombarded on a daily basis with propaganda about all things sexual, and with misinformation about the Church and her teaching. They are under almost constant pressure to get on board with popular culture. With a new "constitutional right" to same-sex "marriage", the pressure to conform will only increase.

Our students live in a world where their Church and school are on record as opposing in principle what the government and many of their own friends, neighbors, coaches, and employers view as a fundamental human right. Their peers in public schools will be subject to an intense propaganda campaign in support of these newly recognized rights, and those who oppose them will be demonized and characterized as religiously motivated, narrow-minded, intolerant bigots. The last thing young people want to experience is being considered intolerant, judgmental, unloving, and mean by their peers. They will need all the help and support they can get from strong, compassionate, and informed adults who are convinced about the Church's teaching—men and women who can serve as mentors. They will need to know why the Church's teaching is an expression of true love and compassion.

Parents will need help as well. From the time inquiring parents enter the school for the open house, the message to them should be clear: the school exists to make disciples of Jesus Christ. That means passing on to students the faith as they have received it, whole and entire. Each family ought to receive at the open house a bullet-point handout of what will be taught about these hot-button issues during their child's time at the school. The principal or appointed staff member should encourage parents to discuss the material with their child and should offer opportunities to speak with teachers or staff if they have any questions. Finally, they should make it clear that enrollment will include a signature of consent by both parents and student that they have read the material and give their full support to it.

Once their children are enrolled, parents will need ongoing support in raising their sons and daughters in the faith. The school can become a significant source of support for them by helping them get engaged in the mission and activities of the school so they can experience being part of a community of missionary disciples. Parents need help from other parents who have successfully raised their children in the faith. They need ongoing teaching, practical help, testimony to what is possible, and the kind of personal support that lets them know they are not alone.

Finally, underlying the clarity of vision, courage to act and practical help is needed to make all of our Catholic institutions places to encounter Jesus, where initial conversion and the awakening to a full relationship with Jesus is a primary goal. It's not enough for our schools to be excellent academic institutions committed to first-rate extracurricular activities. We must all take to heart the words of Pope Emeritus Benedict XVI to Catholic educators: "Fostering personal intimacy with Jesus Christ and communal witness to his loving truth is indispensable in Catholic institutions of learning."[29] It is only from a relationship with Jesus that teachers, parents, and students will be able to rise to the challenge we face today.

This is a moment of opportunity for Church leadership. It is an opportunity to express radical love for God and neighbor. It is a time to teach and lead, to teach by leading, and to model for our people humble, passionate, intelligent, strategic, and courageous leadership. May we who have been "clothed with power from on high"[30] and filled with sure hope[31] rise to the challenge—and live as faithful witnesses to love.

---

[29] "Address of His Holiness Benedict XVI: Meeting with Catholic Educators" (Catholic University of America, Washington, D.C., April 17, 2008), http://w2.vatican.va/content/benedict-xvi/en/speeches/2008/april/documents/hf_ben-xvi_spe_20080417_cath-univ-washington.html.

[30] Lk 24:49.

[31] See Heb 6:19.

AFTERWORD

Pastoral Challenges of Same-Sex Marriages

Janet E. Smith, Ph.D.

As this book was going to print, the Supreme Court decided that all states must open "marriage" to same-sex couples. This book has not addressed political questions and will not do so here. But as always, laws have an impact on culture in general and thus on the way we all perceive things. The particular difficulty this decision presents is that it is based on many erroneous understandings—of the human person, of marriage, and particularly of love.

The decision and discussion surrounding the decision has been cast in terms of "love". Some think that allowing same-sex marriages will help those who experience SSA avoid loneliness by finding love and intimacy within marriage. But is that true? Is that "solution" based on a true or on a false view of human nature and of love?

The Church certainly agrees that love is at the heart of human existence and that all human persons are called to love and be loved. What the Court and our culture seem to have forgotten is that there are many kinds of love and that only one kind of love should be expressed sexually. Parents and children love each other, as do grandparents and grandchildren; brothers and sisters love each other; friends love each other; teachers love their students; and so forth. However, for none of those relationships is sexual expression moral. Sexual expression of love is in accord with God's plan for sexuality only when it is between a married male and female since only they can truly engage in a one-fleshly act that expresses a lifetime commitment to another and one that is inherently oriented to the bringing forth of new life.

Loneliness is a sad reality in our world, not just for those with SSA. The Supreme Court decision reinforces the false view that only in marriage can love and intimacy be found. We must acknowledge that not even marriage provides any sure guarantee against loneliness. The only sure guarantee against loneliness is to live a life of complete self-giving. Fortunately there are abundant opportunities for being a part of loving relationships outside of the marital relationship.

Those providing pastoral care to individuals who experience SSA should help them come to see that they have great powers to love in chastity and that seeking holiness will bring them to become self-givers, becoming bearers of love to others who need love with the result of abundant love in return. They are not at all deficient in being able to live lives of complete self-giving. On the contrary, chaste celibate love has a grand tradition in the Church and a special purity and selflessness about it. All those who never find a suitable spouse, those whose spouses die or leave them, and those who are called to a life of consecrated virginity are not being called to lonely or loveless lives: they are being called to spread their love widely. The Supreme Court decision does not expand the notion of love but, regrettably, narrows it.

Those who would engage in effective relationships with those who experience same-sex attractions are called to love them, to enfold them in a circle of loving relationships, and to call them to extend their love widely.

The Supreme Court decision makes the job of those wanting to provide good pastoral care to those who live with SSA both more difficult and less difficult.

The decision that same-sex marriage is a "right" makes our job more difficult because it increases the confusion of young people and others about the morality and acceptability of same-sex relationships. People will commonly think not only that same-sex marriage is a legal right but a natural right. Many people equate legality and morality and think that if an action is legal, it must be moral. But making abortion legal did not make it moral—nor does making same-sex marriage legal make it moral. Still, future generations will be "educated" to think that same-sex "marriage" and traditional marriage are equivalent and thus that homosexuality and heterosexuality are equivalent. Consequently, fewer of those who live with SSA will choose celibacy and seek holiness. They will be involved in the gay lifestyle for longer periods and acquire more "baggage" that will be difficult to shake.

Young people who may have been very hesitant to entertain the overtures of older seductive people of the same sex may now think that being sought after in this way is just normal and may be more inclined to respond favorably to such overtures. They may then become confused about their sexual identity, whereas in the past they may have made a smooth transition into healthy heterosexual relationships.

People who would be good friends to those who experience SSA will now need to break with their culture to do so. Indeed, that has been true for some time, but the challenge has become greater. For some time, those who recognize that same-sex sexual relationships are not fulfilling for human nature have had to risk being considered hateful for holding that position. How many people will find the courage to seek the truth? Won't most just go along with the law?

How can this decision make the "job" of those who would offer good pastoral care to those who experience SSA less difficult? Brute facts have their own power, and the fact is that same-sex marriages will not, and cannot, lead to true happiness. Many think that permitting same-sex "marriages" will lead to greater happiness for same-sex couples and even for children raised in those relationships, just as many think access to abortion and even pornography can increase happiness. Those of us who understand that the Church's teachings against divorce, fornication, contraception, pornography, abortion, and same-sex "sexual acts" are based on a profound knowledge of human nature know that living in conflict with human nature simply cannot bring true happiness. (We don't even believe that greed brings happiness, for it, too, is in conflict with what is good for human nature!) Our society has become a huge cultural experiment where we are "testing" whether acts judged grievously immoral for millennia by philosophy, Scripture, theology, law, custom, and common sense do in fact bring human happiness when accepted by society, when taught in schools, and when celebrated in the media and entertainment.

Unfortunately, many of us do not seek relief from our bad choices until we have suffered the bad consequences of those choices. It will surely not be long before those who contract same-sex "marriages" are divorcing at a high rate.[1] Same-sex marriages will end by divorce at a high rate since the relationships are not rooted in nature and are not

---

[1] There is evidence that they already do: Jesse Green, "From I do to I'm Done", *New York Magazine*, February 23, 2014, http://nymag.com/news/features/gay-divorce-2013-3/ and Andrew Gellman, "Same sex divorce rate not as low as it seemed," *Washington Post*, December 15, 2015, http://www.washingtonpost.com/blogs/monkey-cage/wp/2014/12/15/same-sex-divorce-rate-not-as-low-as-it-seemed/ accessed June 26, 2015.

supported by sacramental grace. The bad consequences of divorce are considerable and well-known. Arguably the divorces of same-sex couples will be worse—both for the partners and any children. The divorced individuals are likely to be even more prone to self-reproach and despair about their ability to find love, and they may have greater reason to be concerned about the well-being of their children, whose lives are already made very difficult by lack of the presence of parents of each sex.

The negative consequences of contraception, abortion, pornography, and divorce have been terribly corrosive to our culture and detrimental to human happiness. That reality has led some to reconsider their acceptance of such actions and to see the wisdom of the Church. Nonetheless, those who are drowning in the consequences of bad choices often cannot find the right perspective to see what is happening. Those who are blessed to be shaped by Church teaching must become evermore zealous in living out that teaching and promoting it so that others might find the true path to happiness.

True happiness means becoming evermore Christ-like, in becoming evermore selfless and self-giving. Christians know that the self-giving life is one that is infinitely rich in loving relationships, relationships that affirm the deepest part of the person. Our increasingly anti-Christian culture seems to reject the Christian notion of love and sacrifice, which at one time it thoroughly respected. There is no reason that any unmarried person, whether or not they live with SSA, should not be able to achieve love, fidelity, devotion, and sacrifice in selfless chaste relationships. Again, the Supreme Court decision has narrowed the vision of the scope of love, not expanded it. Christ taught the most expansive love of all by teaching that all are infinitely lovable, all are to be infinitely loved, and all are called to love infinitely.

CONTRIBUTORS

Robin Teresa Beck is an author, speaker, and life recovery coach. In February 2009 she showed up to receive ashes at a Catholic Church. At the time of her arrival she had been actively involved in the gay community for thirty-five years with no plans to ever leave (plus the likelihood of her becoming Catholic was slim to none). Six months later she recommitted her life to Jesus Christ, joined the Church in April 2010, and is now on a mission from God to tell the truth concerning same-sex attractions. She is the author of *I Just Came for Ashes* (Dunphy Press, 2012).

Dennis J. Billy, C.Ss.R. is an American Redemptorist of the Baltimore Province. He holds an A.B. in English literature from Dartmouth College (Hanover, New Hampshire), and M.R.E. and M.Div. degrees from Mt. St. Alphonsus Seminary (Esopus, New York). After his seminary training, he went on to earn a Th.D. in Church history from Harvard Divinity School (Cambridge, Massachusetts); an M.A. in medieval studies from the University of Toronto in Canada; an M.M.R.Sc. in moral theology from the Katholieke Universiteit Leuven in Belgium; an S.T.D. in spirituality from the Pontifical University of St. Thomas (Angelicum, Rome); and a D.Min. in spiritual direction from the Graduate Theological Foundation (Mishawaka, Indiana). From 1988 to 2008 he was professor of the history of moral theology and Christian spirituality at the Alphonsian Academy of the Pontifical Lateran University in Rome. He is presently professor, scholar-in-residence, and holder of the John Cardinal Krol Chair of Moral Theology at St. Charles Borromeo Seminary, Overbrook, in Wynnewood, Pennsylvania. He has authored or edited over thirty books, published over three hundred articles in a variety of scholarly and popular journals, and is very active in retreat work and the ministry of spiritual direction.

J. Budziszewski, Ph.D. is professor of government and philosophy at the University of Texas, Austin, and specializes in political philosophy, ethical philosophy, and the interaction of religion with philosophy. Among his research interests are classical natural law, virtue ethics, moral self-deception, family and sexuality, and the problem of toleration. His books include *On the Meaning of Sex* (Intercollegiate Studies Institute Press, 2012); *What We Can't Not Know: A Guide* (Spence, 2003; second edition by Ignatius Press, 2010); *The Line through the Heart: Natural Law as Fact, Theory, and Sign of Contradiction* (Intercollegiate Studies Institute Press, 2009); and, most recently, *Commentary on Thomas Aquinas's Treatise on Law* (Cambridge University Press, 2014).

Robert and Susan Cavera have been involved in EnCourage for 19 years after being invited by Father John Harvey to attend a Courage Conference. Father Harvey then challenged them to begin an EnCourage Chapter in the Diocese of Lansing, Michigan. The couple developed the "Four Ps" (Pray, Prepare, Persevere, and Proclaim) which have since become the heart of their message to other EnCourage members. Robert holds a bachelor of science degree from St. Norbert College and a master of arts degree from Michigan State University. Susan holds a bachelor of science degree from St. Norbert College. With the support of their pastor and bishop, they lead their local EnCourage meeting and serve as coordinators for EnCourage Chapters throughout the United States. Because of their active presence in annual Courage conferences, they are in contact with EnCourage members nationally and internationally.

Father Paul N. Check, S.T.B., S.T.L. was ordained a priest of the diocese of Bridgeport, Connecticut, in 1997. He holds an S.T.B. from Gregorian University and an S.T.L. from the University of the Holy Cross, both in Rome. He served as an officer in the U.S. Marine Corps for nine years prior to entering the seminary. In 2008, he was selected to succeed Father John Harvey as the executive director of Courage International, at the request of Father Harvey and with the approval of Bishop William Lori and Cardinal Timothy Dolan.

Timothy P. Flanigan, M.D. is professor of medicine in infectious diseases at the Miriam and Rhode Island Hospitals and Brown Medical

School. He received a B.A. from Dartmouth College and an M.D. from Cornell University Medical School. In 1991, he came to join Dr. Charles Carpenter to lead the HIV and AIDS program and subsequently was appointed Chief of Infectious Diseases in 1999 until stepping down in 2012. He spearheaded the HIV Care Program at the Rhode Island Department of Corrections and has received NIH funding to develop improved treatments for HIV infection. He has received recognition from the Robert Wood Johnson Foundation and from the HIV Medicine Association for his community-based work with HIV-infected men and women who are in prison and jail, and for providing educational support for their children. In 2013, he was ordained a permanent deacon in the Roman Catholic Diocese of Providence, Rhode Island.

Janelle M. Hallman, Ph.D. is an assistant professor at Denver Seminary and is a licensed professional counselor with over twenty years of clinical experience with faith-based men and women with same-sex attraction, LGB-identified youth and adults, and their families. She directs a counseling clinic in Denver, Colorado, and is the executive director of Desert Hope Ministries, a nonprofit organization providing dynamic retreats for Christian parents of gay-identified children. Dr. Hallman regularly lectures, trains, supervises, and consults other therapists and pastoral caregivers on issues related to sexuality and gender, both nationally and internationally. She is the author of *The Heart of Female Same-Sex Attraction: A Comprehensive Counseling Resource* (InterVarsity Press, 2008) and has contributed several articles to edited books. She completed her M.A. in counseling at Denver Seminary and her doctorate in counselor education and supervision at Regent University.

Peter Herbeck is the vice president and director of missions for Renewal Ministries. For the past thirty years, he has been actively involved in evangelization and Catholic renewal throughout the United States, Canada, Africa, and Eastern Europe. Peter is a cohost for the weekly television programs *The Choices We Face* and *Crossing the Goal*. He also hosts the daily radio show *Fire on the Earth*. He is the author of *When the Spirit Comes in Power* (St. Anthony Messenger Press, 2003) and the coauthor of *When the Spirit Speaks: Touched by God's Word* (coauthored with his wife, Debbie; St. Anthony Messenger Press, 2007). He has also produced CDs and booklets about discipleship and life in the Spirit. Through articles,

CDs, radio and television programs, and conference speaking, Peter has also worked to provide Catholic leaders with the tools to address effectively the challenges in the fight to redefine marriage. Peter is involved with i.d.9:16, an outreach to Catholic young adults that is sponsored by Renewal Ministries.

Timothy G. Lock, Ph.D. is a licensed psychologist in full-time private practice, working within a Catholic anthropology to offer psychological assessment, psychotherapy, and psychological consultation. While Dr. Lock has a general practice, he does specialize in the treatment of clergy and male and female religious, as well as those who have experienced trauma, those who suffer from anxiety disorders, and those who struggle with sexual issues. Dr. Lock serves on the board of directors of Courage International and on the Diocese of Bridgeport Ministerial Misconduct Advisory Board. Formerly, he was the coordinator of an adult sexual offender treatment program, providing psychotherapy to convicted sexual offenders in a large urban area outside of New York City. Dr. Lock has lectured nationally and internationally to seminarians, clergy, mental health practitioners, and the general public on issues including Catholic psychology, Catholic psychotherapy, the psychology of same-sex attractions, and psychotherapeutic treatment of individuals with same-sex attractions. He can be contacted at www.DoctorTimLock.com.

Rachel Lu, Ph.D. is a writer and instructor of philosophy. She has a Ph.D. in philosophy from Cornell University and is a senior contributor at *The Federalist*. Her work has also appeared in *Crisis Magazine*, *Ricochet*, *Public Discourse*, *First Things*, *National Review*, *National Catholic Register*, *Aleteia*, *Touchstone Magazine*, and *Human Life Review*. She teaches philosophy at the University of St. Thomas.

Doug Mainwaring is a marriage, children's rights, and grassroots activist. He cofounded National Capital Tea Party Patriots. Doug has written opinion and commentary for the *Washington Times*, *Washington Post*, *Washington Examiner*, *Baltimore Sun*, *Public Discourse*, *American Thinker*, and others. He has been a guest on Fox News, Sky News, and NPR. He has testified before the U.S. House of Representatives Ways and Means Committee and numerous state legislative bodies, as well as town hall meetings, panels, and rallies. He is cofounder of CanaVox, a grassroots movement to create a vibrant marriage culture, and he recently participated in the Vatican colloquium "Complementarity of Man and Woman in Marriage".

Daniel Mattson lives in the Midwest, where he has a career in the performing arts. He is a member of the Courage Apostolate and is featured in the documentary *Desire of the Everlasting Hills*. He has written about the Church's good news concerning homosexuality in *First Things*, *Crisis Magazine*, and *Catholic Answers Magazine*, as well as other publications. He is also a regular contributor to Chastity.com. He is a frequent guest on Catholic radio, appearing often on *Catholic Answers Live*, the *Al Kresta Show*, and *Catholic Connection* with host Teresa Tomeo. He blogs at LettersToChristopher.wordpress.com. Other writings may be found at JoyfulPilgrims.com. He is currently writing a book for Ignatius Press about same-sex attraction and his conversion to the Catholic Church.

Monsignor Livio Melina, Ph.D., S.T.D. is president and professor of moral theology at the Pontifical John Paul II Institute for Studies on Marriage and Family at the Lateran University in Rome. In addition to numerous articles, he has written, coauthored, and edited several books. Among his English titles are *Building a Culture of the Family: The Language of Love* (Alba House Society of St. Paul, 2011); *The Epiphany of Love: Toward a Theological Understanding of Christian Action* (Wm. B. Eerdmans, 2010); *Learning to Love* (Gracewing, 2011); and *Sharing in Christ's Virtues: For a Renewal of Moral Theology in Light of Veritatis Splendor* (Catholic University of America Press, 2001). He is a member of the Pontifical Academy of Theology and consultor of the Pontifical Council for the Family and the Pontifical Council for Health Care Workers. He is editor of the journal *Anthropotes*.

Jennifer Roback Morse, Ph.D. is the founder of the Ruth Institute, an interfaith organization that addresses the lies of the sexual revolution. She has authored or coauthored four books and spoken around the globe on marriage, the family, and human sexuality. Her newest book is *The Sexual Revolution and Its Victims: Thirty-Five Prophetic Articles Spanning Two Decades* (Ruth Institute, 2015). She earned her Ph.D. at the University of Rochester and taught economics at Yale and George Mason universities. Dr. Morse was named one of the Catholic Stars of 2013 on a list that included Pope Francis and Pope Benedict XVI.

Joseph Prever graduated from the Thomas More College of Liberal Arts with a degree in literature. He has written for *Catholic Phoenix, Catholic Exchange, Our Sunday Visitor,* and his own blog, GayCatholic.com. He currently lives in the Boston area, where he works as a web developer.

David Prosen graduated in 2006 with a M.A. in counseling from Franciscan University of Steubenville. He works at several places, including Franciscan University of Steubenville as a clinical counselor and at the Raphael Remedy of New York, where he offers Catholic phone/Internet counseling and life coaching. As a Catholic therapist he helps others with a variety of issues, some of which include depression, anxiety, gender wounds, co-dependency, and more. As a life coach, David specializes in helping Catholic parents navigate the waters with a loved one claiming a gay or lesbian identity. He has given numerous presentations from a Catholic perspective across the country on same-sex attraction and has had a number of articles published in magazines and Internet sources. David can also be seen in the recently released documentary *The Third Way: Homosexuality and the Catholic Church,* by Blackstone Films.

Deborah Savage, Ph.D. is a member of the faculty at the St. Paul Seminary School of Divinity at the University of St. Thomas in St. Paul, Minnesota, where she teaches philosophy and theology and also serves as the director of the Masters in Pastoral Ministry Program. She received her doctorate in religious studies from Marquette University in 2005; her degree is in both theology and philosophy. Her more recent publications include "The Centrality of Lived Experience in Wojtyła's Account of the Person" (*Annals of Philosophy,* 2013); "The Nature of Woman in Relation to Man: Genesis 1 and 2 through the Lens of the Metaphysical Anthropology of St. Thomas Aquinas" (*Logos, A Journal of Catholic Thought and Culture,* 2015); "The Genius of Man", in *Thinking with Pope Francis: Catholic Women Reflect on Complementarity, Feminism, and the Church* (OSV Publications, 2015).

Bob Schuchts, Ph.D. is the founder and president of the John Paul II Healing Center in Tallahassee, Florida, where he and his team offer healing and equipping conferences for audiences, including priests, seminarians, religious, married couples, and lay leaders in the Church. He is the author of *Be Healed: A Guide to Encountering the Powerful Love of Jesus in Your Life* (Ave Maria Press, 2014) and several journal articles, including "Security, Maturity, Purity: Foundations for a Chaste Celibacy" (*Chaste Celibacy: Living Christ's Own Spousal Love,* 2007).

Janet E. Smith, Ph.D. holds the Father Michael J. McGivney Chair of Life Ethics at Sacred Heart Major Seminary in Detroit. She is the author of *Humanae Vitae: A Generation Later* (Catholic University of America Press, 1991) and *The Right to Privacy* (Ignatius Press, 2008); the coauthor of *Life Issues, Medical Choices: Questions and Answers for Catholics* (coauthored with Chris Kaczor; Servant, 2007); and the editor of *Why Humanae Vitae Was Right: A Reader* (Ignatius Press, 1993). She is best known for her talk "Contraception: Why Not". She has published widely on topics on sexual ethics and bioethics.

Eve Tushnet is a writer in Washington, D.C. She entered the Catholic Church in 1998 and is the author of *Gay and Catholic: Accepting My Sexuality, Finding Community, Living My Faith* (Ave Maria Press, 2014). She has been published in the *Atlantic,* the *American Conservative, Commonweal, Crisis, First Things,* the *New York Post,* the *Weekly Standard,* and online at the *Washington Post* and the *New York Times,* among other outlets, on topics ranging from pro-life horror movies to the U.S. National Figure Skating Championships. She blogs at http://www.patheos.com /blogs/evetushnet/.

Archbishop Allen H. Vigneron, Ph.D., S.T.L. was named archbishop of the Detroit archdiocese on January 5, 2009, succeeding Cardinal Adam Maida; he was appointed by Pope Benedict XVI. Previously, he was coadjutor bishop for the diocese of Oakland, California, for nine months and served as bishop there for six years from 2003 to 2009. Before that he was an auxiliary bishop in Detroit, Michigan, for seven years. He served as rector-president of Sacred Heart Major Seminary from 1994 to 2003. In July 2015, Archbishop Vigneron will become the president of the USCCB Committee on Doctrine.

INDEX

Aardweg, G. van den. *See* van den
Aardweg, G.
abortion, 117, 127, 289, 292, 298, 299,
305, 327, 328
abuse
origins of same-sex attraction and,
54–55, 61, 250, 251
physical abuse of minors, 195, 251
of same-sex attracted persons by
others, 223
of same-sex partners, 268–70, *270*,
280, 285
sexual abuse of minors, 54–55, 63,
68, 195, 229, 250, 251
sexual abuse of women, 66
accompaniment, pastoral concept of,
9–10, 15, 17–19, 26, 48, 64, 102,
156, 170
Acts
13:47, 316n15
14:15–17, 119n3
17:23, 120n8
17:28, 116n1
26:23, 316n15
Adam 4 Adam, 280
Adam and Eve, 8, 62, 74, 75, 81, 84
addictive behaviors
biblical language and, 178
co-morbid with same-sex attraction,
12, 196, 249, *267*, *269*, 277, 279,
280, 281, 282, 285
divine providence, abandonment to,
155
youth support and, 225
adoption, 304

Aelred of Rievaulx, *De speculo caritatis,*
76n11
Aelred of Rievaulx, *De spiritali amicitia,*
73–87
author and persona, gap between, 83
dialogical dimension of spiritual
friendship and, 84
fruits of friendship in this life and the
next, 77–78
goodness, roots of friendship in,
78–79, 85
healing and wholeness in Christ in,
85–86
kiss, theology of, 77, 78, 79n22,
80–81, 85–86
medicine of life, friendship described
as, 77, 81, 84, 85, 87
practical advice in, 81–82, 83, 86
theological context of creation, fall,
and redemption, 74–77, 84–85
thought processes, influence of
relationships with others on, 83
transformation of *eros* and, 189
true friendship and intimacy,
ordering life toward, 113
AIDS/HIV, 279–80, 281–82
Akerlof, George A., 292n10
alcohol abuse. *See* addictive behaviors
Altman, D., 246n5
Amato, Paul R., 292n9, 295n17, 297n21
American Law Institute, *Principles of the
Law of Family Dissolution*, 291
American Psychiatric Association, 264
American Psychological Association,
247–48

*Italics indicate that the reference is found in a table on that page.